Local Government, Local Legislation

In the mid-Victorian period, when British international influence and power were at their height, concerns about local economic and social conditions were only slowly coming to be recognised as part of the obligations and expectations of central government.

Adopting a legal history perspective, this study reveals how municipal authorities of this period had few public law powers to regulate local conditions, or to provide services, and thus the more enterprising went direct to Parliament to obtain – at a price – the passing of specific local Bills to address their needs. Identifying and analysing for the first time the 335 local Parliamentary Bills promoted by local authorities in the period from the passing of the Local Government Act 1858 to the first annual report of the Local Government Board in 1872, the book draws three main conclusions from this huge mass of local statute book material. The first is that, far from being an uncoordinated mass of inconsistent, quixotic provisions, these Acts have a substantial degree of cohesion as a body of material. Second, the towns and cities of northern England secured more than half of them. Third, the costs of promotions (and the vested interests involved in them) represented a huge and often wasteful outlay that a more pragmatic and forward-looking Parliamentary attitude could have greatly reduced.

Dr R.J.B. Morris, O.B.E. is a retired local government Chief Executive and lawyer with over 40 years' interest in local legislation.

Local Government, Local Legislation
Municipal initiative in Parliament from 1858–1872

R.J.B. Morris

LONDON AND NEW YORK

First published 2017
by Routledge
2 Park Square, Milton Park, Abingdon, Oxon OX14 4RN

and by Routledge
711 Third Avenue, New York, NY 10017

First issued in paperback 2018

Routledge is an imprint of the Taylor & Francis Group, an informa business

© 2017 R.J.B. Morris

The right of R.J.B. Morris to be identified as author of this work has been asserted by him in accordance with sections 77 and 78 of the Copyright, Designs and Patents Act 1988.

All rights reserved. No part of this book may be reprinted or reproduced or utilised in any form or by any electronic, mechanical, or other means, now known or hereafter invented, including photocopying and recording, or in any information storage or retrieval system, without permission in writing from the publishers.

Trademark notice: Product or corporate names may be trademarks or registered trademarks, and are used only for identification and explanation without intent to infringe.

British Library Cataloguing in Publication Data
A catalogue record for this book is available from the British Library

Library of Congress Cataloguing in Publication Data
Names: Morris, Roger, 1946– author.
Title: Local government, local legislation : municipal initiative in Parliament from 1858–1872 / Roger Morris.
Description: Abingdon, Oxon; New York, NY : Routledge, 2017. | Includes bibliographical references and index.
Identifiers: LCCN 2016008815 | ISBN 9781138696112 (hardback : alk. paper) | ISBN 9781315525372 (ebook)
Subjects: LCSH: Local government–Law and legislation–Great Britain–History–19th century. | Central-local government relations–Great Britain–History–19th century. | Legislation–Great Britain–History–19th century.
Classification: LCC KD4765 .M67 2017 | DDC 328.4107/709034–dc23
LC record available at https://lccn.loc.gov/2016008815

ISBN 13: 978-1-138-32983-6 (pbk)
ISBN 13: 978-1-138-69611-2 (hbk)

Typeset in Times New Roman
by Out of House Publishing

 Printed in the United Kingdom by Henry Ling Limited

Contents

	Foreword	vi
1	The sources, structure and scope of local legislation	1
2	The context and content of local Bill promotion	31
3	Passing the Bill: Formalities and financing	66
4	Public law and private initiative: The wider context of local legislation	109
5	The texts and technicalities of local legislation	140
6	The powers and purposes of local legislation	174
7	Conclusion	198

Appendices	205
1 Local Bills promoted 1858–1872	205
2 Provisional Orders 1868–1872	226
3 Alphabetical list of places promoting local Bills 1858–1872	229
Bibliography	233
Table of Cases	241
Table of Statutes and Bills	242
Index	247

Foreword

The years between the passing of the first Local Government Act 1858 and the establishment of the Local Government Board in 1872 saw great changes in England and Wales: growing populations brought growing problems in crowded living conditions, but there were also increasing wealth, manufacturing and intellectual resources in a context of major international influence and self-confidence, and rapidly expanding countrywide infrastructure.

Against this backdrop, the municipal authorities of this period had few general law powers to regulate local conditions, or to provide services. While Parliament was still – at least at the outset – broadly antagonistic to centralisation and the enactment of common standards, it was nevertheless willing to grant private Acts – special local Act powers – to those places that sought, and could justify and pay for, the means to improve and invest in their localities. This book identifies and analyses for the first time the 335 local Parliamentary Bills, and the 278 Acts resulting from them, that municipalities promoted in the years 1858 to 1872 inclusive.

Three things stand out from the huge mass of local statute book material which these 278 Acts together comprise – themselves only a small fraction of the total of private Acts passed in the era of railway mania, and of much else besides. The first is that, far from being an uncoordinated mass of inconsistent, quixotic provisions as private Acts are sometimes thought or assumed to be, these Acts have a substantial degree of cohesion as a body of material. Second, the towns and cities of northern England secured more than half of them. Third, the costs of promotions (and the vested interests involved in them) represented a huge and often wasteful outlay that a more pragmatic and forward-looking Parliamentary attitude could have greatly reduced.

These and other matters are examined in detail across the whole spectrum of local legislation for the first time in this monograph as, despite the obvious fact that much of the physical development of Britain in the nineteenth century was built on private legislation, it has been relatively little studied. The common perception of England and Wales – at the height of the empire – includes the rapid growth of urban areas, the construction of railways, widespread pollution and deprivation, the gradual growth (for men at least) of widespread democracy, and the persistent class-consciousness that still shaped most of society. It does not include the thousands of private Acts passed by a Parliament that was willing to allow individual initiative to promote, and pay for, the legal authority needed to do things that neither the common law nor the restricted scope of public Acts would allow. Nor, perhaps, is it widely appreciated that the same Parliament and Government – so significant on the world stage – were, until quite late in Victoria's reign, markedly reluctant to take the lead in reforming public services, establishing proper local government everywhere, and looking after their citizens in a way that later generations would expect. Indeed, at the 1857 general election, more than half of the M.P.s had been returned unopposed.[1] The legislation that Parliament passed then must be judged against the climate of the times, and not merely from the vantage point of hindsight one and a half centuries later.[2]

This book systematically examines local legislation – defined here as private legislation promoted to create or extend the powers of different kinds of municipal authorities – for the first time. The 15 years covered run from 1858, when the first public 'Local Government Act' was enacted, up to and including 1872, when the Local Government Board began its work (and, incidentally, the Ballot Act was passed to introduce secret voting). This is a pivotal period in the local legislation narrative. In 1858, senior Parliamentarians had mostly been born in the eighteenth century and had made their early careers in the wake of the Napoleonic War. By 1872, those then in their early careers would live on into the twentieth century and the advent of the First World War. *Deference*, and the Westminster practice of largely ignoring the needs and opinions of the population at large, was slowly replaced there by *influence*, and the importance – indeed the necessity – of recognising and responding to that population.

Two reasons why local, and indeed all private, legislation of this period has been studied so sparingly involve first, its sheer bulk – some 3,448 private Acts (resulting from 5,468 deposited private Bills) in the years 1858–72 alone,[3] many of them of great length – and second, its inaccessibility. Most private Acts are still not readily available electronically, and sets of bound sessional volumes are relatively few. Moreover, not all the sets that do exist are original composite volumes of Queen's Printer's copies. Some are made up from final prints of Bills as passed, bound alphabetically, and lack chapter numbers or the related index pages. At a time when the alphabetical listing of short titles was not the way in which sessional volumes were prefaced by the Queen's Printers (George Edward Eyre and William Spottiswoode), having to peruse long titles often means that more than one source is necessary to trace and cite a given statute. The Indexes available[4] categorise the subject matters of private Acts, but not the nature of their content.

Just 8 per cent of those 3,448 private Acts – the 278 listed in Appendix 1[5] – come within the 'local' or 'municipal' definition used in this work. In addition, there are also some 57 other local Bills for which formal promotion procedures were started or pursued under the Parliamentary Standing Orders. These are far harder to access, assuming that the Bill texts were ever printed and exist at all. They are listed for each session in *Vacher's List of Private Bills*, a work extremely difficult to find.[6] The Bill titles set out in *Vacher* do not always correspond exactly with the short titles of those that were passed into law. Aside from local Record Offices and chance survivals of individual Bills elsewhere, only the Parliamentary Archives contain copies of those Bills that were printed and formally deposited in the Private Bill Office (or of reprints where Bills were amended after Select Committee consideration etc.).[7] Those Bills that were the subject of petitions or were actually introduced are normally to be found recorded in the Commons and Lords *Journals* – the various stages of any Bill can be traced through the annual indexes. Any references in *Hansard* are very much the exception. Fortunately there is a helpful additional resource; before depositing, would-be promoters had to publish the notices required by Parliamentary Standing Orders. These included publication in the preceding October or November of a fully descriptive notice in the *London Gazette*. Those notices can still be consulted, and are available online. The solicitors and Parliamentary agents acting will have under-signed them. These notices do not set out the precise drafting, but they usually make clear who is promoting. They also provide a full description of each intended Bill's scope and the works involved, and they sometimes run to several pages.

Appendices 1 and 2 accordingly represent the core research that the broad-based analysis in this book has required. The 335 Bills and Acts scheduled there have been distilled from the thousands that were promoted and passed in the 15 years covered. Their provisions have been individually examined – both against prevailing practice and precedent in other local legislation of the period and also against the context of relevant contemporary public legislation. The outcome is an analysis for the first time of the detailed purposes and drafting of *municipal* local legislation, unclouded by the sheer mass of other (primarily railway) local legislation that then filled 92 per cent or so of the private statute book. It also reveals for the first time the extent and nature of the energy and commitment of the leaders and entrepreneurs of local towns and communities all over England and Wales, but primarily in the northern half of England. On those characteristics was so much of the shape of modern Britain built.

As discussed in Chapter 5, the provisions of the local Acts passed (and indeed the clauses of the relevant Bills as deposited on promotion) need to be categorised into those comprising technical and constitutional content – that is, the legislative *means* – and those that represent the legislative *ends* – the actual powers that promoters wanted when they came to Westminster to petition for a private Bill. While a few single-purpose measures might be very short, the 14 local Acts in 1863, for instance, averaged 50 sections. Consolidating Acts would have hundreds of sections. Each enactment, however, is unique, and often technically complex, so that studying its text is both time-consuming and demanding in terms of placing its scope into the context of the body of local legislation as a whole during this period.

This book is based on a Ph.D. thesis accepted by the University of Leicester in 2015. I acknowledge with gratitude the support and thoughtful insights of my principal Supervisor there, Professor Steven King, together with the initiative of Professor Keith Snell in enabling me to undertake a research degree there. I also wish to record the debts I owe to the late Dr Paul O'Higgins and the late Professor Sir David Williams, both of Cambridge University, who encouraged my further studies long after I had left formal education, and without whom my somewhat eccentric interest in local and private legislation over the past 45 years or so would never have yielded any lasting outcome. Jess Farr-Cox has very ably compiled the index.

Roger Morris

Notes

1 Angus Hawkins, *The Forgotten Prime Minister: The 14th Earl of Derby* (vol. II, *Achievement, 1851–1869*, 2008), p. 138. He gives 328 uncontested seats in 1857, and a decade earlier for the 1847 general election 368 M.P.s returned unopposed – more than 55 per cent. These numbers contrast markedly with the totals quoted from other sources in *McCalmont's Parliamentary Poll Book: British Election Results 1832–1918* at p. xix: 236 uncontested out of 400 in 1847 and 219 out of 399 in 1857. The significant point for us here lies not in the exact figure, but in the perspective that in more than half of the constituencies, M.P.s were returned unopposed. Strictly speaking, of course, 'uncontested' and 'unopposed' are not the same thing.
2 As E.H. Carr expressed it: 'If the historian necessarily looks at his period of history through the eyes of his own time, and studies the problems of the past as a key to those of the present, will he not fall into a purely pragmatic view of the facts, and maintain that the criterion of a right interpretation is its suitability to some present purpose?' *What is History?* (1961), p. 21.
3 This total is taken from the Parliamentary *Returns* of 1866, 1872 and 1878 referred to in Chapter 1 under the heading *The Scope of Local Legislation*.
4 See the annex to Chapter 1.
5 Actually, as set out in note 1 to Appendix 1, three of these were printed as private and personal Acts and three as public Acts, but all the latter had been promoted as private Bills.
6 See the second paragraph of Appendix 1.
7 The Parliamentary Record Office copies of Bills of this period often include handwritten leaves of amendments added into the printed texts, and are annotated in Norman French as to whether they were passed, with or without amendments.

1 The sources, structure and scope of local legislation

Introduction

During Queen Victoria's reign (1837–1901), the British Government and the British people both came to expect and assume that central government should broadly look after the welfare and well-being of the whole population, and should take the initiative in doing so. Defence of the realm and the King's (or Queen's) peace might have been part of the unwritten compact between monarch and subjects since medieval times; the governmental climate, however, that still allowed the Irish to starve in their thousands in the 1840s without the then most powerful nation on earth apparently doing much about it was, by the end of that century, long gone – outmoded in part no doubt by the assumptions of a broadening electorate.

Just how the Government should ensure the social and economic wellbeing of its citizens was, however, contentious, and would remain so – but well before Victoria died it was clear that a demographic order mainly based on the pre-eminence and priority of landowners was no longer dominant. There had, however, long been those in both Houses of Parliament who (whether confident because of, or altruistic despite, being landowners themselves) spoke and acted differently. Some peers and M.P.s alike spoke of the public interest, and were concerned for reform. They often had first-hand experience of what happened when self-seeking or vested business interests came up against the power of a state that, while actively ruling much of the globe, was still in the early stages of learning how to control and direct immense social change, rapid industrialisation and urban expansion at home, as well as the rising influence, needs and demands of the wider population, who could no longer be ignored. The Chairman of Ways and Means, John George Dodson M.P. (Liberal, East Sussex), speaking of the members of Private Bill Committees in the House of Commons on 15 March 1872, described them as men 'accustomed to watch and allow for public opinion'.[1]

A very large part of the industrialisation and urban expansion that occurred after around 1840 came about because of private or local initiative, not state direction. Initially at least, there was neither the tradition nor the will in central government for it. (That grew only slowly, until much later the overwhelming needs of the First World War gave rise to a preeminent national control which has never since been significantly reversed.) Individual initiative, whether seeking profit or the improvement of the manifestly intolerable conditions that unbridled development and growing population were bringing, was how projects were undertaken or the state of things was altered.

For a hundred years from the 1790s the national landscape was changed: first by canals, and then by railways, and also by inclosures of hitherto common land. Factories, mills and coal mines changed the landscape too – often even more dramatically and damagingly; they, however, could be built at will by whoever controlled the land involved. Canals and railways on the other hand had to cross many lands over many miles; they needed the ability to override objections and ransom terms, and to appeal to concepts of a wider public good, which cooperation alone could never resolve. That overriding could only come from Parliament, through a statute that could in principle achieve almost anything, and which the courts would uphold. The state would not create the canal or rail network directly; it would not even actively oversee or coordinate it; but it would license the permissions and indemnities needed to build it, and would do so on terms which, considering the general state of public administration at the time, were remarkably exacting, consistent and principled. Furthermore, those presiding over the licensing stood to gain nothing personally from doing so, even though the process was inevitably costly and spawned a specialist industry to meet the needs of those who would be licensed.

What applied to transport infrastructure applied also to thousands of other projects, circumstances and needs – to most things, in fact, that neither the common law nor custom envisaged or encompassed. Early on, local communities sought powers for paving and lighting; other public health requirements followed. In due course, and with the nature and relative speed of the innovations and initiatives varying from place to place, Parliament was asked to license – to give permission for by Act of Parliament – roads, bridges, docks, harbours, markets and much else. The advent of water and gas companies or 'undertakings' was in due course followed by similar ventures about electricity and tramways; meanwhile a whole canon of powers and duties grew up around boundaries, local tax-raising, finance and the associated powers and provisions found necessary in an increasingly sophisticated society whose municipalities possessed only that legal capacity either explicitly or impliedly given to them by statute. As the Law Commissions put it in their 1996 *Report on the Chronological Table of Local Legislation* (Cm 3301):

> Local legislation has played a crucial part in the process whereby the United Kingdom has since the eighteenth century been changed from a predominantly agricultural and rural society into one that is predominantly urban and suburban.[2]

The governance context

The rapidly growing industrialisation and urban expansion of the mid-Victorian years took place amid equally fundamental and lasting change in both national and local governance. At Victoria's accession, both retained the memory, if no longer the detailed imprint, of the late eighteenth century. By the time of her death, the apparatus of both was irretrievably different. When the future or fate of the mass of the people did not matter very much to the state, or to those who guided and governed it, the administrative machinery of regulation could afford to be weak in any context not seen as of compelling national importance. The more, however, that the nation became a cohesive and inter-dependent economic unit, the more that control was required, information needed, and conformity with a planned expectation sought. If you gained the right to vote, you also gained the obligation to pay for that right by playing according to the rules of the new order. The state could pour forth new rules and administrative theory every bit as rapidly as smoke pollution could pour from factory chimneys.

The development of what has come to be known as the 'information state' has been increasingly studied in recent years. Edward Higgs, in *The Information State in England* (2004), contrasts the decentralised state of early modern England – a period he does not define, but which starts for him at least well back in the seventeenth century – when local affairs were largely dealt with locally, and there was a wide gulf, only partly filled by the justices, between those and the affairs of state at Crown and Parliament level. He gives a number of examples of new or nascent administrative systems in the mid-Victorian period; some arise from the Government's need to tax, organise and increasingly to look after its citizens, and some from scandals that could no longer be ignored – but he also shows how the public rationales of the time did not necessarily always tell the full or the real story.[3] Higgs identifies the period from 1830 to 1870 as seeing 'the passage of numerous pieces of legislation that sought to regulate society',[4] and he cites the views of several historians who see the legislation, and the centralising outlook that gave rise to much of it, in widely differing terms – a 'capitalist cultural revolution'; the 'social disciplinarian' role of the Victorian state; the new breed of 'expert'; a revolution in government predicated on the discovery of treatment of 'social ills'; and so on.[5] It was not, however, a novelty for the state to be regulating, and for it to be doing so with an eye to financial gain and political advantage: monarchs back to King John and before had repetitively granted charters to license local privileges and activities, and to gain subservience to the will of Westminster. What was novel was the scale of the regulation, the increasing need also to secure the will of the electorate, and the recognition that the capacity of the centre to administer at local level had never been particularly good. Moreover, it was not the monarch, nor even primarily Parliament, that was doing the regulating – rather it was the newly burgeoning Government administrative machine. Furthermore, the new regulation needed new laws, and new concepts of law. A whole apparatus of decision-making was required, and so was a redefined relationship with the citizenry at large, whose broad consent Ministers of the 1850s – mindful no doubt of the revolutions of 1848 across the Channel – dare not any longer take for granted. The citizenry's willingness to be governed by those new powerful civil servants referred to by Higgs was essential to a fundamental reciprocal respect, without which the business of her Majesty's Government could not be carried on.[6]

Jose Harris, giving an overview of British society in the years after 1870, considers mid-Victorian Britain as having remained 'a society that in numerous ways was fiercely variegated and local'. Contrasting with the European scene, she writes that

> preservation of local autonomy and custom was seen as a quintessential feature of British national character and culture – in marked contrast to the centralization, rationality, and legalistic uniformity imposed on Continental countries by the legacy of the two Napoleons.[7]

That emphasis on the variegated and local is underlined by the enormous numbers of local authorities – public bodies – that existed at this time: among the total were 224 municipal boroughs; 117 sets of improvement commissioners; 637 local boards of health; an extraordinary 15,414 parishes and townships; and various others like poor law unions, county units and burial boards.[8] The extreme complexity of these thousands of local units is illustrated by the evidence printed with the 1873 Select Committee report on *Boundaries of Parishes, Unions and Counties*, and its examples of countless anomalies, such as those places that were associated with a different county from the one within which they were geographically situated.[9]

British politics of the time were dominated by Liberals on the one side, and by Conservatives on the other. 'In general terms' writes Elizabeth Hurren,[10]

> nineteenth-century Liberalism has been characterised by an emphasis on 'individualism'. It personified 'a belief in maximising the individual citizen's freedom from restraint and a corresponding commitment to restricting the role of the state'.[11] It espoused the notion of 'an enabling state' that provided law, order and defence but thereafter left (indeed required) its citizens to get on with their working lives.

'British Conservatism' on the other hand

> saw itself as the guardian of political equilibrium, a role that suited its predominantly agricultural membership prior to 1880. Yet Conservative politicians were often just as capricious as Liberals, sharing many of the same concerns about the need for economic stability, the threat of the coming of democracy and the rise of the left in British politics. There were no easy Conservative social policy solutions to these dilemmas.[12]

At the same time that local communities were trying to demonstrate their independence from over-weening state control, and to persuade an often largely indifferent Westminster that they both needed and could safely be trusted with local reforms, they were also frequently concerned to compete with and outshine their neighbours. Ambition and investment could benefit a community just as it could an individual, and the more connected communities became, so the more that urban and rural rivalries played a part in the outlook and conduct of local affairs. Prestige projects not only required determined local leadership, focus and finance; they might well need special legal powers too – a need readily welcomed by the Parliamentary agents for whom such work was obviously lucrative. Jon Stobart emphasises how town halls, art galleries, and museums and libraries 'were always heavy with symbolism'; their style needed at once to be recognisable but also able to convey the character of a town. Alluding to the civic buildings of Manchester, Crewe and Oldham, he notes that 'These celebrated identity as well as municipal and class-based authority. As such, they combined place promotion with civic boosterism and were designed and built with more than half an eye on rival towns and cities.'[13] It is with those mixed but powerful motivations in mind that we turn to consider what has been written specifically about local legislation, and the extent to which much of the detail of the narrative around local Bills and Acts remains untold.

Historiographical review

An innovative general study of local government-related private Bill legislation was F.H. Spencer's *Municipal Origins* (1911). It covers the period from 1740 to 1835, when the Municipal Corporations Act was passed. The nature of the need for private legislation of this kind in that period is well expressed in the Preface by Sir Edward Clarke, K.C. – social and other changes in the late eighteenth century

> required the erection of new authorities which should do for the community the duties of regulation and administration which were everywhere, but in very different character and degree, found to be necessary. Each locality, sometimes by the general action of its inhabitants, more often by the energetic work of a few of them, suggested its own form of administration and, going to Parliament for authority, was allowed to try its experiment.[14]

In addition to the constitutional aspects of local Acts, and the procedure for obtaining them, Spencer examines at length what was at the time included in what his chapter V titles *The Normal Urban Local Act*, while further chapters consider what he terms 'non-normal clauses' and, in particular, the numerous local Poor Law Acts. No commentary of similar scope and perspective on any period after 1835 has been published.

6 *Sources, structure, scope of local legislation*

There is, of course, a great deal of published description and consideration relating to specific places, about both the local legislation there and the social and political initiatives that usually lay behind it. This is especially the case for the larger cities, and for other towns that have been thought either to offer typical illustrations of the methods and motivations at work in Victorian England, or where the story – often of bitter local political and business rivalry – readily captures the interest. It is much less so for any area that was neither an old borough nor a rapidly growing town in what J.B. Priestley called 'Victoria's heyday'[15] – rural areas waited till 1889 to be given county councils, and many of their histories at the time of which F.H. Spencer was writing were dominated by the arrival of canals, and above all by the depredations (or achievements, depending on one's viewpoint) of the inclosure movement.

Traditionally, a borough history would concentrate, as initial volumes of the Victoria County History published in the earlier part of the twentieth century still tended to do, on medieval charters, the surviving muniments, the formal boundaries and baronies, and the families, trades and traditions that had made the place what it then was. As the emphasis has slowly shifted, much work has been done on the totality of the local population and the significant trends, both local and in the nation as a whole. That has been reflected in a growing canon of research on the political, social, religious and other influences that shaped communities that often grew physically at extraordinary rates, during the middle years of the nineteenth century in particular. Historians have appreciated the wealth of information that is often incidentally contained in an area's local legislation – such as the carefully prepared preambles that would be fatal to a Bill's progress if unable to be proved, or shown to be inaccurate; the names of those local figures who were named as promoters or appointed as commissioners; and the identities of owners of lands or houses sought to be compulsorily purchased.

Although no study of the years since 1835 has matched that of F.H. Spencer in its overall and comparative approach for the period from 1740–1835, some broader-based studies of legislative activity have been published. Sheila Lambert's *Bills and Acts: Legislative Procedure in Eighteenth Century England* (1971), is an important study, though as the title implies, it is less concerned with the terms and texts of the actual measures than with how they progressed through their Parliamentary stages. All works concentrating on this rely considerably on the two volumes of *A History of Private Bill Legislation* by Frederick Clifford (1885, 1887). A useful introduction to the situation prior to the passing of the Municipal Corporations Act in 1835 is provided in *The Unreformed Local Government System* by Bryan Keith-Lucas (1980). His preface noted that

> 'Minor' legislation, in one sense, private statutes no doubt are. Yet if we look at their results in the numerous Acts obtained by Local Authorities, as well as in our canal and railway systems, our water-works, gas-works,

tramways, docks, harbour and river improvements, and other enterprises, we may see how immense an influence they have exercised for the public good ... In bulk and number local and personal enactments far exceed those of a public nature. For example, between the years 1800 and 1884, the number of public Acts has been 9,556; of private Acts 18,497. No connected account of this great mass of private legislation has yet been attempted, although it has had momentous results in promoting national prosperity, and to all historical students should be full of interest.[16]

Clifford's 1880s work was admired 60 years later by O. Cyprian Williams, a former Clerk of Commons Committees, for whom His Majesty's Stationery Office (HMSO) in 1948 published (again in two volumes) *The Historical Development of Private Bill Procedure and Standing Orders in the House of Commons*. Nevertheless, Williams concentrates on procedure, noting of Clifford that

> his main interest lay in the subjects of private bill legislation rather than in the history of procedure ... The great virtue of his book lies in the copious illustration which it provides of the growth, on the parliamentary side, of our civil administration and public services ... accelerating rapidly to a climax in the middle of the nineteenth [century] and then gradually losing speed.[17]

In more recent years, much has been published on local politics and social developments, some of it treating a few cities or boroughs in a comparative or at least a parallel way – such as for example Asa Briggs' *Victorian Cities* (1963, 1968); *Municipal Reform and the Industrial City* (1982, ed. Derek Fraser); *Patricians, Politics and Power in Nineteenth Century Towns* (1982, ed. David Cannadine); Janet Roebuck's more narrowly focused *Urban Development in 19th Century London: Lambeth, Battersea and Wandsworth 1838–1888* (1979); and John Prest's *Liberty and Locality: Parliament, Permissive Legislation, and Ratepayers' Democracies in the Mid-Nineteenth Century* (1990), with its particular focus on the Isle of Wight and the Huddersfield area. There is, however, still no broadly based study of local legislation in the period of this book (or indeed for any other period). Although Joanna Innes' *Inferior Politics: Social Problems and Social Politics in Eighteenth-Century Britain* (2009) is a wide-ranging study, her focus is primarily on public statutes. In her section on *The Pattern of Proposals*, she asserts that 'Categories of bill we are *not* concerned with include all private and local measures'.[18] If they had included them, particularly towards the end of the eighteenth century, she might not have summed up the evidence derived from those public Acts and Bills that she did include by saying 'there seems no reason to read these trends as evidence of declining parliamentary interest in questions of domestic government'. Indeed there was not – but how that interest was manifested was not just to be measured by public legislation activity alone.

8 *Sources, structure, scope of local legislation*

Apart from Spencer's *Municipal Origins*, concluding a generation earlier than the period of this book, the existing published material, and particularly that specifically referred to above, is broadly categorised into two groups. One is very limited; local legislation is either considered as a whole in generalisations that understate the complexity and depth of the subject, or that sweep local Acts aside as does Joanna Innes quoted above. The other is very detailed and specific, related usually to a particular place or development and often purely narrative, drawing few or no wider conclusions or analysis from the material presented to say whether or not this case, these circumstances, presently described were or were not typical of legislative activity of that kind at that time. The studies referred to in the previous paragraph all belong to one category or the other. They may be locally comprehensive – for instance J.S. Phipps' *Leicester in Parliament*[19] – but they do not take the student outside the municipal boundaries in question.

This book accordingly examines for the first time the wider significance, the role and the content of local legislation – that is, local legislation relating to local government, during the municipally significant period in mid-Victorian England from 1858 to 1872 inclusive. Initially, it considers the state of the law about what was then considered to be what came to be termed 'local government' (though the phrase was not in use at that time[20]) in the mid-1830s, when the Municipal Corporations Act came into force in 1836, some 18 months before Victoria's accession. It also considers the role and significance of local legislation (a phrase which, unless the context implies differently, is more fully defined in Chapter 2, and which will be used to mean local legislation *relating to local government*) at that time: local Bills and Acts had already been playing a very significant role in the history and development of many communities by then. What followed during the mid-Victorian period cannot be appreciated or placed in context without an understanding of the continuity of the concept from the eighteenth century. (Indeed, local legislation continues to play a role, though much less prominently now, through to the present day.)

Following the background described in the preceding paragraph, this study considers in much more detail the local legislation promoted and passed in the period 1858–72. The primary purpose is to attempt for the first time to survey the *corpus* of local legislation of this period in an overall way, in contrast to the many studies that have considered the local legislation of a particular area in an individual way. The rest of this chapter accordingly successively considers the historical context of the local legislation with which this book is concerned; its scope in general terms; how it was promoted; and why it was needed. An annex to this chapter provides the sources both for the legislation itself, and for existing principal reference works relating to it.

The historical context of local legislation

In *The Law Relating to Local Authorities* (1934), W.I. (later Sir Ivor) Jennings wrote that

Local authorities were established primarily to carry out the duties which Parliament imposed on them. But from the early days of the nineteenth century there was in many places a local opinion which wanted governmental authority for the provision of services which Parliament had not yet compelled. Specially incorporated improvement commissioners ... were the first public health authorities. They were ad hoc bodies with special powers granted by local Acts. When the public health authorities were established, they followed the precedent thus set. They did not regard themselves as necessarily limited to the functions which Parliament had thrust upon them; they sought special powers for the improvement of their towns.[21]

The trends and developments of many decades cannot be adequately summarised in just a few paragraphs, but the specific context of the second quarter of the nineteenth century can be characterised by brief references to the situations and circumstances of that time. It was, first, a time of growing international power and prestige for Britain, with sustained peace at home, confidence in the Empire, and an apparent stability that contrasted with the revolutions of 1848 in Europe. Manufacturing capacity was growing; it was fuelled by new industrialisation, by the attraction of millions into the burgeoning towns, and of course by the ready availability of raw materials and markets across much of the globe with which the manufacturing could be sustained and developed.

At the same time, Parliament saw itself as the embodiment of enlightened government; there were indeed many altruistic peers and M.P.s, and there was a confidence unlike, perhaps, any that has obtained since. It was the era of Lord Macaulay, of Sir Robert Peel and of a youthful W.E. Gladstone – and while we may also remember that it was a time of rotten boroughs, corrupted elections and a somewhat sanctimonious public morality, the bias for the upright rather than the bent was surely to be preferred.

There was a broad assumption in the minds of many in Parliament that, without necessarily disturbing too much their birthright to be there, some reforms were necessary. Unbridled eighteenth-century licence would no longer be tolerated, though when it came to the supposed interests of the masses, the voices of reaction were still loudly heard. The 1832 Reform Act is inevitably the leading example of this. A few years later, the campaign to create public libraries, led in Parliament in and around 1850 by the Liverpool M.P. William Ewart, could still be opposed by the likes of Colonel Sibthorp, a Lincoln M.P. whose character Surtees or Dickens might have created, and who 'saw no purpose in reading' and had hated it while at Oxford.[22] (He had also opposed aspects of the Bills in 1847 and 1848 that resulted in the latter year's Public Health Act.)

Accordingly the impetus for what became the Municipal Corporations Act 1835, and the reports which led up to it, had much more to do with reining in the licence of most of the old corporations than with fitting the country for the emerging impact of industrialisation. For a nation whose Government was so active and interventionist overseas, it was, on the face of it, remarkable that the pace of structured national reform in municipal affairs was so slow. A contributory factor may have been that, given a perceived public health problem or emergency, our instinct today is to turn to public agencies to tackle it, and to do so at public expense; the early Victorians, however, had not formed that reflex from past experience. The apparatus and infrastructure were not there, and neither were the revenues nor the trained staff. Such facts, combined with the assumption of personal freedom and a more *laissez-faire* outlook, meant that such questions of public policy were either not seen as such at all, or were weighed differently.

In this light, the apparent contradiction between the high ideals expressed in the Parliamentary tradition – of judicial fairness in hearings; of the public interest; of disinterested objectivity on the part of those granting powers and privileges – and a seeming reluctance to tackle so energetically the death, disease and despoliation that industrialisation had brought, becomes less unexpected. The Government, and hence Parliament, reacted to such problems at the behest of others far more than ever itself taking the initiative. That was its most notable characteristic in the area of national life that we are examining.

Yet it could also be said that there *was* in fact a response system. It depended on local and often private initiative, but when petitioned for powers, Parliament took those petitions seriously; considered them carefully according to well-known and published rules of process; and more often than not granted them. If local interests did not want to pave, cleanse, facilitate or whatever, what would the state be doing by trying to force such things on them if the wider national interest were not somehow at stake? It is against this background that we shall consider local legislation in detail during the years 1858–72, and how the sources of initiative and impetus for local reform gradually began to change.

Writing for American students in 1897 in *English Local Government of Today: A Study of the Relations of Central and Local Government*, M.R. Maltbie summed up the changing influence of private legislation ('special legislation' as it was known in America) by saying that

> The first period in the history of all functions that are now under the control of local authorities is that in which private initiative held sway. Poor relief, education, public health and safety were matters of private concern. One by one they passed into the hands of local authorities, but before any general system of administration was created, there was a long period when powers relating to these and other subjects were conferred upon various bodies. In some instances, the associations formed were purely private corporations; in others, the purpose was primarily a public purpose. The characteristic feature of this period was the use of local (or special) acts. General acts relating to these matters were wanting. This period was soon succeeded by one in which the necessity of general

legislation became manifest, and although local acts still remained prominent, the relative importance of general acts constantly increased. Then came the system of central control which took from Parliament and from the local authorities certain powers and duties and conferred them upon central departments. General and special acts continued to be passed, and thus through three avenues could the functions of local bodies be increased. All of these periods did not come at the same moment in all departments of local government, and some subjects once administered by the localities have passed entirely into the hands of the central government, but it is true that the same stages of development have taken place in all and in precisely the same order.[23]

On this side of the Atlantic, and three-quarters of a century later, in *The Growth and Reform of English Local Government* (1971), W. Thornhill described the same evolution from a different perspective, saying that the hundred years from 1832 to 1932

saw the ancient poor law institutions first reformed, and then abolished. It saw the growth of a system of representative, multi-purpose authorities. Yet this was achieved only after a long period in which the ancient but ineffective organs were by-passed by a wide range of *ad hoc* authorities based on the concept of service and efficiency. The reformers were indeed the leading statesmen of the period ... [but] they were defeated by the die-hards of both county and borough who, for the most part concerned to protect their pockets, resisted all attempts to provide more services and more efficient institutions to manage them.[24]

The hundred years from 1835 to 1935 were the subject of a commemorative (and inevitably rather hagiographic) study entitled *A Century of Municipal Progress*, published that year under the auspices of NALGO, the white-collar local government union. The contribution on *Parliament and the Local Authorities* from John Willis includes the verdict that 'The history of the last century reveals nothing to shake one's faith in the ability of Parliament to lead the diversely equipped authorities, stragglers, and hotheads, over the path of progress'.[25] Complex as the reality was, the disparaging implication in this verdict is not one that can be sustained so far as the mid-Victorian period is concerned. The categories and large volumes of legislation during these years are the subject of the next section.

The scope of local legislation

Local legislation is voluminous, and there is a lot of repetitive material. Lawyers and legislators like precedent, so that powers or provisions granted in one place or situation tended to be exactly or very similarly repeated in another. Furthermore, if the provisions had been shown to work well, any case for change or variation would still need renewed justification. Nevertheless, there has been little consistency in how legislation has been passed, printed and categorised over the years.

In 1955, the House of Commons Library published Document No. 1, *Acts of Parliament: Some Distinctions in their Nature and Numbering*. While descriptions varied, particularly before Lord Brougham's Interpretation Act of 1850, the essential division was between *public* – of general application, and always taken notice of by the courts – and *private*. Private Acts originated 'by way of petition from a body or person outside Parliament' (page 3), and royal assent was given by the phrase *Soit fait comme il est desiré* rather than the more familiar (and still used) public Act wording *Le Roy [La Reyne] le veult*. As the word implies, private Acts were of local or personal application. *Statutes* are technically of a general character, 'whereas *Act* when unqualified will cover all legislative decisions made by the King in Parliament' (page 4). The practice and policy on printing and promulgating 'Public Local Statutes' (as they were then termed) had been set out in joint resolutions of both Houses of Parliament in 1797 (page 5). His Majesty's Printer was to print 3,550 copies of every public Act at His Majesty's expense; 200 copies of each public local statute (including Road Acts); and 200 copies of each private statute, but the parties 'interested in' the private Acts were to pay for their printing.

At the beginning of the nineteenth century, there were four categories of Act. Those were *public Acts*; *private Acts declared public* (then termed 'Public Local Acts' as stated above); *private Acts not declared public* but printed by the King's Printer; and *unprinted* (that is, not officially printed) *private Acts* which had to be proved by a certificate from the Clerk of the Parliaments. After 1850 it was enacted that all Acts should be deemed public unless declared otherwise. This was not to contradict the public–private distinction; it ensured that the courts would ordinarily take notice of any Act and apply or enforce it, regardless of how it had come to be passed. From 1869 to 1947 the annual volumes of private Acts were titled either *Local and Private* or just *Local Acts*.

Finally must be noted (since they are very important in the municipal context) *Public Acts of a Local Character*. The House of Commons Library Paper explains this term succinctly[26] as being

> applied to 'Provisional Order Confirmation Acts'. From 1815 until 1868 these were included in the series of 'Public Acts', but from 1869 (when their title changed from 'Provisional Orders' to 'Public Acts of a Local Character') they have been included with 'Local Acts' [or the alternative annual volume title], and numbered as such.

These distinctions described above were potentially very important for private Bill promoters, and an appreciation of them is necessary also if the procedures, limitations and enforceability of local legislation at any period are to be understood. The categorisation, however, particularly before the mid-nineteenth century, was not exact: the Preface to the sixth edition of the

Chronological Table and Index of the Statutes of 1880, referring to 'all Acts classed by the King's or Queen's Printers as Public or as Public General' added that 'Many of these Acts, however, cannot be regarded as public Acts, affecting the community generally, being in their nature special or private Acts, relating to particular persons or places, or to private concerns.'[27] In 1996, HMSO published the Law Commission and the Scottish Law Commission's four-volume *Chronological Table of Local Legislation*. That records[28] that some 26,000 local Acts (as they are now termed) were passed from 1797 to the end of 1973. To refer to an average of nearly 150 per year would be misleading: only one is recorded in 1797, and 36 in 1973 – these two low numbers alone convey some indication of how high the volume of such legislation reached in some years in the mid-nineteenth century. Moreover, there were many other Bills which, for whatever reason, were advertised or promoted but never completed their passage through Parliament, being withdrawn or rejected.[29]

Statistics for the years 1858–72 illustrate the extent to which the numbers of Bills ultimately achieving royal assent differed from the numbers of those promoted. The statistics for the years from 1858 to 1866 inclusive are derived from the *Return showing the Number of PRIVATE BILLS deposited in the PRIVATE BILL OFFICE, for each Year from 1850 to 1866; &c.*, which the House of Commons ordered to be printed on 3 August 1866 and is made under the name of 'Mr. Dodson' – the Chairman of Ways and Means from 1865–72 referred to above. The Return itself, Paper 467, is over the name of W. Hodgkin, then Principal Clerk of Private Bills in the Commons, and is dated 10 August 1866.[30] The years from 1867 to 1872 are set out in the subsequent Paper 68 of 1872, and 1872 in Paper 110 of 1878, both over the name of Hodgkin's successor H.B. Boyne. The names of the individual Bills can be found both in the annual listings in *Vacher's List of Private Bills* and the detailed (and usually annual) Commons returns. Both set out much additional information about which were opposed and which unopposed, the grouping of Bills under separate Committees, and so on.

Initially the tables in *Vacher* were just alphabetical; the Bill number is given, with any plan number, and where relevant the name of the Engineer involved. From 1870, a numerical sequence list is also given. It is also recorded which Bills were withdrawn or not proceeded with; occasionally there were other problems, such as for the Sirhowy Railway Bill [H.L.] in 1868 (Bill 87 and plan 47), which did not pass the Standing Orders. Other Bills were re-submitted either in the same session or sometimes in a subsequent session.

The totals for both Bills and Acts in the official *Return* include Ireland and Scotland as well as England and Wales. The number read a first time in each year is given, along with more detailed categorisation. From 1850 to 1858 inclusive, the numbers of Bills read a first time consistently exceed the numbers of Bills deposited; as stated above, the promotions and procedures were not always neatly contained within one regnal year or one Parliamentary session, so that the numbers given that received the Royal Assent again are not to be compared strictly with the numbers of Bills deposited that year,

14 *Sources, structure, scope of local legislation*

Year	Private Bills Deposited	Read a First Time	Receiving Royal Assent	Private Acts in 1996 Chronological Table
1858	208	216	169	150
1859	272	261	190	174*
1860	311	286	221	203
1861	399	344	266	249
1862	329	293	237	227
1863	381	323	247	238
1864	504	448	343	329
1865	595	520	392	382
1866	633	508	377	363
1867	317	213	222	209
1868	228	140	170	182 (22)
1869	212	129	160	159 (10)
1870	240	159	167	177 (14)
1871	275	182	199	206 (17)
1872	305	188	190	200 (17)

* Two sessions, 35 and 139

or the Acts sequentially numbered and listed in the Law Commission's 1996 *Chronological Table*, which latter are added above as a final column.

In addition, a few Bills were listed in *Vacher* separately against the Lords at the outset; in 1855 there were 19 and in 1856, 14, but these were all estate or personal Bills in character. It was also the case sometimes that plans were deposited for Bills that did not materialise in that session; in 1862, for instance, *Vacher* listed six such cases involving railway schemes and another 11 miscellaneous others, while in 1863 there were a further 12 sets of plans lodged of each kind with no related Bills. After 1848, when the Provisional Order procedure began, those applications too are listed for each session, variously deposited with the Board of Trade in different categories – piers and harbours; tramways; gas and water works. (Provisional Orders Bills were, however, treated as public.) The annual private Act totals above included from 1868 the number of Provisional Order Confirmation Acts given in brackets.

Regard must be had to the impact of the various 'common clauses' that Parliament passed in 1845–47 to ease both the expense and the sheer physical impact of Bill promotion, together with the very considerable burden on Parliamentary time. In 1845 were passed the Companies, Lands, and Railways Clauses Consolidation Acts (Scottish equivalents of all three of which were also passed that year). In 1847 were passed further Clauses Acts for Markets and Fairs; Gasworks; Commissioners; Harbours, Docks and Piers; Cemeteries; Towns Improvement; and Town Police. That for Lands was supplemented in 1860, while further Clauses Acts for Railways, Waterworks and Companies followed in 1863. All these greatly reduced the bulk of individual promotions, which could then both incorporate standardised provisions but also render it much more difficult to justify and be granted provisions which differed from the established norm. The impact of private Bill promotion on both Houses of Parliament not only prompted the enactment of common clauses; it also prompted significant examinations of the requisite practices and procedures. In fact the Commons in particular had always given extensive and repeated attention to private Bill procedures;[31] this intensified in the 1830s and 1840s as the demands of the business grew.

The Commons ordered the printing of the first report from the Select Committee on Private Business on 25 February 1839, the second report following on 9 August that year. The full impact of 'railway mania' was yet to be felt, but already there was unease about the practicalities and proprieties of the procedures involved.[32] The Committee employed 'two professional men' – Mr. James Booth and Mr. Arthur Symonds – 'to classify the Private Bills, and prepare drafts of General Bills', which was done. Letter no. 3 in the Appendix to the second report lists the nine Bills that Mr. Booth had drafted: General Inclosure; Special Inclosure; General Railway; Special Railway; Joint Stock Companies; Lands Acquisition; General Companies' Suitors; Special Companies' Suitors; and Commissioners of Public Undertakings. He also records that he had prepared them alone, as Mr. Symonds, while cooperative, had differed as to the plan and approach to be adopted. The Committee recorded, however, that hopes that the Bills might be taken forward imminently had not materialised. Nevertheless, the Committee recommended that they should be further considered in the next session; meanwhile they also recommended that Mr. Booth be permanently appointed as an Officer of the House to continue the preparation of Breviates of Private Bills that he had been hitherto retained by the House to provide from his private practice.

Eventually a statutory response did result from the previous discussions and the mounting concern about the existing system. 'Whereas it is expedient that Facilities should be given for procuring more complete and trustworthy Information previous to Inquiries before either House of Parliament on Applications in certain Cases for Local Acts...' Accordingly was passed in 1846 'An Act for making preliminary Inquiries in certain Cases of Application for Local Acts'[33] – provisions requiring intending promoters to serve notices on the requisite Government Department, thereby allowing Commissioners to be sent at the expense of promoters to survey and find out about local circumstances before the Houses considered applications for local Acts involving waterworks, town paving, cleansing and improving, as well as burial and cemetery powers and extensions, and anything affecting ports or navigable rivers. The reports of these preliminary inquiries were published as Parliamentary papers. The 1846 legislation was replaced in 1848.[34] The preliminary inquiry initiative, however, was not adjudged a success,[35] and this Act was in its turn repealed by the Preliminary Inquiries Act 1851,[36] which confined the approach to Board of Admiralty matters.

In 1847, the House of Commons appointed a Select Committee on Private Bills, which published three short reports and took extensive evidence. The reports considered the impact of the consolidating Acts referred to above that were then beginning to rationalise, and curtail the need for, some local legislation; fees and costs; and what had been the impact of the Act of 1846 requiring preliminary inquiries before many private Bills could proceed. In 1858 a Select Committee of the House of Lords reported on the 'system of proceedings in Parliament on private Bills'. The Committee recommended that compliance with Standing Orders should ordinarily be proved before Examiners before such Bills were introduced into Parliament, and how cases of non-compliance should be dealt with. They also made recommendations *inter alia* about opposed Bills where there were no petitions against them, and how questions of *locus standi* should be decided.

Subsequently in 1863 another *Select Committee on Private Bill Legislation* took extensive evidence and published a further report.[37] It was almost entirely preoccupied with the mass of railway Bills, but is revealing also about the general body of promotions at that time. (The Select Committees of 1858 and 1863 are both extensively considered in Chapter 3.) James Booth, by then a Joint Secretary to the Board of Trade, but (as noted above) from 1839 until the end of 1850 Counsel to the Speaker, was the first witness to give evidence to the 1863 Select Committee, on 12 March, and he gave the history of the 1845 Consolidation Acts.[38] He had had 2 years' experience prior to 1839 preparing Breviates – summaries – of private Bills in the Speaker's service, and considered that the private Bills in 1839 'were in a very rude state indeed; they were of enormous size and great verbosity, and there was no principle of order in the arrangement of the clauses ...' He went on to describe how, encouraged by the Chairman of Committees in the House of Lords, the sixth Lord Shaftesbury, he analysed the kinds of clause being promoted, and obtained authority to have model clauses 'printed and circulated among the Parliamentary agents'. 'The effect of all this was', he continued

> that the bulk of a Railway Bill, which before that time was something like 100 folio pages, was reduced to somewhere about ten pages, with the great advantage that what was in the Bill was matter special to the undertaking under consideration ... these public Acts were framed with a great deal of consideration, and with a view to the interest of the Public, which a Private Bill is not, for, of course, the object of the promoters is to take as large powers as they can.[39]

The impact of consolidation – or more accurately, of requiring Bills to be drafted conforming to a template and incorporating a standard apparatus of clauses and provisions – was considerable. In the next year, 1846, Booth recollected[40] that

> there were between 600 and 700 Railway Bills, and where the type would have been obtained for all those Bills with the amendments which were

required to be printed, and the Bills re-printed as they came out of Committee, I do not know ... to say nothing of the fee upon drawing the Bill, which is generally measured in some degree by its length.

Nor was this unusual; in 1863, although not all were promoted separately, Booth stated that there were 'more than 300 [railway] lines, which are less than three miles long, asking for the sanction of Parliament'.[41] Later, William N. Massey M.P., a member of the Select Committee and the Chairman of Ways and Means, who gave evidence on 19 March, gave the number of Private Bills in the previous session referred to Committees as 198, detailing how many fell into each category of procedural outcome.[42] Among these, 54 were unopposed; 15 were withdrawn; and of the 129 Bills that were 'tried', 20 were rejected because their preambles were not proved.

Although the 1863 Select Committee report was almost entirely concerned with railway legislation, there were some references to other areas of promotion and the moves made similarly to rationalise and consolidate the processes involved. Lord Redesdale, Chairman of the Committees on Private Bills in the Lords, had earlier that same day[43] referred to public health promotions:

> The Public Health Acts, and more recently the Local Government Act, 1858, have invested the Secretary of State, acting on the requisition of the local authorities of towns, with large *quasi* legislative powers, extending to almost every object previously attainable only by Private Acts, and including even the compulsory purchase of lands, subject only to a confirmation of the Provisional Orders by a Public Act of Parliament. This measure has gone very far to supersede private legislation, so far as regards the local management of towns, hereto effected by 'Improvement Bills'.

The subsequent growth in the ambit and ambition of municipal activity overtook this verdict, but Lord Redesdale was no doubt correct in contrasting purely local concerns with the wider geographical and policy implications of railway Bills. When asked, however, whether delegating this local government business had proved inconvenient to the public or to Parliament, he partially contradicted his previous implication by adding

> I am not aware that it has been attended by any inconvenience to Parliament. In some instances I think it has been attended by inconvenience to the public, because I find in a great many instances that the parties, after having tried the application of the Improvements Acts, have had to come to Parliament to put matters straight when they wanted to do anything in the least out of the ordinary and general way.[44]

Contained in these exchanges are matters of considerable significance for the subject of this study: the implications of consolidation, the changing mood of central government and the growing aspirations of local government have never before been considered in the context of private legislation.

Mr. Percy Wyndham M.P. (Cumberland West) mentioned the marked reduction in the numbers given in the table above in the context of the 1866 monetary crisis, in a resumed debate about the private legislation system on 22 March 1872.[45] Undoubtedly several factors influenced the numbers of promotions annually – prominent among them no doubt the coming to an end of the 'railway mania' era and the increasing availability of consolidating provisions, as well of course as the economic climate. Promoting a Bill was in itself, however, no simple matter; it was a usually costly and intricately articulated process, partly established for the public good with its quasi-judicial overtones; partly structured to suit the requirements and convenience of Parliament; and partly driven by the fees that those engaged in this Westminster 'cottage industry' could earn. Just how private legislation was promoted was important in all these quarters.

How local legislation was promoted

It was the traditional right of the citizen to petition Parliament, and that right could be exercised by other legal entities also, providing that they had the power to do so. That is to say, provided they were legally competent to petition in the first place, Parliament would hear that petition so long as preliminary qualifying conditions were met. Petitioning was commonplace at this time: it was no mere footnote or arcane byway in the annals of Parliamentary procedure. In relation to the eighteenth-century turnpike movement, Eric Pawson cautioned that 'Petitions presented to Parliament are not the best measure of local feeling that preceded or accompanied a request for turnpike authority'.[46] Nevertheless, in the record year of 1843, Parliament received 33,898 petitions, and the average across most of the nineteenth century was some 10,000 a year. From 1832 onwards, there were moves to modify procedures to enable Parliament to cope with the tide by restricting 'the radicals' freedom to use parliamentary time to debate radical issues on the floor of the House on any day they pleased and before the government could proceed with the business for the day'.[47]

The procedures were very detailed, and continually changed and evolved as Parliament struggled to deal not only with the sheer volume of business that dealing with local Bills entailed, but also with their technical and jurisprudential demands. The first formal publication of the Standing Orders of the two Houses 'Relative to Private Bills' was in 1836; they were republished thereafter 'as annually altered and amended'[48] at the close of each Parliamentary session. The following references to the outlines of the procedures are all taken from the 1866 edition of the Commons Standing Orders.

Both Houses identically divided private Bills into two classes; the first comprised most Bills that may be considered primarily municipal in nature, whereas the second concerned various kinds of public works – the 'making, maintaining, varying, extending or enlarging' of what would today be termed infrastructure. The requirements for each class differed. The promoters of private Bills were required to prove to the appointed Examiners compliance with the Standing Orders of both Houses before they could proceed (a necessity that usually gave the recitals in Bills and subsequent local Acts very reliable authenticity). Petitions had to be deposited in the Private Bill Office on or before 23 December (S.O. 38), and were numbered consecutively. Each was separately examined, starting on 18 January, at not less than seven clear days' notice: S.O.s 72 and 73. No private Bill could 'be brought into this House' for consideration without a duly deposited petition 'indorsed by one of the Examiners': S.O. 182.

Memorials could be deposited complaining of non-compliance with the Standing Orders (S.O. 75); in relation to the actual provisions of any Bill,

> No petition against a Private Bill shall be taken into consideration ... which shall not distinctly specify the ground on which the Petitioners object to any of the provisions thereof; and the Petitioners shall be only heard on the grounds so stated.
>
> S.O. 128

The question of standing, of the right to be heard – technically known as *locus standi* – was very technical and legalistic; James Mellor Smethurst devoted some 200 pages to it in *A Treatise on the Locus Standi of Petitioners Against Private Bills in Parliament* (1866, 1867). From 1846 the House of Commons, and from 1856 the Lords, referred private Bills to Examiners to ascertain whether they complied with Standing Orders, or whether some dispensation might be applicable. *Locus standi* was extremely important; for promoters, concerned at the costs and uncertainties that petitions and opposition could involve, disqualification of potential objections could make all the difference between affordable success and possible rejection outright of the whole Bill; for objectors, the converse applied; if they could afford to petition Parliament against a Bill, but still could not establish the right to be heard, their only chance of blocking unwelcome proposals probably lay in whatever local influence they could bring to bear. Smethurst began his preface to the first edition of 1866 by saying that it was generally admitted that Parliament's practice about whether a petitioner had the right to be heard was 'most unsatisfactory', and that it was

> clear to all that the present system in the House of Lords, and the former one in the House of Commons, have been the cause of enormous and unnecessary expense both to the promoters of private bills and to the petitioners against them.[49]

The general rules of entitlement to be heard as a petitioner are summarised on the first two pages of his second edition of 1867, and are further discussed in Chapter 3: we may particularly notice here Rule IV, 'Parties Petitioning Under Standing Order H.C. 133', which reads

> That the municipal or other authority having the local management of the metropolis, or of any town, or the inhabitants (as a body) of any town or district, will be allowed a *locus standi* against a bill injuriously affecting their interests, if an allegation to that effect is made in their petition.

Once it was established that a Bill had been validly brought to Parliament, and the rights of any objectors had been established, each House could consider it. Committees had been necessitated when the volume of business meant that the evidence for or against a Bill could no longer be heard at the bar of the House. Initially, any member of the relevant House who wished to attend could do so, but the numbers were reduced when this open-ended participation proved unsatisfactory, and in 1855 the limit was set at five.[50] While the Committee hearings were crucial, other more formal stages in a Bill's progression could not be overlooked; they provided additional opportunities in particular for objectors with the support of M.P.s or Lords to upset the progress of a contentious promotion.

The rapidly rising tide of private promotions had soon convinced Parliament that they needed help to deal with the circumstances and contexts of Bills as well as the processes of their formal consideration, leading to the Act of 1846 referred to above that required formal preliminary inquiries to be made. The House of Commons *Select Committee on Private Bills* printed, as Appendix 7 to their Third Report of 1847,[51] the transcript of an investigation into how the new Act was working and was being perceived by those required to comply with it. The 1846 Act was, however – as noted above – not considered a success; it was repealed and replaced 2 years later by 11 & 12 Vict. cap. CXXIX, and replaced yet again in 1851 by 14 & 15 Vict. cap. XLIX, requiring Admiralty involvement where a promoted Bill proposed works on tidal lands. As time went on, both Houses sought to rationalise and streamline the Parliamentary processes; these steps sometimes were of considerable consequence for promoters and objectors, who not only wanted to know whether and when their Bills would become law, but had of course to bear the mounting costs involved.

The questions of costs and fees are further considered in Chapter 3. They could be very considerable, particularly if objections were lodged against the proposals. Both, however, were tightly regulated so far as Parliament was concerned. Edward Webster published *Parliamentary Costs: Private Bills, Election Petitions, Appeals, House of Lords* (3rd edition, 1867), with examples of how to draw bills of costs. Webster worked in the Commons Taxing Office and in the Examiners' Office of both Houses; his Preface included advice 'that it is safer and more economical to employ Parliamentary Agents than to try to do without them, as the latter course sometimes results in loss of money to the client and of professional reputation to the solicitor'. In 1847 and 1849 respectively, very similar Acts were passed 'for the more effectual

Taxation of Costs on Private Bills'.[52] After 1865, promoters had at least some protection against unjustifiable expense; if the promoters of a Bill whose preamble had been proved had been, in the unanimous opinion of a Committee, 'vexatiously subjected to expense in the promotion of the said Bill by the opposition of any petitioner or petitioners against the same' they could be awarded appropriate costs under section 2 of the Parliamentary Costs Act of that year.[53]

The fees that Parliament derived from considering private Bills were considerable. The Lords did not alter the scale of fees that they had laid down in 1725 until 1824. Many of the Houses' office-holders were at least in part remunerated by fees, and it was only when this system, undesirable even when not open to abuse, was effectively discontinued, that the whole procedural structure – for both Standing Orders, fees and process generally – could be reformed so as to be both defensible and better fitted to cope with the enormous business demands now being made of it. It was evident to many also, that while they sat unpaid through endless Committees and Readings of countless Bills, the counsel and other professionals who appeared before them were in some cases earning many thousands of pounds per year from the status quo.

In 1844 the Commons cancelled the several different fee streams that had hitherto existed, and a new table was drawn up. The Commons received £40,963 for private Bills in 1844, £30,681 of that being paid on 159 Bills that eventually received the royal assent. This year 'was taken by the Speaker as a fair average year on which to base a new scale', and 'The scale of 1847 was arranged so as to produce, with a corresponding quantity of business, the same proportionate income'.[54]

For promoters, of course, and sometimes for objectors, fees and costs in Parliament were only part of the outlay – or investment – that they were likely to have to make, and with no guarantee of eventual success. Promoters probably needed to do some research; take legal and probably other kinds of advice, such as surveying and engineering expertise; prepare plans and other preliminaries; consult local opinion and negotiate with those directly affected, especially potential objectors; give necessary public notice; ensure that they would be able to comply fully and minutely with the Parliamentary Standing Orders; and – depending on the nature of their objectives – then finance whatever purposes they intended if the local Act were passed. Prior to 1849, Bills had to be ingrossed, or as Clifford put it, 'transcribed by hand in beautiful characters', while it was 1851 before Breviates, summaries of each Bill's chief objectives, were discontinued.[55]

In 1883 were published some Returns of the costs incurred in Parliament by local authorities on obtaining local legislation. Clifford considered them misleading, as tending not to include the legal costs incurred among all the other preliminary expenses (though the accounts of those municipal authorities involved should presumably have recorded a more complete picture). Nevertheless, he adds that

Taken as a whole, the Returns only prove what hardly required proof, namely, that when the sanction of Parliament is sought for changes in the existing law, usually involving large pecuniary issues, affecting to a greater or less degree the status and welfare of rich and powerful companies and communities, and demanding, on all sides, the services of skilled witnesses, the very highest in their respective professions, the costs of obtaining or opposing such legislation cannot fail to be heavy.[56]

Reliable and comprehensive information on the total costs of Parliamentary promotion is hard to obtain. What information is available tends to refer only to the Parliamentary aspects of what was involved – not to the all-up costs to the promoters of their enterprise. The average cost of getting an improvement Bill through Parliament in 1848 was estimated by S.E. Finer at over £2,000, while John Garrard quotes page 7 of the *Bolton Chronicle* for 17 February 1855 for the assertion that getting a much-reduced Bolton Bill to royal assent was £9,000.[57] Civic pride, where it was part of the motivation for promoting a Bill, could be a very costly factor – but at the same time those behind the initiative could speak of investment for the future, and of keeping up with other municipalities in what modern parlance would call 'the race for jobs and growth'. Indeed this was not fanciful – many towns were expanding very fast indeed during the mid-Victorian era, and could reasonably expect to recoup from growth in the product of a penny rate the outlay incurred by local Bills. Where civic pride spilled over into outright competition with towns seen as economic or social rivals, costs could be driven well beyond the already heady heights of the Parliamentary process itself. Jon Stobart, in the article already referred to,[13] has illustrated the wider repercussions of a drive for civic culture by instancing that in the Potteries in the nineteenth century were built 14 town halls, 5 museums and schools of art, 9 libraries, 5 public parks and over a dozen theatres.[58] These were not, of course, all the products of local legislation, but they demonstrate the momentum behind civic ambition, pride in one's place, and – no doubt – the grand ambitions of particular individuals. For all these motivations the cost and commitment entailed in promoting a local Bill were just parts of a wider policy and programme of civic investment – and the more that local feeling was behind the aspirations of those leading these initiatives, the less likely they were to face costly opposition if they went to Parliament for increased powers.

The House of Commons Select Committee on Private Bills in 1847 had looked carefully at the costs of Bill promotion. On 8 March 1847 the Chairman, Joseph Hume M.P., asked G.B. Gregory, a Parliamentary agent, about the preliminary expenses of improvement Bills. He was told[59] that they typically cost some £300, occasioned mainly by the length of Bills, although that would be reduced by the proposed consolidation measures. Much time was spent by the Committee on the high costs that its promoters had recently had to meet in obtaining the Bury Improvement Act 1846 (9 & 10 Vict. cap.

ccxciii), and the solicitors', Parliamentary agents' and witnesses' bills of costs were printed in detail in Appendix 3 to the Third Report.[60] A petition had been sent to the House complaining about the costs incurred; William Bowman, a Bury Improvement Commissioner who had opposed the Bill, said that there had been no more than three days of hearings, the opponents having attended only on two. The bill of costs for the Parliamentary stages amounted to £3,696 6s. 3d.[61] On the other hand, it was asserted that the local investigation procedures under the Preliminary Inquiries Act of 1846[62] had saved the expense of investigation before a Parliamentary Committee in the case of the Colchester Improvement and Navigation Bill.[63]

A decade later the Select Committee appointed by the Lords to consider private Bill procedures also considered the questions of fees and costs. George Pritt, a Parliamentary agent, gave evidence on 1 July 1858 to the effect that in 1855, 1856 and 1857 he had dealt with a total of 17 unopposed Bills. His own charges had averaged £139 1s. 11d. Parliamentary fees had averaged £282 4s. 6d. and printing costs had brought the overall average – this in cases where the promoters ordinarily did not require counsel, as their proposals were unopposed – up to £474 15s. 9d.[64] Another agent, C.E. Thomas, giving evidence on 5 July about 40 unopposed Bills with which he had dealt, gave the same categorised information, yielding an average total in his experience of £362 3s.7d.[65] These averages were not of course derived from wholly municipal or similar instructions, and neither did they obviously include all the other costs that the relevant promoters had had to pay. Chapter 3 further considers the evidence given about different aspects of the costs involved.

Why local legislation was needed

Before the mid-nineteenth century, the doctrine of *ultra vires* ('beyond the powers') was not well developed, though it had long been understood that the great seventeenth-century jurist Lord Coke had opined in the *Sutton's Hospital* Case[66] that a common law corporation has power at common law to do everything that a natural person may do. By the 1850s, however, this approach, and the creation of increasing numbers of statutory companies given specific powers for explicit purposes, was inadequate. The courts began to decide cases based on challenges to the validity of company and corporation powers. At the same time the careful detail inserted into so much legislation was indicative of a general view that implied powers were open to question and challenge, so that explicit provision was necessary for the avoidance of doubt.

In 1875 the House of Lords essentially settled the law in *Ashbury Railway Carriage and Iron Co. v. Riche*.[67] Although it was many years before a similar approach was judicially confirmed as applicable in local government, in *London County Council v. Attorney-General*,[68] it had long been clear in practice that local authorities, in the main creatures of statute, could do only what was given to them to do.

Those who promoted local Bills usually needed Parliamentary approval for one or more of four reasons. First, if they did not already comprise a legal entity, a new corporate body would probably need to be created. Second, existing common law or statute might need disapplying, amending or reforming in the local context. Third, and probably most contentiously, exceptional authority might be needed to do something that would otherwise be unlawful or impractical – such as interfering with private rights or land ownership; enforcing some control; or giving the right to raise local revenue or impose enforceable charges and penalties. It was, and still is, the essence of private legislation that it is about the conferring of, or interfering with, private rights in specific ways that cannot be done under the general public law. The fourth reason was civic pride. It might be that the powers sought were more or less already available to them in other ways; it might be that they felt the need to display growing municipal power and wealth by projects designed for show as well as for practical utility, or to consolidate the applicable local legislation into their own separate code. Any of these might be seen as justification for going to Parliament for direct authority to undertake whatever it was that the city fathers wanted.

This was not only a matter of vainglory. This was not a time of municipal innovation at the hands of central government; there were reforming moves in Parliament, but they tended to rely on determined individual pioneers, like William Ewart for public libraries, or the seventh Earl of Shaftesbury for child labour. In local legislation the promoters were by definition proactive, and Parliament largely reactive. The promoters might be the municipal equivalents of the pioneers in Parliament, but without their initiatives their localities would not simply be gratuitously awarded the kinds of powers on which cleansing old communities and building new ones depended. The state did not universally incorporate the Towns Improvement Clauses Act 1847 (where there was no special local Act applicable) until it was included as section 160 of the great reforming Public Health Act 1875.

Annex

The Sources for and Existing Discussion of Local Legislation

The Chronological Table of Local Legislation referred to above lists on pp. xxvii–xxiv the major collections of local legislation in the U.K. Apart from the Parliamentary Archives and British Library, most collections – with varying degrees of completeness – are, as would be expected, in the libraries of Government Departments and universities, though a number of county councils also possess extensive holdings.[69]

In addition, other local authorities generally possess copies of at least the principal or modern local Acts which apply to them, or which either they or their predecessor councils promoted. It is, however, often far from easy to trace all currently applicable provisions for two main reasons. The first is that in the twenty-first century, local legislation is far less significant in day-to-day applicability and use, so that practitioner knowledge of it is generally limited. The second reason is that, in order to reduce the *corpus* of local legislation without undertaking the enormous task of specific repeals, Parliament has resorted to the device of *cesser*. This declares that particular classes of legislation shall, without being individually itemised, be repealed. It was most recently used for local government in general in s. 262 of the Local Government Act 1972. The example, however, of s. 26(1) of the Municipal Corporations Act 1883 (which abolished a number of local government corporations) – 'So much of any Act, law, charter, or usage as is inconsistent with this Act is hereby repealed' – demonstrates how uncertain the state of the law could be rendered by such an ill-defined and expedient approach.

The sheer bulk and complexity of local legislation (and maybe to some extent the relative inaccessibility of copies, compared with the availability of the public general Acts) has undoubtedly inhibited comparative study. As they were then defined, the 1866–77 and 1878–87 respective *Indexes to Local and Private Acts*[70] covered 2,649 and 2,228 Acts respectively – 212 per year on average, or rather more than one every two days. Without rigorous categorisation, and some means of distinguishing the innovative from the purely repetitive, it is almost impossible to distil significant trends or conclusions from such a mass of material. In consequence there is little published commentary or analysis of the *genre* as a whole, as opposed to what can be found from published indexes, local knowledge or particular specialisation. Local Acts from 1797, though not all private and personal Acts, are now available online at www.justis.com on a subscription basis.

As early as 1813, George Bramwell published *An Analytical Table of the Private Statutes* passed between 1727 and 1812, the first such work in its field. Volume II for 1813–34 followed. During the nineteenth century more such works were published, initially by private enterprise. They included Thomas Vardon's *Index to the Local and Personal and Private Acts 1798–1839* (1840).[71] An *Index to Private Acts 1483–1831* (accompanied by *Road Acts 1753–1797* and *Local and Personal Acts 1797–1831*) was followed by a second volume covering both public and local/private Acts for the period 1801–65.[72] Under the aegis of the Select Committee on the Library of the House of Lords, *An Index to the Statutes, Public and Private*, categorised into 21 classes, was published in 1860 covering the years 1801–59 – the first official compilation of this kind. A further official compilation down to 1900 was published in 1901. In 1949, HMSO published the *Index to Local and Personal Acts 1801–1947* (to which a *Supplement 1948–66* was published in 1967). In addition, the Parliamentary Archives contain a *Classified Index to the Journals of the House of Lords: From 1833 to 1863, both inclusive*, the first part dating from 1865. Part V dealing with *Local and Personal and Private Bills* was printed in 1869.

The 1949 HMSO publication was again a categorised index, with the listed Acts divided into 15 subject areas (the 1967 Supplement was categorised slightly differently; the last subject area XV included personal Acts). In that respect it differed from the 1996 Law Commission *Chronological Table*, which, as the title implies, listed all the Acts serially year by year and also sought to include repeals (though without necessarily including all cross-references and other repeal implications like the effect of cesser). Finally, in 1996, HMSO published the four-volume *Index to the Local and Personal Acts 1850–1995*, complied by Rosemary Devine, who had been Examiner of Private Acts in the House of Lords. Her two further volumes covering 1797–1849 were published in 1999. For London a helpful additional source is *London Statutes. A Collection of Public Acts Relating Specially to the Administrative County of London and of Local and Personal Acts Affecting the Powers and Duties of the London County Council From 1750 to 1907* (vol. I, 1907). This was prepared by G.L. Gomme and Seager Berry, Clerk and Solicitor respectively to the L.C.C.

Apart from indexes, several treatises on aspects of private Bill procedure have appeared over the years, usually originating from the desire of practitioners (particularly in the early years) to capture and record their personal experiences at a time when there was generally no official or authoritative material available. The 77-page work *Local and Personal Acts of Parliament in the United Kingdom* (ed. Carleton Olegario Maximo, 2012), however, is a largely peripheral collection of Wikipedia articles.

The *Parliamentary Papers* for 1860[73] (vol. LVII, pp. 203 and 219 – Papers 325 and 578) contain two sets of correspondence prompted by Mr. James Bigg, who suggested to the Treasury a plan for publishing a composite revised set of all the public statutes. He did not propose to include private statutes, but the correspondence contains detailed information about current and potential printing costs etc. and the scale of what would be required. At the close of the second 1859 session, apparently, he stated that 6,988 public Acts containing 62,620 folio pages had been passed since 1801; of these 3,734 with 35,849 pages were wholly repealed, expired or spent, leaving 3,254 with 26,771 pages wholly or partly in force. Bigg suggested in his letter of 10 December 1858 that altogether 'The public statutes extend to near 90,000 foolscap folio pages, of which the larger part have been repealed, or have expired, or are spent'. (Bigg's compilation of public railway Acts was published by Waterlow's in 1872; he edited a number of volumes of public Acts at this period.)

Notes

1 *Hansard*, 3rd series, vol. 210, col. 18. See also Chapter 3. John Dodson was created Lord Monk Bretton in 1884.
2 Para. 3.1.
3 He instances the legislation passed in 1874 about the registration of births and the certification of deaths, ostensibly to improve the quality of medical and demographic statistics, but also in fact prompted by 'baby-farming' concerns voiced in Parliament: pp. 76–7.
4 Higgs, *op. cit.*, p. 65. He mentions against this point (in this order) the Poor Law Amendment Act 1834, the Public Health Act 1848, the Metropolitan and County and Borough Police Acts of 1829 and 1856, and the Education Act 1870.

Sources, structure, scope of local legislation 27

5 Higgs, *op. cit.*, p. 65, referring to the cited work of respectively Corrigan and Sayer, Philip Harling, Harold Perkin and Oliver MacDonagh. See also Tom Crook and Glen O'Hara (eds.), *Statistics and the Public Sphere: Numbers and the People in Modern Britain, c. 1800–2000* (2011).
6 See Chantal Stebbings, *Legal Foundations of Tribunals in Nineteenth Century England* (2006); and also her *The Victorian Taxpayer and the Law: A Study in Constitutional Conflict* (2009).
7 Jose Harris, *Private Lives, Public Spirit: Britain 1870–1914* (1993), pp.17–18. She adds on p. 18 that

> Utilitarian efforts of the 1830s and 1840s to shift the locus of Government away from small communities had proved largely a failure; and, far from dwindling in the face of economic change, the culture and philosophy of localism had enjoyed a tremendous resurgence in the 1840s and 1850s, as part of a nationwide reaction against bureaucratic rationalization.

8 Theodore K. Hoppen, *The Mid-Victorian Generation: England 1846–1886* (1998), p. 107, citing Sir Norman Chester, *The English Administrative System 1780–1870* (1981), pp. 347–8. This illustrates how source information may acquire the authority of those through whose hands it passes: Chester in turn took the totals from V.D. Lipman, *Local Government Areas 1834–1945* (1949) pp. 72–4, but also cites what is in fact Paper 308 in the following note below (though giving the wrong date of 1878, and no *Parliamentary Papers* reference at all), while drawing attention to unexplained small differences between the quoted totals and those of Dr Farr, the Registrar General's Superintendent of Statistics, in his evidence to the Select Committee (qq. 1069–1221). Lipman's direct sources are the relevant Parliamentary reports and returns.
9 1873, *Parliamentary Papers*, vol. VIII, p. 1 (Paper 308 – also printed as Paper HL252). The whole Paper is fascinating, and makes one wonder that there was any systematic local administration anywhere. See for instance qq. 261–71 and qq. 1457–87.
10 Elizabeth T. Hurren, *Protesting About Pauperism: Poverty, Politics and Poor Relief in Late-Victorian England, 1870–1900* (2007), p. 32.
11 Quoting S. Collini, *Liberalism and Sociology: L.T. Hobhouse and Political Argument in England, c. 1880–1914* (Cambridge, 1979), p. 1.
12 Hurren, *op. cit.*, p. 39.
13 Jon Stobart (2003), 'Identity, competition and place promotion in the Five Towns', *Urban History*, vol. 30, p. 2. In his 12-page May 2002 article 'A central role for local government? The example of late Victorian Britain', at www.historyandpolicy.org, Simon Szreter summarises the period 1870–1914 as experiencing 'a flowering in British civic activism'. He also considers that, 'Between 1865 and 1875 the prestige of local government was revolutionised and a model for popular, effective public services was developed by provincial business and community leaders'. Such dates are usually indicative rather than specific, and the article concentrates on the larger conurbations for what he terms 'the provincial sources of civic revival' rather than that proportion of the population who still lived outside the reach of such civic energy – indeed some places like Glossop still had no local authority at all in 1865 – see note 6 to Appendix 1 – but there is no doubt that after the Local Government Acts of 1888 and 1894 the importance, scope and effectiveness of the municipal contribution to the national life had been transformed for the better from what had obtained only one generation earlier.
14 Page v.
15 *Victoria's Heyday* by J.B. Priestley was published in 1972.
16 Pages vi–vii.

28 *Sources, structure, scope of local legislation*

17 Page 3.
18 Page 27.
19 1988, Leicester City Council.
20 See note 67 to Chapter 4.
21 Page 323.
22 *Parliament and the Public Libraries* (1977) by R.J.B. Morris, p. 26. Sibthorp's obituary in the *Lincoln, Rutland and Stamford Mercury* of 21 December 1855 noted that 'though eccentric in his extreme tory views, even his opponents allowed that he was honest and consistent in his political conduct'.
23 Pages 244–45.
24 Pages 2–3.
25 Page 410.
26 Page 7.
27 Page v.
28 Page vii.
29 The numbers of all Acts passed in the years 1800–1884 were published as Appendix A to Frederick Clifford, *A History of Private Bill Legislation* (1885), vol. I, pp. 491–2, based partly on a Return printed as House of Commons paper 34 in 1857. In a footnote Clifford adds, 'Since 1867 the Acts for confirming Provisional Orders, and a few other public Acts of a local character, have been transferred from the list of Public General to that of Local and Personal Acts'. The journal *Archives* published an article by John Sheail entitled 'Local Legislation: Its Scope and Content' in vol. XXX, no. 113 (October 2005) at pp. 36–50; it is useful, and illustrative of the difficulties at Preston in the 1880s when they had exceeded their local Act powers in relation to the river Ribble, but is mostly concerned with a later period, from then on into the early 1900s, than we are here. On the Parliamentary Archives see Maurice F. Bond, *Guide to the Records of Parliament* (1971), and also the House of Lords Record Office Memorandum No. 16 on *The Private Bill Records of the House of Lords* by E.R. Poyser (1957).
30 There were also other returns: for instance, Paper 0.101 for 1857–8 provides a categorised analysis of that session's private Bills (see *Parliamentary Papers*, vol. XLVI, p. 777; this Paper is listed on p. xci of Paper 483 at vol. LXII, p. 1, the annual accumulated *List of the Bills, Reports, Estimates, and Accounts and Papers* for the 1857–8 session). To place the start of the period 1858–72 in context, 1858 followed on fairly consistently from the years before; 249 Bills were deposited in 1857 for instance, and 255 were read a first time, with 185 receiving royal assent and 162 listed that year in the *Chronological Table*.
31 This is illustrated by the 59 pages occupied by the Calendar of Select Committee appointments and other private Bill legislation consideration set out in *The Historical Development of Private Bill Procedure and Standing Orders in the House of Commons* by O.C. Williams (HMSO 1948), vol. I, pp. 262–320.
32 W.E. Gladstone, as President of the Board of Trade, chaired a Select Committee whose fifth report, in 1844, considered that 'railway schemes ought not to be recommended as mere projects of local improvement, but that each new line should be viewed as a member of a great scheme of communication'. A special department of the Board of Trade was established accordingly, but would-be promoters raised such clamour that at the opening of the 1845 Session of Parliament, the Prime Minister Sir Robert Peel announced that railway Bills would be left as before to the judgement of the Private Bill Committees. The 'Railway Mania' followed. Edwin A. Pratt, *A History of Inland Transport and Communication in England* (1912), notes at p. 271: 'By the summer of 1845 the country had gone railway mad.' He goes on the give the statistics – 24 railway Acts passed in 1843; 37 such Acts in 1844; then 248 railway Bills in 1845; and in 1846 the total of Bills deposited with the Board of Trade was 815 for 20,687 miles of track and £350 million

worth of capital powers, with some 700 of them reaching the Private Bill Office. So James Booth somewhat underestimated. See Pratt's narrative generally about the *Railways and the State*, which comprises his chapter XXI, pp. 258–93. He considered that previous experience with the canal companies from the outset fostered distrust in the attitude of the state towards railway companies: p. 258. A return of the fees paid on railway Bills in the previous session was printed at pp. 171–6 (actually only four pages as the printed page numbers omit 172 and 173) in the Report from the 1846 Select Committee of the House of Lords on *Railways* at *Parliamentary Papers*, vol. XIII, volume p. 217 at pp. 411–14, Paper 489. (The printed title of this paper began *Report from the Select Committee of the House of Lords Appointed to take into Consideration the best Means of enforcing one uniform System of MANAGEMENT of RAILROADS in operation or to be constructed ...*)
33 9 & 10 Vict. c. CVI.
34 By 11 & 12 Vict. c. CXXIX. A four-part list of papers on *Preliminary Inquiries: 9 & 10 Vict. C. 106* was published in *Parliamentary Papers*, (1847), vol. XXXIII, p. 87 (Paper 33, ordered to be printed 1 February 1847). It included instructions and guidance to the surveying officers; a summary of cases deposited up to 30 November 1846; and the arrangement of cases as at 30 January 1847.
35 See *Minutes of Evidence of the House of Lords Select Committee on Proceedings on Private Bills*, 29 June 1858, paras. 78–87: evidence of Mr T. Erskine May, Clerk Assistant of the House of Commons (*Parliamentary Papers*, 1857–8, vol. XII, pp. 15 and 273: Papers 450 and 450-I).
36 14 & 15 Vict. c. XLIX. The measure was introduced as Bill 532, 'Mr. Wilson Patten' being one of the three M.P.s bringing it in.
37 *Parliamentary Papers* (1863), vol. VIII, p. 205: Paper 385, ordered to be printed on 24 June 1863.
38 *Op. cit.*, q. 5.
39 *Op. cit.*, q. 5.
40 *Op. cit.*, q. 19.
41 *Op. cit.*, q. 43.
42 *Op. cit.*, q. 812.
43 *Op. cit.*, q. 713.
44 *Op. cit.*, q. 713.
45 *Hansard*, 3rd series, vol. 210, col. 522.
46 Eric Pawson, 'Debates in Transport History: Popular Opposition to Turnpike Trusts?', *Journal of Transport History*, (1984) 3rd series, vol. 5, no. 2, pp. 57–65 at p. 59. See also note 66 to Chapter 2.
47 Colin Leys, 'Petitioning in the Nineteenth and Twentieth Centuries', *Political Studies*, vol. III, pp. 45–64 at p. 48 (1955). The numbers of petitions presented and printed in the preceding 5 years were the subject of Commons Paper 0.108 in 1857–8: *Parliamentary Papers*, vol. XLVI, p. 773. The Prime Minister, Viscount Palmerston, thanked the Committee upon Petitions by name on 25 August 1860 for their onerous labours after 24,264 petitions involving some three million signatures had been received during the 1860 session, the largest total since 1843: H.C. Deb. 3rd series, vol. 160, cols. 1815–17.
48 *The Standing Orders of the Lords and Commons Relative to Private Bills* (1878 edn., for the 1879 session), p. iii. (*Parliamentary Papers*, 1878–9, vol. LVIII, p. 113, printed as Paper 379). The process in 1836 is described in the extensive commentary *A Practical Treatise on Passing Private Bills Through Both Houses of Parliament* by John Halcomb (London, 1836).
49 Smethurst, *op. cit.*, p. v.
50 The limit for opposed Bills was further reduced; by 1878 in the Commons it was a Chairman, three members and a referee. For unopposed Bills the limits were even lower, but were different according to whether the Bill had originated in the

30 *Sources, structure, scope of local legislation*

Commons or the Lords. *Standing Orders* (1878 edn, *op. cit.*): Commons, nos. 116–17 and 137. Throughout this period the Lords kept their limit at five, though unlike the Commons the Chairman did not have a casting vote: see Frederick Clifford, *A History of Private Bill Legislation* (two vols., 1885 and 1887) vol. I, p. 256.
51 Pages 299–307, *Parliamentary Papers*, 1847, vol. XII, p. 357 (Paper 705).
52 10 &11 Vict. c. 69 and 12 &13 Vict. c. 78 respectively.
53 The 1865 Act was repealed and replaced by the Parliamentary Costs Act 2006. As to how 'unanimously' it had been interpreted, see the Law Commissions' report on the *Parliamentary Costs Bill*, Cm6846 (June 2006).
54 Clifford, *op. cit.*, vol. II, p. 744.
55 Clifford, *op. cit.*, vol. I, p. 258.
56 Clifford, *op. cit.*, vol. I, pp. 259–60.
57 S.E. Finer, *The Life and Times of Sir Edwin Chadwick* (London, 1952) p. 433, and quoted with the *Bolton Chronicle* reference in John Garrard, *Leadership and Power in Victorian Industrial Towns 1830–80*, p. 101.
58 Jon Stobart, 'Building an Urban Identity. Cultural Space and Civic Boosterism in a "New" Industrial Town: Burslem, 1761–1911', *Social History* (2004) vol. 29, no. 4, pp. 485–98 at p. 488. The diversity of the requirements of actual building development is portrayed by Roger H. Harper in *Victorian Building Regulations: Summary Tables of the Principal English Building Acts and Model By-laws 1840–1914* (1988).
59 First Report from the Select Committee on Private Bills (*Parliamentary Papers*, 1847, vol. XII, p. 347, Paper 116), q. 482.
60 *Third Report from the Select Committee on Private Bills* (1847, *Parliamentary Papers*, vol. XII, p. 357, Paper 705), pp. 253–67). The Act was 9 & 10 Vict. c. ccxciii. Section 334 of the Bury Improvement Act 1846 provided for the yield from rates to be applied 'in the first place in paying Three Fourth Parts of the Costs and Expences of obtaining or passing this Act, or incidental thereto', leaving the Bill's promoters accordingly with a very large sum still to find elsewhere.
61 *Op. cit.*, qq. 2043–6 (26 April 1847).
62 9 & 10 Vict. cap. CVI.
63 16 April 1847; Capt. J. Vetch, R.E. at q. 1536 (16 April 1847), and H.C. Paper 124–50.
64 *Report from the Select Committee of the House of Lords, Appointed to Inquire into the present System of Proceedings in Parliament on Private Bills*, qq. 563–79 (*Parliamentary Papers*, 1857–8, vol. XII, pp. 15 and 273: Papers 450 and 450-I).
65 *Op. cit.*, qq. 729–42.
66 (1612) 10 Co. Rep. 23, at p. 30b.
67 (1875) L.R. 7 H.L. 53.
68 (1902) A.C. 165.
69 Subordinate legislation presents much greater problems of access; there is no fully complete set in existence. See 'Finding and Using Local Statutory Instruments' by R.J.B. Morris, *Statute Law Review* (Summer 1990), vol. 11, no. 1, pp. 28–47.
70 Law Society Library, Chancery Lane, London, WC2.
71 Vardon records in his Preface that

> An Index to the Local and Personal Acts had been compiled in pursuance of the recommendation of the Committee on the Library of the House of Commons; but the MS, when nearly completed, was destroyed in the Fire of the Houses of Parliament in October 1834. The Committee, in the following year, ordered that a similar Index should be re-compiled and completed to the close of the Session preceding the printing of the Work.

72 Law Society Library, Chancery Lane, London, WC2.
73 The letter of 10 December 1858 is letter no. 1 in Paper 325.

2 The context and content of local Bill promotion

In *A Century of Municipal Progress 1835–1935* (1935), John Willis comments in a deceptively simple statement that 'local legislation consists, in the main, of applying old principles to new facts'.[1] Whatever its truth in 1935, or its continuing validity 80 years later, it did not then adequately describe the situation as it had been 80 years earlier in mid-Victorian times. In 1935 the growing – and widely accepted – role of central Government in shaping and regulating local government was long established; in the mid-Victorian era it was not, and while the relative situation was quite quickly evolving, the pre-eminent national role in the emergence of local government was still played by Parliament rather than by Government.

Chapter 1 has suggested that local legislation was sought for four principal reasons: the need to create a new corporate body; the necessity of disapplying, amending or reforming the common law; seeking authority to do something otherwise unlawful or impractical; and finally from civic pride. There was, of course, an even more fundamental and obvious reason – that the existing law did not provide for or authorise what the promoters now wanted or were required to do. Accordingly we must first consider – as no existing commentary explicitly does – the state of public municipal or local government law as it stood in 1858, at the start of this study's period, and what made continuing dependence on local initiative, rather than central Government direction, still so important at this time. Also we shall examine the nature and scope of the vast archive of private Bill promotions in the mid-Victorian period – rarely considered material that will illuminate the context within which specifically local legislation was sought and granted.

Public law and public mood

'What' asked Oliver MacDonagh in *Early Victorian Government 1830–1870* 'did the reform of local government accomplished by the statutes of 1831 and 1835[2] amount to? The answer is, a great deal in terms of "civil and religious liberty" and egalitarian principle, but almost nothing in terms of day-to-day living.'[3] In the early nineteenth century there were incorporated towns, and there were unincorporated ones lacking charters and corporations, and coming, like the rest of England, under county benches of magistrates and paying county rates. There was no *system* of local government proper before 1835,[4] and while the Municipal Corporations Act 1835 for the first time enacted a deliberate – if partial – structure of authority (rather than the previous arrangements that had 'just growed'), it did not, as some writers have rather given the impression,[5] create a new paradigm or structure of local authorities; rather it *regulated* the 'divers Bodies Corporate at sundry Times [that had] been constituted within the Cities, Towns, and Boroughs of *England* and *Wales*' and held it expedient that their 'Charters ... should be altered'.[6] A total of 178 closed corporations were abolished. Areas outside the ambit of a municipal corporation were not covered, and some places were excluded from the Act's operation. A further weakness was that it remained voluntary for improvement commissions to merge with municipal corporations, with the result that duplication of local responsibilities persisted.[7] It was, however, concerned with the election, constitution, regulation and operation of the corporations themselves rather than the provision of services – it had after all been primarily the perceived abuses of the old order that had prompted the appointment of the Royal Commission shortly before.[8] Similarly the Highway Act 1835 also accepted the existing parishes (as then defined), and conferred on them powers and duties relating to the highways and bridges in their areas. Much the same at this time was true of the poor law. It was not until the 1840s and the passing of the various Clauses Consolidation Acts – referred to in Chapter 1 – that national, or at least Parliamentary, initiative began, at least in principle, to confer *generally available* powers and capacity on municipal authorities that had neither acquired them by charter nor secured them by some individual local initiative. It is seldom noted, however, that the early consolidation Acts did not in themselves directly confer powers, so that they represent a partial transition, rather than a direct change, towards a climate where Parliament and central Government saw it as their duty to legislate compulsorily about local government and its services, rather than leaving it in the hands of any local initiative that there might be.

For municipalities, the Acts relating to lands (1845) and cemeteries, commissioners, gas, markets and fairs, towns improvement and town police (1847) were potentially the most significant. They were passed, as already noted, more to relieve pressure on Parliament than to obviate the need for local Bill promotions, but there were advantages from the perspective of Government in some standardisation, and the establishing of legislative norms from which it would require special pleading to depart.

The phrase 'generally available' was used above advisedly. These Acts were not immediately applicable, but municipalities could qualify to avail themselves of them. They were enabling – voluntary – for those areas that wanted, and were able, to use them, whether in whole or in part. The tradition of enablement rather than prescription was already long established, and prevalent in diverse areas of what would now be termed public policy, from the Poor

Law to prostitution. The Towns Improvement Act 1847 was *An Act for consolidating in One Act certain Provisions usually contained in Acts for Paving, Draining, Cleansing, Lighting, and Improving Towns.* Its application extended (section 1) 'only to such towns in England or Ireland as shall be comprised in any Act of Parliament hereafter to be passed which shall declare that this Act shall be incorporated therewith'. It accordingly removed the need for the given powers to be promoted and obtained by another, largely repetitive local Act, but those powers (the Act had 216 sections and two schedules) were given to 'the commissioners'. The commissioners were the persons or body corporate given improvement powers by a 'special Act'; in turn, a 'special Act' was (section 2) 'any Act which shall be hereafter passed for the improvement or regulation of any town or district, or of any class of towns or districts, defined or comprised therein, and with which this Act shall be incorporated ...'

The Common Clauses Acts, therefore, while a step forward, were enacted in a form that made their availability still dependent on having already obtained a special (local) Act; far from empowering improvement commissions or other local bodies at large, when passed by Parliament they were measures of convenience and conformity only for those entitled to rely on them. (It should not be overlooked that the Clauses Acts, like those for gas and water etc., also applied in many cases to private, as opposed to public or municipal undertakings; there were, for instance, far more places whose water or gas supplies came from a private company, incorporated and empowered by its own special Act, in which all or most of the relevant Clauses Consolidation Act was incorporated, than there were municipal corporations or Local Boards.) The Town Police Clauses Act 1847 was not made widely available without the special Act qualification until it was incorporated with the Public Health Act 1875 (section 171). It would be wrong, however, to stigmatise what may seem a lost opportunity – a lack of vision – simply on the basis of later standards. The nation was, after all, rich and powerful, with a dominant role in much of the world – the state of municipal government and law were largely as they were, not because of inertia or ignorance, but because in general they suited the vested interests and the dominant people of the day. As soon as that began to change, reform usually followed. So once the eighteenth-century excesses of the old corporations became untenable, they were swept away, but the appetite for doing so did not also predicate an immediate appetite for similarly drastic action to provide for better social conditions in which the majority of the subjects of those old corporations lived.

As late as the mid-1840s, the state of what we now call local government law in relation to the population at large – as opposed to the municipal corporations themselves – requires little description, because it was so limited in extent.

> Until about the middle of the nineteenth century the local authorities, i.e. parishes, boroughs and counties, had little or no statutory responsibilities for such matters as education, public health, housing, etc. In fact,

no general Acts of any kind relating to these were to be found on the Statute Book.[9]

It is only necessary to consider the chronological *List of Statutes* pages included in most legal commentaries to see the truth of this. The new municipal corporations, like their abolished predecessors, had the common law powers of any landowner; they also had certain charter powers and the benefit of custom in most cases; but they had no general legal competence. While the crucial doctrine of *ultra vires* ('beyond the powers') was not formally articulated in legal precedent relating to local government until early in the twentieth century,[10] it was impossible for a municipality to behave freely according to whatever a majority of its members wanted. That was not the outlook of the times – nor was it the outlook of ratepayers, who generally resented paying the proliferating sums levied on them for various activities. The municipal corporations were only part of the picture – M.D. Chalmers wrote as late as 1883 that 'Local government in this country may be fitly described as consisting of a chaos of areas, a chaos of authorities, and a chaos of rates'.[11]

Clarke gives the situation in the mid-1830s as consisting of '27,069 local authorities levying as many as eighteen different kinds of rates'.[12] He comments (under the general heading of 'Nineteenth Century Chaos and Reform') that 'It is difficult to understand today [1955] how the borough councils failed to appreciate their responsibilities for the paving, lighting, watching, and cleansing of their towns'.[13] There will have been many reasons for this, but an obvious one in many cases – particularly in the early years – was that they did not actually have any such responsibilities. Unless there had been an improvement commission or special Act, there were not only no *duties* to do these things, there were no *powers*, a distinction and limitation insufficiently appreciated by historians. Local conditions might be regarded as acceptable to the people of the day who mattered in the local scene, and who would have to pay more rates if more works and commitments were undertaken.[14] Gradually, however, everything began to change; the links between local conditions and sickness or death began to be recognised; urban populations grew far beyond the confines of the old boundaries; and the leading lights in local communities began to have much more personal interests in the availability of healthy workforces, healthier places, and the kind of civic pride that could make a borough far more than the sum of its original parts.[15] These changes were, however, often slow in coming – and with a Parliament that began the 1830s with no tradition of social legislation, and also a Government with no sense of any obligation to insist on local standards of paving and lighting, etc., reform where it occurred was bound to be led primarily by strong local initiative, vision and determination. Those with such qualities looked to Westminster not to solve the problems for them, but to allow or enable them to tackle those problems for themselves.

As early as 1840 W. Cooke Taylor wrote that 'the use of steam as a motive power, the progress of machinery and manufactures, and the rapid accumulation of large masses of people in manufacturing districts, are formative powers, almost created before our eyes.'[16] Quoting that passage, R.A. Forsyth opined that

> The emergence of industrial cities is the predominant historical fact of the Victorian age. Their proliferation stands as a visible symbol of what Karl Polyani calls 'the great transformation', unprecedented in the life of any nation, from a rural to a market economy.[17]

He adds

> The true nature of Disraeli's 'two nations', that is to say, was a type of spiritual 'apartheid'.[18] In the context of local improvement, however, and the promotion of special legislation, more significant than the famous concept of two nations of haves and have-nots is the description of 'the rural town of Marney' – its situation 'one of the most delightful easily to be imagined' with its 'merry prospect' from across the dale, yet this 'beautiful illusion' contrasted with the reality that 'behind that laughing landscape, penury and disease fed upon the vitals of a miserable population'.[19]

Many writers of the time echoed the sense of physical, and also personal or spiritual, hopelessness and wretchedness of Cooke Taylor's 'rapid accumulations of large masses of people'. 'They leave all hope behind who enter there'[20] declared the poet James Thomson; while William Wordsworth wrote and campaigned passionately (and successfully) to keep railways out of the Lake District: 'Mountains, and Vales, and Floods, I call on you/ To share the passion of a just disdain'.[21]

Historians indeed have identified this time as a key period in the progression of urban poverty and welfare – this was a time when on the one hand, there was evident misery, degradation and disease in the rapidly growing towns. Yet also on the other hand, the pollution associated with much of the new infrastructure that was at the same time both bringing prosperity, and growing the urban areas even faster, was resented by those who saw the old ways and the old certainties threatened for ever by the railways, the mines, the factories and the docks that were outstripping the established and largely *laissez-faire* outlook of the state, with its limited capacity and will to regulate and restrain.[22]

The Health of Towns Association was formed in 1844, just as Disraeli was working on *Sybil*. The Government in 1847 had introduced a Public Health Bill, but despite extensive compelling evidence, it ran into a good deal of opposition, including whether it would or should apply to the metropolis. Just before the session ended, it was withdrawn, but another Bill was reintroduced in the following year. Speaking on this second Public Health Bill in

1848, Lord Morpeth (First Commissioner of the Board of Woods, Forests and Land Revenues), stated that 13 years after the Municipal Corporations Act 1835, 62 of England's 187 incorporated towns had no means of draining and cleansing, and only 29 had power to act through their elected local government. Of the towns with a population of over 5,000, 276 were 'left to complete anarchy' so far as sanitation, streets and water were concerned.[23] Lord Morpeth read out extracts from several reports when he moved for leave to bring in the Bill; these included average ages at death in 1840 in the parish of St. Margaret, Leicester – 23½ in well-drained streets, 17½ in those partially drained, and 13½ in streets without drains.[24] He also said later in the Bill's progress that he could state 'on accurate information, that there were about 300 towns in England without any local Acts'.[25] When later Mr. Newdegate MP referred to the '100 local Acts in London' and asked about 'the number of local Acts in the country which were to be placed at the discretion of the Privy Council by the Executive', Viscount Morpeth replied very shortly 'It is not the number of scattered Local Acts which makes the difficulty; it is the 100 in the lump'.[26] Historians have generally underestimated just how much of an obstacle the wealth of accumulated local legislation presented: with limited administrative support, and no tradition of central government intervention, the problems of assessing and reviewing or replacing private legislation anywhere, let alone in London, could be daunting.[27]

The variety of local authorities – in itself not a phrase ordinarily current at that time – described by Clarke[28] makes generalisation both inevitable and difficult. On the principle alluded to above, that places understandably tended to concentrate on what they felt they needed to do and often little else, there was an increasing focus during the 1830s and 1840s on the demands of poor law relief. Law and order had always been important, and was largely in the hands of the magistrates. So, too, had the state of the highways and bridges, and the obligations of maintaining them (particularly for those places that found themselves maintaining through routes). Highway law was well developed, and had been consolidated by the Highway Act 1835. The Highway Act 1862 supplemented that, and there was a further important Highway Act in 1864.[29]

This was the situation and context of municipal law after 1835, and in the earlier years of Victoria's reign. What, however, was the public mood in which that law had come to be as it was in 1858? What were the attitudes and aspirations that were prevalent at that time – and more to the point in the context of the appetite for, and the manner of, reform – what were the attitudes and aspirations that *mattered* in how events developed, and what got done? The state of municipal law generally is considered in Chapter 4, while the next part of this chapter considers these complex questions which, while often the subject of specific local histories,[30] seem never to have been fully generally addressed in the specific context of the growing mood for – and reliance on – local initiative and individual Bill promotion. Better understanding that mood will help to define the point of balance between the contrasting and conflicting motivations of the time, and how an incipient national movement for reform still largely aspired and expected to deliver by means of local initiative, and saw no contradiction in doing so.

The appetite for reform

Public mood is not always exactly the same as popular opinion, though they are generally supposed to be similar. In 1858, most commentators would largely have gauged or defined *public mood* by reference to what was said in Parliament, in the counsels and Clubs of the nation, and in publications like *The Times* that recorded what the class of those whom today we would call the Establishment was saying. *Popular opinion*, however, might well have been very different. Few men, and no women, could vote; the heyday of national popular newspapers was still ahead, and – although some will see it as contentious to say so – the mass of the population still counted for relatively little in forming received opinions, steering reforms, and on occasion turning out Governments. While that was still true – if reducing – at national level, it was not necessarily also true, however, at local level. The local 'Establishment' were closer to, indeed were part of, the local community, and the power to influence was not necessarily congruent just with the power to vote. As Garrard states:

> The expense involved in obtaining improvement legislation ... made municipal leaders anxious to conciliate both opposition and potential opposition ... Moreover, almost any opposition might become worth conciliating – even when ... it emanated from within the town and from some way down the socio-economic scale.[31]

The municipal governments of the day varied greatly; perhaps the only valid contemporary generalisation was that of James Hole, who wrote of councils in 1853 (in the context of the cautious and limited new powers to provide public libraries) 'We have no hope for them at present ... The truth is, they represent the *ignorant prejudices*, quite as much as the good sense, of their constituents.'[32] Although clearly the willingness and wherewithal for reform were overall predominant – we have hindsight to tell us that – it is instructive to look for some of the contrasts and comparisons that illuminate the mood of the age from differing perspectives. Chapter 1 included reference to the work of Higgs and the concept of the information state, and his allusions to

> the views of several historians who see the legislation, and the centralising outlook that gave rise to much of it, in widely differing terms – a 'capitalist cultural revolution'; the 'social disciplinarian' role of the Victorian state; the new breed of 'expert'; a revolution in government predicated on the discovery of treatment of 'social ills'; and so on.[33]

All of these phrases speak of an assumption of, and a mood for, change – as if it were merely the method and the timing, rather than the principle, which were in question.[34]

Certainly there was much gathering of evidence about discovering how to treat perceived social ills. (Redlich and Hirst commented that 'the old system of English administration collapsed before the unavoidable demands of an industrial development'.[35]) The *List of Commissions and Officials*[36] for the period 1815–70 reveals the scope of official interest: Improvement of the Metropolis 1842–51; Health of Towns 1843–8; Popular Education 1858–61; Children's Employment 1862–7; Water Supply 1866–9; and so on including many with more narrowly specific terms of reference. There was of course also much other work going on at both national and local levels, exemplified by the two probably most famous welfare reformers of their day – Lord Shaftesbury and Edwin Chadwick.[37] This was not, however, the whole story. Although a new class of 'professionals' and administrators was beginning to evolve,[38] there was in the 1850s still very little tradition of state-sponsored social intervention, and only a rudimentary 'information state', in terms of administrative resource and capacity, by which much of it could be done. Moreover, if the concept of 'Victorian values' has any resonance today it is likely to be in the contexts of hard work, high moral tone (whatever that means), and self-reliance – coupled with a preference for shutting or sending away the uncomfortable and the incorrigible (the disabled, the convicted), and of assuming that hardships were far more the fault of the individual than ever they could be the responsibility or the accountability of the community or of the state. The Marquess of Granby, in the debates on the 1848 Public Health Bill, uttered a telling sentiment about his attitude to this kind of legislation at this time:

> He despaired of the Bill, as long as it contained the un-English, unconstitutional principle of centralisation. There was no chance of being able to eradicate this odious principle in time to enable them to pass the Bill as it ought to be.[39]

'Odious principle' or not, the passing of the Public Health Act in 1848 was a triumph for Edwin Chadwick and others who thought like him, but the debates on that Bill, and its unsuccessful predecessor the year before, underscore the ambivalence of the age towards what came to be seen later as inevitable and long overdue reform.[40] Earlier that year there had been revolution and disturbance on the European mainland; there was anxiety about whether England might be drawn into that. Unlike many other social reforms, the Bills of 1847 and 1848 were introduced as Government Bills, and not as individual initiatives. The 1848 Act also introduced the first of what became the modern local authorities – bodies created to regulate, and to some degree at least to provide services for the population at large. These were the Local Boards of Health. There had been temporary or limited national

Boards of Health in 1805–06 and 1831–32, but these had faded away, along with any local activities, as soon as the fears of disease and epidemic that had prompted them subsided. Now a General Board of Health was established; initially created until the end of the Parliamentary session sitting 5 years after Royal Assent on 31 August 1848, it was reconstituted in 1854 by 17 & 18 Vict. c. 95 and eventually lasted for 10 years until superseded in 1858.[41] Local Boards of Health were also introduced, but they were generally to be voluntary – a petition was required of one-tenth of those rated to relief of the poor in any area with a defined boundary and at least 30 such ratepayers. Only if the death rate exceeded 'Twenty-three to a Thousand' could the General Board impose a Local Board.[42] The Local Board members would either be chosen by the corporations of municipal boroughs wholly containing them, or otherwise elected by plural property votes elsewhere.[43] They had powers relating to the kind of paving and cleansing provisions often found in earlier local Acts, but the emphasis was still on local leadership rather than national direction, and all the powers were essentially permissive.[44]

Significant and symbolic though it was, the 1848 Act was not as successful as its progenitors hoped. By 1854, 182 Local Boards of Health had been established, though in many of those, the commitment and competence to achieve much was wanting. In particular, the opportunities to require improved building standards were often missed or not enforced.[45] In some instances, those with influence in local affairs wanted things kept largely as they were; James Hole wrote in 1866 of the local sanitary bodies that

> They and those who elect them, are the lower middle class, the owners, generally speaking, of the very property which requires improvement … Every pound they vote for drainage, or some other sanitary improvement, is something taken out of their own pocket.[46]

In others, the inhabitants affected were worried about the increased rents that they expected improvements to bring. At the same time, the supply of people qualified and able to do what needed to be done was limited, and while medical and public knowledge was increasingly making the connections between insanitary conditions and death and disease, these things were not yet universally accepted, still less acted on.[47]

Nevertheless, R.A. Lewis[48] presented a more positive picture; by the end of 1853, 284 towns had applied to establish a Local Board of Health, and the 182 successful places covered some 2.1 million people and were a high proportion of the 243 by then reported on. Of those 182, surveys had been completed in 126, with seventy plans of public works prepared – and these numbers might have been higher but for problems at the Board of Ordnance who were doing the surveying. Lewis moreover makes a further point about why this outcome is significant in the context of local legislation: 'By the Act a place could, for little more than a hundred pounds, arm itself with powers which, if sought by Local Bills, might cost several thousands.'[49] That cost was usually less; but while the initiative lay with local ambitions, and the powers available were permissive in accordance with that outlook, for the first time a community might for an accessible price in effect obtain from a Government agency the authority to do things – principally cleansing and draining works, and to raise the money necessary for them – which formerly it had taken Parliament (and much else besides) to grant. The General Board of Health stated in its 1854 report[50] that 'In some instances, one-third of the permanent rates are required to defray legal and parliamentary expenses'. At the same time, while the availability of public general Acts powers would change the nature of the local Bills henceforth promoted, there were still significant limitations: 'The Local Boards are generally under difficulties, on account of their want of legal powers for carrying sewer pipes beyond their immediate jurisdiction …'[51] The General Board was often asked for advice: requests for legal opinions alone were 'not far short of 2,000, and the Board have reason to believe that much expense and litigation has thus been saved to Local Boards'.[52] C. Fraser Brockington reprints the House of Commons return of Local Boards of Health established up to 4 June 1856.[53]

The issue of finance was, as ever, significant for local communities. While some, as noted above, might be fearful of increased rents, others saw the 1848 Act, with its powers in section 108 for the Government to make loans, as heralding a more flexible policy, whereby long-term funding could be obtained for works that – under the regime commonly available to improvement commissioners – would previously often have had to be paid for at the outset, with costs falling on owners and those liable to rating.[54] If, to quote Hamlin again,[55] 'A great range of motives led towns to seek the act', there were also many motives that led towns *not* to seek it. If local Acts were expensive, and the advent of public general laws might obviate the need for them, so too were the implications of that new public legislation – and it must be remembered, from earlier in this chapter, that at this time the supposed generally applicable powers of the Towns Improvement Act 1847 depended for their individual availability on the existence already of a relevant 'special Act'. This, however, is in the nature of *local* government: different places will come at the same issues from different angles, driven by different local priorities, personages or perspectives – so we should not be surprised if cause and effect in one town cannot be extrapolated even to apparently similar places.

On 1 September 1858, the Local Government Act of that year augmented the 1848 Act, but on commencement it came into force only where Local Boards of Health were already constituted. Far from superseding its predecessor, the new Act was to be 'construed together with and deemed to form Part of the Public Health Act 1848'.[56] It shortened the title just to 'Local Board', and termed the areas of these authorities 'local government districts'. At the same time the General Board of Health was abolished, to be replaced (until the Local Government Board was created in 1871) by the Local Government Act Office, under the Secretary of State for the Home Department (at that time S.H. Walpole). Once again, the Act was both adoptive and permissive – and indeed the former power to create a Board where the death rate exceeded 23 per thousand was not continued. Improvement commissioners could now adopt the Act, thereby also constituting the Local Board, and there were changes to the petitioning procedure both to include places with no 'known or defined boundary' and also to allow the right to petition against the creation of a Local Board where more than 1 in 20 of the defined ratepayers objected to it.[57] The 1858 Act was much more successful than its predecessor, and the public mood had been changing; in the decade to 1868 there were 568 adoptions.[58] Notices of adoptions were published in the *London Gazette*.[59] Three important and very detailed Parliamentary returns in 1867, 1868 and 1874 provided information about adoptions, relevant authorities and local Acts in force.[60]

How, one and a half centuries on, do historians assess the effectiveness or success of the public health legislation of 1848–58? Bernard Harris considered that the importance of the 1848 Act could 'easily be exaggerated',[61] citing the relatively low rate of adoptions – 192 applications for inspection up to 5 March 1850, but only 50 involving towns or districts with populations exceeding 10,000, out of a national 1851 census population of 16.9 million. Nevertheless, Chadwick's capacity for setting people against him, and his rather narrow view of the causes of disease, 'began to give way to a range of new ideas' in the 1850s and 1860s, which 'laid the foundations for a much more wide-ranging approach to public health policy than that envisaged by Chadwick'. A new mood engendered a 'growing willingness to introduce, and accept, compulsory public health legislation'.[62] Despite this, however, Szreter notes that '… it was primarily local government that initiated, staffed, sometimes devised and mostly funded the enormous expansion in urban infrastructure and social services that occurred during the period, 1858–1914'. He goes on to quote H.J. Hanham's observation that 'the extent of local self-government during the nineteenth century appears stupefying. As a matter of principle Whitehall thrust every type of administration on to elected bodies.'[63] Hamlin, however, approaches the degree of importance of Chadwick and the 1848 Act differently. He acknowledges 'that there were no well-developed institutional alternatives to the public health Chadwick chose to offer' but he insists 'that choices were being made and that they involved profound and permanent questions that continue to need to be recognized. For what is most important about the debate of the 1830s to the 1850s is its scope.'[64] Whatever one's perspective on the first Public Health Acts, another tide of new, private legislation whose lasting influence – and scope – could hardly be denied was the tide of railway Bills.

The coming of the railways

Before the coming of large-scale industrialisation and the building of the railways in the early Victorian period, there had been four historical developments that might be assumed to have set precedents for both public mood and popular opinion about the new landscape. None of these four had, however, really been a precedent for what was to come – or had prepared the country for the scale and impact of the changes. The first had been the gradual introduction of mechanised processes from the mid-eighteenth century: what local marketing now calls 'the birthplace of industry' at Ironbridge in Shropshire; the different scale of activity possible following the invention of steam engines; and all the many mines, works and other plants set up where the necessary raw materials or favourable local conditions existed. While they offered new kinds of employment and sometimes prosperity, they also often brought about much offsite air and water pollution, or other problems like subsidence or excessive noise. These might be restrained or compensated by the law of nuisance, but that law was about personal, not public, losses. Moreover these factories and plants could only be operated on lands owned or controlled by the business proprietors. When in 1772 a 'planked and railed road' was to be constructed from the Sankey Navigation to the Warrington Company's copper works, the Company had to promise to compensate the landowner's tenants for any crops or buildings damaged or affected in any way by the copper smelting processes.[65]

The second development had been the onset of the canal age from the opening of the Duke of Bridgewater's canal in 1761. The canals required Parliament's authorisation because of the extensive lands required, so unlike the mines and factories there was a vital state contribution required for their coming about. Once dug, however, the canals – though working facilities with none of the leisure overtones of two centuries later – were relatively tranquil places, with horse-drawn barges and limited environmental impact beyond their towpaths. The third development had been the turnpike trusts, whereby under numerous individual Acts – initially in the seventeenth century, but principally in the eighteenth and nineteenth centuries – road tolls were collected.[66] The fourth, and probably often the most bitterly resented, was the inclosure movement, whereby thousands of special Acts authorised the conversion of open common land to fenced, defended estates, with irreversible consequences for the mass of those affected, and their relationship with the people or pastures whereon they depended to make their livings.[67]

Neither the nature nor the numbers of the factories, canals and turnpikes built before 1825, nor even the conversion of common lands to private estates, could have prepared for what was to come. Railways were vastly more extensive and disruptive than the canals, and while they brought economic growth, goods and employment, they also brought clamour and smoke pollution on an unprecedented scale. In turn towns began to grow at extraordinary rates, as did the populations to fill them. Railways had both of the eighteenth-century elements – the self-centred tendency to pollution and the state licence respectively of early industry and the canals – and had them to a degree that far outran what had gone before.[68] In addition the 'railway mania' – the craze for promoting railway schemes after the more obvious routes had been claimed, and often in apparent defiance of business logic – was evident to all, and was seen to be motivated by factors often seemingly based on self-interest to the exclusion of public interest.[69] While Parliament was wrestling in 1863 with the problems caused by the sheer volume of business,[70] it was also recognised that the private Bill promotion circuit was a lucrative cottage industry in and around Great George Street in Westminster, where in 1845 it appeared that there were 157 people in Parliament 'whose names were on the registers of new [railway] companies for sums varying from 291,000*l.* downwards'.[71]

The impact of all the lines now built, authorised but yet to be built, and still being promoted – augmented by the rapid urban growth and other changes in the countryside that the railways were directly or indirectly fostering – had, after three decades or so, a marked effect on public attitudes. A reference from the very industrial St. Helens (not incorporated as a borough till 1868) makes the point in relation to the impact of noxious works:

> Twenty or thirty years before, when the population was relatively small and there was no local government body with power to act on its behalf, public opinion was ineffective and could be ignored. But by the early 1860s the town was growing quickly and was soon to acquire borough status. The alkali maker, as the Act of 1863 made plain,[72] could no longer be a law unto himself ... with public opinion becoming more outspokenly hostile and possessing an increasingly effective weapon of attack in the developing machinery of local government.[73]

Tom Crook and Glen O'Hara make two points about public expression in the early Victorian period:

> First ... the press was widely recognized as a significant source of public accountability ... Secondly, the authority of public opinion altered the practice of political leadership. The art of statesmanship, for instance, was increasingly conceived as one of careful accommodation and balance.[74]

The more that people *could* read, and the more they *actually* read through the medium of cheap newspapers and pamphlets, the more they were likely to form opinions of which, increasingly, those in positions of power would come to take account for obvious practical reasons.[75]

Opposition to railway schemes had also become more widespread and more determined as time went on. It was expressed at different levels.

> Railways were a symbol of change and progress. They also seemed to epitomize popular resentments toward a changing world picture: the depersonalization of workers and passengers, the altering of an established social pattern, and of course, their tendency to mow down anything that happened to get in their way, be it public opposition, family land, natural beauties, national history, or even unwary passengers on [their] tracks.

But public outcry did have a direct impact on railway development, and the popular conception of the railway in Victorian society.[76]

The response to the railways

The relevance for this study of attitudes to the promotion and building of the railways lies in the context they provide for efforts to promote local powers to regulate and develop communities – and particularly of course the rapidly burgeoning urban areas, which many saw as dens of filth, degradation and iniquity (often with no clear concept of any boundaries between the physical and the moral). Improvement commissioners had been created by Parliament from 1765 onwards,[77] but the first railway mania years were well over – and public attitudes formed accordingly – before the heyday of the establishing by local Acts of most improvement commissions in towns and cities. The prevalent attitudes to the obtaining of local powers of improvement (or of interference with the existing order of things, depending on one's perspective) were for the most part not the same as those engendered by railway developments. The nature of municipal or local government Bill promotions as a class in the 1850s and 1860s was very different. Historians, who have not much studied the overall field of private Bill promotion in this period, have accordingly failed to characterise the distinct purposes and content of municipal promotions sufficiently clearly. Had they done so, there would be a better understanding of the range and depth of promotions; of the links, precedents and rivalries – and also the limitations – that the world of private Bill promotion engendered; and of the economic and business impact that the 'local Westminster industry' of Parliament's private business had during the time of what was arguably the zenith of the country's wealth and influence in the world. While local promoters may often have had mixed motives, they were at least officially using private Bills for public purposes, in contrast to the more usual commercial motives that lay behind railway, dock, inclosure and similar promotions, for which the whole concept was different. Improvement and other municipal Bills were not based on creating and operating joint stock companies. Improvement commissioners would together be constituted a body corporate, but of quite a different kind from the A to B Railway Company. The latter needed to raise capital, and persuade investors of the likelihood of dividends and capital gain, to finance its constructing and operating. The former needed resources too, of course, but the principal basis of that was taxation and charging of local ratepayers. Both might speak of the public good in making the case for being granted the powers that they sought, but whereas the one was wholly fed by investment and trading, the other sought improvement, public welfare and health as ends in themselves – even though there were undoubtedly vested interests in the economic well-being that improvements were anticipated to bring about.

Were not railway promotions so dominant among private Bill promotions in the first three decades of Victoria's reign, it would scarcely be necessary to consider them so extensively as comparators and paradigms for other municipally based local Bills. There were many other promotions of private Bills for docks and harbours, for instance, but railway promotions not only far outnumbered the others, but the processes and procedures for dealing with them in Parliament preoccupied both Houses, and the rules and practices thereby developed influenced and affected how all other private Bill promotions were handled. Moreover, docks and harbours were more limited in number; they were intended to attract economic activity, but they usually lacked the environmental impact of railways, and affected many fewer landowners.[78]

Improvement commissioners might well have expectations that their actions in improving their local town would eventually bring them personal profit (and perhaps also reputation and standing). Many improvements could not, however, be sold as such to the consuming or benefiting public – though ratepayers might well find themselves paying for better accommodation and better facilities. Parliament might grant the improvement powers, but the money to use them would have to be found locally. E.P. Hennock considered that improvement commissioners 'were primarily concerned with the comfort of the wealthier citizens' – he thought their value as measures of sanitary reform marginal, and 'not conclusive evidence that there existed an effective public opinion in favour of sanitary reform'.[79] Sidney and Beatrice Webb's verdict was that their powers were anyway usually inadequate, with insufficient capacity to borrow money and levy rates to make much impact on their supposed purpose[80] – an argument which does not explain why, in that case, so many commissions were established by local Acts on similar footings after repeated Parliamentary Bill hearings.

Private companies were set up to provide water, gas and more – and did not necessarily always require statutory authority to do so. As time went on, municipal trading enterprises developed, but in 1858 most of this lay in the future. The answers to the question 'When private companies were set up to run the railways, why were such companies not similarly set up to run the towns?' are essentially twofold. First, it took Parliamentary authority to establish improvement commissions with the requisite powers; Parliament granted railway companies their privileges to take land and run enterprises, but it did not in the first place establish the railway companies themselves. Second, the financial realities, as described above in relation to private investments and returns, were different. A prosperous railway company could pay dividends to the people that owned it by virtue of having bought its shares; a prosperous town simply could not work that way.

The political philosopher and thinker Herbert Spencer (1820–1903) published an extensive essay on 'Railway Morals and Railway Policy' in October 1854 in the *Edinburgh Review*. Nominally a review,[81] it was not anti-railway in principle – Spencer had himself been an engineer on the London and Birmingham Railway from 1837–41 – but it attacked what he saw as the cynical and manipulated conduct of railway company meetings; the vested interests; the lack of justification and rigour in supplementary undertakings and uneconomic additional lines; and the fault of Parliament in using its constitutional authority (a 'State-warrant' as he called it) to override realities, and so justify 'what without it would be unjustifiable'.[82] At the root of all his strictures were money and self-interest. Landed opposition had at first defeated the Liverpool and Manchester line, and a second Bill had succeeded, he noted sardonically, 'only by keeping out of sight of all mansions, and avoiding the game preserves'.[83] In a passage which pre-dates a field of legal argument that occurs to the present day, he analyses what kinds of activity are incidental to the originally authorised lawful purposes, and finds no logical restraint in the trend: '... if it is a sufficient excuse for accessories of this nature, it may be made a sufficient excuse for any accessories whatever.'[84] He concludes by recording:

> Prompted by jealousy and antagonism, our companies have obtained powers for 2000 miles of railway which they have never made. The millions thus squandered in surveys and parliamentary contests – 'food for lawyers and engineers' – would nearly all have been saved, had each supplementary line been obtainable only by an independent body of proprietors with no one to shield them from the penalties of reckless scheming.

The total authorised capital of these companies would soon reach £300 million.[85]

Herbert Spencer did not confine himself to commentary on railway legislation. He viewed what he saw as 'over-legislation' in other contexts equally disparagingly, writing in the *Westminster Review* in 1853 that

> while every day chronicles a failure, there every day reappears the belief that it needs but an Act of parliament and a staff of officers, to effect any end desired. Nowhere is the perennial faith of mankind better seen. Ever since society existed Disappointment has been preaching – 'Put not your trust in legislation'; and yet the trust in legislation seems scarcely diminished.[86]

While he exaggerates to make a point ('... if ... the State had proved itself a capable agent in some other department – the military for example – there would have been some show of reason for extending its sphere of action'[87]), the degree of cynicism greatly weakens his argument. It is amusingly written; the reference to the military seems prescient ahead of the imminent conduct of the Crimean War; yet when the prevailing wind of reform is blowing, it lacks political awareness to imply that almost all legislation or Parliamentary initiative is somehow inherently bad or over-provided. This contrasts with his attitude to the railways described above. He stigmatises the Nottingham Inclosure Act 1845;[88] because it prescribed the structure of working-class dwellings, and the size of their yards or gardens, the Act had rendered it impossible to build working-class dwellings at such moderate rents as to compete with existing ones ... as a consequence, 10,000 of the population are debarred from the new homes they would otherwise have, and are forced to live together in miserable places unfit for human habitation.

He also approves of private enterprise to the apparent exclusion of the state – though when he refers to judge-made codification of the law, he seems to refer to its systematic recording rather than to its rationalising and consolidation.[89] Finally, he concludes that

> The enthusiastic philanthropist, urgent for some act of parliament to remedy this evil or secure the other good, thinks it a trivial and far-fetched objection that the people will be morally injured by doing things for them instead of leaving them to do things themselves.[90]

Social evolutionist, but also utilitarian and libertarian, he seems not to have been able, in this context at least, to see that principles must often be applied with pragmatism if progress is to be made – and it is unclear whether he classed those 'urgent for some act of parliament' as in the camp of private enterprise or the state when they raised their own money to promote private Bills that required legislative steps to be validated. Without a clear categorisation, any analysis of this kind of initiative is likely to be flawed.

These, we may think, were neither the usual views of those who promoted local Bills nor of those who were likely to be subject to them. Philanthropists, like philosophers, tend to espouse views that will serve their own aims, ideals and interests – or at least will not undermine them. It was appropriate to warn against vested interests; and to remind those whom John George Dodson was in 1872 to call 'men accustomed to watch and allow for public opinion'[91] that Parliament could not legislate for everything, and that merely because Parliament legislated at all the ends it desired would automatically be achieved. Yet it must have been obvious to all but the most reactionary of mind that, in the situation of England as it was, progress and reform were unattainable without what Spencer had called a 'State-warrant' – the power and authority of Parliament to achieve whatever was required. It was with the need to seek that authority that so many promoters came with local Bills to Parliament. The number and nature of those Bills is the subject of the next section.

Defining 'local' private Bills

The table on page 14 has given the totals of private Bills, taken from the House of Commons returns, for the years 1858–72. This section analyses 1858, as a year illustrative of the mid-Victorian period, to portray for the first time the breadth and purposes of private Bill promotion, to which – as a class – historians appear to have given scant attention. The number of deposited Bills in 1858 – 208 – was rather lower than the 249 deposited in the 1857 session, and appreciably less than the rapidly growing totals in the years following, when it reached an extraordinary 633 in 1866. In the same year – actually, 21 & 22 Vict. was the sessional year 1857–58 (20 & 21 Vict. having been 1857, when there were two Parliamentary sessions) – there were 248 public Bills introduced or re-numbered,[92] and 110 public Acts given the royal assent. There were also 11 purely private Acts, 10 of which were concerned with estates or other land and leasing interests[93] and one, not printed, a naturalising Act.

The total 208 refers to the number of Bills deposited in the Private Bill Office. Not every Bill would proceed (and in some cases notice was given and published of Bills that were never deposited). The correlation of totals was not exact – indeed, more private Bills were actually read a formal first time than were deposited in both 1857[94] and 1858 as there could sometimes be carrying forward. Some 216 were read a first time in 1858 – the date refers to the session of that year – and 169 eventually received the royal assent and thereby passed into law.[95] In 1859, 272 Bills were deposited but only 261 were read a first time: usually a small number failed to proceed, or were withdrawn. The annex to this chapter lists all the 1858 deposited Bills to show the extent and variety involved – and at this time, the growing dominance of railway promotions in the total. We are primarily concerned in this book with *local* (or *municipal*) private Bills and legislation. What kinds of Bills are included in the definition of *local*?

Local or municipal authorities were not defined in 1858 in a manner consistent with the later pattern after the legislation of 1888 and 1894.[96] It was also the case that individual promoters who, following enactment, would become participants in an incorporated body – as improvement or sewerage commissioners for example – were not technically promoting in that capacity at the outset. Bills (and where enacted, the relevant Acts) are therefore included here that were promoted in England and Wales by existing municipal corporations; or by parishes; or by justices of the peace for county areas; or by equivalent bodies in London; by improvement commissioners and other entities already possessing separate legal identity and status; and by individuals who, if successful, would bring about a new corporate body for municipal objectives. Other bodies are included according to the nature of their purpose and creation: Highway Boards created in highway districts under the Highway Act 1835, and later the Highway Act 1862, are included, being a traditional part of the municipal spectrum; Local Boards[97] under the Local Government Act 1858 are included; so too for the same reason are Burial Boards (set up for parishes by vestries under section XI of the Burial Act 1852[98]), and Boards of Education following their creation under the Education Act 1870. Overseers of the Poor, however, are not included, because while local in application they were part of a national system of poor law relief.[99] Nor are public general Acts confirming Provisional Orders (though from 1868 they were placed with private rather than with public Acts, and those are the subject of Appendix 2), and neither are Turnpike Acts.[100] Private companies formed to undertake other activities that in later years commonly (but not always) became municipal undertakings, such as gas and water supply, markets and piers, are not included unless the Bill promotion was done by a municipal authority.[101] Conservators are excluded also – so that (for example) the private Acts of 1871 set up for Wandsworth Common and for Wimbledon and Putney Commons[102] are outside our scope.

It is not possible to define the bodies included by reference to democratic election, or indeed any other means of membership election or selection, since those circumstances varied. Nevertheless, there was considerable interrelation; as K.B. Smellie said of the situation in 1830: 'The Boroughs were often merely a combination of the leading tradesmen of a town.'[103] This could have been said for long afterwards. Furthermore, the same people often served on more than one of the bodies or Boards that together made up the government of a town, just as in the counties the squires and landowners were often the magistrates and mainstays of the public weal.[104]

The nature and analysis of private Bills

In 1858 the 208 promotions in the House of Commons return included 16 Bills coming within the definition above. All received the royal assent in 1858, so can conveniently be listed with their 21 & 22 Vict. local and private Acts chapter numbers:

xii	The Merthyr Tydfil Water Act
xxiv	The Manchester Assize Courts Act
xxv	The Manchester Improvement Act
xxxi	The Malvern Improvement Amendment Act
xxxii	Vauxhall Bridge Road
xxxviii	The Victoria Park Approach Act
lxiii	The Wallasey Improvement Act
lxix	The Chiswick Improvement Act
lxxvi	The Bradford Corporation Waterworks Act
lxxx	The Liverpool Improvement Act
lxxxv	The Birkenhead Improvement (General Mortgagees) Act
lxxxvii	The Manchester Corporation Waterworks Act
xci	The Halifax Park and Improvement Act
cxx	The Hove Improvement Act
cxxi	The Birkenhead Commissioners Gas and Water Act
cxl	The Middlesbrough Improvement Act

These Acts therefore comprised just over 10 per cent of the 150 private Acts passed in the 1858 Parliamentary session, while the Bills from which they came comprised just over 9 per cent of the 1858 promotions that were eventually to achieve royal assent.[105]

It is noticeable immediately that two-thirds of these Acts concerned the north of England. There were three from London;[106] one from the west; one from the south coast; and one from Wales. That reflects a key theme of

50 *Context and content of local Bill promotion*

the history of local government generally in the century between 1850 and 1950 – much of the energy and innovation came from the industrial towns and cities of the northern half of the country, which through their natural resources and manufacturing capacity often had both the social and environmental conditions that demanded legislative and governmental initiative, as well as the financial resources to achieve it. Moreover, in 1858, the city fathers in these places no doubt observed that Westminster seemed less than wholeheartedly committed to their welfare and prosperity, and they were not temperamentally inclined to rely on 'them down south' anyway. Accordingly they looked to their own communities, and at what other towns around were doing, to serve their needs and further their interests.

What did the other 90 per cent or so of the 1858 private Acts comprise, together with the other promoted Bills of that session? No systematic detailed analysis appears ever to have been undertaken of this kind before – and exactness is extremely difficult to achieve, because not all Bills proceeded at all through the required Parliamentary stages, or necessarily achieved royal assent (if they achieved it at all), in the same year. For similar reasons the totals appearing from examination of Vacher's annual *List of Private Bills* differ from those of the official Commons returns. Vacher's *Lists*, however, give much additional information, including the grouping of opposed private Bills, and the Committees to which they were referred. The memberships of those Committees are also given, with the initial dates of meeting, providing an additional source of information that would otherwise usually only be available from the official Parliamentary *Journals* and similar sources.

For the 1858 session, *Vacher* records 211 Bills,[107] as against the 208 of the official return. Against each is first given the number on the Petition List, which 'indicates the order in which the respective Bills will be taken up by the Examiners'. A second number 'is the Private Bill Office No. of the Plan which has been deposited there'. Over half, 110, are concerned with railway works or railway companies, occasionally combined with canal or other ancillary concerns.[108] Occasionally, Bills are concerned with more than the principal subject, making exact categorisation difficult: Part II of the *Index to Statutes 1801–1859*, published in 1860, categorised the local and private Acts under 21 headings. Of the 101 non-railway Bills in this 1858 session, 15 concerned gas- and 13 water-works or their associated companies; 14 concerned various local improvement powers; 10 concerned bridges and roads; 8 concerned docks; 6 harbours; 5 land or estate issues of various kinds; 4 canals; 3 the poor; and 2 each were about markets, municipal corporations, tramways and turnpikes. There were 15 miscellaneous others, such as the Edinburgh Life Assurance Company; the Edinburgh &c. Annuity Tax; the St. Leonard, Shoreditch, Parish; and the Tay Fisheries Bills. The annex to this chapter lists them all. Although a few firms predominated, between them the Bill promoters employed no fewer than 33 different Parliamentary agents.

Vacher also gives the groupings of the opposed Bills, with the Committees to which they were referred, with the associated memberships. The Groups were styled from A to T (with I omitted); thus the Group A Committee were to consider four of the Gas Bills; Group B had four Water Bills (including the Malvern Improvement Bill); and so on. Group F had three Bills, two Gas and one Water, but all three were municipal promotions, and Group G had four of the non-railway-related Manchester promotions. In this way not only did the Committee members gain particular experience in these topics – they were also better able to compare provisions and aspirations, and ensure that the drafting of clauses was reasonably consistent unless there were very compelling reasons in any case for departure or variation. The railway and canal Bills went to the General Committee on Railway & Canal Bills; among the other regular Committees were ones on Standing Orders and Public Petitions.

It is interesting also to note from the following annex how many railway companies, and indeed others, promoted more than one Bill in the same session. Outside London, the proportion of all Bill promotions coming from the south of England is less than might be expected on average. Overall it is Manchester that is the most remarkable, with no fewer than a dozen Bills (including one entitled the Rochdale and Manchester Road Bill) connected in one context or another with that community. This contrasts with the assertion of Harris in relation to the era of the late eighteenth century, that 'although significant improvements may have been made to the urban environment in London and many southern market towns, the pace of reform in the industrial towns of northern England was much slower'.[109]

Chapters 5 and 6 will consider more specifically for subsequent years those Bills that come within the 'local' or 'municipal' definition given above, and the nature of their provisions, as well as their success in passing into law the provisions that their promoters wanted. As the number of railway Bills grew in the years immediately following 1858, the proportion of local municipal ones diminished, but their significance in the developing Victorian local government system – for now it may be called a system – continued to increase. In this year, however, while the development of national, prescriptive local government legislation was beginning, it was still the era of local initiative so far as reforms, developments and standards were concerned. Alongside local Acts may be placed the process of *adoption* of public Acts – still a matter of local will, even when the accessibility of desirable legal powers was gradually becoming easier. The extent to which the growing national mood for reform was still so dependent on local response, which it has been part of the purpose of this chapter to show,[110] is seldom fully realised by most commentators, and will be further demonstrated in the succeeding chapters.

Annex

List of private Bills originating in the House of Commons, Session 1858

This alphabetical title list is derived from *Vacher*, which also in the original gives each Bill's number on the Bill petition list; the Private Bill Office number of the deposited plan; the date of second reading (to which there were a few exceptions); and the Parliamentary agent involved. Information about the progress of individual Bills can of course be found in the Commons and Lords *Journals*, and sometimes also in *Hansard*.

Aberdare Water
Aberdeen, Peterhead and Fraserburgh Railway
Allendale Stinted Pasture
Alyth Railway
Andover Canal Railway
Athenry and Tuam Railway
Atlantic Telegraph Company
Ayr and Dalmellington Railway
Balby and Worksop Road
Ballymena, Ballymoney, Coleraine and Portrush Junction Railway
Banbridge, Lisburn and Belfast Junction Railway
Barnstaple New Waterworks
Belfast and County Down Railway
Belfast (Town) Improvement
Belfast (Town and Borough) Improvement – *Withdrawn*
Besselsleigh Road
Birkenhead Improvement Commissioners (Bondholders' Arrangements)
Birkenhead Improvement Commissioners (Gas and Water)
Birmingham Canal Navigations
Birmingham and Staffordshire Gas
Blackburn Railway
Blyth Harbour and Dock
Bognor Railway
Border Counties Railway
Bradford Corporation Water
Brentford Gas
Brentford and Richmond Railway
Brimspill Harbour
Burghead Harbour
Burton-upon-Trent Railway
Bury and Radcliffe Water
Caledonian Railway (Branch to Port Carlisle Railway)
Caledonian Railway (Dalmarnock Branch)
Carlisle, Langholm and Hawick Railway
Carron Railway
Cheltenham Water
Chester Gas
Chester and Holyhead Railway
Chiswick Improvement
Clyde Navigation

Cornwall Railway
Corris, Machynlleth and River Dovey Railway
Cromford and High Peak Railway
Crystal Palace District Gas
Darenth Valley Railway
Dean Forest Turnpike Trust
Devon Valley Railway
Dublin Iron Road or Tramway – *Not proceeded with*
Dublin and Meath Railway
Dundalk and Enniskillen Railway
Durham and Cleveland Union Railway
Eastern Counties Railway
Eastern Steam Navigation Railway
East Kent Railway (Dover Extension)
East Kent Railway (Western Extension)
East Suffolk Railway
East Suffolk, Yarmouth and Haddiscoe, and Lowestoft and Beccles Railway Companies Amalgamation
Eden Valley Railway
Edinburgh and Glasgow and Stirling and Dunfermline Railways
Edinburgh Life Assurance Company – *Read first time in Lords, 25 March*
Edinburgh, &c., Annuity Tax – *Read first time, 22 March*
Electric Telegraph Company
Ely Valley Railway
Exeter and Exmouth Railway
Fife and Kinross and Kinross-shire railways
Fishguard Harbour Improvement – *Petition, 22 February*
Folkestone Water
Formatine and Buchan Railway
Garngad Road
Globe Insurance Company
Gorbals Property and Liabilities – *Withdrawn*
Gosport Water
Great Northern and Western (of Ireland Railway)
Halifax Park and Improvements
Hampstead Heath Park
Haslingden and Rawtenstall Water
Hesketh Marsh
Horsham Turnpike Trust
Hove Improvement
Imperial Continental Gas – *Not proceeded with*
Inverury and Old Meldrum Junction Railway
Isle of Wight Poor
Knighton Railway
Lancashire and Yorkshire and East Lancashire Railway Companies

Lancaster and Carlisle Railway
Leitrim Railway and Lough Allen Pier
Limerick and Castle Connell Railway
Limerick and Foynes Railway – *Petition, 23 March*
Liskeard and Looe Union Canal Company's Railway
Liverpool Docks Rating
Liverpool Exchange
Liverpool Improvement
Llandaff and Canton District Markets
Llanelly Harbour
London (City) Union – *Not proceeded with*
London Corporation – *Read first time, 8 February*
London Dock Company
London Tramway – *Postponed*
London and North Western Railway (Additional Works) (No. 1)
London and North Western Railway (Additional Works) (No. 2)
London and North Western Railway (Extension from Longsight)
London and South Western Railway
London, Brighton and South Coast Railway (Capital, &c.)
London, Brighton and South Coast Railway (Shoreham to Henfield)
Londonderry and Coleraine Railway – *Petition, 16 February*
Luton Gas
Luton, Dunstable and Welwyn Junction and Hertford and Welwyn Junction Railway
Companies Amalgamation
Madras Irrigation and Canal
Maidstone Gas
Malvern Improvement
Manchester Assize Court House
Manchester Corporation Water
Manchester Improvement
Manchester Poor
Manchester, Hyde and Mottram Road
Manchester, Sheffield and Lincolnshire and Great Northern Railway Companies
Manchester, Sheffield and Lincolnshire Railway (Garston to Liverpool)
Manchester, Sheffield and Lincolnshire Railway (Newton to Compstall)
Manchester, Sheffield and Lincolnshire Railway (Station at Manchester)
Manchester, South Junction and Altrincham Railway (No. 1)
Manchester, South Junction and Altrincham Railway (No. 2)
Mersey Docks and Harbour Board
Mersey Docks and Harbour (Consolidation of Acts)
Mersey Docks and Harbour (New Works)
Merthyr Junction Railway – *Not proceeded with*
Merthyr Tydfil Water

Metropolitan Board of Works (Victoria Park Approach)
Metropolitan Railway (Abandonment of Undertaking, &c.)
Middlesbrough Improvement
Middlesbrough Water – *Read first time, 22 March*
Mid Kent Railway (Bromley to St. Mary Cray)
Mid Kent Railway (Croydon Extension)
Midland Great Western Railway of Ireland
Newport, Abergavenny and Hereford Railway
Newport (Salop) Markets, Town Hall, &c.
Northampton Gas
North British Railway (Consolidation, &c.)
North British Railway (Hawick and Carlisle Junction Railway)
North Staffordshire Railway – *Petition, 22 February*
North Yorkshire and Cleveland Railway
Nottingham Gas*
Norwich Gas
Oude Railway Company
Oxford, Worcester and Wolverhampton Railway
Peniston, Thurlstone and Oxspring Gas
Plymouth Great Western Docks
Portsmouth Railway
Portumna Bridge (Ireland)
Redditch Railway
Rochdale and Manchester Road
Royal Mail Steam Packet, and European and Australian Royal Mail Companies
St. Andrew's and Quebec Railroad Company (Class A. Shareholders) and New Brunswick and Canada Railway and Land Company
St. Helens Canal and Railway
St. Leonard, Shoreditch, Parish
Salisbury and Yeovil Railway
Sculcotes and Kingston-upon-Hull Gas
Selkirk and Galashiels Railway
Severn Valley Railway (Abandonment) – *Not proceeded with*
Severn Valley Railway (Extension of Time)
Shoreham, Horsham and Dorking Railway
Shrewsbury and Welchpool Railway
South Devon and Tavistock Railway
South Eastern Railway (Dartford, New Cross, &c.)
South Eastern Railway and Mid Kent Railway (Bromley to Saint Mary Cray Companies)
South Wales Railway (Further Powers, &c.)
South Wales Railway (New Railway, &c.)
Staffordshire Potteries Gas
Staines, Wokingham and Woking Railway

Stanhope and Wolsingham Rectories – *Not proceeded with*
Stockport, Disley and Whaley Bridge Railway
Stockton and Darlington Railway (Durham Lines)
Stockton and Darlington Railway (North Riding Lines)
Stockton and Darlington, Wear Valley, &c., Railway Companies Amalgamation
Stockton, Middlesbrough and Yarm Water
Stoke Fenton and Longton Gas
Stokes Bay Railway and Pier
Sufferance Wharves, Port of London
Sunderland Dock
Symington, Biggar and Broughton Railway
Taff Vale Railway – *Not proceeded with*
Taunton Water
Tay Fisheries
Tees Conservancy
Tramore Embankment
Trent Navigation
Tyne River Improvement
Ulverstone and Lancaster Railway
Vale of Towy Railway
Vauxhall Bridge Road
Victoria Station and Pimlico Railway
Wallasey Improvement
Ware, Hadham and Buntingford Railway
Warrington and Stockport Railway
Warrington and Stockport Railway (Capital)
Waterford Gas
Waterford and Kilkenny Railway (Capital)
Waterford and Kilkenny Railway (Power of Purchase, &c.)
Waveney Valley Railway
Wem and Bronygarth Roads – *Withdrawn*
West End of London and Clapham and Norwood Junction Railway (Abandonment)
West End of London and Crystal Palace Railway
West Metropolitan Railway – *Not proceeded with*
Westminster Improvements (Appointment of Managers, &c.)
Westminster Improvements (Sale and Lease, &c.)
Wexford Harbour Embankment
Whitehaven Harbour – *Read first time in Lords, 25 March*
Whitehaven Junction Railway
Wimbledon and Dorking, and Epsom and Leatherhead Railway Companies   *Not proceeded with*
Windsor New Road

Worcester and Hereford Railway
Yar Bridge

* *Printed out of alphabetical order*

Notes

1. Page 410.
2. 1 & 2 Will. IV, c. 60 (Hobhouse's Vestries Act) and 5 & 6 Will. IV, c. 76. See also K.B. Smellie, *A History of Local Government* (4th edn, 1968).
3. London, 1977, p. 126.
4. London, 1977, p. 126.
5. E.g. John J. Clarke, *A History of Local Government of the United Kingdom* (1955), pp. 44–5: 'This Act established a uniform system of government in 178 incorporated towns ... New elected bodies were set up ...' See also Sir Norman (D.N.) Chester, *The English Administrative System 1780–1870* (1981), esp. at pp. 329–31.
6. The preamble to the Municipal Corporations Act 1835, 5 & 6 Will. IV, c. LXXVI (76).
7. See section LXXV (75). Sidney and Beatrice Webb, *Statutory Authorities for Special Purposes* (1922), p. 346, noted that

    It was in vain that Francis Place pointed out that such a clause would inevitably prove quite inoperative. There was no time for a Parliamentary fight with three hundred bodies of Commissioners, which might all have claimed, like the Municipal Corporations, to be heard in defence of their statutory rights.

    The boundaries of many cities and boroughs were uncertain; a Government Boundaries of Boroughs Bill (no. 348) was introduced in 1837 in the last days of William IV, but that Bill was not passed. See also J.R. Somers Vine, *English Municipal Institutions: Their Growth and Development From 1835 to 1879, Statistically Illustrated* (1879), pp. 16–20.
8. See Bryan Keith-Lucas, *The Unreformed Local Government System* (1980).
9. Clarke, *op. cit.*, p. 48.
10. *London County Council v. Attorney-General* [1902] A.C. 165. See W. Ivor Jennings, *The Law Relating to Local Authorities* (1934), pp. 20–21 and 252–6. In the mid-Victorian years the modern concept of *ultra vires* appears to have been discussed differently; see generally for instance the approach of Thomas James Arnold and Samuel George Johnson, *A Treatise on the Law Relating to Municipal Corporations in England and Wales* (1883), and by way of example the statement on p. 7 that 'When a council is acting as an urban sanitary authority there must be strict compliance with the provisions of the Public Health Act, 1875'.
11. Quoted without citation by Clarke, *op. cit.*, p. 49. For a more contemporary view of the developments after 1832 and 1835, see J.R. Somers Vine, *English Municipal Institutions: Their Growth and Development From 1835 to 1879, Statistically Illustrated* (1879), pp. 10–12. This is followed by a list of the 31 Acts 'directly applicable to municipal corporations' passed between 1835 and 1878. Much of the rest of this very valuable work comprises schedules and analyses of the corporations of 1835, those reformed, those excluded, and much else besides.
12. *Op. cit.*, p. 48. See also note 8 to Chapter 1.
13. *Op. cit.*, p. 49.
14. Perhaps the comment is meant rather to refer to the responsibilities that Clarke believes that boroughs *ought* to have felt. Strictly speaking also, the municipal corporation and the improvement commission were not the same legal entity; the overlaps and rivalries between the two would make a major study in themselves. The electorates for boroughs were of course usually small, whereas improvement commissioners were appointed.

15 See the sources cited in notes 7 and 13 to Chapter 1.
16 *The Natural History of Society* (London, 1840), vol. II, pp. 261–2.
17 'Nature and the Victorian City: the Ambivalent Attitude of Robert Buchanan', Essay 6 in *The Lost Pattern: Essays on the Emergent City Sensibility in Victorian England* (University of Western Australia Press, 1976), p. 71.
18 *Op. cit.*, p. 72.
19 Benjamin Disraeli, *Sybil or the Two Nations* (1845); Oxford World's Classics paperback edition re-issued 2008, p. 51.
20 *The City of Dreadful Night* (1874).
21 *Proud were ye, Mountains* (published in protest against the projected Kendal and Windermere Railway in the *Morning Post* for 17 December 1844). This and the preceding quotation come from *The Industrial Muse: The Industrial Revolution in English Poetry* (1958), an unusual and compelling anthology compiled by Jeremy Warburg, pp. 65 and 27 respectively. (Warburg also records, however, that Wordsworth had himself previously invested in railway stock.) Writing in 1932, Frederick S. Boas held that 'the period saw important changes in the conception of the scope of historical study, and no less important changes in the methods by which it was pursued'. See 'Historians in the 'Sixties: A New Era' – one of the essays (pp. 175–200 at p. 175) contributed by Fellows of the Royal Society of Literature to *The Eighteen-Sixties* (1932).
22 See for instance Bernard Harris, *The Origins of the British Welfare State: Society, State and Social Welfare in England and Wales, 1800–1945* (2004).
23 This is quoted without citation in *The Book of the Country Town* by E.W. Martin (London, 1962), p. 92. The words do not appear in Viscount Morpeth's introductory speech (see note 24), and remain untraced.
24 Viscount Morpeth's speech is at *Hansard*, 3rd series, vol. XCVI, cols. 385–403 (footnoted as 'From a pamphlet published by Ridgway'). The Leicester mortality rates appear to be quoted from the most recent quarterly report of the Registrar-General; they had also appeared, however, at p. 151 of the appendix to the *First Report of the Commissioners of Inquiry into the State of Large Towns and Populous Districts* of 1844 (*Parliamentary Papers*, vol. XVII, p. 1, Paper 572). It is commented there that '1840 was remarkable for the increase of disease and the number of deaths throughout the town'. St. Margaret's parish appears to correspond exactly with the 'East District' of the appendix, which gives information for 1841 and 1842 also. It is remarkable what information certain pioneers, often at great personal risk, were collecting at this time. In 1842, the difference between deaths in culverted and unculverted streets in the West District was an extraordinary 11½ years – 29 to 17½. The *Report* itself characterised these Leicester streets as 'almost exclusively occupied by the manufacturers of stockings' (p. x).
25 H. C. Deb. 3rd series, vol. XCVIII, col. 875 (12 May 1848).
26 H.C. Deb. 3rd series, vol. XCVIII, col. 798 (8 May 1848). Charles Newdigate Newdegate was a large landowner, and MP for North Warwickshire.
27 For example, Christopher Hamlin makes this point, but without explicitly referring to the wealth and variety of local legislation:

> ... often adopting the Act [of 1848] had little to do with public health in any sense. Many towns sought relief from a tangle of jurisdictions and procedures that had grown up over the centuries and that might make widely desired changes almost impossible.
> *Public Health and Social Justice in the Age of Chadwick: Britain, 1800–1854* (1998), p. 282.

He had, however, also commented on p. 277 that 'in most respects sanitary improvement under the General Board of Health would be indistinguishable from what towns were doing under private acts'.

28 *Op. cit.* p. 48.
29 Respectively 5 & 6 Will. IV, c. 50; 25 & 26. Vict. c. 61; and 27 & 28 Vict. c. 101. The 1835 Act did not, however, apply to highways under local Acts (section 113). The public authorities with highway responsibilities were originally parishes, and later counties, but the definitions of these were both complicated and evolving as the century passed: see W.C. Glen, *The Law Relating to Highways, etc.* (2nd edn, 1897) and *Foot's Highway Acts* (properly James A. Foot, *Consolidated Abstracts of the Highway Acts, 1862, 1864; etc.* (1879)).
30 Good examples are *Municipal Reform and the Industrial City* (1982, edited by Derek Fraser, concerning Manchester, Leeds and Bradford); and John Garrard, *Leadership and Power in Victorian Industrial Towns 1830–80* (1983, a general study supported by specific essays on Rochdale, Bolton and Salford). An example of a study concentrating on a different aspect is Part II, *A Local Study: Wolverhampton, c. 1860–1914* in Jon Lawrence, *Speaking for the People: Party, Language and Popular Politics in England, 1867–1914* (1998). For an example of a study of an area with different considerations, where any references to local legislation or similar Parliamentary initiatives are seemingly not part of the story at all, see Richard W. Davis, *Political Change and Continuity 1760–1885: A Buckinghamshire Study* (1972).
31 Garrard, *op. cit.*, p. 103.
32 *An Essay on Literary, Scientific and Mechanics' Institutions* (1853), p. 178. The new powers were those of the Public Libraries Act 1850.
33 Higgs, *op. cit.*, p. 65, referring to the cited work of respectively Corrigan and Sayer, Philip Harling, Harold Perkin and Oliver MacDonagh.
34 For essays analysing how statistics developed and influenced nineteenth-century society and beyond, see Tom Crook and Glen O'Hara (eds.), *Statistics and the Public Sphere: Numbers and the People in Modern Britain, c. 1800–2000* (2011). There remained, however, much ambivalence in both Liberals and Conservatives in Parliament around their attitudes to municipal reforms and improving sanitary and other standards: see notes 10–12 to Chapter 1.
35 *Local Government in England* (1903), vol. II, p. 240.
36 *Office-Holders in Modern Britain* vol. IX, *Officials of Royal Commissions of Inquiry 1815–1870* compiled by J.M. Collinge (University of London, Institute of Historical Research, 1984).
37 J. Wesley Bready, *Lord Shaftesbury and Social-Industrial Progress* (1926); Roger Watson, *Edwin Chadwick, Poor Law and Public Health (Then & Now)* (1969). A broader recent study is that of Benjamin Ward, *The Health of Nations: A Review of the Works of Edwin Chadwick* (vol. I, 2008). The classic study was R.A. Lewis, *Edwin Chadwick and the Public Health Movement, 1832–54* (1952). See also the Introduction by M.W. Flinn (and particularly the section at pp. 3–18 under the sub-heading *The deterioration of public health conditions*) to his 1964 edn of Edwin Chadwick's *Report on the Sanitary Condition of the Labouring Population and on the Means of Its Improvement* (1842); Anthony Brundage, *England's 'Prussian Minister': Edwin Chadwick and the Politics of Government Growth, 1832–1854* (1988); and Christopher Hamlin, *Public Health and Social Justice in the Age of Chadwick: Britain, 1800–1854* (1998).
38 See the essay by Gavin Drewry 'Lawyers and statutory reform in Victorian government', which comprises chapter 1, pp. 27–40, of the first part, 'Ways and Means', of *Government and Expertise: Specialists, Administrators and Professionals, 1860–1919* (1988, paperback edn 2003) edited by Roy MacLeod. A specialist study is Gloria C. Clifton, *Professionalism, Patronage and Public Service in Victorian London: The Staff of the Metropolitan Board of Works 1856–1889* (1992).
39 *Hansard*, 3rd series, vol. XCVIII, cols. 797–8 (8 May 1848).

60 *Context and content of local Bill promotion*

40 See for instance Christopher Hamlin, *op. cit.*, pp. 266–74. There had been Government Bills about sanitary improvement in 1841, 1845 and 1846 (summarised by Hamlin at p. 267), but public health was not a state priority or preoccupation, and the Bills easily fell prey to vested interests, debate about detail, and overriding political events.
41 Public Health Act 1848, 11 & 12 Vict. c. 63, ss. 4–7.
42 Public Health Act 1848, s. 8.
43 The size of Boards was to be fixed by Provisional Order: ss. 12–15. Those having property worth up to £50 annually had one vote, up to a maximum of six over £250: see s. 20. Votes were cast by signing, though an illiterate could make 'His mark': s. 25.
44 Public Health Act 1848, ss. 39–83. There was, however, a duty on Boards under s. 46 that sewers vested in them by the Act were not to be injurious to health.
45 See the excellent short survey by S. Martin Gaskell, *Building Control: National Legislation and the Introduction of Local Bye-laws in Victorian England* (1983), p. 22.
46 *Homes of the Working Classes*, quoted in Anthony S. Wohl, *Endangered Lives: Public Health in Victorian Britain* (1983), p. 170.
47 Gaskell, *op. cit.*, p. 33.
48 *Op. cit.*, pp. 339–40. His statistics were taken from the *Report of the General Board of Health on the Administration of the Public Health Act, and the Nuisances Removal and Diseases Prevention Acts, from 1848 to 1854*; *Parliamentary Papers*, (1854), vol. XXXV, p. 1 (Paper 1768).
49 The 1854 Report at p. 38 quoted one return as putting the average cost of a local improvement Act as £1,627, and another as £2,000.
50 *Op. cit.*, p. 17.
51 *Op. cit.*, p. 35. The Report recorded at p. 35 (and see also pp.37–43) a far more significant obstacle to progress north of the border:

> The extension of the Public Health Act to Scotland was barred by the passing of the Scotch Police and Improvement Act, which may be adopted by the vote of a majority of ratepayers, and which confers powers enabling towns to execute the improvement works themselves. But it is reported to us that this Act has been adopted by hardly any towns in Scotland, so that, in general, these merely permissive powers are a dead letter, and even where town drainage works are attempted, they are of the character of the works so decidedly condemned by the Health of Towns Commissioners.

The report, addressed to Viscount Palmerston (then at the Home Office), was signed by Lord Shaftesbury, Edwin Chadwick and T. Southwood Smith.
52 *Op. cit.*, p. 55.
53 *Public Health in the Nineteenth Century* (1965), Appendix III, pp. 185–6. The *Parliamentary Papers* reference is 1857 Session 2, vol. XLI, p. 3 (Paper 328). A note refers to the subsequent 1867 return at vol. LIX, p. 141 (Paper 80) of districts where either the Public Health Act 1848 or the Local Government Act 1858 was in force.
54 See Hamlin, *op. cit.*, pp. 255fn., 277 and 292. For a detailed exposition of early borrowing rules and techniques under the Public Health Act 1848, see Sir Harry Page, *Local Authority Borrowing: Past, Present and Future* (1985), pp. 132–3; annuities had been widely used before this date in private Acts, though the 1848 Act made no reference to them.
55 *Op. cit.*, p. 282.
56 21 & 22 Vict. c. 98, s. 4 (and see also the discussion of the 1858 Act in Chapter 4). The metropolis, s. 3, and Oxford and Cambridge, s. 82, were excluded from the operation of the Act (see also s. 31 of the 1848 Act). For the Poor Law background to London, see David R. Green, *Pauper Capital: London and the Poor Law, 1790–1870* (2010).

57 Local Government Act 1858, ss. 12–17. Section 24 prescribed the constitution of Local Boards, the mode of election being that of the 1848 Act. This section was strangely drafted, starting with types of Local Board and ending with detailed rules for warding 1848 Act districts. The principal powers for services, as opposed to supplementary matters, were in ss. 29–53.
58 Gaskell, *op.cit.*, p. 37. The need for cleansing had been forcibly brought home to Parliament when in 1858 the 'Great Stink' caused by the foul condition of the Thames forced suspension of a sitting: see Stephen Halliday, *The Great Stink of London: Sir Joseph Bazalgette and the Cleansing of the Victorian Metropolis* (1999), pp. 71–6. Disraeli introduced the Metropolis Local Management Act Amendment Act 1858, 21 & 22 Vict. c. 104, which was swiftly passed and 'gave the Board all it needed to carry out the main drainage' (p. 75). The Act amended was 18 & 19 Vict. c. 120. The condition of the Thames was frequently alluded to in *Punch* at this time (from 1874–80, its Editor was Tom Taylor, who was also – improbably perhaps – the Secretary of the Board of Health before it was abolished in 1858). See for instance the *Essence of Parliament* feature for 31 July 1858 at p. 42 –

> Wednesday. Never mind if it was, the Lords sat, and LORD WYNFORD complained on the Public Health Bill debate that the measure gave no remedy against the Manufacturers who carry on their filthy and noxious trades on the south bank of the river. LORD HARDACRE made the spooney reply, that the Bill empowered the Privy Council to inquire into such matters; but WYNFORD stuck to his text, that what was wanted was power of suppression, as no inquiry was wanted beside a sniff, especially on a Friday.

59 For three typical examples, involving Bootle-cum-Linacre, Bury and Askern, see the *London Gazette* for 8 July 1870, pp. 3308–9.
60 *Returns of Districts where 'The Public Health Act 1848', or 'The Local Government Act 1858', or both are in force; and districts or places where any public, or local Act, is in force; date of passing or adoption of Act; populations and rateable value in each case*: Parliamentary Papers ordered to be printed on 22 February 1867, vol. LIX, pp. 141–66 (Paper 80). There is also a list of Local Boards of Health 'acting under the authority of the Public Health Act or Local Government Act' ordered to be printed on 31 July 1868 at 1867–68 vol. LVIII, pp. 789–822 (Paper 489); and a differentiated list of Boroughs which had become Urban Sanitary Authorities etc. ordered to be printed on 17 July 1874, vol. LVI, pp. 853–6 (Paper 304). These sources are very valuable, being virtually impossible to replicate now from other sources, and may be presumed to have been compiled with a high degree of accuracy before being presented to Parliament.
61 Bernard Harris, *The Origins of the British Welfare State: Social Welfare in England and Wales, 1800–1945* (2004), pp. 109–10.
62 Harris, *op. cit.*, p. 111.
63 Simon Szreter, *Fertility, Class and Gender in Britain, 1860–1940* (1996), p. 193; H.J. Hanham, *The Nineteenth Century Constitution 1815–1914: Documents and Commentary* (1969), p. 373.
64 Hamlin, *op. cit.*, pp. 339–40.
65 T.C. Barker and J.R. Harris, *A Merseyside Town in the Industrial Revolution: St. Helens 1750–1900* (1959), p. 77. The experience of the industrial revolution in the settlements that in 1868 formally became St. Helens is indicative of its environmental impact, as the town seemed to have it all – mining, chemicals, an iron foundry, glass-making and other manufacturing, a canal and – later – two principal railway lines.
66 See Eric Pawson, 'Debates in Transport History: Popular Opposition to Turnpike Trusts?', *Journal of Transport History*, (1984) 3rd series, vol. 5, no. 2, pp. 57–65. At the trusts' peak in the 1830s, there were said to be about a thousand trusts, with

30,000 miles of road and 8,000 tollgates. See William Albert, *The Turnpike Road System in England, 1663–1840* (1972). Pawson's 1984 article was followed in the same journal by another by Albert, 'Popular Opposition to Turnpike Trusts and its Significance' at pp. 66–8, somewhat critical of Pawson's outlook and referring to his *Transport and Economy: The Turnpike Roads of Eighteenth Century Britain* (1977).

67 See Charles Hadfield, *The Canal Age* (1968), esp. pp. 140–54; and J.R. Ward, *The Finance of Canal Building in Eighteenth-Century England* (1974). The total impact of the inclosure movement, and the acreages involved, Act by Act and county by county, can be seen from the chronological *Return* (H.C. Paper 399), ordered by the House of Commons to be printed on the eve of the First World War, 29 July 1914 (*Parliamentary Papers*, vol. LXVII, p. 325). It runs to 93pp. For a specific example – Northamptonshire – of poor people's attitudes to enclosure, where 'debates about common rights never receded', see Elizabeth T. Hurren, *Protesting About Pauperism: Poverty, Politics and Poor Relief in Late-Victorian England, 1870–1900* (2007), pp. 85–6. A general study is Mark Overton, *Agricultural Revolution in England: The Transformation of the Agrarian Economy* (1996); see also Jeanette M. Neeson, *Commoners, Common Right, Enclosure and Social Change, 1700–1820* (1993).

68 Perhaps a hint of some of the attitudes, whether of rival promoters or the affected populace, can be gleaned from the last words of the long title of James John Scott's 1846 manual on *Railway Practice in Parliament. The Law and Practice of Railway and Other Private Bills … The Order of Proceedings in Both Houses, With Plain and Full Practical Directions; the Formula; and the Most Useful and Successful Modes of Conducting or Opposing.*

69 While the literature on railways is vast (the 1983 2nd edn of George Ottley's *Bibliography of British Railway History* runs to 683pp.), there appears to be no significant monograph study of the history and process of railway Bill promotion itself. While histories abound of individual companies and lines, and many of these give much detail about the surveying and Parliamentary processes, the sheer volume of Bills, including so many unsuccessful ones, is probably at least partly responsible for this. A limited exception is provided by the treatment in M.C. Reed, *Investment in Railways in Britain 1820–1844* (1975), but its sub-title *A Study in the Development of the Capital Market* shows that its focus and perspective are elsewhere. More broadly based is Ernest Carter, *An Historical Geography of the Railways of the British Isles* (1959), appendix 1 to which lists at pp. 569–601 the *Unregistered; Registered, but Unauthorized by Act of Parliament; Defunct; and Abandoned Railways in Great Britain.* R.S. Joby, *The Railway Builders: Lives and Works of the Victorian Railway Contractors* (1983) presents a fascinating picture of how the works authorised by so many railway Acts were delivered, while Robert Keith Middlemas had earlier profiled five great Victorian contractors, including Thomas Brassey, in *The Master Builders* (1963), and John Neville Greaves published a biography of *Sir Edward Watkin, 1819–1901: The Last of the Railway Kings*, 2005). Set beside them, however, should be Terry Coleman, *The Railway Navvies* (1965). For a well-told example of the story of a series of Bill promotions, see E.T. MacDermot, *History of the Great Western Railway*, vol. I, 1833–1863 (1927). Vol. II, 1863–1921, was published in 1931. For a detailed archive of correspondence and accounts, see vol. 70 of the Lincoln Record Society series, *Letters and Papers Concerning the Establishment of the Trent, Ancholme and Grimsby Railway, 1860–1862*, edited by Frank Henthorn (1975). The associated 1861 and 1862 Acts were 24 & 25 Vict. c. clvi and 25 & 26 Vict. c.cxxix. As the railway era unfolded, there was some overlap in Bill promotions with canal companies: the Second Report from the Select Committee on Railways and Canals

Amalgamation (*Parliamentary Papers*, 1846 vol. XIII, Paper 275, qq. 28–40) sets out lists of the amalgamations of railway companies (24 Bills); power to lease or sell to some other railway (106 Bills); and amalgamations of railways with canal companies (30 Bills).

70 *Report from the Select Committee on Private Bill Legislation*, ordered to be printed 30 June 1863 (*Parliamentary Papers*, vol. VIII, p. 205, Paper 385). W.E. Gladstone (not a member of the Select Committee) was one who reportedly lost a lot of money investing in railways in the 1860s; see the Denault and Landis article cited in note 76 below.
71 See 'Railway Morals and Railway Policy' by Herbert Spencer, *Edinburgh Review*, vol. C, no. CCIV, October 1854, pp. 420–61 at pp. 429–30. 'The supporters of new projects boasted of the number of votes they could command in the House.' For the background and influence of the *Edinburgh Review* at this time, see Rosemary Ashton, *142 Strand: A Radical Address in Victorian London* (2006, a study of the publisher John Chapman).
72 The Alkali Act 1863, 26 & 27 Vict. c. 124, required the registration of alkali works under s. 6 and provided in s. 7 for the appointment of inspectors.
73 Barker and Harris, *op. cit.*, p. 353.
74 *Op. cit.*, p. 11.
75 Parallels may be drawn with the advent of mass television in the 1950s and 1960s, and again with the advent of so-called 'social media' in recent years, which those in authority cannot afford to ignore. For the Victorian period, however, see Jon Lawrence, *Speaking for the People: Party, Language and Popular Politics in England, 1867–1914* (1998).
76 See the valuable and illuminating December 1999 article 'Motion and Means: Mapping Opposition to Railways in Victorian Britain' by Leigh Denault and Jennifer Landis. This appears not to have been separately published, but is available at https://www.mtholyoke.edu/courses/rschwart/ind_rev/rs/denault.htm and was related to a module nod. *History 256* at Mount Holyoke College, Massachusetts. A list is included of railway schemes, opposition to which attracted public attention.
77 5 Geo. 3, c. 81. It was bound with the Road Acts for 1765, and described in a handwritten index at the front of the Law Society Library's volume as the 'Manchester & Salford Cleaning Lighting & C. [Act]'. The Act (sections were not then numbered) constituted some 178 people by name as Commissioners, together with the Fellows of the College of Christ in Manchester and 'the Borough Reeves and Constables of the Towns of Manchester and Salford for the time being'. They were not created as a body corporate, but any nine or more could act together, and indeed any one commissioner or more could prosecute for stealing lamps or damaging the street furniture etc. that the Commissioners might provide. They had powers to raise money by rating (at the Law Society Library, see pp. 869–71 as bound), but had to defray their own 'expences' of meetings. This first Act was repealed and replaced along similar lines by 32 Geo. 3, c. 69. Birmingham obtained a similar Act in 1769, 9 Geo. 3 c. 83, also listing a huge number of Trustees rather than Commissioners. Not being corporate bodies as such, these long lists of names have more the character of membership organisations.
78 E.P. Hennock, 'Urban Sanitary Reform a Generation Before Chadwick', *Economic History Review* (1957), vol. 10, pp. 113–20 at p. 117, quoted in Bernard Harris, *op. cit.*, p. 106.
79 The impact and complexity of railways and their regulation is well told in Frederick Clifford, *A History of Private Bill Legislation* (1885), vol. I, pp. 43–184. Perhaps the most telling comment in this context is on p. 181: 'The text-books on railway law set forth about eighty general statutes relating to railway, passed since 1837.

64 *Context and content of local Bill promotion*

Not fewer than four thousand private railway Acts have been sanctioned since 1830, many of them after prolonged investigation.'
80 *Statutory Authorities for Special Purposes* (1922), p. 348. Their verdict on improvement commissioners overall (pp. 345–9) is, however, less dismissive – they remark on the general lack of contemporary popular criticism, despite the adverse opinions of radicals and reformers; they note the 'mass of wage-earners who, paying no rates, remained stolidly indifferent to the whole business', and 'conclude that such work as was done by the Improvement Commissioners was a clear gain to the community. Their sins were sins of omission.'
81 Spencer, *Edinburgh Review*, October 1854, vol. 100, no. CCIV, pp. 420–61 at p. 451. His article was prompted by the *Reports from the Select Committee on Railway and Canal Bills* (1853) and *A History of the English Railway; its Social Relations and Revelations, 1820–1845* (1851) in two vols. by John A. Francis. Spencer was born in Derby, soon to become a principal railway town. (See also notes 17, 41 and 52 to Chapter 3.)
82 *Op. cit.*, pp. 450–1. The table on p. 440 of preference shareholdings and votes cast in a third attempt to secure company approval for a major extension scheme is particularly revealing, though Spencer does not identify the company.
83 *Op. cit.*, p. 428.
84 *Op. cit.*, p. 449.
85 *Op. cit.*, pp. 459 and 461. In this financial climate, speculation was inevitably added to the business objectives of actually building and opening profitable railways. Anthony Trollope based much of his 1875 novel *The Way We Live Now* on a fraudulent scheme involving $3 million in share capital (then about £600,000) for the supposed 2,000-mile 'Great South Central Pacific and Mexican Railway' – a plot that he clearly thought his readers would find plausible.
86 *Westminster Review*, July 1853, republished in Herbert Spencer, *Essays: Scientific, Political, and Speculative* (1854), vol. 3, and in an expanded edition by Williams and Norgate, London, 1891, vol. 3, pp. 229–82. The original article was unattributed, and in what was fully titled *The Westminster and Foreign Quarterly Review*, vol. LX (no. CXVII), New Series vol. IV, no. 1, pp. 51–84 at p. 53.
87 *Op. cit.* (original 1853 publication), p. 54.
88 This was the private Act 8 & 9 Vict. c. 7, relating to the inclosure of St. Mary's, Nottingham, which amended 2 & 3 Vict. (1839), c. 28, whereby 34 acres had been enclosed. A further 18 acres had been inclosed by 8 & 9 Vict. c. 32. Spencer did not comment on whether this land was available to house anyone before the inclosure; indeed this passage did not occur at all in the original article. It is inserted at pp. 240–1 in vol. 3 of the 1891 edn (see note 81 above).
89 *Op. cit.* (original publication: see note 81 above), pp. 70–1.
90 *Op. cit.* (original publication), p. 80.
91 *Hansard*, 3rd series, vol. 210, col. 18, 15 March 1872.
92 After substantial amendment and reprinting, public Bills would be re-numbered, so that Bill 248 (the highest number recorded in the Commons *Journal*, for the first reading of Mr Mackinnon's Equitable Councils of Conciliation Bill on 30 July 1858 at vol. 113, p. 359), does not reflect the number of different Bill titles. The public Bills in a session were indexed and published in returns, but not usually in the numerical sequences that can be found in *Vacher* for later sessions for private Bills.
93 As it happened, one of these, no. 4, was for a lease by the Westminster Improvement Commissioners of land in Victoria Street and Tothill Street to the Westminster Palace Hotel Company. The hotel opened in 1861, on the traditional site of William Caxton's press in the Almonry.
94 In 1857, 249 private Bills were deposited, and 255 read a first time. Chapter 3 explains further the private Bills procedure.

Context and content of local Bill promotion 65

95 Only 150 received royal assent in time to be included in the statute book for 21 & 22 Vict. and dated 1858.
96 Local Government Acts 1888 and 1894; 51 & 52 Vict. c. 41 and 56 & 57 Vict. c. 73.
97 The 1858 Act, 21 & 22 Vict. c. 98 replaced the Public Health Act 1848 and, as noted earlier in this chapter, the authorities for their local government districts were simply styled 'Local Boards' rather than, as hitherto, 'Local Boards of Health'.
98 Burial Boards were distinct corporate bodies by virtue of section XXIV of the 1852 Act, which was 15 & 16 Vict. c. 85. Vestries controlled the membership, who were not elected; Burial Board expenditure was funded under section XIX out of 'the Poor's Rate'. Burial Board law became excessively complicated; there were 13 public Acts from 1852 to 1900; and nice distinctions between 'cemeteries' under the Cemeteries Clauses Act 1847 and 'burial-grounds' under the Burial Acts. By 1894 'there were 919 Burial Boards, and there were 86 Town Councils, 58 Local Boards, and one body of Improvement Commissioners acting as Burial Boards, making a total of 1064' (William Blake Odgers and Edward James Naldrett, *Local Government*; one of the Macmillan series *The English Citizen: His Rights and Responsibilities*, second edn, 1913, pp. 192–3).
99 No classification is without its exceptions and qualifications. The Manchester Overseers Act 1858, 21 & 22 Vict. c. lxii, while primarily creating four separate systems of Overseers for Manchester, Ardwick, Chorlton-upon-Medlock and Hulme, also included section XXX, ending the former Gas Directors' exemption of what were now Manchester's gasworks from rating by the Overseers.
100 The term 'local Act' in s.7 of the Highway Act 1862 did not include Turnpike Acts: see s. 1 of 26 & 27 Vict. c. 94. The Highway Act 1835 had not been applicable to local Acts, though that changed after the passing of s. 144 of the Public Health Act 1875, when former local and private Act powers came under the newly created urban authorities.
101 An 1858 example from the list of local Acts above would be the Bradford Corporation Waterworks Act 1858, 21 & 22 Vict. c. lxxvi.
102 34 & 35 Vict. c. clxxxi and c. cciv respectively.
103 *Op. cit.*, p. 22.
104 See the cited work of Jon Stobart in notes 13 and 58 to Chapter 1.
105 By way of comparison with an earlier age (and when public and private Bills were not distinguished in the manner of subsequent years), see the large numbers of unsuccessful Bills recorded in *Failed Legislation 1660–1800: Extracted From the Commons and Lords Journals* (1997), edited by Julian Hoppit, with an Introduction by Julian Hoppit and Joanna Innes. Some 7,025 failures are recorded across this period.
106 Victoria Park was in Middlesex, the Bill having been promoted by the Metropolitan Board of Works.
107 The return totals and *Vacher's Lists* both include Bills for Ireland and Scotland, as well as England and Wales. One railway Bill related to two Canadian companies.
108 Such as the St. Helens Canal and Railway Bill (no. 58), or the Stokes Bay Railway and Pier Bill (no. 120).
109 Bernard Harris, *op. cit.*, p. 106.
110 See also James Thompson, British Political Culture and the Idea of 'Public Opinion', 1867–1914 (2013).

3 Passing the Bill
Formalities and financing

The process whereby a private person, company or corporation might seek to obtain an Act of Parliament for their own special benefit was closely regulated. There were exacting requirements to be met before the merits of a Bill could be considered at all by either House of Parliament. The procedures of the two Houses were not particularly well coordinated, but they were interrelated while also differing – Commons Standing Order 81 of the 1866 edition (the edition generally referred to here) required the Commons Chairman of Ways and Means to confer at the start of each session with the Lords Chairman of Committees about which Bills should commence in each House. The costs of Bill promotion (and indeed of objections) could in some instances be crippling, and there was much that could be stigmatised as either monopolistic or restrictive practice among the relatively closed circle of the Westminster 'village'. On the other hand, the procedures gave, and had to give, much regard to the rights of objectors and the public, as well as to the interests of the promoters, and the quasi-judicial reputation of Parliament in considering private Bills stood quite high, even while the system itself was thought to be unduly expensive and cumbersome. Petitioning Parliament had always been regarded as a privilege, and it was not desirable that obtaining the ultimate legal authority of an Act of Parliament for private advantage should be too easy, or lack rigorous safeguards. When an M.P. sought to raise in the House his personal interest under a railway Bill, the Speaker made it clear that that was inappropriate.[1]

The House of Commons had made a standing order on 18 June 1811 'That all Petitions for Private Bills, be presented within Fourteen Days after the first Friday in the next, and every future Session of Parliament'. Accordingly, last dates were thereafter set each session for receiving Bill petitions, first Bill readings, and private Bill reports. The Standing Orders had, by the mid-1850s, become elaborate codes of process, the navigating of which required specialist expertise and professional support. The growth in the number of railway Bills in particular had its effect, not only in providing lucrative work for the firms of Parliamentary agents established from 1836[2] – and giving them vested interests in its continuance – but also in imposing severe over-loading demands on the resources of Parliament and its membership. There were consequential effects too for the promoters of other Bills that were not about building, consolidating or abandoning railways. They had to work within the same framework, but by no means necessarily with the same levels of financing available to the promoters of supposedly profitable schemes. Building a railway was not necessarily inherently very expensive – in 1863, sums of £5,000 or £6,000 per mile were quoted to that year's Select Committee for cases where the ground was flat, there were no significant cuttings and bridges to make, and the land was readily available.[3] To obtain powers to build, and then actually to construct, a contentious line with demanding terrain could, however, easily become ruinously expensive.

This chapter explores how private Bill procedures developed and were scrutinised in Parliament; how in outline those procedures worked; and some of the many aspects and facets of the business of trying to get such Bills through both Houses successfully. While commentators like Clifford,[4] O.C. Williams[5] and Rydz[2] have written on the history and application of the relevant Parliamentary procedures, there has been little modern published detailed examination of the Select Committee reports of 1858 and 1863 on private Bills, or collated information about the costs and commitments involved in endeavouring to get Bills passed. From the several hundred pages of these reports has not only come much otherwise undiscoverable information, presented here for the first time; they also provide that information from the different perspectives (and vested interests) of the practitioners involved. The practitioners giving evidence were, naturally, generally of long experience; they were drawing on that in a heyday age of public petitioning and growing public concern and militancy about matters that concerned them. For those in Parliament, it was not merely that they could or should listen to what the Standing Orders quaintly termed 'voices' – increasingly in mid-Victorian England they *had* to listen.

The evolution and examination of private Bill procedure

The unprecedented growth in private Bill business after 1830 necessitated several examinations by Parliament of how this overwhelming new burden of work should be handled, none of which has been fully explored by other commentators. Neither the numbers of inclosure Bills, nor the enthusiasm for canal Bills, had previously given rise to the quantity and complexity of issues that the railway age brought – nor indeed to the levels of capital investment to be raised and spent.[6] The environmental implications too were both extensive and controversial, while the scope for lobbying was boundless.

Back in 1824 the Commons had appointed a Select Committee on Private Business.[7] The 12 recommendations were mostly about adjusting timetables and detailed procedural requirements, including replacing Standing Orders from 1700, 1794 and, in one case, 12 April 1604.[8] Yet already the business was growing: in the previous 5 years, it was reported, there had been 864 private Bills, but only 199 contested (and Standing Orders dispensed with in

192 cases). In the current session of 1824, however, 75 out of 225 had been contested, while what were termed 'voices' had been admitted in Committee in 40 of those 75. A Lords Committee took evidence on the fees and charges for private Bills in 1827, and a Commons Committee did likewise in 1834. The growth in private business, which became much more rapid as railway Bills arrived, was the subject of two further Commons Committee reports in 1838, and three more from another Committee in 1840. A generation or so after 1824, so much outside Parliament was different, yet the conduct of private business had not kept up. Limited changes in internal procedures were not proportional to the number, the environmental impact, and the contentiousness of so many hundreds of Bills – and plainly the high costs and fees of promoting seemed to be having little effect on many who, while they opposed these costs, resisted still more the notion that they might be left out of the rush to secure the best routes and the large profits that the new railways seemed likely to bestow. Accordingly in 1846 and 1847 Select Committees reported on the implications of all these new promotions, and considered afresh how private Bills should be handled. Joseph Hume was Chairman of the 1846 Select Committee on Private Bills, whose report drew attention to the disregard of the public interest in the promotion of needlessly expensive, uncontrolled and unnecessarily inconsistent Bills.[9] (The 1846 Railways Committee's supposed Report was, it appears, published by accident without authorisation: a Select Committee reported on the circumstances on 29 March 1847.[10])

In 1847, a further Select Committee on Private Bills, appointed to continue the previous year's inquiries, took extensive evidence. The first report, ordered to be printed on 26 February, was merely a recommendation that no overlapping private Bill should be considered until Parliament had decided on the various general Clauses Consolidation Bills that were coming forward.[11] The second, which was ordered to be printed on 29 March, recommended that the complicated fees structure should be simplified; that there should be a proper system for taxing – that is, adjudicating – costs; and that Bills of Charges should be expeditiously delivered. (The House of Commons Costs Taxation Act 1847 was passed shortly afterwards.[12]) The third and principal report, ordered on 21 July 1847,[13] was wide-ranging. The Committee considered – and applauded – the reputation of the Examiners of Standing Orders; they reviewed the overly complex rules on posting notices;[14] they considered a more equal distribution of Bills between the two Houses, and a better timetabling balance instead of many Committees having to sit all at once; and they noted with satisfaction the several Clauses Consolidation Acts which by that time had been passed during the 1847 session. They also supported the idea that willing communities should be able to obtain powers for improvement without the expense of a special local Act, citing the successful general lighting powers of 3 & 4 Will. IV, c. 90 by way of precedent. Finally, among a number of other matters, they considered at some length the expenses of Bills, quoting a few examples particularly, and most notably the £432,620 spent by the Great Northern Railway Company up to 26 June 1846 'without a spade having been put into the ground'.[15] A barrister, Alexander Pulling, writing a few years later, quoted the number of local, personal and private Acts in the first decade of Victoria's reign as 2,200 – twice the number of public general Acts. 'In the Session of 1846' he said

> there were no less than 500 sittings of Select Committees; as many as thirty-four being held in one day, and the average number sitting daily seventeen. Such a consumption of time, coupled with an ill-concealed disrelish of Honourable Members for the business which consumes it, tend to justify the opinion, that a Select Committee on a Private Bill is about the most objectionable tribunal that could be devised.[16]

He added later, 'The Clauses Acts of 1847 produced much good; but to be an effectual substitute for the clauses in Private Acts, they should be equally obligatory in all cases'.[17]

Pulling later published in 1862 *A Proposal for Amendment of the Procedure on Private Bill Legislation, in a Letter Addressed to Colonel Wilson Patten, M.P.*,[18] with whom he had evidently had some discussion, but he was not one of those giving evidence to the Select Committee in the following year. His solution was to advocate 'the appointment of Commissioners or Examiners, to enquire into and reduce into an authentic form all the facts and circumstances with which Select Committees have to deal ...' He considered that the abortive preliminary inquiries briefly introduced in 1847 had been 'not effectually carried out'.[19] (Wilson Patten in fact advocated such an approach to the 1863 Select Committee, though without referring to Pulling, and the Committee's report alluded specifically to the proposal, but entertained 'strong doubts whether it is possible to say, beforehand, what are the facts in respect to classes of Bills which, when found, a Select Committee would consider material for the determination of the particular case before them'.[20])

The apparent reforms of the Clauses Consolidation Acts of 1845–7 and their two Costs Taxation Acts of 1847 and 1849 did not prevent both Houses needing to reconsider the machinery of private Bills again within a few years. The 165 sections of, and three schedules to, the Railways Clauses Consolidation Act 1845 did not mean that promoters did not still need to come to Parliament for authority to raise capital; to take land compulsorily; to construct earthworks, cuttings and bridges; and so on. Meanwhile, the process of preliminary inquiries, introduced in 1847 with the aim of foreshortening the process of assessing the technical issues surrounding individual promotions, was soon seen to be failing to work as intended; no doubt protective of their powers, and dismissive of the status of those appointed to conduct the inquiries, neither House took much notice of their deliberations.[21] A Committee examined the process and produced two reports in 1850, while yet another Commons Committee in 1851 considered private business again, and the duties of the office of Counsel to the Speaker. The House of Lords appointed a Select Committee in 1858, and the Commons in 1863; much of the evidence taken then, and the attitudes of witnesses (some of whom had given evidence in the 1840s) are very reminiscent of the earlier hearings. The Commons agreed in 1867 that Board of Trade reports on private Bills were costly, usually of little impact, and should be discontinued except in the case of those affecting tidal waters.[22] Finally in the period before 1872, further Committees considered the Court of Referees on private Bills in 1865, and in 1867 there were two Joint Committee reports of both Houses on Parliamentary deposits. Throughout all of the Reports and evidence it is inevitably the railway schemes and their implications that dominate the evidence and the concerns of those involved; other kinds of Bills – and in particular municipal Bills – are either virtually ignored or included within procedures and considerations that are driven by the principal and over-reaching priority of railways.

In moving the appointment of the Select Committee on Private Bills, 'to consider whether any Improvement could be effected to facilitate such Legislation and diminish its Expense', Lord Stanley of Alderley (who became its Chairman) said that

> the great evil of the existing mode lay in the expense to promoters of such Bills consequent upon their having to prove their case first before a Committee of the House of Commons, and then before one of the House of Lords.[23]

Despite the need for practical reforms and reduction in both the costs of promotion and the scale of Parliamentary resources demanded by private Bill promotions, the 1858 Lords Committee's conclusions were of limited procedural scope; they principally recommended that compliance with Standing Orders should be proved before the Examiners prior to the introduction of Bills; that any Bills against which petitions had been withdrawn be treated as if originally unopposed; that questions of *locus standi* – the standing or right to be heard – should be referred to a special Committee; and that witnesses before both Houses should give evidence on oath. Limited conclusions of this kind were not what some at least in the Commons desired: a few weeks before 18 June, when the 1858 Select Committee was appointed, Lord Robert Cecil had moved in the Commons that private Bills should henceforward 'be conducted by a paid and permanent Tribunal'. There was insufficient support for the principle, and after a lengthy debate he withdrew his resolution.[24]

The 1863 Commons Committee took in a broader sweep of evidence; its members readily agreed the obvious – 'that the present system on which the Private Business is conducted is not satisfactory, chiefly on the ground of the length and costliness of the proceedings in contested cases' – but there was 'a great diversity of opinion amongst them as to the changes that are required'. This is reflected in several pages of individual views. The 15 agreed resolutions of 24 June 1863 amount to surprisingly little. Several are relatively incidental to the scope or scale of the business involved – the size of Committees, the timing of meetings, how often M.P.s could be expected to sit on such Committees, that Minutes of Evidence be printed, and so on. The Committee was able to agree that reporting on opposed Bills must be kept within Parliament.[25] They also agreed that a way should be found of hearing the issues on opposed Bills once jointly instead of separately in each House, and that the way that fees and payments were made to counsel and solicitors should be reformed.

As President of the Board of Trade, and Chairman of the 1863 Select Committee, Mr. Milner Gibson was questioned in the Commons by Mr. R. Hodgson M.P. on 17 July 1863 about what course he intended to pursue. For the most part his response was lacklustre, and playing for time at the end of the session, he concluded by saying that 'he had not yet been able to make up his mind as to the best and most useful course to take'.[26] Six days later Mr. Darby Griffith M.P. tried again, and also made specific reference to solicitors' charges for copies of evidence, and to the *ad valorem* duties on private Bills in the Commons. Again he equivocated, and when pressed by Mr. Whalley said that

> it was intended to introduce a Bill at the commencement of next Session to enable promoters of undertakings, when all parties were assenting, to carry out certain works, and accomplish certain objects by complying with the provisions of a general measure, such compliance to be certified by a department of the Government.[27]

The conclusions of the Select Committee eventually came before the Commons in a lengthy debate on 16 February 1864. After several discussions around motions and amendments, a series of resolutions[28] around process and costs was agreed, but the more fundamental reforms for which some had called were not. Lord Robert Cecil for one remained persuaded that

> when it had to decide upon its Report the Committee shrank from applying any adequate remedy to the enormous evils with which it had been expected to grapple. He spoke of the Committee in its corporate capacity, but the Report which decided that the system so generally condemned should continue, was only passed by a majority of a single voice.

Several of those who spoke in the debate were M.P.s who had served on the Committee, and inevitably much similar ground was trodden.[29] Some progress was made, however, in relation to costs: supported by Mr. Massey, 'Mr. Scourfield presented a Bill for awarding Costs in certain cases to Opponents and Promoters of Private Bills' on 18 July 1864. He withdrew it two days later,[30] but in the following year the Parliamentary Costs Act 1865 to similar effect made it onto the statute book.[31] Meanwhile the *Solicitors' Journal and Reporter* for 27 August and 17 September 1864 carried two articles on private Bill legislation: No. I dismissed the notion that the 'Parliamentary Bar' had a monopoly on the rights of audience before Select Committees while defending the higher rate of fees that such practice commanded, while No. II dismissed the notion of House of Commons Referees that had been experimentally introduced, adding at the end rather patronisingly that 'as an experiment, the harm done in one session cannot be great'.[32]

Writing in the *Edinburgh Review* in 1867, John George Dodson M.P., the Chairman of Ways and Means since February 1865,[33] was also scathing about the outcome of the 1863 Select Committee. 'Parliament', he wrote,

> loath to part with its jurisdiction, has called in the aid of Examiners, has had recourse to panels of Chairmen, has reduced the quorum and multiplied the number of its committees, has divided and sub-divided inquiries and remitted some to the Chairman of Ways and Means, and other to the new Courts of Referees, but all in vain ... The private business, lopped and shorn of all the heads we have enumerated, attacked with all the weapons we have described, has risen up each successive year more formidable than before.[34]

His dismay was understandable; he refers to '648' private Bills in 1866, of which 377 had become law, and to the 392 private Acts of 1865, 256 of which concerned railway schemes. The various Committees and Referees in 1865 had held 60 sittings, more than 80 per cent of them railway-related.[35] As it happened, the years 1865–66 proved to be the apogee, but his indignation was clear:

> The Blue Book which was the result of the labours of the Committee of 1863 sufficiently illustrates the hopeless diversity of opinion that prevails. That Committee consisted of fifteen members, by whom, after the evidence had closed, twelve different reports or sets of resolutions were submitted for approval. Thirteen witnesses were examined as to the conduct of private business, who proposed minor twelve [*sic*] different schemes of reform, besides making innumerable suggestions. Finally the Committee reviewed twelve propositions for improving or superseding inquiries by Parliamentary Committees; of these it condemned eleven, and the twelfth, which it approved, has never been adopted by either House. The cause of the failure of so many attempts at reform is not far to seek. Railways present the great difficulty, and the public does not know its own mind about railways ... Parliament ... knows what it wants, but then it wants an impossibility – namely, to retain its jurisdiction over private Bills, and at the same time to be relieved of a laborious and distasteful task.[36]

The large numbers of railway promotions are put into a different perspective if Dodson was right, as apparently he was, when he averred that in 1864, 13 companies commanded three-quarters of the whole U.K. railway traffic, and that total railway receipts that year exceeded £35 million, involving some 110,000 employees. 'Some companies' he said 'singly represent a capital of

40,000,000*l*., while their annual income vies with that of the greatest and most powerful corporation in the world, the established church of Great Britain and Ireland'.[37] That this 'private business' was in truth very public indeed was beyond argument. We shall return again to the 1863 Select Committee report later in this chapter: it is the most authoritative contemporary investigation and analysis of the private Bill world in its Victorian heyday, and the information it reveals – and the picture it presents – seems to have been largely overlooked by those modern historians who, while emphasising the torrent of private Bill promotion in the second age of 'railway mania', have not trawled its pages as a means of revealing how that huge and almost unmanageable legislative burden was regarded by those whose business it was to handle or deliver it.[38]

Hybrid Bills

Hybrid Bills are those having characteristics of public and private Bills, and the process for considering them has long combined elements of each. Speaker Hylton-Foster defined a hybrid Bill as a public Bill that affects 'a particular private interest in a manner different from the private interests of other persons or bodies of the same category or class'.[39] Once enacted they are classed with public Acts, and accordingly fall outside our scope here.[40]

The accumulation of private Bill procedure

As with public Bills, private Bills had to pass three readings in each House. The Standing Orders of the Lords and Commons that governed how promoted private Bills must qualify to be considered by Parliament, and then the rules according to which that consideration would be conducted, were published annually at the end of each session from 1836. By the 1870s they provided an elaborate code not only of process but also of safeguards as to what must appear. For example, if 15 or more houses occupied by 'the labouring classes' were to be taken, that Bill must contain a clause stipulating a duty to provide sufficient accommodation for those displaced.[41] Similarly, a Bill for 'making a burial ground or cemetery, or the erection of works for the manufacture of gas' must contain a clause defining the limits of such grounds or works.[42] In most years, the Standing Orders were debated and amended, often in quite minor ways, by each House, as is readily evidenced by the annual *Hansard* Indexes to each session.[43]

A private or local Bill had three principal hurdles to clear. The first involved persuading the Examiners that the deposit and preliminaries of the Bill had satisfied the Standing Orders. The other two were the separate Committee stages in each House, where arguments were heard afresh and success in one was no guarantee of success in the other. If there were major objections to the Bill's proposals, these stages could take many days and, in such cases, would probably cost enormous sums.

Both the Lords and Commons Standing Orders divided private Bills into two classes. The first comprised most municipal powers, and also Bills for incorporating, regulating or giving powers to companies; those about courts and public order matters; and those for improving land. The second class involved works of construction and enlargement of various kinds (including railways), of which most would more usually be promoted by other than municipal authorities, but did include bridges, sewers, streets and waterworks. Occasionally a Bill would be presented for something wholly new, 'such as the introduction of the system of electric telegraph, which was a novelty' as Lord Stanley of Alderley, Chair of the 1858 House of Lords Select Committee on Private Bills, put it.[44]

The Examiners were Officers of the House, appointed by the Speaker in the Commons and by the House itself in the Lords. Standing Orders compliance – for each House – had to be proved to their satisfaction on such matters as the serving of notices to owners and others, naming parishes involved, publication of proposals, and listing landowners who were for, against or neutral about the Bill's proposals. There was accordingly scope for opposition on points of process. Bills and plans – and all 'Memorials complaining of non-compliance with the Standing Orders' – had to be deposited, and all the requisite notices served, within the strict timetables laid down: these dates mostly fell in December, and the *General List of Petitions* would be made out in the Private Bill Office, with at least seven clear days' notice given 'of the day appointed for the examination of each Petition'.[45] It might take several days to satisfy the Examiners in the case of complex Bills – for instance in the case of a Railway Bill the intended route for which stretched across many miles, parishes and land ownerships. The examinations were held in public, and in contentious or disputed cases might be attended by any number up to 200 people.[46] Some felt that Examiners should have discretion to allow or overlook trivial non-compliances with Standing Orders, but the requirements were strict,[47] although Parliamentary agent Thomas Coates averred that by 1863 there were 'very few memorials complaining of non-compliance with the Standing Orders', and he thought 'that they are disposed of in the most satisfactory manner possible'.[48] Those with long familiarity with Bill promotions generally felt that the processes could readily be improved, to render them more effective both in terms of notice to the public and less cost to the parties.[49] There were, however, those who were essentially supportive of things as they were, and made practical arguments against, for instance, the suggestion that hearing objections separately in both Houses was wasteful and unnecessary: the head of Parliamentary agents Martin and Leslie, Theodore Martin, wrote in 1872 that

> the real merits of the cases of Opponents are frequently not appreciated by the Promoters themselves until disclosed in the first House. And, although the opposition may have been unsuccessful there, the Promoters become satisfied that it is not groundless; and so, rather than imperil their

Bill by a second discussion, they wisely concede points which might have been settled by a Joint Committee irrevocably in their favour. Hence it is that not more than one-third of the Bills opposed in the first House are opposed in the second.[50]

Cash deposits were required for certain Railway Bills under Commons S.O. 63. Because of the care that was taken to ensure that compliance was complete, and that Bill preambles were accurate, those preambles provide particularly valuable historical evidence; in 1858 for instance, the Birkenhead Improvement (General Mortgagees) Act had five-and-a-half folio pages of preamble, and the Halifax Park and Improvement Act had nine pages.[51] Herbert Spencer provides an unusual insight into the process in 1845, when his employers, the Birmingham and Gloucester Railway Company, required him to help them pass Standing Orders for an extension Bill; he refers to the row of temporary wooden structures erected beside the Thames for those engaged on Railway Bills while the new House of Commons was being built after the fire of 16 October 1834.[52]

It was critical whether a Bill was opposed. An unopposed Bill was of course not guaranteed to be passed, but where there were significant and well-resourced petitions against a Bill, the scene was set for an expensive and protracted Committee stage likely also to be repeated in the other House. A Bill might become unopposed if petitions against it were withdrawn. In 1866, the Committee size for opposed Bills was a Chairman and three Members, and for unopposed Bills comprised the Chairman of Ways and Means and two others.[53] To be heard, petitioners against Bills had to have the standing to be allowed to sustain their arguments; they had to have what was termed *locus standi*. This might be either general or limited *locus*: 'The general principle of *locus standi* is that petitioners shall not be heard merely for the purpose of getting some advantage conferred on them by the Bill, but for the purposes of meeting some injury which will be caused to them by the provisions of the Bill.'[54] The notion of *locus standi* developed into an extremely complex concept of entitlement to be heard, in particular where objections were taken to Bill proposals based not on intrinsic arguments but on grounds that the competition would have an adverse effect on the petitioner's interests. Colonel Wilson Patten, later the Chairman of the 1863 Select Committee, told the 1858 Lords Select Committee in evidence that he thought that the issue about competition should be directly decided: 'I think that you cannot get uniformity with regard to Railways' he said 'unless you lay down one of two principles, either that you will conduct the Railway legislation of the country upon the system of competition, or that you will conduct it upon the system of protection within certain districts.'[55] Issues of this kind were more likely to affect Railway Bills and those for commercially based schemes, but could have an impact in municipal and other contexts too. 'How and at what stage' asked Clifford rhetorically, 'should this issue be raised?' answering that –

Before the year 1864 the practice of the two Houses was uniform on this point. When an opposed Bill came to be heard in Committee, counsel for promoters, at the end of his speech, or when opposing counsel rose to cross-examine the first witness, took objection to the petitioners' *locus standi*. ... In 1864 the House of Commons came to the conclusion, after inquiry, that its procedure in this respect might be amended. One reason for amending it was the needless expense incurred by petitioners, whose right to be heard should, it was thought, be determined at an earlier stage of a Bill. Still stronger grounds for change were found in the time occupied before Committees in discussing *locus standi* questions, and the uncertainty of decisions then given upon more or less technical points by fluctuating bodies suddenly called upon to deal with each case as it arose.[56]

The general rules on *locus standi* were summarised by Smethurst in 1867,[57] and are worth setting out at length because of their importance in portraying the approach of Parliament as to who might take part in the promotion process in some way (and thus potentially create risk and expense for the promoters), and who might not –

Owners, lessees and occupiers of property – anyone who has a vested interest in property that would be taken, or is entitled to Parliamentary notice, has *locus standi*, 'not so, however, where their property is not proposed to be taken, but will be injuriously affected by proposed works'.

Traders, freighters, shipowners, &c. – people in business on whom rates and tolls will be imposed have *locus standi*, 'if they petition as a class; not so, however, a single trader, &c., petitioning alone'.

Competition – railway and other companies petitioning against a Bill authorising competition 'will be allowed a *locus standi* under Standing Order H.C. 130, but not against a bill merely extending competition, or making it more effectual'. S.O. 130 reads 'It shall be competent to the referees on private bills to admit petitioners to be heard upon their petitions against a private bill, on the ground of competition, if they shall think fit'.

Parties petitioning under Standing Order H.C. 133 – 'That the municipal or other authority having the local management of the metropolis, or of any town, or the inhabitants (as a body) of any town or district, will be allowed a *locus standi* against a bill injuriously affecting their interests, if an allegation to that effect is made in their petition'.[58]

Shareholders – when their interests are not distinct from those of their company, they will generally be refused *locus standi* under S.O. 131, but will be allowed it 'in either House if they have been dissentients at a Wharncliffe meeting'.[59]

Smethurst then provides more than a hundred pages of precedents. Those concerning municipalities and local inhabitants[60] clearly demonstrate that a petition was likely to fail unless it was demonstrably made on behalf of, and with the properly constituted authority of, the municipality – and also that the petition clearly asserted the injurious effect on the township or area that the intended powers were expected to have if granted. Both circumstances were required: the Abergavenny Improvement Commissioners, for instance, petitioned against the Vale of Crickhowell Railway (Eastern Extension) Bill of 1865[61] but *locus standi* was denied; the Commissioners did not appear to control the turnpike roads that they claimed the Bill's passage would affect, and 'there was no statement in the petition that the town of Crickhowell would be injuriously affected'.[62]

George Pritt, a very experienced Parliamentary agent whose father had acted in the original Liverpool and Manchester Railway Bill, explained to the 1858 Lords Select Committee how unfairly the *locus standi* issue might be played: counsel for the Bill might open the case, and comment freely and disparagingly on the petitions presented against the Bill and the petitioners, whose *locus* would be questioned. Then as soon as the petitioners' counsel sought to speak, the question would default to determining that *locus*, 'so that, practically, the minds of the Committee have been directed to the whole matters at issue by the counsel for the Bill, the counsel for the petitioners having no means of answering him'.[63] He went on to allude to a case that had occurred in the Lords only that week whereby Stockport Corporation had petitioned against the Manchester Corporation Waterworks Bill; Stockport had clearly had no *locus standi*, but he had had to be prepared, and even though the evidence involved 'was not heavy' he thought that

> from 70 to 100 guineas would have been saved if that question of *locus standi* could have been decided before the Committee was appointed, so as to save the necessity and expense of going prepared to fight the case as an opposed Bill.[64]

Locus standi in the Lords could be affected by decisions taken on Bills in the Commons, or *vice versa*, giving new parties rights to be heard or taking them away from those formerly entitled.[65] Evidence was given on oath in the Lords, but not in the Commons.[66]

The question of whether competition could in itself legitimately be a ground of *locus standi* remained contentious. Mr. Dodson opened a debate on the subject in the Commons on 24 March 1868 in relation to what was then Standing Order 131 – currently capable, he said, of two different constructions:

> It might be taken to mean that the proprietors of existing works might be admitted before Committees to argue that the proposed new works were not required for the public advantage; or, without denying that the works were for the public advantage, that they might be allowed to oppose the construction on the ground that those works would interfere with their private interests ... He believed it would be best to revert to the old law

of Parliament, and not to allow one company to oppose another except in case of interference with its works ... he would substitute for it a new Standing Order, rendering it competent to the Referees on Private Bills, if they thought fit, to admit the proprietors of existing works to be heard upon their petition against any Private Bill relating to similar works within a town or district served by them, on the ground of the absence of public advantage.[67]

The House was, however, not persuaded, and after a short debate he withdrew his motion.

One who would not withdraw was John Rea, a Belfast solicitor apparently described in *The Scotsman* for 29 April 1864 as 'the person notorious for his strange freaks in the meetings of the corporation of the town that is cursed with him'. After ten days arguing with the committee in opposition to the Belfast Town Improvement Bill and finally being told to withdraw, he refused and had to be forcibly removed by three constables, one of whom sustained a broken wrist. *The Solicitors' Journal and Reporter* printed a verbatim account of the final exchanges prior to this altercation, which it described as a 'scene perfectly unprecedented in the annals of Parliament'. Justified or not, it belies the image of select committees as uniformly decorous proceedings rationally analysing the legal arguments advanced before them![68]

Despite the care taken over the formalities, Parliament itself was not immune from error. Sir John Trelawny records his irritation on 16 July 1863, when 'the Speaker might have saved much time had he read at an earlier moment one of our standing orders, which applied to 2 bills'. The editorial note records that 'The Great Eastern and North British railways (steamboats) bills had to be recommitted as the companies' plans to acquire steamboats were not permissible unless recommended by the committee'. William Massey, M.P., the Chairman of Committees, also on the same occasion successfully had steamboats removed from the Morayshire Railway Bill, when another standing order had been violated because acquiring steamboats had been added in committee, and had not been part of the original Bill.[69] It was understandable that most M.P.s would be unfamiliar with the highly specialised private Bill procedures (though better would be expected of the Speaker and the Clerks); Robert Baxter – who had also given evidence to the previous year's Select Committee on *Standing Orders Revision* – gave evidence to the 1863 Select Committee that the sheer numbers of Bills had resulted by the early 1860s in there being far less debating of private Bills on the floor of the Commons.[70]

Objections outside Parliament

While the Standing Orders provided Parliament's formal processes for objecting to deposited Bills, other avenues were of course open to opponents in the local government setting. If the local Board or corporation could be

Passing the Bill: Formalities and financing 79

persuaded to drop a particular measure or clause, there would be no need for an expensive intervention at Westminster – and there would be no niceties about *locus standi* to consider.

A number of writers have already described a few of the local campaigns of this kind,[71] but there remains enormous scope for research, as most local Bills were likely to be the subject of claim and counter-claim. Just as voices were raised in Parliament against public general legislation that now seems urgent or unarguable, so too were local communities (or at least the more articulate and determined within them) often vociferous about proposed local reforms that they saw as leading directly both to unwanted social consequences and, more immediately, to increases in the various local rates that they were liable to pay.

One case will serve here to illustrate the kinds of events and local narratives that underpin the purely Parliamentary history of a Bill's progress towards enactment. In 1869, the Northampton Corporation decided to give notice for what became the Northampton Markets and Fairs Bill in 1870. Their existing markets and fairs were, as the preamble of the eventual Act put it, 'at present held in the streets and public places, so as to cause obstructions thereof' and they sought powers to move them and to provide 'new markets and fairs, and slaughter-houses'. The Bill was confined to this purpose, and did not seek wider powers beyond what were also incidentally required to acquire the necessary land and money, and to regulate the new facilities that were to be established. On Monday 6 September 1869 the Market Committee was reported to the Town Council as having recommended that notice be given of the intention to apply for a Bill, and 'that the town clerk prepare a draft bill, to be submitted to the Council at the earliest practicable period'.[72]

On suggestion of a delay, the Town Clerk told them, as the weekly *Northampton Herald* reported, that they must decide at once: 'Before the notices were given, they must know what they were going to apply for, and a bill must be drawn up embodying what they wanted. That would take time.'[73] Much of the essence of the local story of the next few months – too detailed to follow here – is contained in the following report of some of the exchanges that shortly followed –

> Mr. DORMAN said if the Committee came before the Council with a well-digested scheme, and were prepared to point out a suitable site which could be obtained at a cost within their means, there would something for them to consider, and they should know what to do; at present it seemed to him they were as far off bringing the matter to a successful issue as they were ten years ago.
>
> The MAYOR said this was merely a preliminary measure to put the Corporation in a position to get an Act of Parliament for what might be required if they thought proper to apply for one. Unless the notices were given now, the matter must stand over for another year.

Mr. Alderman ERRINGTON said it was proposed to take powers, he believed, to take a site for a covered market, but he did not understand that any particular site would be named?

The TOWN CLERK could not tell how that would be until he had consulted his Parliamentary agent. If they were compelled to specify a site, of course, they would specify one, or as many as they might think desirable.

Mr. WILLIAM THOMAS HIGGINS hoped it was not intended to take the market from the centre of the town; if it was he should oppose it.

Mr. DENNIS said that would be a matter for the Council to decide.

Mr. ALEXANDER MILNE said that it would be premature to give the proposed notices.

Matters were unresolved only a few days before the closing date for the statutory notices: the *Herald* reported on 20 November that the Council (having inconclusively considered another Market Committee report) would meet again on 22 November. Subsequently, however, the statutory notices did appear, and were published a week later on the *Herald*'s front page on 27 November (and in the *London Gazette* for 26 November[74]). They included the intention for either the Corporation or the Bedford and Northampton Railway Company to extend the railway to accommodate the intended cattle market site, and to make requisite contractual and other arrangements; these clauses, however, were not included in the deposited Bill, and therefore not enacted when the Bill eventually received the royal assent on 20 June 1870.

Meanwhile, arguments had continued. 'A Ratepayer' wrote to the *Herald* on 27 November decrying the idea of building a cattle market at all, while others disputed the siting. Earlier that week, at the 22 November Council meeting, there had been a long and contentious debate about the proposed new covered market and cattle market, with the associated legal powers to be promoted. Mention was also made of the former Town Clerk John Jeffery, removed from office a year earlier by the Liberals, who was present to hear the debate.[75] Finally, after a failed amendment, authority to proceed further was given. Letters, often anonymous, continued to appear in the *Herald*,[76] and there was further debate on 6 December, when 'Mr. VERNON's motion for postponement of the bill until 1871 was lost by a majority of 13 to 7'.[77] It was not until 11 June 1870 that the Town Clerk William Shoosmith was able to say that the Bill had passed the House of Lords and merely awaited royal assent, while 'In answer to Mr. Vernon, the Town Clerk said a few amendments had been introduced, but they were merely of a formal character'.[78]

This issue, covered at length in the local press (the *Herald* was not the only local newspaper published at this time) vividly illustrates the importance of the local story in fully considering any local Bill promotion. This Bill was hurriedly prepared, and its promotion that year in doubt until the last minute; not merely the principle, but also the siting of the envisaged facilities was fiercely debated and – somewhat contrary in this case to the notion discussed in Chapter 1 that civic pride was a major factor in local promotions – while some were envious of Peterborough's cattle market, others thought that a purpose-built Northampton competitor would prove a loss-maker for the Corporation, and quoted statistics of local cattle trading to support their arguments. Merely to read the statutory notice, the Bill as deposited, and the resulting Act of Parliament is to miss entirely all the local context and the party-political undercurrents in which, narrowly and belatedly, the authority to promote was given and the formal Parliamentary consideration accordingly began.[79] (The Corporation was back in Parliament in the following session promoting the Northampton Improvement Bill.)

The passage of private Bills

Detailed study and observance of private Bill procedure was vital for those who practised before the relevant Committees;[80] they knew that the climate had changed markedly in the first 15 or so years of the railway age. As J.J. Scott put it in 1846, explaining why the early opposition of landowners to the unwarranted trespass of railways had already more usually become their enthusiastic welcome:

> Immense speculation, from the accumulation of wealth, resulting from good harvests, extended commerce, and national successes in China, and elsewhere, has taken place during the last year in railway projects. The monetary world is deeply involved. The sound and legitimate railways are as secure investments as either the funds or the land. Those who heretofore opposed them from a contrary opinion, have not only abated their hostility, but have become ardent advocates. The history of the Liverpool and Manchester line, with the opposition of powerful noblemen ... testifies to the fact. This conviction has led to greater impulse for railways than was the previous resistance to them. Over-speculation has been the natural result. Much evil may exist in consequence.[81]

Knowledge of the procedure itself, however, no more tells the whole story than knowledge of the relevant law and the Highway Code describes road traffic conditions in general, still less those of a particular journey. Moreover the demands, and the sheer number, of Railway Bills shaped the whole machinery and context of private Bill procedure at this time. There was already concern about the working conditions of those who were physically building the new railways: the reformer Edwin Chadwick, who read a paper on this and related subjects to the Statistical Society of Manchester on 16 January 1846, proposed that the Railway Bill Committees should impose conditions on the promoting companies about controlling and caring for the men who would be employed.[82] In 1858 just over half of all the private Bills promoted – 110 out of 211 listed in Vacher's annual *Lists of Private Bills*[83] – concerned railways; in the peak year of 1866, when some 633 Bills were deposited, almost 400 – some

396 – concerned railways in one way or another, and that proportion had reached around 62.5 per cent. A Select Committee had reported on Private Bills in 1847, following on from a Committee on Private Bills the year before. It was already evident by 1846, following the early years of so-called 'railway mania', that the means of dealing with these Bills was not only inadequate but was unsustainably distorted by their number, by the promoting and investing money behind them, and by the environmental impact that the proposed works would have. The 1847 Select Committee repeated the comment of their predecessors, that 'no provision is made for furnishing the Committees which sit upon them with complete and trustworthy information', and that

> the Committee, when the Bill is unopposed, are wholly dependent for information on the interested representations of the promoters, and where it is opposed, they have, in addition, only the representations of parties not in the least more likely to be disinterested than the promoters.[84]

In July 1858, when the Select Committee of the Lords reported on Private Bills,[85] there was further consideration of how this problem might be overcome, but that Committee 'deemed it more expedient' to confine themselves to suggesting improvements to the current approach 'without entertaining the larger question of an entire alteration in the existing system'.[86] The Commons appointed a further Select Committee in 1863.[87] Its Report and Minutes ran to more than 400 pages, and provide extensive insight into the practice of private Bill legislation as the number of promotions was reaching its zenith. Several aspects of the evidence given to the Committee require consideration here, in five groupings.

First, it was unsurprising that the Parliamentary authorities felt the need by 1863 to review private Bills again. 'The Committee will be surprised, I dare say' said their first witness James Booth, Secretary to the Board of Trade,

> to hear of the number of small branch lines, and extensions, and little deviations which are passed. In the present year there are more than 300 lines, which are less than three miles long, asking for the sanction of Parliament.[88]

From 1847 to 1857, 'the number of days on which Committees sat on opposed Railway Bills was altogether 167; that is the average'.[89] In the 1862 session, 198 Bills had been referred to Committees, of which 54 were unopposed and 15 had been withdrawn.[90]

Second, since 1830 a small, but lucrative, industry had grown up at Westminster to serve the needs of those who sought private legislation. They consisted of companies, corporations or associations of individuals (purely personal Bills about matters such as estates and landholdings, divorce, and naturalisation comprised a separate category). The Parliamentary Bar, comprising barristers whose business was solely or mainly about seeking or opposing private Bills, had largely developed to meet the demands of Railway Bills.[91] Etiquette and restrictive professional practice largely controlled the costs and arrangements according to which counsel worked, so that fees were maintained at levels of which those obliged to pay them had little control – if the customary daily refresher were ten guineas, no counsel would appear for less.[92] A solicitor, whose fees would likely be less, could not appear as such before a Parliamentary committee; that was a rule, although since more or less anyone (that is, anyone male) could set himself up as a Parliamentary agent, it was not a practical barrier – he had 'merely to go and sign a book in the House and make himself responsible for the fees'.[93] In fact, however, a good deal of the work 'in the case of Gas Bills, Water Bills and that class of business' was acknowledged to be well done before Committees by Parliamentary agents.[94] According to Thomas Erskine May, their costs and those of the solicitors involved had reduced by a third since changes made in 1847 following the House of Commons Costs Taxation Act.[95] Nevertheless, one such agent, Thomas Coates, opined that the fees paid to Parliamentary agents were sufficient only if they had enough Bills: '... if a man had only one or two Bills, it would be a very bad trade.'[96] He explained that the subjects dealt with by private Bills were 'very considerably' reduced in number, being now dealt with by Provisional Orders.[97] These were a more straightforward alternative to local Bills, whereby usually several Orders made under statutory powers, and making different provisions for separate communities, were then confirmed in legal effect by a single authorising statute.[98]

Third, questions of the costs faced by promoters or incurred by petitioners were directly related to their legal expenses, as well as to the fees that Parliament itself charged. Under 10 & 11 Vict. c. 69 and 12 & 13 Vict. c. 78, the Speaker and the Clerk of the Parliaments together fixed a scale of charges for solicitors and Parliamentary agents. They were set out in Edward Webster's *Parliamentary Costs: Private Bills, Election Petitions, Appeals, House of Lords* (3rd edition, 1867).[99] Webster provides 11 model Bills of Costs, detailing and annotating the sums allowable for every aspect of the process of taking a Bill through Parliament.[100] He also thereby provides a detailed breakdown of the duties, commitments and likely activities and expenses inherent in a Bill's passage, and cautions in his *Preface* 'that it is safer and more economical to employ Parliamentary Agents than to try to do without them, as the latter course sometimes results in loss of money to the client and of professional reputation to the solicitor'. James Blenkinsop expressed grievance over the requirement to pay *ad valorem* fees on the amount of capital proposed to be raised under a Bill, making the contrast that fees to raise £2 million were about ten times those to raise £100,000, 'and yet the Parliamentary offices have no more trouble, and are put to no more expense'.[101] G.K. Richards, the Speaker's Counsel, quoted the Parliamentary fees on a Bill to raise £750,000 as £520, and to raise any sum below £50,000 as £65.[102] The Parliamentary agent Thomas Coates sought to clarify what the whole private Bill business actually cost Parliament to administer. He understood that it cost the

84 *Passing the Bill: Formalities and financing*

Commons about £18,000, out of their total budget of £51,000, and the Lords £12,000. Fees amounted to about £76,000, so that the surplus on the Fee Fund was apparently some £25,000, which he considered amounted to a tax on those seeking Bills. The minimum fee for an unopposed Bill would be about £200 – in theory £87 in the Commons and £101 in the Lords.[103] When his evidence resumed three days later, he provided much more detail, and handed in papers, printed with his evidence, setting out his assessments of the private Bills costs of both Houses and his proposals for how the fees structures should be reformed. He quoted the fees for various kinds of Bills, and the highest fee – £182,000 – that had been incurred in the House of Lords alone.[104] Later, Joseph Gurney, who ran the team of Parliamentary shorthand writers, provided extensive information about their earnings, and the pressures that they worked under.[105] Petitioners against a Bill, or against a specific provision in a Bill, also of course incurred costs in doing so, and could not recover them from the promoters if successful: Thomas Coates told the 1858 Lords Select Committee –

> The great hardship is in oppositions: a landowner *bonâ fide* striving to get protection of a particular sort even by a clause, not desiring to oppose the preamble at all, but desirous of protecting some especial portion of his property by some particular means, cannot have a counsel in the room for a single day under 35*l*. Now that seems to me an extreme hardship.[106]

It was by no means easy to ascertain exactly how much a particular Bill had cost its promoters, or what it had cost objectors to petition against it.[107] Even where costs had been taxed – adjudicated – more might still be paid in practice than was formally allowable. 'I know as a fact' said the solicitor John Swift to the 1858 Lords Select Committee[108]

> that the engineer, for instance, whose charge is the highest, generally charges 10 guineas a day, and is paid the same in private business, or in the courts, or anywhere. That is not allowed on taxation, probably only half of it … if you want the man you must pay him his price.

Page 3 of *The Surrey Advertiser* for 30 December 1865 carried a report, under the heading *The Water Supply Opposition*, about the Dorking Water Bill,[109] which is indicative of the costs of what appear to have been spontaneous local objections:

> The report of the committee appointed to oppose the Dorking Water Bill in the late session of parliament, has recently been published, together with a list of subscribers and a statement of the receipts and expenditure. From a perusal of it we find there were 146 subscribers to the fund, whose united subscriptions amounted to £118 8s. The sum paid to parliamentary agents and solicitors was £91 17s., the balance being made up by

sundry payments to professional witnesses in attendance at the committee room of the House of Lords, disbursements made by members of the committee, and printing, &c.

Extreme examples of particular costs or charges merely distorted the averages without necessarily giving any useful guidance for anyone wanting to estimate the likely costs of any particular promotion. Regulations imposing multiple fees, charging each aspect of what was termed a 'Single Bill' £27, had also had a pernicious effect, as the Clerk of the Parliaments Sir John George Shaw Lefevre, who had the management of the fees under his direction, told the 1858 Lords Select Committee:

> The effect of the regulations was to charge some Bills with very large fees, especially some which ought not to be very highly charged, such as Improvement Bills, which latterly (more especially) have contained a variety of distinct objects; as, for example, water, gas, cemeteries, police, and other objects quite distinct one from the other; those were each considered separate objects, and the 27*l.* had to be paid in respect of each of them; so that on some of those Bills the fees amounted to several hundred pounds, whereas upon a Bill simply for making a railway, however large the amount of its capital was, and however important the railway, the Bill only charged 54*l.*[110]

Some of the most detailed information available about an individual Bill had been published already. In appendix 3 to the evidence they took, the 1847 Select Committee had printed 15 pages of itemised promotion costs of the Bill that became the Bury Improvement Act 1846. The solicitors' bill of costs was £3,696. 6s. 5d., and gives fascinating detail about all the elaborate work, much of it behind the scenes, that was required: 'Attending upon Mr. Entwistle ... explaining to him the nature of the Bill, and requesting him to oppose its summary rejection before having brought it before the Committee' – and seven more M.P.s the same, each at 6s. 8d. 'The Committee having been postponed, writing six letters to witnesses, countermanding their attendance for the present: £1 1s. 0d. Messengers therewith at midnight ...: 10s. 6d.' 'Mr. Harper's journey to London to give evidence on preamble of the Bill, out 14 days: £44 2s.'[111] The Parliamentary agents Dyson & Co. charged an itemised £1,393 8s. 10d., while ten other witness bills of costs amounted to well over £500, making an overall total exceeding £5,500. The 1858 Lords Select Committee heard much evidence about the average costs of Bills as perceived from different points of view. Bartholomew Adam, the Lords Principal Clerk for Private Bills, spoke of 63 Railway Bills both 'heavy and light' as having incurred an average of £230 in Parliamentary agents' charges; of those charges being a maximum of £150 for an unopposed Estate Bill; and of the average cost of an unopposed Turnpike Bill being from £250 to £300, with the latter sum 'being quite the maximum'.[112] The Parliamentary agent George Pritt, however, instanced his own costs for 17 unopposed Bills in 1855–57 as having averaged £139 1s. 11d., with the total costs including printing costs, counsel's fees and so on reaching an average £335 13s. 10d. He gave the professional charges for an unopposed Turnpike Bill as £110–130, with the total cost 'under £200, say £180'.[113] Another Parliamentary agent, Charles Evan Thomas, indicated that

> about 100 copies of Bills are required to be deposited at the offices of the two Houses in the first instance ... No copy of a Private Bill can be bought ... the promoters of the Bill must in practice supply all the copies that are required by opponents and for use in the country. The total number of copies actually required in practice varies from 240, which would be sufficient in a Naturalization Bill, to 1,200, which might be required in a Bill such as a Liverpool Docks Bill, but the number usually ranges between 500 and 800.[114]

In considering all these estimates, it must be recognised that very few if any witnesses had a detailed grasp of the whole costs issue – they were each expert in their own field, but often disclaimed authoritative knowledge beyond it[115] – and Bills of course incurred solicitors' fees, and those of the agents, counsel and the Houses of Parliament, as well as all the other costs of preparation, complying with Standing Orders and bringing witnesses to London. It must also be recognised – as part of the context against which private Bill costs may be viewed – that despite relatively stable prices, the costs of governing generally were rising in this period as the demands of the 'information state'[116] grew.[117]

In the 1863 Select Committee hearings, G.F. Whalley M.P. asked the Secretary to the Board of Trade James Booth to accept that since the system had changed in 1848, so that Inclosure Acts were passed by schedule in a Public Bill, the average expense of each had been £15 4s. 9d.[118] In the 1862 session 'a very important drainage Bill was conducted through both Houses entirely without counsel; the Committee knew perfectly well that the expenses of that Bill were to be defrayed by ratepayers'.[119] Another, however, 'to prevent rubbish being thrown into a river' reportedly cost £9,000.[120] George Parker Bidder, an engineer with 38 years' experience of the promotion of Bills, said that it had taken 22 days and cost £10,000 to get the Stone and Rugby Bill through Standing Orders.[121] Thanks to delaying tactics, the Bill was apparently 62 days in Committee.[122] Apart from delaying tactics by objectors, spoiling and speculative Bills were also sometimes put up by railway interests, usually seeking to divide (or threatening to divide) the available traffic.[123] Another Select Committee member, Colonel John Wilson Patten, M.P., considered that 'The great defect of the present system is, that before a private Bill Committee of the House of Commons, there is not a single individual who appears before it who has not a pecuniary interest in prolonging the proceedings'.[124] Making a railway did not in itself require the sanction of Parliament: if the land was available, it could be done spontaneously or consensually. Sometimes Bills came to Parliament simply because of the difficulty in acquiring land that was part of a settled estate, or where one or more landowners objected, without which problems there would have been no need to come to Parliament at all.[125] On the other hand, there were also occasions where a wealthy objector could afford to fight off a proposal which another party could not fight; James St. George Burke, Q.C. instanced 'a very rich landowner, namely, Dulwich College' successfully defeating the Brighton Railway Company's wish to take a line through the College estate: '... there was nothing but landowners' opposition.'[126] Sometimes the opposition of those landowners might be subsidised, which 'would never appear at all except it was backed by some competing railway company whom the Committee would not have heard' – that is, which would not have had *locus standi* – 'if it had appeared directly'.[127] Again, a well-resourced party might try again and again to achieve success: he further instanced his own involvement with a Bill for the Doncaster and Wakefield Railway, passed at the fifth attempt.[128]

Fourth, the Select Committee considered the repute of the private Bill process. The outlook within Parliament would by no means necessarily be the same as that of promoters or practitioners, whose vested interests were different. Further, the concept of value for money could not apply if it implied that the legislative constitutional authority of Parliament could be bought as of right if certain conditions were met and certain fees paid. Nevertheless, if that process were not to be brought into disrepute, the costs of petitioning Parliament for or against a Bill had to be demonstrably reasonable in themselves, and clearly and consistently proportionate to the work and the issues involved. Hugh Edward Adair, M.P., a member of the Select Committee who had sat as a Chairman of Railway Committees for nine sessions, was in no doubt that both 'the suitors' and the public at large had 'very great reason' to make their complaints and objections.[129] G.F. Whalley, M.P. read to Earl Grey a passage from the 1846 Report from the Select Committee on Private Bills that concluded

> under the present system the interests of the public at large, who have neither the means of obtaining detailed information as to the proposed measures, nor the means of defraying the expenses of opposition, are often prejudiced by the Local Acts.

He received the response 'I quite concur in the opinion'.[130] On the other hand, George Parker Bidder – perhaps not without regard to the interests of his long career in private Bill business – when asked if the Committees were satisfactory as tribunals, answered

> Yes. I do not mean to say that the decisions on all occasions are right, because no one has any right to expect that from any tribunal, but

> there is one satisfaction which we all feel who have any practice before Committees, namely, that we have the contest fairly fought out, and although we often retire defeated and dissatisfied with the conclusion, yet, on the whole, we feel that we have had a fair and an uncontrolled hearing.[131]

Whether those to whom the passage from the 1846 Report referred would have concurred in that view is another matter; it was an important consideration in reviewing private Bill practice in 1863 to take into account that, whether or not that process broadly satisfied the immediate and often well resourced participants, it had not been designed to serve the interests either of the poorly resourced or the public at large. Earl Grey was one who considered the outcomes often inconsistent: 'The policy of Parliament at present fluctuates very much' he said, 'because in point of fact it is not the policy of Parliament, but it is the policy of small Committees, composed of different persons, varying every day.'[132] Colonel Wilson Patten (who had been a member of the 1847 Select Committee) cited a famous railway example when, in the context of whether a joint Select Committee on a Bill could guide both Houses, he referred to the wish of each House to exercise its own judgment, and what he considered

> wrongly determined between the two Houses, namely, whether there should be the broad or the narrow gauge. It was discussed with different views in each House of Parliament. I believe that there was one view in one House and the other view in the other, and that it ended in the broad and the narrow gauges both being maintained.[133]

Finally arises the question of how effective was the concept of private legislation, assuming that given Bills were passed. Considered simply as texts, much had changed in James Booth's experience since he had been appointed Counsel to the Speaker in 1839, when 'Bills were in a very rude state indeed ... of enormous size and great verbosity, and there was no principle of order in the arrangement of the clauses'.[134] Every issue before the Select Committee was principally seen in the context of Railway Bills – they obviously were the dominant concern in terms of time taken, costs incurred, and above all of economic and environmental impact.

Bills for other purposes were viewed very differently. In the 1858 Lords Select Committee, the Chairman Lord Stanley of Alderley asked T. Erskine May, referring to the Public Health Act 1848, 'With respect to the Health of Towns Improvement Act, has it not been practically the case that parties have not been so generally willing as might have been expected to obtain powers under that Act, but have applied to Parliament for separate Bills?' May responded

> Yes, that is frequently the case; there are local peculiarities everywhere, which suggest some variation from the general Act which has been passed by Parliament to meet all cases, and hence there are numerous

applications to Parliament in spite of these general Acts, which would, at first sight, appear to be unnecessary.[135]

An extract from Mr. George K. Rickards' paper[136] to the 1863 Select Committee, however, quoted by Mr. G.F. Whalley M.P. to Lord Redesdale, is revealing in its tone:

> The Public Health Acts and more recently the 'Local Government Act, 1858' have invested the Secretary of State, acting on the requisition of the local authorities of towns, with large quasi-legislative powers, extending to almost every object previously attainable only by Private Acts, and including even the compulsory purchase of lands, subject only to a confirmation of the Provisional Orders by a Public Act of Parliament. This measure has gone very far to supersede private legislation, so far as regards the local management and sanitary regulation of towns, heretofore effected by 'Improvement Bills'.

Revealing also is Lord Redesdale's response, with its rather patronising approach to local choice: he responded that he found in a great many instances

> that the parties, after having tried the application of the Improvement Acts, have had to come to Parliament to put matters straight when they wanted to do anything in the least out of the general and ordinary way. But allowing people to deal a little with their own matters in their own town or place, is a very different thing from allowing parties to deal with the interests involved in a Railway Bill.[137]

Certainly there was a wider view that, as Earl Grey expressed it, 'the more it is possible to reduce those provisions in General Acts, the better, and that additional Acts upon the principle of the Lands Clauses Consolidation Act would be very useful'.[138] The Provisional Order approach, applicable for improvement purposes but also in other contexts,[139] was generally welcomed, but Thomas Coates alluded to the abolition of the General Board of Health by the Local Government Act 1858. This had reformed matters, but 'the Provisional Orders of the Board of Health, and the practice of the Board of Health in the preparation of those Provisional Orders, were found to be so objectionable, that the Board of Health was abolished by public acclamation'.[140] It was his view that

> whether it is under a Provisional Order, confirmed by a General Act, or whether it is by a Private Bill, which becomes a Private Local Act, it is a privilege to the promoter; it enables him to take land, and to do other things which his neighbour cannot do; then I say that the only fit tribunal to grant that privilege is Parliament, and not a department of the executive Government.[141]

The Committee did not follow very far the limitations on the practical enforceability of clauses included in private Acts for public benefit, but it was clear that – if a party did not comply with legal duties – there might well be no public agency with the duty to make them do so. In London, the Home Office was charged by Act of Parliament with the administration of the Smoke Acts; 'but with respect to railways in general' said Earl Grey,[142] 'I believe that there is no public authority to prevent the companies having locomotive engines with smoke; and in travelling by a railway now, persons are very often very much annoyed by smoke.' The likelihood, or degree of risk, that requirements of that sort would, or would not, be effectively enforced cannot have been lost on promoters, objectors or Parliamentarians.

The continuing case for reform

After the 1860s the volume of private Bills promoted was never so large again. As we have seen, however, the various debates and Select Committees, in both Houses, combined with the continual adaptation and amendment of the Standing Orders, were scarcely enough to cope with the quantity of Bills, let alone to meet the aspirations of those who felt that the principles of the system still needed fundamental reform. Mr. Dodson remained one of the most influential of them.

As the period of this study closed, his efforts and those of other would-be reformers continued. On 27 June 1871, Mr. Jonathan Pim, M.P. for Dublin, proposed a motion –

> That a Select Committee be appointed to inquire into the operation of the present system of legislation as regards Local and Personal Bills, and to consider whether means may not be devised for the improvement of such legislation.

The Chairman of Ways and Means Mr. Dodson agreed with the spirit, though not the methods, of this proposal, but after a short debate, the House was counted out at 10.30p.m. (initially at the instigation of Mr. George Leeman, the M.P. for York), there being fewer than 40 present, and accordingly this proceeded no further.[143] The following summer, Mr. Dodson himself moved four carefully crafted resolutions in the Commons on 15 March 1872 –

1. That, in the opinion of this House, the system of Private Legislation calls for the attention of Her Majesty's Government, and requires reform.
2. That it is expedient to substitute, as far as possible, an extended and improved system of Provisional Orders for Local and Personal Bills.
3. That Provisional Orders should be obtainable in England, Scotland, and Ireland on application to a permanent tribunal of a judicial character, before which Promoters and Opponents should be heard in open

Passing the Bill: Formalities and financing 91

Court, and the decisions of which should be subject to confirmation by Parliament.
4. That, in case of either House of Parliament admitting an Appeal against a decision of the tribunal in the matter of any Provisional Order, such Provisional Order should be referred to a Parliamentary tribunal, composed, in the manner recommended in 1869 by the Joint Committee of the House of Lords and the House of Commons on the Despatch of Business in Parliament, of Members of both Houses.[144]

After considerable discussion, conducted with considerable respect for his eminence (he remained Chairman of Ways and Means till the month following), debate was adjourned for a week, and resumed on 22 March, the day after Dodson had sent his scheme for reforming private Bill legislation to M.P.s.[145] From the beginning there were objections, led by Mr. Leeman; eventually, however, Mr. Dodson accepted an amendment to include a reference to Parliament in the first resolution, on the basis that the remaining three would be adjourned, though 'he had no idea of bringing them on unless some disposition should be shown on the part of the House for their discussion'.[146] That caution was justified; he asked formal questions about progress on 17 June, and again on 17 June a year later, on both occasions receiving what he no doubt considered as stalling answers from Mr. Chichester Fortescue, the President of the Board of Trade.[147] On the first occasion, the Minister referred to what he rather patronisingly called resolutions 'of an interesting character' put to the House on 13 June 1872 by Mr. F.S. Powell, to the effect –

1. That the range of Local Legislation affecting Towns and other Places ought to be contracted.
2. That the existing system of passing Local Bills on the same subjects as Public General Acts is inconvenient, works injustice between different Towns, and leads to unnecessary complication in the Laws affecting Local Government.
3. That no such Bills shall be introduced or passed unless upon proof (to the satisfaction of the Minister within whose department the subject matter lies) that the circumstances are exceptional and are not provided for under the Public General Statutes.[148]

This motion was agreed, and the debate was adjourned for a week, although in fact it resumed on 4 July. Mr. Dodson gave provisional support, while Sir Charles Adderley (who had brought what became the Local Government Act 1858 to the Commons, and had received the K.C.M.G. in 1869) thought that the second resolution should be omitted under any circumstances, and the third required to be very much modified. The motion was further adjourned, but eventually the order for the resumption was discharged on 26 July without more. All these events gave the impression that, in the face of both other priorities and the vested and objecting interests both inside and outside Parliament, the Government had very little will to do much beyond stalling. Moreover, there were still those who spoke up for the existing state of things.[149]

The following year, in 1873, Mr. Heron and Mr. Serjeant Simon introduced a public Local Legislation Bill 'to establish a Court for the Local Legislation of the United Kingdom', while shortly before four other M.P.s had introduced a public Local Legislation (Ireland) Bill 'to facilitate the obtaining of Powers for legislating on Public Local Matters in Ireland'. Neither proceeded beyond a formal first reading.[150]

Conclusion

The term 'private business' usually conveys an impression of activity with minimal, if any, significance for outsiders. That term is, however, used in a very special sense in the Parliamentary context. We have seen that the Committees handling it typically had only five members, and sometimes fewer; and that during the period 1858–72 very little private legislation was ever discussed on the floor of either House. Yet it was far from peripheral, even though there was an Empire and much other national business to consider. This chapter has centred largely on railway Bills, because they comprised the mass of the private Bill business at this time, and the procedural considerations that they engendered overlaid and drove the way in which all similar private business was conducted. To the House authorities and the Chairmen of the Bill Committees, municipal local Bills were almost incidental, and indeed viewed often as a class of promotions that the Public Health Act 1848 and the Local Government Act 1858 had rendered unnecessary.

Whatever the setting for local Bills, the setting for 'private' railway Bills could in fact hardly have been more public. Personal interests in the investment potential of the new transport revolution were serving, in every sense of the word, a national interest. Railway lines – built, authorised and proposed – ran over the whole kingdom. No M.P. could have been unaware of the lines that crossed or affected his own constituency; no more could a peer in relation to his own estate. Many (if not most) in Parliament must themselves have been involved or invested in railway schemes. The capital theoretically involved added up to hundreds of millions of pounds, while large numbers of people often came to hear contentious Bills examined in public. It was obvious at the time that railways were transforming the landscape, and that their promotion was having a huge impact on the market for capital, on the capacity of the construction industry, and on the mobility and attitudes of the wider public. An interesting historical question, given the effect of this 'private' business on the nation as a whole and on Parliament in particular, is the extent to which the principles and procedures developed then influenced the development of analogous processes elsewhere. *Locus standi* remains a familiar concept today (especially in the fields of judicial review and public enforcement); so too do the codes of compulsory purchase, injurious affection, blight and

Passing the Bill: Formalities and financing 93

betterment. It is arguable that the standards that Parliament set – and that Parliamentarians set for themselves – in the early and mid-Victorian period in handling private Bills, and in responding to workloads of promotions far beyond anything expected or experienced in earlier days, remained influential long after.

That alone makes it surprising that legal historians have not hitherto given more attention to the structure and drafting details of private legislation. The actual words whereby Parliament gave both effect and effectiveness to new powers for communities, and to new scope for railway and other promoters and investors, comprise an important part of the fabric of reform and industrialisation; millions of pounds were spent on formulating, justifying and enacting them, and they give an insight into a small but critical part – indeed one amounting virtually to an industry in its own right – of the history of public affairs in a pivotal era of the Victorian Parliament.

It is also important to set Parliamentary private business against a wider context: although attitudes were slowly beginning to change, this was still at this time a Parliament – and certainly a House of Commons – opposed to centralisation,[151] resistant to the notion that central Government should be prescriptive about, or providing of, most local or individual public services, and sceptical both of the needs of the ordinary or 'common' people to benefit from improved living standards, and of their capacity to improve themselves. Yet in 1858 in the House of Lords a Select Committee – including two Dukes (Newcastle and Somerset) and seven Earls – were spending days contemplating the niceties of *locus standi* and the mechanism whereby the whole infrastructure and economy of the country were being transformed.

Meanwhile, a mile or so away, most of the population lived in abject and disease-ridden poverty. Within a year the 'Great Stink'[152] was to come to the very portals of Parliament itself. While a few M.P.s and peers put in long hours in what were often dull and unrewarding Private Bill Committees, the majority on the floors of each House usually took little interest in them.[153] It can never be known what effect or influence this shortage of talent and commitment may have had on the whole private Bill situation. The Select Committees of 1858 and 1863 – and indeed of 1847 – valued the Clauses Consolidation Acts, and discussed the potential for more standardisation of that kind, yet focused hardly at all on the national 'business case' (as we would term it) for coordinating the provision of railway lines and the different company interests involved. To do so was not within their terms of reference. Gladstone's Committee in 1844[154] had seen the case for some central direction: individual company competition was certainly an issue much discussed, yet despite the lack of remit in the Select Committees of 1858 and 1863 (the lack of *locus standi* in that context, one is tempted to say) the need to take the step between the national interest and the sum of the parts of local or company interests, within Parliament at least, seems hardly to have been overtly recognised. This was quite different, for example, from the second report of the 1846 Select Committee on Railway Acts, with terms of reference that included the wording 'to promote and secure the Interests of the Public'. That Committee noted in its report, drawing comparisons with the situations elsewhere in Europe, that

> In this country no comprehensive system has ever been traced. The lines promising the most ample returns were, as a matter of course, first selected by companies; but the best mode of communicating the benefit of railways to the kingdom, considered as a whole, was only incidentally, considered by Committees in deciding between rival projects. The Committee of the Board of Trade, in some of its Reports, first attempted to lay down principles more worthy of the legislature of a great country, by which it should be governed in regard to its railways.[155]

Asked by the Chairman in the 1858 Lords Select Committee whether he thought 'that the railway legislation of the House of Commons has been unsatisfactory or satisfactory?' the solicitor John Swift replied 'Unsatisfactory to those who have failed, and the contrary to those who have succeeded; I think everybody must say that it has been entirely uncertain, and that there has not been anything like the application of principles or anything of that sort'.[156] The exchange that followed from Lord Stanley of Alderley's next question represents almost the only direct comment in all the evidence given to both the 1858 and 1863 Select Committees on considerations of national policy as opposed to the practice and procedure of the system of private railway Bill promotion. 'Would the country have been in a better position' he asked, 'supposing some principle had been laid down before railways were begun to be made, as to what ought to pass and what ought not to pass?' John Swift responded –

> I think it would; you would not perhaps have had so many railways made; you would not have had two or three railways made to one place, but you would perhaps have had the best railway to that place, and the other two or three made somewhere else where they were wanted. The result has been that people are now alarmed, and do not want to touch railways, because there is no sort of certainty whether when they have invested their money there is anything like a return to be had for it.

Lord Redesdale went on to ask, 'The railway interest are very much concerned in some definite principles on the subject being laid down by Parliament, are they not?'[157] Swift replied that he thought that 'they' – referring as Lord Redesdale had done to shareholders generally – evidently were but, pressed further as to whether they had drawn up any such principles, he acknowledged that they had apparently not done so. To do would be 'very difficult, but not impossible'. Further exchanges ensued about competition, and whether the country might be divided into large districts for the purpose of defining or confining competition in the promotion of alternative interests.[158] They were inconclusive, however, and no similar debate occurred in the 1863 Select Committee. The rising numbers of railway Bills that followed in the early and mid-1860s may have undermined Swift's point that people did 'not want to touch railways'; the nature of these exchanges underlines, however, the reluctance of these Parliamentary inquiries to consider the overall issues from the point of view of the state or the national interest in that context, and their predisposition to focus primarily on the issues for Parliamentarians and for shareholders.[159]

From the extensive scrutiny of these little-explored Reports have come layers over the bare bones of procedure in the Houses' Standing Orders. In Chapter 4 following, we consider the state of general local government law in the 1850s and 1860s, and how the public general legislation and common law of the time related to private legislation – and thereby provided the context within which arose the desires and needs of local Bill promoters to come to Parliament.

Notes

1 *The Parliamentary Diaries of Sir John Trelawny, 1858–1865*, edited by T.A. Jenkins, p. 88 (Royal Historical Society, Camden Fourth Series, vol. 40, 1990): 'A member (Whalley) complained that the Lords had passed a clause in a railway Bill giving a company power to take an unnecessarily large slice of his park ...' This was annotated as the Vale of Llangollen Railway Bill. G.H. Whalley, who was M.P. for Peterborough, did secure a clause in the Act limiting (but not very tightly) deviation within his land without consent: see s. 21 of 22 & 23 Vict. cap. lxiv. Interestingly, he was later a member of the 1863 Select Committee on Private Bill Legislation and himself gave evidence to it (see qq. 2806–57; 23 April 1863). At this time he was 'Chairman of six different Railway Companies in Wales' – q. 2806 – totalling nearly 300 miles, and the narrative of his evidence reveals a fascinating interplay between the various interests and standpoints involved.
2 See D.L. Rydz, *Parliamentary Agents – A History* (1979), esp. chapter 4, *Matters of Procedure, 1836–1868* (pp. 82–109). A concise synopsis of the creation of the business of Parliamentary agency is given by Mr Bartholomew Samuel Rowley Adam in his evidence to the 1876 Joint Select Committee of both Houses on *Parliamentary Agency* (*Parliamentary Papers*, vol. XII, p. 539, Paper 360), q. 155 (and see note 93 below). Rydz narrates what happened at pp. 69–79.
3 *Minutes of Evidence*, 1863 *Report from the Select Committee on Private Bill Legislation* ('the 1863 Select Committee', *Parliamentary Papers*, vol. VIII, p. 205, Paper 385), qq. 3308–11 and 3353–9. (The title-page numbers it as Paper 176-I, but that is not carried on.) Slightly lower rates – £3,000 or £4,000 a mile – had been quoted by the railway industry solicitor Robert Baxter in the *Report from the Select Committee of the House of Lords* on private Bill proceedings ('the 1858 Select Committee'), ordered to be printed by the Commons 20 July 1858, *Minutes of Evidence*, qq. 1074–5 (1857–8 *Parliamentary Papers*, vol. XII, pp. 15 and 173, Paper 450 + 450-I). He added that 'Common roads only cost about 1,000*l.* a mile, but canals will cost from 2,000*l.* to 3,000*l.* a mile, according to the country through which they pass'.
4 Frederick Clifford, *A History of Private Bill Legislation* (two vols., 1885, 1887).
5 O.C. Williams, *The Historical Development of Private Bill Procedure and Standing Orders in the House of Commons* (HMSO 1948), vol. I, is a particularly important

96 *Passing the Bill: Formalities and financing*

procedural commentary, though his chapter VI, pp. 125–75, rather understates the significance of this period by titling it *Further Adjustments, 1852–81*. See also note 29 to Chapter 1.

6 In 1860 there were some 4,000 miles of canals, and already by that time around 7,500 miles of constructed railways. Michael E. Ware, *Britain's Lost Waterways* (1979), vol. I, *Inland Navigations*, Introduction.

7 Paper 432, ordered to be printed 18 June 1824 (*Parliamentary Papers*, vol. VI, p. 497).

8 This 1604 Standing Order required eight Members to be present at a private Bill Committee; the Committee of the Whole House on 22 June 1824 concurred that the number should be reduced to five.

9 See the summary in O.C. Williams, *op. cit.*, pp. 284–6.

10 *Parliamentary Papers*, vol. XII, p. 41, Paper 236, including some unusual and personal detail. The Committee Clerks involved are named:

> That Mr. Stone ... took the Draft Report ... to Mr. Chalmers, but before Mr. Chalmers could make further and more particular inquiries, there being a sudden call for a Committee Clerk to attend some other Committee, and before Mr. Stone had time to give Mr. Chalmers any further information, Mr. Stone was called away to attend that other Committee.

11 On the 1845–47 Clauses Consolidation Acts and 'common clauses', see Chapter 1.

12 A House of Lords Costs Taxation Act was similarly passed in 1849 (12 & 13 Vict. c.78.).

13 The three Reports were numbered 116, 235 and 705 respectively: *Parliamentary Papers*, vol. XII, pp. 347, 351 and 357.

14 To make Lime Street Station in Liverpool, the North Western Railway Company had been obliged to publish notices in nine counties, although the Bill affected only one. See q. 639 and p. v of the Report.

15 Q. 156 and p. xi of the Report, together with appendix 5. They had served about 9,000 notices, and had objected to 26 other lines (listed on p. 297) comprising 1,051 miles.

16 Alexander Pulling, *Private Bill Legislation: Can Anything Be Now Done to Improve It?* (1859, London, Longmans), p. 7. This 16pp. pamphlet was reviewed in the *Law Magazine and Law Review, or Quarterly Journal of Jurisprudence* (May to August 1859), 3rd series, vol. VII, pp. 447–9. (See also note 90 to Chapter 4.) In the same issue of this Journal he also published an article on 'The Failure and Fate of the Statute Law Commission' at pp. 122–45. This Commission, the successor of several failed consolidation attempts, had been appointed in 1854 (see p. 127 as to its august membership).

17 Pulling, *op. cit.*, p. 16. In a footnote to this, Pulling refers – but without reference – to his Bill for the Statute Law Board on canals, in which such a provision was included. He had been appointed a Senior Commissioner under the Metropolis Management Act 1855; that year he also published an unattributed article on 'Private Bill Legislation' in the *Edinburgh Review* (vol. CI, no. CCV for January 1855, at pp. 151–91; see also note 90 to Chapter 4) advocating the transfer of private Bill business to local authorities, with a further pamphlet *Proposal for Amendment of the Procedure in Private Bill Legislation: In a Letter Addressed to Colonel Wilson Patten M.P.* in 1862. Frederick Clifford (*op. cit.*, vol. II, p. 904) credits Pulling with first using the term 'private Bill legislation' in his *Edinburgh Review* article: 'Being referred to in Parliament, it has gradually come into general use.' Pulling's January 1855 article is approvingly quoted by John Joseph Murphy in an equally well argued article 'The Private and Local Business of Parliament' in the *Journal of the Dublin Statistical Society*, vol. 1, part VI (1856), pp. 311–21 at p. 312. Murphy thought,

contributions then being unattributed, at p. 315 that the same author had probably written on *Railway Morals and Railway Policy* in October 1854, though in fact that was by Herbert Spencer – see note 81 to Chapter 2).
18 This was also reviewed (see note 16 above) in the *Law Magazine and Law Review*, or *Quarterly Journal of Jurisprudence* (May to August 1862), 3rd series, vol. XIII, p. 367, while the same journal issue also included a long article 'Private Bill Legislation – Local Statute Law' at pp. 235–45 adapted (at a time when contributions were often unattributed) from a paper that Pulling had read to the Jurisprudence Section of the Social Science Congress.
19 *Op. cit.*, p. 9. This 1862 'letter' comprised 12 pages as printed. Pulling referred at the outset to 'the appointment of a Committee of the House of Commons, on the Standing Orders' but he was actually referring to what became the 1863 Select Committee on Private Bill Legislation, of which of course Col. Wilson Patten was a member.
20 1863 Select Committee, p. iv and qq. 3139–40. See *Parliamentary Papers*, vol. VIII, p. 205, Paper 385.
21 1858 Select Committee, qq. 81 and 204 (evidence of T. Erskine May). The Third Report of the 1847 Select Committee on Private Bills (*Parliamentary Papers*, vol. XII, p. 357, Paper 705), chaired by Joseph Hume, has several appendices (see esp. app. 7–13) on the Preliminary Inquiries Act, 9 & 10 Vict. c. 106, including the views of 12 Admiralty Surveying Officers to whom specific queries were sent.
22 H.C. Deb. 3rd series, vol. CLXXXV, col. 1800, 14 March 1867 (Mr Stephen Cave, Vice-President of the Board of Trade, whose own office was abolished a few weeks later in favour of a Parliamentary Secretary position).
23 H.L. Deb. 3rd series, vol. CLI, cols. 3–6 (18 June 1858).
24 H.C. Deb. 3rd series, vol. CL, cols. 455–73 (11 May 1858).
25 There had been several suggestions that the Houses should accept the findings of others. The preliminary inquiries instituted in 1846 (see Chapter 1) had been largely disregarded in Parliament, and so proved ineffective. The Houses wanted at the same time to reduce the burden of considering so many private Bills in detail, but without forfeiting any practical discretion elsewhere. See also the points made in Lord Belper's Memorandum, submitted to the 1858 Select Committee on 12 July, and printed at pp. viii–x.
26 H.C. Deb. 3rd series, vol. CLXXII, col. 950; also *The Solicitors' Journal and Reporter*, vol. VII, 25 July 1863, p. 723. Mr Richard Hodgson, who had been a member of the 1863 Select Committee, was at this time the Conservative M.P. for Tynemouth and North Shields 1861–65.
27 H.C. Deb. 3rd series, vol. CLXXII, cols. 1284–85; also *The Solicitors' Journal and Reporter*, 25 July 1863, vol. VII, p. 725. Mr Christopher Darby Griffith was one of two M.P.s for Devizes.
28 The six agreed resolutions (see H.C. Deb. 3rd series, vol. CLXXIII, cols. 645–80) were as follows –

1. 'That the Committee of Selection and the General Committee on Railway and Canal Bills, at any time after the committal of any Bills, be empowered, with the consent of all parties promoting and opposing, to refer the same, wholly or with reference to particular Clauses, to the Chairman of the Committee of Ways and Means, and that such Chairman, together with Members to be appointed in like manner as Members of the Committee on Unopposed Bills, be empowered to hear the parties promoting and opposing such Bills or their agents, and to report upon the same to the House.
2. That in lieu of the Fees to be paid by the Opponents of a Private Bill for proceedings before any Committee, the following Fee be hereafter paid:- For every day on which the Petitioners appear before any Committee £2 0s. 0d.

98 *Passing the Bill: Formalities and financing*

3. That in lieu of the ad valorem Fees to be paid by the Promoters of Private Bills for proceedings in the House, where money is to be raised or expended under the authority of any Bill for the execution of a work, the following Fees be hereafter paid: – If the sum be £100,000, and under £500,000, twice the amount of such Fees. If the sum be £500,000, and under £1,000,000, three times the amount of such Fees.
4. That in the Table of Fees to be paid on the Taxation of Costs on Private Bills, the third paragraph – namely, 'For every Bill under £100, £1' be omitted.
5. That Mr. Speaker be requested to revise the List of Charges for Parliamentary Agents, Solicitors, and others, with a view especially to the reduction of the Charges allowed for Copies of Documents.
6. That the *Minutes of Evidence* on Opposed Private Bills be printed at the expense of the parties – whenever Copies of the same shall be required.'

29 H.C. Deb. 3rd series, vol. CLXXIII, cols. 645–80. This debate was also reported at some length in *The Solicitors' Journal and Reporter* for 20 February 1864: vol. VIII, pp. 305–7. An editorial had preceded it in the same issue (p. 297). Quoting Lord Robert Cecil at some length again, and disparaging Mr Milner Gibson's proposals, it concluded that

> The real remedy will not be resorted to until Parliament is prepared to relinquish so much of its legislative capacity as will be necessary to constitute a proper tribunal for dealing with such business. In truth, it has already taken many steps in this direction. The Copyhold Commission, the Tithe Commission, the Inclosure Commission, and the jurisdiction of the Court of Chancery under the Leases and Sales of Settled Estates Act, are standing proofs how much better and more safely this kind of work can be done by regularly constituted tribunals than by Parliament.

30 House of Commons *Journal*, vol. 119, p. 437 (when it was in fact after midnight) and pp. 443 and 444. This public Bill was no. 221; J.H. Scourfield was M.P. for Haverfordwest. *The Solicitors' Journal and Reporter* also briefly covered this on 23 July 1864 at vol. VIII, p. 768.
31 28 & 29 Vict. c. 27. The Private Bill Costs Act included in section 2 words added by way of amendment at the behest of the Duke of Cleveland:

> Provided always, that no Landowner who *bonâ fide* at his own sole Risk and Charge opposes a Bill which proposes to take any portion of the said Petitioner's Property for the Purposes of the Bill shall be liable to any Costs in respect of his Opposition to such Bill.

The wording was slightly less formally drafted as originally moved on the Lords third reading: H.L. Deb., 3rd series, vol. 178, col. 767–78 (6 April 1865), and *Solicitors' Journal and Reporter*, 8 April 1865, vol. IX, p. 483.
32 *Op. cit.*, vol. VIII, pp. 849–50 and 894–5 respectively. The *Solicitors' Journal* also defended the prevailing practice in securing and providing legal services in a strongly worded and sardonic article on 13 April 1867 entitled 'Salaried Solicitors', vol. XI, pp. 545–57: the eventual introduction of in-house solicitors employed by the larger railway companies – long resisted as beneath professional dignity in a climate where lucrative fees were at stake – is discussed at length in R.W. Kostal, *Law and English Railway Capitalism 1825–1875* (1994), pp. 349–57.
33 J.G. Dodson, 'The Private Business of Parliament', article in the *Edinburgh Review*, vol. CXXV, no. CCLV, January 1867, pp. 85–107. See also Chapter 1, note 1. He remained Chairman of Ways and Means until April 1872.
34 *Op. cit.*, p. 87.

35 *Op. cit.*, p. 90.
36 *Op. cit.*, p. 91.
37 *Op. cit.*, pp. 97–8. There is an interesting discussion of how some other countries, including America, approach the issues presented by the promotion and development of railways at pp. 101–04.
38 *Parliamentary Papers* for 1857–8 contained several documents on railway and canal promotions. Paper 132 at vol. LI, p. 425 set out the Acts passed in the two sessional periods of 1857 with the lengths of lines, capital stock and loans authorised 'and the other principal Provisions contained therein', while Paper 411 at vol. XIV, p. 1 comprised the Select Committee report on railway and canal legislation.
39 H.C. Deb. 1962; 5th series; vol. 669, col. 45 (10 December 1962, following a speech by Mr G.R. Mitchison M.P. urging that the Local Government Bill relating to the reform of London Government ought to be treated as hybrid).
40 Examples in the period include the Falmouth Borough Act 1865; the County of Sussex Act 1865; the Chester Courts Act 1867; and the Bath City Prison Act 1871. See Erskine May, *The Law, Privileges, Proceedings and Usage of Parliament* (20th edn, 1983), p. 903, note 11. Part of the Liverpool Licensing Bill 1865 should have been contained in a public Bill: see p. 907.
41 Herbert Spencer commented sardonically, on a Lords Standing Order applicable where a Bill if enacted would displace 30 or more houses, that the House was 'apparently not believing in the relationship of supply and demand': *The Westminster and Foreign Quarterly Review*, July 1853, vol. LX (no. CXVII), New Series vol. IV, no. 1, pp. 51–84 at pp. 83–4.
42 Commons S.O.s 184–85 (1878 edn) and 178 (1866 edn) respectively.
43 A particularly extensive entry, reflecting to a degree, no doubt especially, the rising numbers of railway Bills, is in vol. CLXXX for 1865 under both Houses' *Private Bills* headings. Each revision of Standing Orders was printed in *Parliamentary Papers*.
44 Q. 221.
45 Commons S.O.s 220, 219 and 224 respectively (1866 edn).
46 1858 Select Committee, q. 45: T. Erskine May, Clerk Assistant of the House of Commons, to the Duke of Somerset.
47 Evidence given to the 1863 Select Committee on Private Bill Legislation by James Blenkinsop, Solicitor to the London and North Western Railway Company, 23 April 1863, q. 2752.
48 *Op. cit.*, q. 1481. Compliance with Standing Orders, however, was not necessarily a guarantee of probity in the overall promotion: see Adrian Vaughan, *Railwaymen, Politics and Money: The Great Age of Railways in Britain* (1997), p. 115 – they 'demanded that [railway] companies compiled share subscription contracts, to prove that they had the required shareholders, and these lists frequently included fictitious names or those of people without resources: "men of straw"'.
49 *Op. cit.*, q. 2217, where George Parker Bidder, a freelance engineer with 38 years' promoting experience, stated at length how he believed improvements could be made. (See also note 121 below.)
50 See Theodore Martin, *Notes on the Present System of Private Bill Legislation* (1872, J.B. Nichols and Sons, 25 Parliament Street, p. 12). See also note 112 to Chapter 4. Martin gave evidence to the Joint Select Committee on Parliamentary agency on 3 July 1876 – see note 93 below.
51 22 & 23 Vict. c. lxxxv and xci respectively. This was by no means one of the longer preambles in the private statute book: the British Plate Glass Company Act 1862, 25 & 26 Vict. c. xvi, has 17 such pages, while the Westminster Life Insurance Society (Dissolution) Act 1861, 24 & 25 Vict. c. ccxxv, has a remarkable 45 pages of preamble.

100 *Passing the Bill: Formalities and financing*

52 Herbert Spencer, *An Autobiography* (two vols., 1904), vol. I, pp. 272–3. The previous chapter, pp. 257–71, describes *A Parliamentary Survey*. The resultant Act was presumably 8 & 9 Vict. c. clxxxiii. Another insight into working conditions comes from the evidence of Robert Baxter to the 1863 Select Committee, mentioning at *op. cit.* q. 3300 that 'the atmosphere of the Committee-rooms is most intolerable' because of the lack of ventilation; this was, however, also the period when works to deal with the 'great Stink' of the Thames were under way. Robert Baxter (1802–89), of Baxter Rose & Norton, was a leading railway industry solicitor. He was in practice for 65 years: for a study of him and the context within which he worked, see R.W. Kostal, *op. cit.*, pp. 325–33 and 340. For an interesting (and disparaging) judicial view of his firm's reputation, see the remarks of Vice-Chancellor Stuart in *In re London, Chatham, and Dover Railway Arrangement Act, Ex parte Hartridge and Allender* (1869) 5 Ch. App. 671 at pp. 675–6ff. As to the losses of documents and records in the 1834 fire, see Caroline Shenton, *The Day Parliament Burned* (2012), *passim* and pp. 180–90.
53 Commons S.O.s 110 and 111 (1866 edn). This decision to have four members dates from 25 July 1864: H.C. Deb. 3rd series, vol. 176, cols. 2011–12, also reported in *The Solicitors' Journal and Reporter* for 30 July at vol. VIII, pp. 786–7.
54 Gerald John Wheeler, *The Practice Of Private Bills: With The Standing Orders Of The House Of Lords And House of Commons, and Rules As To Provisional Orders* (1900), pp. 45–6. A general commentary published at the start of the period with which we are concerned here was Samuel Boteler Bristowe's *Private Bill Legislation, Comprising the Steps Required to Be Taken by Promoters or Opponents of a Private Bill Before & After Its Presentation to Parliament: & the Standing Rules of Both Houses* (1859).
55 Q. 319. Lord Redesdale then asked him whether he did not think 'that that is precisely the principle which it is impossible now to lay down in any broad form?' He replied (qq. 320–21) 'I think so … the further we get in the Railway system with our varying districts, the more difficult it becomes to determine any principle at all.' Wilson Patten was created Lord Winmarleigh in 1874.
56 Clifford, *op. cit.*, vol. II, p. 805. This passage and pp. 805–11 generally provide a useful and knowledgeable commentary on the technical and practical aspects and implications of *locus standi* (as other passages do about other aspects of private Bill promotion) by someone who was himself a contemporary practitioner. The Commons inquiry referred to was the 1864 Committee on Standing Orders. For Clifford's tribute to the role of Colonel Wilson Patten (later Lord Winmarleigh) in the field of private legislation over some 40 years, see vol. II, p. 810fn.
57 James Mellor Smethurst, *A Treatise on the Locus Standi of Petitioners Against Private Bills in Parliament* (second edn, 1867), pp. 1–2.
58 It will be noticed that this is apparently the only heading that might cover what we would term environmental considerations. See 'Did the Victorians Count Social Costs?' in John R. Kellett, *The Impact of Railways on Victorian Cities* (1969), pp. 25–59. The Huddersfield Water Bill of 1866 provides a good example of how the interests of local inhabitants might be viewed; a petition signed by 27 inhabitants was refused *locus* out of a population of 34,000, and 'there was a body of commissioners to represent the town'. (Bill 172; Smethurst, *op. cit.*, p. 177.)
59 A Wharncliffe meeting involved the right to be heard of shareholders not in accord with the decision taken by the majority. See Commons S.O. 131, introduced in 1853 in favour of shareholders whose 'interests … shall be distinct from the general interests of such company'. It remained S.O. 131 in the 1866 edn. (This contrasted with the situation in 1846, where J.J. Scott (see note 80 below) had declared at pp. 144–5 that there was no *locus* in these situations.) A 'very large proportion' of the Bills thrown out in the Lords Standing Orders Committee before 1858 were said to be for non-compliance with Wharncliffe Orders: 1858 Select Committee,

per Charles Evan Thomas, a Parliamentary agent, at q. 701. The Wharncliffe Order originally stemmed from Lords S.O. 185, requiring the assent of four-fifths of the proprietors of a railway to any Bill for proposed amalgamation with another railway company. It was defended by Lord Redesdale on 24 June 1852 (*Hansard*, 3rd series, vol. CXXII, cols. 1259–64), when the House resolved to appoint a Select Committee to consider the propriety of altering it (which Committee reported later that year).

60 Smethurst, *op. cit.*, pp. 168–84.
61 Bill no. 125. The Commissioners had supported the earlier Vale of Crickhowell Railway Bill in the previous year (H.L. Bill no. 456 of 1864), which was enacted as 27 & 28 Vict. c. clxxxviii.
62 Smethurst, *op. cit.*, pp. 168–9.
63 1858 Select Committee, q. 656. The reference to his father is at q. 592.
64 *Op. cit.*, q. 660. He was speaking on 1 July 1858. The Bill achieved Royal Assent on 12 July 1858 as 21 & 22 Vict. c. lxxxvii.
65 *Op. cit.*, qq. 55–7, T. Erskine May. George Pritt also gave evidence on the *locus standi* issue to the 1864 Select Committee on *Standing Orders Revision* (*Parliamentary Papers*, vol. X, pp. 747 and 863; Paper 510 and 510-I, ordered to be printed 21 July): see paras. 192–203 of Paper 510-I. Thomas Coates had earlier also given evidence to that Committee, and from a somewhat different standpoint, at paras. 192 ff.
66 *Op. cit.*, q. 165 (T. Erskine May).
67 H.C. Deb. 3rd series, vol. CXCI, cols. 139–45. (This is wrongly recorded as vol. 190 in the 1868 sessional Index.) The brief debate is also interesting because of the personal explanation of his remarks therein by Mr Stephen Cave, Vice-President of the Board of Trade; see vol. CXCI, cols. 351–56 (27 March 1868).
68 7 May 1864, vol. VIII, pp. 519–20. The committee meeting was on 28 April on the Belfast Town Improvement (No. 2) Bill, no. 284 (the first Bill of that number having been withdrawn). The Bill was passed as the Belfast Award Act 1864, 27 & 28 Vict. c. cxcviii; the history behind its contentious passing can be judged from the 25-page award of the arbitrators comprising the first schedule to the Act – one of those to whom the award was addressed being John Rea. He also features in the second schedule arbitration award of the Umpire the Rt. Hon. Edward Cardwell. The *Journal* reported criticism of Mr E.P. Bouverie, M.P., over his alleged influencing by John Rea in an earlier failed Belfast Improvement Bill in 1858.
69 *Parliamentary Diaries*, *op. cit.*, p. 266.
70 1863 Select Committee, q. 3273. The report 1862 Select Committee on *Standing Orders Revision* was ordered to be printed on 24 July 1862 (*Parliamentary Papers*, vol. XVI, pp. 207 and 333, Paper 444); Baxter's questions are nos. 399–541. In q. 433 in 1862, Baxter had said

> a Bill may be conducted through Parliament for 300*l.*, but of that 200*l.* are fees paid to the House. If there be no opposition to the Bill, and no particular circumstances rendering expensive journies [sic] necessary, a Bill will not cost more than 300*l.*, of which 200*l.* are fees paid to the House, so that it is exceedingly cheap. Then, if people aggravate the cost of it by opposition, nobody can help that in this free country; every man has a right to come here and oppose. As I said before, the system is absurd as it stands, but where the remedy is I cannot tell. The amount of money spent in Parliamentary contests is something enormous, but who is to remedy that? If they will have those great fights, and will pay the best men to conduct the case, nobody can quarrel with them if they choose to do it; all that you can say is, that the result is that there are hundreds and thousands of pounds spent which, with rather more calmness and consideration, might almost altogether be saved.

102 *Passing the Bill: Formalities and financing*

71 See, for example, those works cited in the *Historiographical Review* section of Chapter 1.
72 *Northampton Herald*, Saturday 11 September 1869, p. 6. The Bill as introduced had 36 clauses and 4 schedules, with the eventual Act having the same. The population of Northampton in 1871 is given as 45,080 with an electorate of 7,063 in *McCalmont's Parliamentary Poll Book: British Election Results 1832–1918* (1879; 8th rev. edn, 1971) at p. 219.
73 This remark and the exchanges immediately following all come from the same report as the preceding note.
74 At pp. 6599–601.
75 This was before the time when the office of Town Clerk was expected to be apolitical; John Jeffery (who before appointment had three times been elected a Northampton Liberal councillor) wrote crossly to the *Herald* to defend his reputation over an allegation that before being dismissed he had authorised money to be spent on a Town Hall kitchen, referring to two 'Liberals' as he referred to them dismissively in inverted commas. His successor William Shoosmith responded vigorously a week later, also correcting Jeffery's statement that the now current Mayor had moved his dismissal: Saturday 15 and 22 October 1870, p. 3 and p. 8 respectively. (By agreement in 1880 Shoosmith resigned and was reappointed on a non-political basis.)
76 See for instance those letters against, or sceptical of, the proposals in the *Herald* on 25 September (market tolls), 23 October, and 4 and 18 December 1869 (all at p. 3), and the supportive letter on p. 8 on 4 December. A councillor wrote anonymously what he termed 'a calm and dispassionate review of the merits of the cattle market question' – he was in favour of it as 'really an investment to get more trade to the town, instead of losing what we have' – printed on p. 8 of the *Herald* for 26 March 1870, above a letter from the Town Clerk accompanying an explanation from the Mayor as to why he had refused 'a public meeting of the ratepayers of the borough, to take into account the decision of the Committee of the House of Commons with reference to the Northampton Markets and Fairs Bill'. There had already been one such public meeting, and 'after a patient and exhaustive hearing of four days, the committee has found the preamble of the Bill proved'.
77 *Northampton Herald*, Saturday 11 December 1869, p. 6.
78 *Northampton Herald*, Saturday 11 June 1870, p. 6. The 1870 Act was eventually repealed by the Northampton Act 1988.
79 On 28 April 1870 the Lords *Journal* records the petition of Thomas Pressland seeking an amendment (vol. 102, p. 181); this was withdrawn shortly afterwards (2 May, vol. 102, p. 192) and a week later the petition of the Northampton and Northamptonshire Chamber of Commerce was recorded, in favour of the Bill's passing (9 May, vol. 102, p. 205). The Bill was specially reported with amendments on 12 May (vol. 102, p. 228); the Commons agreed the Lords' amendments on 20 May (Commons *Journal*, vol. 125, pp. 213–14), and the Bill received the royal assent on 20 June.
80 This need was met by several practitioners' commentaries and editions. In addition to Smethurst, James John Scott in 1846 published *Railway Practice in Parliament: The Law and Practice of Railway and Other Private Bills*. The author's fascinating 'Prefatory Remarks', pp. v–xiv, comment on the state of things, 'Parliament itself being in nearly as much uncertainty, on various points, as the various persons who look to it as a guide and protector' (p. v).
81 *Op. cit.*, pp. vi–viii.
82 See Terry Coleman, *The Railway Navvies* (1965; Readers Union edn 1966), p. 126. In 1846 the celebrated contractor Thomas Brassey alone was employing 25–30,000 men, as he told the Select Committee on Railway Acts Enactments (q. 954). The *Select Committee on Railway Labourers* that year took evidence *inter alia* from

Brunel and Chadwick. After Brunel at qq. 2046–162, Chadwick, who advocated a law to protect workers from injury such as applied in France, was scathing about his attitude:

> Mr. Brunel, whose examination I have just heard, is the only person of the many to whom I happen to have spoken, and that have had time to consider the first superficial impressions on the subject, who has expressed any doubt on the practical operation of the proposed law ... English workmen are peculiar.
> *Parliamentary Papers*, vol. XIII, p. 425
> (Paper 530); q. 2207

Evidence taken included the testimonies of some witnesses who had themselves worked as labourers; see the hearings of John Sharp (qq. 2768–2927); Richard Pearce (32 years a labourer; qq. 2928–77); and Thomas Eaton (27 years a labourer; qq. 2978–3041).

83 See note 107 in Chapter 2. Mr Thomas Brittain Vacher gave evidence about his business as a Parliamentary stationer to the Select Committee on *Standing Orders Revision* (see note 65 above) at qq. 542–93 – particularly about copying and lithographing the *Minutes of Evidence* of Private Bill Committees.
84 *Third Report From the Select Committee on Private Bills*, ordered to be printed 21 July 1847, p. xiv (*Parliamentary Papers*, vol. XII, p. 357, Paper 705).
85 Brought from the Lords 19 July 1858; ordered to be printed 20 July 1858, (Paper 450).
86 *Op. cit.*, preamble to Report recommendations.
87 *Report from the Select Committee on Private Bill Legislation*, ordered to be printed 30 June 1863 (Paper 385).
88 *Op. cit.*, q. 43. He had also given evidence to the 1858 Lords Select Committee (qq. 1108–56).
89 1863 Select Committee, q. 533 (George K. Rickards, Counsel to the Speaker).
90 *Op. cit.*, q. 812 (William Nathaniel Massey, M.P., a Select Committee member.) Massey returned to the detailed statistics of how these Bills had been dealt with in qq. 1048–55, commenting that there had been nearly 400 private Bills altogether in that year. In fact the official return gave the 1862 deposited total as 329, and 399 for 1861.
91 *Op. cit.*, q. 2864 (Sir William Atherton, Attorney-General).
92 *Op. cit.*, q. 2863 The Attorney-General set out in qq. 2858–63 the current practice on the briefing and remuneration of Counsel in Parliament and some higher courts. A different outlook on the restrictive practices in respect of counsel's fees was expressed in the evidence of Fereday Smith, who appeared 'as representing the canal interests of Great Britain': see qq. 2040 and 2052–86. His comments on solicitors' fees followed at qq. 2087–2120. The Parliamentary agent Thomas Coates quoted an extreme case to the 1858 Lords Select Committee of as many as five counsel being employed on a Bill by one party (q. 878).
93 *Op. cit.*, q. 2687 (James Blenkinsop, Solicitor to the London and North Western Railway Company). Clifford, *op. cit.*, vol. II, p. 880–81, notes that since 1836 anyone had been able to practise before the Lords as a Parliamentary agent, and that although a Joint Select Committee of both Houses on *Parliamentary Agency* had in 1876 recommended a special examination for agents, this was not adopted and (in 1887) 'the profession ... remains an open one'. (This report was ordered to be printed by the Commons on 17 July 1876; *Parliamentary Papers*, vol. XII, p. 539, Paper 360).
94 *Op. cit.*, qq. 2679–80 (James Blenkinsop).
95 *Op. cit.*, qq. 2940 and 3070. May had been one of the first appointments made of Examiners of Petitions for Private Bills in 1846. The 1847 Act was 10 & 11 Vict. c. 69.

104 *Passing the Bill: Formalities and financing*

96 *Op. cit.*, q. 1613.
97 *Op. cit.*, q. 1777. The reference here is to *subjects*, not of course to the absolute number of deposited Bills.
98 Typical examples are (1860) 23 & 24 Vict. c. xliv (Southampton, Leicester, Epsom, Coventry, Ipswich, Fareham, Wells, Tormoham, Scarborough, Ludlow, Banbury, Boston, Penrith, Barnsley and Shipley); (1861) 24 & 25 Vict. c. xxxix (Brighton, East Cowes, Preston, Morpeth, Bromsgrove and Durham); (1861) 24 & 25 Vict. c. cxxviii (Plymouth, Weston-super-Mare, Llanelly and Llandilo); (1866) 29 & 30 Vict. c. xxiv (Winchester, Burton-on-Trent, Longton, Accrington, Preston, Bangor, Elland, Halstead, Wadsworth, Canterbury, Dartmouth, Dukinfield, Stroud and Bridlington). These Acts at this time were generally styled Local Governmental Supplemental Acts. For illustration of the purposes of these Provisional Orders, taking the above Local Governmental Supplemental (No. 2) Act 1861: Plymouth was drawing on the Lands Clauses Consolidation Act 1845 to buy land compulsorily for street improvements; Weston-super-Mare was repealing some local Acts, consolidating debts and altering rating powers and, in a second Order, altering the district boundaries for the purposes of the Local Government Act 1858; Llanelly was extending the borrowing powers of the Local Board of Health; and Llandilo was similarly extending the powers of the Local Board.
99 See pp. 140ff.
100 At pp. 170–1 is set out the 'great dissatisfaction' about counsels' fees, and that the 1863 Select Committee, 'after hearing the evidence of the Attorney-General on the subject, reported against the system as then existing'. It was preferred that the Parliamentary Bar should respond, so no formal action was taken directly on the Committee's recommendation. Subsequently the Parliamentary Bar had 'abolished all rules which were previously considered as restricting counsel from accepting a lower fee than those above enumerated ...'
101 *Op. cit.*, q. 2748.
102 *Op. cit.*, qq. 349–50. Discussion followed on the high fixed costs allowed to Parliamentary agents and solicitors of copies of evidence, 8d. per folio, which were recognised as about four times their actual cost and a significant element both of the income of the recipients and the costs to promoters.
103 *Op. cit.*, qq. 1490 and 1493. His evidence at qq. 1487–1504 gives much more detail about his estimates of Parliamentary costs, how solicitors approach Parliamentary agents and how counsel come to be instructed. In evidence to the 1858 Select Committee, Parliamentary agent Charles Evan Thomas gave much similar detail and breakdown of his costs and charges at qq. 729ff. His highest charge had been for the Birmingham Gas Bill; 'there happened to be a great deal of trouble with it' (qq. 739–40) and he had charged his maximum sum of £185 18s. 8d. His evidence was based on the last 40 unopposed Bills passed into Acts through his firm and, he said, 'I may add, that in every one of the 40 cases the House fees exceed the Parliamentary agents' charges'. (The Gas Bill reference was no doubt to what became the Birmingham Gas Act 1855, 18 & 19 Vict. c. xlviii.)
104 *Op. cit.*, qq. 1584–92.
105 He had succeeded his father in the role in 1851, and was paid a daily attendance fee of two guineas, plus '9d. per folio of 72 words for the transcript of the evidence'. *Op. cit.*, qq. 3364–9. The ninepence had been reduced from one shilling in 1851. Much additional information was provided in answering the following questions, including the totals of shorthand fees paid in the preceding 3 years: q. 3382.
106 1858 Select Committee, q. 861. Asked in q. 862 how the £35 was made up, he instanced five guineas for the retainer; ten guineas (and probably more) put upon

the brief; five guineas for consultation; ten guineas for the first day; and clerk's fees of about 7½ per cent.
107 Where a municipality obtained an Act that included the usual section that its costs could be paid from the rates, its accounts would in due course record the relevant promotional costs.
108 *Op. cit.*, qq. 956–7.
109 Bill 582. The Bill was promoted to establish a company, so is not within our definition here, but provided an interesting non-Parliamentary illustration of the costs involved in local protest. It was not passed, though Bill 197 of 1869 (also involving incorporation of a company) was more successful, and was passed as the Dorking Water Act 1869, 32 & 33 Vict. c. cxxv.
110 Much more detail of the amounts and breakdown of these fees is given in qq. 1088–9. Sir John was equal to their intricacies: he had been Senior Wrangler in the Mathematics Tripos at Cambridge in 1818.
111 Mr Harper was the Bury Superintendent Registrar of Births and Deaths. These three items are on pp. 258 and 261. Between 1846 and 1863 costs fell by an average of 0.4 per cent annually, so that £1 in 1847 was the equivalent of only about 18s. 6d. (92p.) in 1863, but these costs, made up of hundreds of small amounts, are broadly comparable across the period with which we are concerned. The Bury Improvement Act was 9 & 10 Vict. c. ccxciii. £1 in 1846 is considered to be the equivalent of almost £100 now, after average inflation of about 2.8 per cent p.a., so putting its cost of promotion at over £0.5 million in today's terms. The four attorneys involved had in fact charged as if they were only one attorney: see q. 2102 of the evidence given to the 1847 Select Committee. The passing of the 1846 Bill and its aftermath is described in a valuable article by M. Whittaker, M.A. on *The Bury Improvement Commissioners* in the *Transactions of the Lancashire and Cheshire Antiquarian Society* (1935), Vol. XLIX for 1933, pp. 113–49.
112 1858 Select Committee, qq. 536–51. Subsequently Sir John George Shaw Lefevre gave further detailed evidence of the previous excessively complicated fees system; a Bill's second reading had until shortly before required seven separate fees, almost all since commuted, 'to the Lord Chancellor, to the clerk of the Parliaments, the gentleman usher, the clerk assistant, the yeoman usher, the reading clerk, and the doorkeepers' (q. 1088).
113 *Op. cit.*, qq. 563–4 and q. 650 respectively.
114 1858 Select Committee, q. 745.
115 Though we may view with some scepticism the statement by the prominent solicitor Robert Baxter to the 1858 Lords Select Committee that 'the principals never see the bills [of costs]': q. 1063.
116 See Chapter 1.
117 In 1855, 1865 and 1875, general government expenditure went from £2.9 million to £3.1 million to £4.0 million, while total public expenditure was respectively £69.1 million, £67.1 million and £116.9 million.
118 The witness responded 'Still, I think that to spend fruitlessly £15 4s. 9d. is not a thing to be encouraged'. Lord Redesdale, Lords Chairman of the Committees on Private Bills, told the Committee that he did 'not believe that a Bill for inclosure was ever rejected' (1863 Select Committee, q. 704). Giving evidence to the 1858 Select Committee, an Inclosure Commissioner, William Blamire, referred to having had 'nearly 800 [Inclosure] cases without an appeal', an experience which led him support that other kinds of Bills, like Gas, Cemetery and Improvement of Towns Bills might also be referred to a similar Commissioners procedure (qq. 372–8), although in the latter case he acknowledged that this approach had been tried and discontinued under the Commissioners of Woods and Forests (qq. 379–80).

106 *Passing the Bill: Formalities and financing*

119 1863 Select Committee, q. 1556 (Thomas Coates, Parliamentary agent). This Bill is not certainly identified; it may have been 25 & 26 Vict. c. clxiv, the Nene Valley Act 1862, which had been introduced as Bill 25.
120 *Op. cit.*, q. 2049–50 (Fereday Smith). This was identified as referring to the Irwell navigation; the Mersey, Weaver, Irwell, &c. Protection Bill was passed as 25 & 26 Vict. c. ccxxii.
121 *Op. cit.*, q. 2297. Bidder submitted a paper *Suggestions as to Statement and Counter-Statement by Promoters and Opponents of Private Bills*, printed as appendix 9 to the 1863 Select Committee report. His reputation as a civil engineer led to his appointment under section 2 of the Torbay and Dartmouth Shipping Dues Act 1870 (33 & 34 Vict. c. xxxiii) as a commissioner for the purposes of the Act. Some idea of the scope and scale of his involvement in railway developments around the time of the 1840s 'mania' can be derived from Vaughan, *op. cit.*, pp. 141–2. The Retired Chartered Engineers' Club of Exeter installed a wall plaque, commemorating Bidder (1806–78) in Moretonhampstead, Devon as 'The Calculating Boy' – 'A child prodigy who was born nearby and became a distinguished engineer'.
122 *Op. cit.*, q. 2342. He could not remember the total cost of it all: q. 2349.
123 *Op. cit.*, q. 2733 (James Blenkinsop).
124 *Op. cit.*, q. 3102.
125 1858 Select Committee, q. 1066, *per* the solicitor Robert Baxter. Asked by Lord Redesdale how without statutory authority railways might cross roads, he replied at q. 1067:

> Perhaps your Lordship will be astonished when I tell you that there is no law to prevent it; it is a singular thing, but the Act of Parliament which prevents the level crossing of roads does not apply to a railway constructed without the authority of Parliament.

He went on at q. 1070:

> The protection of the public lies in this: that you cannot open a passenger railway without coming to the Board of Trade for a certificate, and they will not pass your line unless you have erected lodges at the level crossings to protect the level crossings; but they make no objection to the fact of your not having the authority of Parliament for the crossing.

126 1863 Select Committee, qq. 1260–2.
127 *Op. cit.*, q. 1030. The Chairman, Thomas Milner Gibson, M.P., put this more vigorously as a 'notorious' practice; the witness, Earl Grey, attending by permission of the Lords, answered much less decidedly that it was 'very possibly the case'. T. Erskine May stated at q. 2991 that 'the reason why competition was admitted as a ground of opposition, was to get over the practice by which landowners were invariably resorted to to raise an opposition, being backed by the Railway Companies'. The same point about opposition from landowners that was really from other railway companies had been made in the 1858 Lords Select Committee during the evidence of the Parliamentary agent Thomas Coates (q. 855).
128 1863 Select Committee, q. 1274.
129 *Op. cit.*, q. 1086, giving a long critique of the whole system as he saw it, and making suggestions for its reform, continued particularly at qq. 1090 and 1107. He had sat for 56 days in the previous session, and thought that no Member should be expected to sit for more than ten days. In an unusual case in that session, seven Bills had been taken together 'without deciding on the preamble of any': qq. 1091 and 1094.

130 *Op. cit.*, q. 916. The reference is to the Report from the 1846 Select Committee on Private Bills, *Parliamentary Papers*, vol. XII (Paper 556), at p. iv. The last few words of the original were actually 'often greatly prejudiced by Local Acts'. (This passage was repeated in the Third Report from the 1847 Select Committee on Private Bills, p. xiv.) Appendix 13 to the 1846 Report set out in full detail at pp. 175–85 the £1,985 2s. 2d. that comprised the solicitors' bill for what became 8 & 9 Vict. c. 73, the Newcastle Coal Turn Act 1845, while earlier appendix 1 had revealed that from 1836 to 1844 the Corporation of Liverpool had spent £24,124 11s. 4d. on obtaining 16 local Acts, not including two more still in progress.
131 *Op. cit.*, q. 2213. He was working at this time for the Great Eastern Company: see q. 2249.
132 *Op. cit.*, q. 1017.
133 *Op. cit.*, q. 3090. In 1845–46 Parliament appointed a three-member Railway Gauge Commission to consider whether future Bills (and railways already constructed) should have a uniform gauge. Their three-part report was presented to the Commons on 17 February 1846: *Parliamentary Papers*, vol. XVI, pp. 1, 29, 383 (principally Papers 699 and 700: the full report of the Gauge Commissioners comprised 829pp.). In the 1858 Select Committee at q. 153, T. Erskine May, appearing alongside Colonel Wilson Patten, had commented that

> There was a Commission appointed to inquire into the broad and the narrow gauge, and certain recommendations were made by that Commission upon which a statute was founded; and nevertheless that question has been quite open ever since; one Committee has decided in one way, and another in another, and no general principle with regard to gauge has been adopted.

The statute was the public Act 9 & 10 Vict. c. LVII (57), stipulating – subject to exceptions – 4ft. 8½ ins. in Great Britain and 5ft 3ins. in Ireland. For a good example of a company already authorised to build the broad gauge being granted powers to lay additional rails so as also to accommodate the narrow gauge, see the preamble to the Somerset Central Railway (Narrow Gauge) Act 1859, 22 & 23 Vict. c. lvi. Both gauges, however, were still very much in evidence 15 years later: section 33 of the Launceston and South Devon Railway Act 1862 provided that 'The Railway shall be constructed, maintained and worked upon the Broad Gauge'. For an extensive narrative of these and other gauges in early railway legislation, see Frederick Clifford, *A History of Private Bill Legislation* (1885), vol. I, pp. 72–9.
134 1863 Select Committee, q. 5. James Booth remained Counsel to the Speaker till 1850, and in 1863 was Secretary to the Board of Trade. In qq. 5–8 he sets out the background to his drafting of the Clauses Consolidation Acts. His work had reduced the bulk of typical Railway Bills from around a hundred to about ten folio pages. In q. 11 he instanced about ten standard clauses 'providing for the case of the bursting of a reservoir' commonly included in Waterworks Bills, as a good example of provisions still needing to be consolidated into a general Act.
135 1858 Select Committee, q. 72. May went on to add in q. 73 that 'there is great local opposition in improvement Bills'.
136 Printed as appendix 3 to the 1863 Select Committee Report, but quoted by Mr G.F. Whalley at q. 713.
137 *Op. cit.*, q. 713. Similar language was occasionally used in the 1858 Lords Select Committee deliberations, as when for instance the Chairman Lord Stanley of Alderley referred at q. 1072 to 'Bills of a comparatively inferior importance, such as Gas Bills and others'.
138 *Op. cit.*, q. 905. See generally qq. 904–06 and 909.

108 Passing the Bill: Formalities and financing

139 For other contexts, see the references at *op. cit.*, qq. 58–60 in James Booth's evidence.
140 *Op. cit.*, qq. 1789–91.
141 *Op. cit.*, q. 1786.
142 *Op. cit.*, q. 1005.
143 H.C. Deb. 3rd series, vol. CCVII, cols. 686–95.
144 H.C. Deb, 3rd series, vol. CCX, col. 17. The report continues to col. 30.
145 Dodson had courteously declined to accede to this, justifying a request for further postponement of debate till after Easter from Mr William P. Price, the M.P. for Gloucester: H.C. Deb. 3rd series, vol. CCX, cols. 402–03.
146 H.C. Deb. 3rd series, vol. CCX, cols. 507–29.
147 H.C. Deb. 3rd series, vol. CCXI, cols. 1853–54 and vol. CCXVII cols. 497–98 respectively.
148 H.C. Deb. 3rd series, vol. CCXI, cols. 1666–68. At this time Mr Francis Sharp Powell was M.P. for the Northern Division of the West Riding.
149 Theodore Martin, *op. cit.*, *passim*.
150 The U.K. Bill was nod. 137, and read a first time on 23 April, but the second reading was dropped: see the Commons *Journal*, vol. 128, pp. 158 and 251. The Ireland Bill was nod. 72 and read a first time on 19 February; see the Commons *Journal*, vol. 128, p. 58. Its second reading was deferred four times.
151 See note 39 to Chapter 2 (Marquess of Granby).
152 See note 58 to Chapter 2.
153 See for instance the comment of Colonel Wilson Patten (then Chairman of the Commons Standing Orders Committee and of the Committee of Selection that selected Committees for the investigation of different Bills) to the 1858 Lords Select Committee at q. 303: '... the investigation of Railways, for instance, is so laborious that we cannot get Members to take it'.
154 See note 32 to Chapter 1.
155 See p. ix. At pp. xv–xvi are given the cost per mile of some of the principal lines then built.
156 *Op. cit.*, q. 929. In his evidence to the 1846 Select Committee on Railway Acts Enactments, Robert Stephenson, asked to give examples of 'injury arising from the present system' of railway private Bills, responded

> I can quote a case at Wisbeach, where within half a mile of that town there were actually 14 schemes intersecting the land in every possible direction; hedges cut down and crops interfered with ... Now all the legal expenses and the expenses of engineers and surveyors have been thrown away, because only one Act has been obtained.
>
> (q. 2868)

The Committee quoted this example from him again in their second Report (p. x).
157 1858 Select Committee, q. 998.
158 *Op. cit.*, qq. 1000–1015.
159 The reports of 1846 and 1847 were more wide-ranging, but their recommendations were more concerned with railway companies and promotional considerations than any outlook of overall economic or transport policy from the point of view of Government or Parliament. Of course, the network was far less extensive at this time, and the situation much less developed.

4 Public law and private initiative
The wider context of local legislation

Although, as we have seen in Chapter 1, civic pride played a part in the motivations that led to the promotion of private Bills, the usual answer as to why a given Bill was promoted was simply and obviously that without a private Act the existing law did not allow to be done (or to be done on suitable terms) that for which the promoters sought powers. As typical 1860 preambles put it: '... for the Purposes aforesaid the Authority of Parliament is necessary' (Wigan Waterworks Act); and '... the same cannot be effected without the Aid and Authority of Parliament' (Metropolitan Meat and Poultry Act). Before the following chapters consider in more detail, therefore, the content of local legislation in the years from 1858, we need to examine the overall state of general local government law as it stood on the day that the Local Government Act 1858 came into force, and how that evolved in the decade following. The importance of this lies not only in what it says about the attitudes of Parliament and people alike to the municipal world of the time – a theme comparatively well studied already by historians of social conditions and governmental relations – but also lies in how much was lacking in the limited and unprescriptive statute book of that time. Communities needed to take the initiative not only to obtain special powers in exceptional circumstances, but also to be given basic and essential powers for minimal standards of health, well-being and public regulation. The scope of those individual local demands, and in particular the legal mechanisms and drafting provisions whereby they might be met, have hitherto received at best scant historical attention.

We also need to bear in mind the wider context, discussed particularly in Chapter 2, against which local government law had come to be as it then was. The formal construction of statutes, and indeed the whole approach and apparatus of the law, was only slowly evolving from its elaborate and essentially unplanned condition. Bills, and hence Acts, were lengthy and – particularly prior to the Consolidation Acts of 1845–47[1] – repetitive, with the categorisations between public and private not always well defined. Short titles were traditionally not provided, although after 1804 – in addition to the annual *Table* that had always been included since private Acts had been separately numbered from 1797 – there was at least an *Index to the Local and Personal*

Acts, and to the Private Acts printed by the King's/Queen's Printer (as it was styled from 1816) prefacing the annual sessional volumes (private Acts not having been included in the earlier years). There was no subordinate legislation as it would later come to be understood; that is, there were none of the statutory rules, orders and instruments which later came to be an integral part of the Parliamentary process, though municipal charters and local customs (also traditional sources of law, as well as the common law itself) still retained considerable importance. Just as public Bills were drafted, as always, in the swim of current practice, so private Bills similarly were promoted in a form that complemented that practice; such Bills sought to provide whatever legal powers the promoters claimed they needed in a form that they hoped came within the limits of both content and drafting approach that Parliament was willing to sanction.

Legal historians, despite the attention paid to particular local Acts in particular places in monographs and other commentaries, have never examined overall the nature of that content and drafting style. No doubt this is largely because of the sheer bulk of thousands of Bills and Acts in the decades after 1835; despite the similarly voluminous attention, however, that historians of public services and social developments have paid to the state of local government, to its gradual reform, to central–local relations, the Local Government Board, and so on, the nuts and bolts that – largely out of sight – held the machinery together have been for the most part overlooked. It is the intention of this study to repair that omission, and to reveal not only their intrinsic interest as an aspect of legal history, but also the light that they shed on what local Bill promoters had to do – and hence what they had to be able to persuade a Parliamentary Committee to allow – to achieve their objectives in this period of rapid social, industrial and of course municipal expansion. Because there has been no previous systematic study of this legislation and its content, there has been no real recognition of its true character, of the kinds of provisions that promoters had individually to win in default of general statutory coverage, and of the differing ways in which the whole practice of private Bills at this time played a part in the rise of the so-called 'information state' (on which see further the conclusions in Chapter 7).

The state of local government law in the mid-1850s

It was neither the physical state of towns and communities nor the needs of their inhabitants that had occasioned the reform of municipal corporations in 1835; rather it was how those corporations were constituted, and what they did (or did not do) with the often substantial funds at their disposal. Moving the Address on the King's Speech on 24 February 1835, Viscount Sandon declared that

> it will be said that the Reform Bill is not to be left a mere barren measure of constitutional law; what, then, are to be its fruits? Perhaps that

which has most attracted public attention, is the Reform of Municipal Corporations. No doubt much in those Corporations does require correction, much both in the management of the funds and the constitutions of the various bodies; but it is a question of great complication, and one on which Lord Grey's Government thought it necessary to institute a minute inquiry before it proceeded even to suggest a remedy.[2]

Two days later, in the same adjourned debate, Sir James Graham repeated the point: for him,

The question of Corporate Reform divided itself naturally into two parts – the one relating to the application of trust property, the other, the mode of appointment of those by whom the affairs of the several Corporations were conducted ... At present the governing party in the corporations were self-elected; the people desired, that the mode of their election should be popular, and as the public mind was evidently made up on that subject ... whoever might be Minister, a removal from our Municipal Corporations of the vice of self-election was, in his opinion, a matter fully and completely decided.[3]

As we have seen in Chapter 2, in the mid-1850s there was still relatively little public local government or municipal law, as it would later come to be understood. Local improvements or investments in significant projects – like delivering water supply, providing gas or building a new market – all required discrete local initiatives and, usually, specific authorisation. The various new Clauses Acts of the 1840s were public Acts, but they were not available for use without that additional and specific local authorisation. When the pre-1835 corporations had been notorious for unaccountable and profligate expenditure in the pursuit of self-interest, it was perhaps hardly surprising that their successors were not from the outset trusted or allowed by Parliament to spend money on new schemes without crossing a threshold of independent approval. There were some important areas where national legislation applied, for example weights and measures, and highways (consolidated in 1835, and extended for instance in 1862 and 1864[4]), but there was little that would have been regarded even 50 years later as 'service provision'. What the individuals owed locally to their corporation was far more important than what the corporation owed to them. Where general legislation for local services was beginning to be passed – for instance, for free public libraries, hesitantly introduced by the Public Libraries Act 1850 – it was often adoptive, the fruit of zealous reformers in Parliament, and hedged about with severe constraints.[5] The notable aspect in these cases was that any legislation was passed at all.

Even where there was legislation, there was often little appetite in Westminster to use and exploit it fully. This was summed up in 1852 in the attitude of the Prime Minister the Earl of Derby. He identified overcrowded burial places, the lack of clean water, inadequate sewage disposal and the accumulation of waste and rubbish in the capital as four major causes of disease, but

> He opposed bringing these problems under the provisions of the 1848 Board of Health Act. Although solutions sought through a single statutory authority, such as the General Board of Health, might appear desirable, he believed enforced obedience to new sanitary regulations would be difficult to secure and that voluntary compliance was preferable. To this end, he amended Shaftesbury's call for the government's interposition in these matters to the statement that they required the ministry's attention. The compulsory powers enjoyed by the General Board of Health, established in response to Edwin Chadwick's campaign for the centralized regulation of public health, were already generating a political reaction to state control of social issues. Derby promised further discretionary powers to enhance the authority of local bodies to deal with the sanitary afflictions of London, but he declined to pursue statutory state solutions.[6]

The overall position of local government law throughout our period is well illustrated by the table provided by J.R. Somers Vine in *English Municipal Institutions; Their Growth and Development From 1835 to 1879, Statistically Illustrated* (1879).[7] He lists the 31 'legislative measures, directly applicable to municipal corporations' added to the statute book in this period. Apart from the Municipal Corporations (Bridges) Act 1850, the short titles of these Acts are about the regulation of municipal corporations, the levying of rates, the administration of justice, elections, byelaws, charters, and the like. They may reflect a continuing concern, as the Municipal Corporations Act 1835 did, with the constitution, status and process of these corporations, but they hardly reflect the urgency and overwhelming need for the nation that could run an Empire on which 'the sun never set' to provide decently for its populations at home. Somers Vine notes that the 124,710 burgesses (electors) on the rolls of the 1835 Act corporations exceeded by 100,765 the number of those qualified to vote immediately before for the old corporations, while the total number of municipal electors in 1879 had risen to 1,312,796 – a more than tenfold increase in 35 years.[8]

A generation after 1835, the motivation for passing what became the Local Government Act 1858 – after several confusing attempts to legislate on public health and how it should be overseen nationally – was rather more focused on local need, or at least on local decision. Charles Adderley, a Staffordshire M.P. and the responsible Minister for the General Board of Health, initially explained his outlook to the Commons on 22 April 1858 while seeking leave to introduce a Public Health Act 1848 (Amendment) Bill. The Board's existence had been successively and temporarily continued after its initial five-year life, but other intended replacement measures had more than once failed to pass into law. He had no embarrassment in explaining this, as he had been appointed in the Earl of Derby's new Conservative Government only a few weeks earlier. Adderley briefly summarised the various efforts that had been made in the preceding 4 years or so to put public health legislation on a more permanent footing, and *Hansard* reported him, after referring to these previous failed legislative attempts, as saying that

> He had under those circumstances felt it to be his duty to introduce a Bill upon the subject, and in doing so he had done his best to deal with it upon a permanent footing. The general principle of the measure which he was about to ask the House for leave to introduce was one the object of which was to decentralize the whole system; to allow the General Board of Health to expire in September; and to enable all those towns which desired to possess the power of self-administration to constitute local boards through the medium of meetings of owners and ratepayers, two-thirds of whom must consent to the adoption of such a course; it being open to town councils or commissioners, who fairly represented the inhabitants of large towns, to exercise similar powers in that respect as the owners and ratepayers to whom he had just adverted. ... He also proposed that the boards which might be constituted under the Act, as well as all the local boards now in existence, should have the amplest powers of self-administration extended to them, and should be no longer subjected to the necessity of referring to a central board in London. Those powers of self-administration would, however, be placed under proper check by granting to individuals who might feel themselves aggrieved by the action of those local hoards a power of appeal, and also by rendering it necessary that they should annually undergo re-election.[9]

Leave to introduce the Bill was given without further debate, but it was withdrawn on the following day, and Adderley introduced instead a Local Government Bill.[10] When the second reading came up on 30 April, he did not speak of his measure as a landmark of reform; indeed he spoke almost dismissively of the Bill:

> the Second Reading could hardly be necessary to discuss at that stage, as it was not a new measure, nor founded on a new principle. It was merely an Amendment of the Board of Health Bill of 1848. The only novel provision in it was the abolition of the General Board of Health in London, and leaving it to every town in the kingdom to adopt the powers of local Government which it conferred.[11]

His mention of previous Bill failures was a reference to the several recent attempts to legislate. To appreciate fully the context in which Adderley was speaking, an outline of some of those attempts is necessary. Mr. William F. Cowper (later Cowper-Temple, M.P. for Hertford; President of the General Board of Health from August 1855 to February 1857, and again from

September that year till March 1858) had presented his General Board of Health Continuance Bill[12] on 29 July 1857; it was swiftly passed, receiving royal assent on 17 August. Meanwhile on 15 July 1857 William Massey, M.P. for Salford, had presented a Public Health Act (1848) Amendment Bill, with 181 clauses.[13] It was not passed. A second version of this Bill, with the same title and with six further clauses, was introduced on 10 December.[14] The later version *inter alia* added clause 6, continuing the existence of the General Board of Health for five more years, and accordingly substituting the General Board for reference to the Committee of Council for Health[15] as well as adding four more General Board clauses, 37–40, under the heading of *Application of Act by Parliament*. Parliament rejected this Bill; the same two M.P.s brought in a further similarly titled Bill in 1858, but it was withdrawn on 24 March.[16] Why were they unsuccessful when so shortly afterwards what was for the first time styled the Local Government Bill passed? There had been a change of Government – the Conservative Earl of Derby became Prime Minister on 21 February 1858 – but there had also been a very significant alteration in tone and in scope in Charles Adderley's approach, which may be judged from the following examples.

In the December 1857 Public Health Act (1848) Amendment Bill, no part of the London area, 'the Metropolis', was included 'unless the Public Health Act, 1848, has already been applied to such Place' – clause 3). In Mr. Adderley's original 1858 Local Government Bill and subsequent Act, however, the Metropolis was completely excluded (and the Government also failed to proceed in summer 1858 with a Bill for the Corporation of London).[17] The 1857 Bill had contained a clause declaring as a duty that 'The Local Board shall cause their District to be effectually drained', and would also have given powers to construct sewage reservoirs and connecting sewers; the 1858 Act contained no such duty or additional powers.[18] What the Victorians called 'scavenging' was vital to the health and well-being of any populous area: the 1857 Bill included a duty properly to cleanse and water all streets; that 'all Dust, Ashes, and Rubbish shall be carried away from the Premises of the Inhabitants' and that 'All Privies, Cesspools, and Ashpits shall be from Time to Time emptied and cleansed'. In the 1858 Act this positive Parliamentary direction to cleanse was replaced by discretionary powers to the same ends.[19] Yet again, consider public streets (which were distinguished from highways): clause 87 of the 1857 Bill vested their management in the Local Board, and declared that 'The Local Board shall make good and maintain in proper Repair all such streets'. Section 38 of the 1858 Act merely provided extended powers, based on those earlier provided in sections 69 and 70 of the Public Health Act 1848. Finally, the 1857 Bill had expressed clear powers to provide a market place and construct a market house, and also would have given extensive water supply powers – provisions repetitively sought by local Act powers in the years that followed. The 1858 Act much more modestly amplified the existing 1848 Act provisions, and expressed the reference to markets more conditionally.[20] It did, however, follow the drafting of the

1857 Bill in extending two groups of provisions of the Town Police and Towns Improvement Clauses Acts 1847, even extending the latter group by adding references to the supply of water and to slaughterhouses.[21]

These examples amply demonstrate the mood of the times in relation to local initiative, the health of towns, and the limits on central direction. Parliament would grant general powers, but only on a discretionary and often conditional basis.[22] The concept of national oversight of public health was often the subject of fierce debate, and opposing matters of principle. The 1858 Local Government Act was not generally applicable: it was adoptive, and indeed might be only partly adopted.[23] Rights of individual objection still played an important part in what might be sanctioned, and duties, as opposed to powers, to act – especially if they demanded universal standards – were objectionable to such a significant proportion of those in Parliament that any Bill that contained them was likely to fail. The emphasis remained firmly on what local initiative wanted, rather than on what Parliament expected or central government demanded. As President of the Board of Health, Mr. Adderley did not make any mark for introducing a Bill that wholly changed the face of local government and local environmental reform, but at least, by removing or diluting the provisions that had so recently been rejected, he succeeded in getting his Bill passed. (He was able to tell the House on 30 April that there was no opposition to the principle of the Bill.[24]) The General Board of Health was finally allowed to expire, its statutory approvals being rendered unnecessary in future,[25] while the important development of the Provisional Order process contained in section 77[26] was secured. The Secretary of State for the Home Department issued a 'Minute of Information' – later termed a circular – on the Act. It explained the new Provisional Order procedure, but it did not even mention the General Board.[27] Adderley also secured a further Public Health Act that vested public health powers in the Privy Council.[28]

Chapter 2 has already discussed the various Clauses Acts that Parliament had passed in the mid-1840s just prior to the Public Health Act 1848. Undoubtedly a step forward, they were nevertheless still only applicable to qualifying communities which had also obtained a 'special Act', so that in the years immediately following their passing they merely facilitated, rather than removed the need for, individual local promotions of Bills for the various kinds of improvements that the Acts covered – companies, lands and railways in 1845; cemeteries, commissioners, gasworks,[29] harbours and docks etc., markets and fairs, town police, towns improvement and waterworks in 1847.

Of these, the Act most broadly concerned with community betterment, the Towns Improvement Clauses Act 1847, was of course largely permissive in its approach. In its 216 sections it provided for a variety of powers, addressed to the improvement commissioners, trustees or other corporate body 'intrusted by the special Act with Powers for executing the Purposes thereof'. They were not new powers, but a consolidation in one place of 'sundry Provisions usually contained in Acts of Parliament' to avoid repetition and encourage greater uniformity. Accordingly they dealt with such matters as making and maintaining streets, providing and connecting sewers, preventing houses being built without drains, and so on. Commissioners were required to sweep and cleanse all streets and pavements from time to time (section 87), but a duty such as this was one that the then Commissioners, by virtue of the 'special Act', had in effect volunteered to have thrust upon them. That was different in the eyes of Parliament from a duty compulsorily imposed. There were other directive provisions – for example, that there must be at least twice as many baths for the working classes in any public bathing house as for the baths 'of any higher Class'.[30] There were also incidental powers, required to be specified for corporate bodies who could only do what it was specifically or impliedly given them by Parliament to be able to do. Section 143, for instance, allowed the provision (and removal) of public clocks, and for lighting the clock faces at night; rather more importantly, there were extensive provisions about paying, and setting allowances against, rates, and for how long and in what context money could be borrowed.[31]

The other Clauses Acts had similar approaches. The preambles recited the objective of ensuring greater uniformity in the law, but complete uniformity could of course have been achieved by the simple expedient of a generally applicable measure not dependent upon the existence, then or later, of a 'special Act'. In the Markets and Fairs Clauses Act 1847[32] there were sixty sections of ancillary provisions about the process of constructing and operating markets and fairs, and in the Waterworks Clauses Act 1847 ninety-four sections similarly about the building of reservoirs and the business of supplying water and providing 'fire-plugs' and keys, and much else besides.[33] Yet neither Act in itself directly authorised the building of any new market, nor the construction of any new waterworks: both depended on the existence of a separate authorising 'special Act'. Why did they not do so? The answer is simply that the times were not ready. Commissioners could not be given that kind of latitude or discretion: it required specific justification at Westminster, with all the resources of time and money (and the uncertainties and vested interests) that such a step involved. A modest step forward however – though assuming greater significance in later years – was made in 1848 by the creation of the 'Provisional Order'.

Provisional orders

Section 141 of the Public Health Act 1848 had provided for *Provisional Orders*: these were Orders made by the Secretary of State on request by a Local Board, but which were of no effect, and therefore 'provisional', until confirmed by Act of Parliament. Section 77 of the Local Government Act 1858 repealed and replaced that section. (No equivalent provision, incidentally, had been made in the failed 1857 Bills.) Technically, the powers to petition thereby were given not only to the Local Board of any district, but also to the majority of owners and ratepayers in any parish, township, hamlet, or place maintaining its own roads or its own poor, adjoining any district, or to the majority of owners and ratepayers in any part of a district, such majorities to be ascertained in the way herein provided for voting with respect to the adoption of this Act.

Provisional Orders enabled an area to be added to, or separated from, an existing district, or for changes to be made where it was considered desirable that

> provision should be made for the future execution of any local Acts in force within such district, having relation to the purposes of this Act, and not conferring powers or privileges upon corporations, companies or undertakers, or individuals, for their own pecuniary benefit; or that any such Acts, or any exemptions from rating derived therefrom, or any provisional order or Order in Council applying the Public Health Act, 1848, or Act confirming such provisional orders, should be wholly or partially repealed or altered.

The Secretary of State might accept the petition entirely, or modify its objectives, and then had the duty to 'take all necessary steps for the confirmation of such order by Act of Parliament', but there could be petitions against such Orders and reference to a Select Committee, in which case 'the petitioner shall be allowed to appear and oppose as in the case of private Bills'.[34] Provisional Orders were accordingly very useful in obtaining statutory approvals by a generally less troublesome and expensive route, but like the Clauses Consolidation Acts they had clear limitations. Existing boundaries and local Acts might be modified, but this procedure could not be used to obtain wholly new powers, or even powers well precedented elsewhere but not in force in the petitioning district. On the other hand, for the first time the Local Boards were empowered to acquire land compulsorily by Provisional Order, again of course subject to Parliamentary confirmation.[35] Under an Act of 1861, the Secretary of State could recover all costs associated with the furthering of a Provisional Order.[36] From 1868 Provisional Order Confirmation Acts 'and a few other public Acts of a local character' were moved from the public to the local statute book, much reducing the bulk of the former.[37] An Act of 1871[38] empowered Committees on Bills confirming or giving effect to Provisional Orders to award costs, and to examine witnesses on oath. The Public Health Act 1875[39] would later consolidate and re-state the provisional order process. Where Provisional Orders were inappropriate or inadequate, however, and the public general law would not allow something that needed specific and individual authorisation, the promotion of private legislation was the only alternative. The capacity and entitlement to promote Bills, however, were of course themselves matters of law.

Clifford[40] provides an extensive and more or less contemporary survey of the attributes and scope of Provisional Orders, commenting in 1887 that

118 *The wider context*

> By far the most important branch of jurisdiction exercised by the Local Government Board [who had inherited the powers of previous Government Departments] in the grant of Provisional Orders is that relating to sanitary and kindred subjects.

In each case a public inquiry would be held in the locality. We may derive the scale and significance of the Provisional Order approach from the statistics he provides –

> From 1848 until 1882, the total number of Orders issued under the Sanitary Acts by the Local Government Board, and the departments to whose jurisdiction they succeeded, was 1,205, including 503 issued under the Public Health Act 1875. Of the 1,205 Orders, 1,114 were confirmed by Parliament without opposition; 84 were referred to Select Committees on adverse petitions; 71 of these were afterwards confirmed by Parliament with or without amendment; 13 were withdrawn or rejected. Of the Orders granted under the Public Health Act 1875, 19 were amended by Select Committees; 12 were considered and not altered; Parliament refused to confirm five, and one fell through, as both the sanitary authority promoting, and the petitioners opposing it, objected to the frame of the Order itself.[41]

The powers of the courts relating to private Bill promotion

Promoting a private Bill is about pursuing private advantage; the expanding railway industry was not the only one to depend upon Parliamentary authority for its existence and much of its growth. Sometimes individuals or companies, as in some of the cases quoted below, would bind themselves contractually to seek Parliamentary powers, or to refrain from seeking competing powers, or to refrain from objecting to a particular Bill's promotion or specific clause. It was unsurprising that cases began to come before the courts where those undertakings had allegedly been broken – thereby giving rise to difficult constitutional conflicts between the proper jurisdiction of the courts on the one hand, and on the other the right to petition Parliament, and Parliament's privilege that its jurisdiction should not be externally fettered.

In *Heathcote v. The North Staffordshire Railway*,[42] the defendants had been restrained by an injunction from applying to Parliament to seek an Act allowing them to abandon the Silverdale and Apedale Branch Railways, contrary to a covenant entered into in 1846. On appeal, however, the Lord Chancellor, Lord Cottenham, dissolved the injunction and said

> it has been suggested that this Court could not interfere without infringing upon the privileges of Parliament: so the Courts of Common Law thought at one time; and there is as much foundation for the one as for the other supposition. In both cases, this Court acts upon the person,

and not upon the jurisdiction. In a proper case, therefore, I have said here and elsewhere that I should not hesitate to exercise the jurisdiction of this Court by injunction, touching proceedings in Parliament for a private bill or a bill respecting property; but what would be a proper case for that purpose it may be very difficult to conceive.[43]

This contains the kernel of a number of similar decisions in the period. Lord Cottenham observed that while courts enforce legal rights, Parliament through enacting private Bills abrogates existing rights, and creates new ones.[44] Not long before, he had been similarly specific in *The Stockton and Hartlepool Railway Company v. The Leeds and Thirsk and the Clarence Railway Companies*[45] that

a party who comes to oppose a railway bill in Parliament does so solely in respect of his private interest, not as representing any interest of the public ... He is not even allowed to be heard as a Petitioner against the bill, unless he has a *locus standi* ... This Court, therefore ... has just the same jurisdiction to restrain a party from petitioning against a bill in Parliament as if he were bringing an action at law, or asserting any other right connected with the enjoyment of the property or interest which he claims. About that there can be no question whatever.[46]

Other decisions followed. In *The Lancaster and Carlisle Railway Company v. The North-Western Company*[47] the plaintiffs, in contravention of an earlier agreement following which the defendants had obtained an Act, sought an injunction to restrain them from seeking another Act to authorise a connecting railway. It had been a key term of the earlier agreement that they would not do this, and the plaintiffs had refrained from petitioning against the earlier Bill on the strength of it. The court refused to intervene, distinguishing applications to Parliament on private grounds from those on public grounds, and averring that the second Bill, if passed, would be passed 'on public grounds, which this court could not try, and with full knowledge of the agreement'.[48] Two shareholders were similarly unsuccessful – following a Chancery Appeal decision in *In re London, Chatham, and Dover Railway Arrangement Act, Ex parte Hartridge and Allender*[49] – in restraining company directors from proceeding with a Bill that had been materially modified during its passage through the Commons in a manner that they opposed.

In the event (and sometimes after appeals), despite the reaffirming of the court's jurisdiction in principle to intervene, no party was successful in achieving that. 'How far it is expedient or proper for the Court to exercise this jurisdiction is a totally different question', as Vice-Chancellor Page Wood put it in the *Lancaster and Carlisle Railway Company* case referred to above.[50] He cited Lord Cottenham as saying back in 1839 that 'No case has been cited in which this Court has interfered to restrain parties from petitioning Parliament, or applying to Parliament for any law which they supposed would be granted'.[51] Lord Cottenham considered such a case, as we have seen, 'very difficult to conceive',[52] and it remained true at the end of the period of this study that no such case was known to have occurred. Indeed, that remains true to this day.[53]

A different issue – with different outcomes – concerned cases where the challenge was not directly about the approach itself to Parliament, but about paying for the costs of such an approach. In 1850 in *Attorney-General v. Andrews*[54] it was held that commissioners under a Southampton local Act of 1836, while empowered to do various things 'and in otherwise carrying the Act into execution',[55] could not use rates income from that Act to promote a Bill seeking more extensive powers to carry out that existing Act's objectives. A year later in 1851 in *Stevens v. The South Devon Railway Company*[56] the court declined to prevent an application to Parliament to alter the position as between two classes of shareholders, but ordered that (for the time being at least) the company's funds should not be used to pay for the relevant Bill clauses. In 1870, in circumstances similar to those in *Attorney-General v. Andrews*, the West Hartlepool Improvement Commissioners were restrained from using rates income to promote a Bill to extend their district.[57]

Funds might also need to be expended in opposing, rather than promoting, a Bill. The Corporation of Dublin spent money opposing the Dublin Markets Bill empowering construction of a new cattle market and marketplace etc. before a Lords Committee; the Court declined to intervene, Hayes, J. saying

> Where a public body gets property for public purposes, they have a right to protect and defend that property; and if it were shown that that property was likely to be injured by any measure this would be sufficient indication to them that they should, by opposing it, protect and defend that property.[58]

The rationale of this approach is similar to that of Smethurst in relation to *locus standi*,[59] although of course two separate legal issues, the right or otherwise to appear in Parliament and the lawfulness or otherwise of spending public money, were involved.

What is the relevance of these decisions for us here? It lies in how the law was perceived in the period after 1858, and how that perception would affect what occurred. Local promoters and objectors alike might often want, or be obliged, to make agreements that would further their objectives. They would be advised that, although in principle the courts could interfere if they went to Parliament in breach of undertakings, in practice there was little risk of an injunction – certainly at the appellate level. On the other hand, they could not just disregard past promises; they would also be advised that they still might be liable in damages for breach of contract even if the Parliamentary process went ahead regardless. Furthermore, and very importantly, money raised under one private Act could not be used to promote a Bill to modify or extend that Act, since doing so was not one of the powers directly or impliedly granted under it. This latter point lies behind many local Act provisions stipulating how the costs of passing the Bill were lawfully to be met. Parliament might give retrospective approval to using local rates, but were a Bill to fail for any reason (or to pass without that clause) the risk and the costs would of course fall back on the promoters.[60]

Judicial consideration of private Acts

The successful promoters of local Acts had (save for whatever amendments might have been made to their Bill during its passage) presumably placed the law in their context explicitly on the footing that they desired. Despite that, cases turning on the construction of such Acts were regularly reported before, during and after the period 1858–72. Mr. Justice Mathew commented in one instance some years later that 'The case is not free from difficulty; few cases are which turn on the construction of private Acts of Parliament which are sought to be blended with public Acts'.[61] This decision involved the protection of market rights; an auctioneer selling on his own field was held entitled to do so without penalty, despite the fact that had the Abergavenny Improvement Act 1854 not been passed he would have infringed the Markets and Fairs Clauses Act 1847 that had been incorporated with it.

Because local Acts often elaborated on basic powers granted by general Acts, duplication or overlapping of powers was likely to occur if the local Acts had provided a self-contained code of provisions. In *The Earl of Derby v. The Bury Improvement Commissioners*, the Court of Exchequer Chamber held that the defendants had power to build a new sewer under either the local Act or the general Act at their option; as Willes J. put it, 'the local Act conferred upon the commissioners a power conditional upon giving notice, and the General Act gives power ... to do the same thing without such notice'. Nor was the power contained in the Bury Improvement Act 1846 impliedly repealed by the later Nuisances Removal Act 1855:

> many cases were cited to show that special privileges conferred by statute upon individuals, or special constitutions imposed upon limited bodies are not to be considered as repealed by subsequent general legislation nor expressly or by necessary inference inconsistent with the former. These authorities are only so many illustrations of the rule, *generalia specialibus non derogant*.[62]

The Court of Exchequer had already decided a more tricky case also involving a repeal earlier in the decade. A conviction under section 101 of the Hull Improvement Act 1848, for starting to build houses before the Local Board of Health had approved the plans, was upheld in *Pearson v. The Local Board of Health of Kingston-Upon-Hull*. Section 101 incorporated section 53 of the Public Health Act 1848, but that section had been repealed and replaced by section 34 of the Local Government Act 1858, Martin B. saying 'It seems to me that the repeal of this 53rd section by the 34th section of the Local Government Act 1858 does not at all affect the absolute enactment of the 101st section of the Hull Improvement Act 1854'.[63]

Rating powers were always a fertile source of litigation, scrutinised as they were with particular exactness by those liable to pay. The Liverpool Corporation had the power, under a local Act for public libraries, etc.[64] to levy a yearly rate not to exceed one penny in the pound on the rateable value of all the liable property in what was then a borough. The amount in cash purported to be levied exceeded what the overseers could collect, because some rateable premises were unoccupied or had insolvent occupiers. The Court of Queen's Bench were clear, Cockburn C.J. finding that 'The intention of the Act was that each occupier should be liable to pay a rate not exceeding $1d.$ in the pound' and Crompton J. added that 'The meaning was to limit the rate to $1d.$ in the pound upon each house. The council must take care not to make an assessment that will require a taxation of more than $1d.$ in the pound upon each house.'[65]

Promoters will have expected their advisers not only to be aware of decisions of this kind, and how problems might be mitigated, but also to take account of changes in general municipal legislation as they evolved. As referred to later in this chapter, section 29 of the public Local Government Act (1858) Amendment Act 1861 was passed to clarify the interrelation of public and local Acts where they overlapped. Throughout the period of this study, whenever private Bill promoters were considering what provisions and drafting terms were required, they had continually to take into account the slowly changing public local government legislation, and what those changes might mean for the attitudes of Parliamentary Committees. As we have seen in Chapter 3, there were no restrictions on who could set up as a Parliamentary agent,[66] and *Vacher*'s sessional lists of deposited Bills reveal the wide range of firms involved. The costs were likely to be considerable, and the procedural requirements intricate and easily fatal if followed incorrectly. Mistaken assessments of the technical aspects of any given promotion could just as easily confound promoters and their investors. Then, as now, the reputation for integrity and professionalism of the most sought-after practitioners came at a premium.

The evolution of public municipal legislation after 1858

Adderley did not, it seems, regard his Local Government Act 1858 at the time as a major step in municipal reform. In his own notes about his work that year he said only that it 'was chiefly consolidating the accumulated Minutes of Council on Education, and, helped by Tom Taylor, carrying a large Local Government Act, the title "Local Government" being my own invention'.[67] Tom Taylor was then Secretary to the soon-to-be-abolished Board of Health; surprisingly from 1874–80 he was also the Editor of *Punch*, which may be relevant for the frequent references there in 1858 to the state of the Thames, and the last line in a sketch piece on 10 July 1858 that 'What made the matter more aggravating, we had not even continued for another year the Public Health Act!'.[68]

It is clear, however, looking back to the decade or so following its passing, that from then on significant change was afoot. It was archetypical *laissez-faire* politics to refer to 'leaving it to every town in the kingdom to adopt the powers of local Government'[69] as Adderley did, but both the volume and tone of public Acts (as well as other unsuccessful Bills) demonstrated that slowly the outlooks of both Government and governed were changing. This was soon widely recognised. Well before the nineteenth century ended there was also a large body of opinion that public provision, and direct delivery of municipal services by municipalities themselves at their own discretion, was either appropriate, desirable or necessary – an outlook that, as Mr. Cowper had found in 1857, could not at that time get through Parliament. This was expressed in different ways, from Frederick Clifford's high-flown phrase about 'accomplishing these ends by measures of local self-government in harmony with the best English traditions'[37] to the sentiment of Sidney Webb, the standard-bearer of public provision, who wrote of London in 1891 (and might well have said the same of all local government) that

> The Reform of London Government is, therefore, no mere matter of cleaner streets or better drains. We should 'municipalize' our metropolis, not only in order to improve its administration, but as the best means of developing the character of its citizens.[70]

Clifford, writing just a few years before Webb, clearly felt that by 1885 municipal initiative had proved itself. He cited, with evident approval, the fact that over 270 local authorities had water supply, and about 150 had gas supply, in their own hands –

> By far the larger proportion of these transfers have been made by means of private legislation, after due inquiry, during the last fifteen years ... More striking proofs of the growth of wealth and public spirit in our provincial towns could hardly be given than by the legislation which has thus gradually handed over great commercial undertakings from private to public bodies ... good and economical management, though unpaid is the rule.[71]

The period after 1858 witnessed mostly consequential changes to formal law about the structure and overall ground rules of local government and its authorities. The Municipal Corporation Mortgages, Etc. Act 1860[72] made some technical changes about mortgages outside the scope of local Acts, followed by a broadening of some aspects of the Lands Clauses Consolidation Act 1845 in the similarly titled Amendment Act 1860.[73] The Local Government Act (1858) Amendment Act 1861 provided *inter alia* for how expenses were to be paid when the 1858 Act was unsuccessfully adopted;[74] its section 18 also defined the term 'special Act' for the purposes of the Lands Clauses Consolidation Act 1845 and Provisional Orders. Particularly interesting here, however, was section 29 of this 1861 Act, which begins:

> And whereas Doubts exist whether Local Boards of Health, constituted under or by virtue of Local Acts, are affected by the Provisions of 'The Local Government Act, 1858', or by the Provisions of 'The Nuisances Removal Act for England, 1855', and 'The Diseases Prevention Act, 1855' and it is desirable to remove such doubts.

It is indicative, perhaps, of the gulf between public and local legislation at this time that any potential interrelation or overlap between them had previously been overlooked. Section 28 confirmed that all the recited Acts did apply to Local Boards constituted under local Acts, but with two qualifications:

(1) Provisions of the General Acts opposed to or restrictive of the Provisions (whether adopted or original) of any such local Act shall be of no Force in the District for which the Local Act was passed;
(2) Wherever the General Acts and a Local Act contain Provisions for effecting the same or a similar Object, but in different Modes, the Local Board of Health may proceed under the General Acts or a Local Act:

with the section concluding by adding that

> And every future Act for amending or repealing any of the General Acts aforesaid shall, subject to the aforesaid Qualifications, also apply to every such Local Board of Health.

Local Acts are public in the sense that judicial notice will be taken of them; unlike personal Acts, they do not have to be proved in court. There was (and still is) a presumption against implied repeal, so that a local Act would not usually be deemed repealed by implication were a contradictory public Act later passed. Once enacted, a local or private Act remains in force.[75] Its necessity in 1861 may indicate some lack of familiarity in the draftsmen of public legislation both with the need to take account of local provisions – which were usually drafted by or on behalf of their promoters – and with the principles of statutory construction by which that might be best achieved. It will be recalled that this question of overlap would later be considered by the courts in the case involving the Bury Improvement Commissioners, reported in 1869,[62] and in other cases.

The Local Taxation Returns Act 1860[76] sought to create a comprehensive record of local taxation by requiring the clerk of any body levying taxes, charges, tolls and the like to submit an annual return to the Secretary of State, who was required to lay the abstract of the responses before Parliament. The ratepayers of a parish with more than 500 inhabitants, that was maintaining its own poor were, together also with any borough of at least that size, given adoptive powers for certain improvements by the Public Improvements Act 1860.[77] The 31 sections of the Local Government Act (1858) Amendment Act 1861[74] referred to above suggest that no sooner had the 1858 Act begun to be operated than numerous practical shortcomings in its provisions had become apparent. The short Municipal Corporations Act Amendment Act 1861[78] altered the provisions about Commissions of the Peace. The Local Government Act Amendment Act 1863[79] ordinarily restricted adoption of the principal 1858 Act to 'places' (as the Act called them) having more than 3,000 in population, amended the law on petitions appealing against the resolution of adoption, and provided for the possible abandonment of the Act in places with populations below 3,000. (At the same time the confusingly named Public Works (Manufacturing Districts) Act 1863[80] temporarily provided in section 7 for marked reductions in the time periods required in the adoption procedures for the Local Government Act 1858.) The Local Stamp Act 1869[81] enabled local authorities to collect fines and fees by means of stamps, while the Municipal Corporation Elections Act 1869[82] lowered the time period to qualify as a local elector to one year. The County Property Act 1871[83] provided for the vesting of county property in that county's Clerk of the Peace. The Municipal Corporations Act, 1859, Amendment Act 1871[84] provided for dividing electoral areas into wards.

In *The Queen v. The Mayor and Town Council of Sheffield*, expenditure by Sheffield Corporation in preparing to oppose a Sheffield Water Company Bill, that was in the event withdrawn, was reluctantly declared invalid. Cockburn C.J. considered

> that it must be taken that the opposition of the corporation [to the Bill] was meritorious and in the true interests of the borough ... I very much wish I could protect the corporation against the expenses which must now fall upon the individual members; but we cannot strain the words of the statute so as to include these expenses within the terms 'carrying into effect the provisions of the Act'.[85]

Subsequently, the Municipal Corporations (Borough Funds) Act 1872[86] was passed. It required a local vote, including possibly a poll, before a local Bill could be promoted. In the same session the Borough and Local Courts of Record Act 1872[87] amended the law relating to them.

None of the Acts described above in this section gave any more real scope to local initiative; rather they were primarily concerned with safeguards, limitations on what was lawful, and matters of process. It was understandable that as more and more – and many extremely small – communities adopted the 1858 Act and established Local Boards, the enabling Act would be found in need of elaboration as experience grew.[88] The tenor of much of the Acts, however, is of constraints and conditions, of the need for Treasury or

126 *The wider context*

Secretary of State approval, and of increasing complexity in terms of the types and circumstances of local authorities that could now be brought into existence. As power in some hands grows, so power in other hands tends to diminish; we have seen what was the mood in Parliament about legislating overall publicly for municipal development and advancement, and how some spoke out against the centralising tendencies that they so much deplored. There can, however, be an interesting debate about the creeping growth of centralising and administration that was built up by apparently minor provisions, about seeking Treasury sanction for this, and Secretary of State approval for that. The means to respond to those duties demanded increasing Government capacity, often in matters of detail, to an extent not required before. Historians have elsewhere extensively canvassed issues such as these in recent years – particularly in the context of the evolution of the so-called 'information state'.[89] The trend was also the subject of direct contemporary comment in the context of private Bill legislation; assessing for the *Edinburgh Review* in 1855 the various Select Committee reports of 1846–54 on railway Bills and legislation, private Bills and the 1854 edition of the *Standing Orders* of both Houses, Alexander Pulling observed that –

> Despite the outcry against 'Centralisation' the public feeling in this country is getting every year more strong in favour of efficient government in every department, – of the establishment of system even at the cost of individual independence, – the strong authority of one responsible Court in lieu of the uncurbed tyranny of innumerable boards of directors.[90]

By later standards, however, the years from 1858 to 1872 actually saw relatively few significant developments in what could now formally be called *local government* service provision, though a greater emphasis on the basics of public health, and increasing provision of water supply and sanitation, had other consequences, and a succession of Acts about sewage collection and disposal were required in the 1860s. Leave was given to introduce a Public Improvements Bill in 1859 'to enable a majority of Two-thirds of the Ratepayers of any Parish or District, duly assembled, to rate their District in aid of Public Improvements for general benefit within their District'. It did not make progress,[91] but a public Act to that effect was passed in 1860.[92]

Section 3 of the Sewage Utilization Act 1865[93] defined sewer authorities (essentially boroughs, improvement commissions and parish vestries). The sewage utilisation powers were quickly broadened by the Sanitary Act 1866,[94] and the following year – under the Sewage Utilization Act 1867[95] – the powers to store, distribute or otherwise dispose of sewage were extended again, and provision was made for special drainage districts. Yet more extension ensued in 1868 under the Sanitary Act[96] of that year, while the Sanitary Loans Act 1869[97] gave the Secretary of State power to borrow money to defray the costs of anyone appointed to perform the duties of what section 4 called 'a defaulting local authority'. At the same time as basic health and hygiene needs were being addressed, the Artizans and Labourers Dwellings Act 1868[98] gave boroughs, improvement commissions and Local Boards (as defined in schedule 1) the powers for the first time in public general legislation to survey and take action on houses that were found unfit for human habitation.

The Elementary Education Act 1870[99] was, of course socially very significant in the longer term, and enacted in section 5 the duty to provide sufficient schools for every district, but that was exceptional. Parliament passed some 25 similarly titled Local Government Supplemental Acts from 1859 up to and including 1867, confirming a total of 193 Provisional Orders.[100] A few of these also included some limited ancillary local provisions. Some districts or local authorities obtained two or more separate Provisional Orders. (As noted above, Provisional Orders were later transferred out of the public and into the local Acts.) Where developmental public legislation was passed, empowering further local powers, it was usually about the structures rather than the services: the Public Libraries Act, 1855, Amendment Act 1871, for instance, empowered Local Boards to adopt the Public Libraries Acts, but it did not compel them to do so, and its section 5 (that this power was not to apply to any district wholly within a municipal borough or under improvement commissioners) was inserted during the Bill's passage.[101]

Although the initiative for public legislative reform was likely to come from the Government, or in the event to be overseen or controlled by Ministers, others might be interested in it too. That applied even to municipal reform in the metropolis, always a complex and exceptional matter with particular powerful vested interests with a special profile as the capital city of the Empire. The Commons *Journal* for 8 March 1870[102] lists leave given for three Bills to be introduced by Mr. Buxton and Mr. Thomas Hughes entitled Municipal Boroughs (Metropolis), Corporation of London and County of London. Immediately following are the entries for Mr. Buxton's presentation of these three Bills, respectively numbered 65, 66 and 67. None was enacted.

As the period of this study closed, the onset of another shift of approach can be seen in the advent of the Local Government Board in an Act of 1871, operative from 1873, which also took over the functions of the Poor Law Board.[103] Meanwhile the Public Health Act 1872, in a further structural move, merged Local Boards into those municipal boroughs and improvement commissions that shared the same district – numerous examples had been enacted in local legislation of provisions about essentially the same municipal entity in different capacities.[104] England was to be divided into either urban or rural sanitary districts.[105] The Local Government Board's creation, however, was a poor compromise in the minds of those who had hoped for so much more – J.G. Goschen, the President of the Poor Law Board, had introduced two Bills in 1871 for a systematic provision of rural and urban sanitary authorities, together with sweeping rating reforms. 'But he had offended too many interests to pass his Bills ... Only the clauses providing for the establishment of the Local Government Board were saved.'[106]

The Local Government Board Act 1871 had just eight sections, with a schedule listing the powers and duties transferred there. Those hitherto with the Secretary of State were mainly the public health, local government, drainage and improvement matters, with those with the Privy Council relating to disease prevention and vaccination transferred also. The Board was given no new powers, but we can recognise a distinct step towards centralisation of standards, and hence greater central government concern and control, in the bringing together of these activities. (Not long after, however, section 303 of the Public Health Act 1875[107] gave the Board power by order, if a local authority applied, for any local Act to be wholly or partly repealed or amended, or for its area of application to be varied, including extension.) Bellamy, noting that the Board lacked 'certain key powers' said that 'Instead it was entangled in a mass of detailed procedural checks in which strategic direction was unavailable'.[108] Redlich and Hirst, writing while the Board was still operating, and with the Germanic outlook of Redlich, opined that

> The Local Government Board is emphatically not a motor engine; it does not supply power to set in motion the machinery of local government; and in practice the Board takes the initiative even less than the letter of the law might lead one to suppose, the reason really being no doubt that the statesmen who preside ... share more or less in this traditional abhorrence of the nation from any and every kind of administrative direction over public life. Nothing is so jealously guarded in England as this trait of national life.[109]

This was what, in the 1858 second reading debate, Adderley had called 'leaving it to every town in the kingdom to adopt the powers of local Government'.[69] There was still room for surprise that so much repetitive material went before Parliament, or that simple steps to reduce that material went untaken, but throughout the period from 1858 to 1872 it was clear that any community that wanted to take the initiative, to extend its scope and to raise local standards had primarily to bring that about for itself in Parliament, on a publicly justified and costly basis. Although section 7 of the Artizans and Labourers Dwellings Act 1868 did provide a duty to take action in prescribed circumstances, public Acts were essentially permissive and, during our period here at least, there was a contrast between the incipient growth of the controlling and overseeing 'information state' and the *laissez-faire* attitude to municipal advancement expressed by Adderley. The Local Taxation Returns Act 1860 sought to collate the immense variety of local circumstances into a systematic public record, but it was no part of that Act to command Ministers directly to *do* anything much with all the information collected, except to present it to Parliament in a manageable form. At this time, the 'traditional abhorrence' of central direction to which Redlich and Hirst alluded 40 years later was undoubtedly the prevalent motivation of many in Parliament.

Frederick Clifford, however, was in no doubt about another reason why chartered municipalities had not been readily entrusted with new responsibilities either by Parliament or their local citizenries. Had it not been for the reputation of self-serving indifference of most of them to the true state of their localities – 'supineness' as he called it – the passing of local Acts 'would hardly have been intelligible'. These Acts for the most part 'did not recognize these corporations, but created bodies of trustees or commissioners for many purposes of municipal government'. The corporations

> should have been natural guardians of the interests of the whole community in all matters pertaining to local government. But by their prolonged neglect of those duties, their exclusiveness, and political demoralization, they were left with hardly any duties to perform, and only nominally responsible for health and good order in their towns.[110]

Clifford, however, by 1887 came to regret 'the party spirit which of late has generally ruled in local elections'. He thought it

> another reason why local legislation should remain subject to Imperial control, and to searching and public inquiry before Committees in Parliament, as a guarantee against the jobbery and extravagances which have arisen under local and party rule in kindred institutions elsewhere, and for which there are fresh temptations and opportunities now that so many local authorities have become large traders ... local government involves that branch of private legislation which is of by far the greatest moment to the nation. Local laws and administration, indeed, concern a community more directly and intimately than most Imperial measures.[111]

It would take a couple of generations after 1835 for municipal corporations to recover from a reputation then so poor that even before the death of William IV they had to be reformed. As the case came to be made for improving the health of towns, so new means of achieving those ends were considered essential. That reality had helped to inform the outlook of Parliament by the time that Adderley made his remarks in 1858 about 'leaving it to every town in the kingdom'.

The outlook of Parliament in 1858

This chapter has described the setting and situation of local government law in 1858. There had been a slow recognition of the desperate state of public health, based partly on the obvious and self-evident, and partly on the rapidly developing state of medical understanding. There was, however, other than in limited (though important) areas like highways and poor law provision, no tradition of public services in what would later be recognised as a municipal context. The way that things were done was that local communities had to approach Parliament for permission to help themselves. If permission were given, there would be no Government grants: the costs involved had to be either raised or borrowed, invested and repaid locally. There was at best only an embryonic principle that the wider interests of people or 'society' at large, however defined, might sometimes – even at the price of compensation – outweigh the private interests of individuals (and particularly of the well born and landed classes).

Parliament would, subject to conditions and if the mood were right, authorise local initiatives where a borough or improvement commission sought to cleanse, regulate and invest in their community, but there was no bias for action. There were some reformers at Westminster, but in 1858 there was no irresistible expectation in the minds of the electorate, or therefore of the Government, that it was for them to require and legislate for improving standards for the people at large. Egregious excesses like those of the unreformed municipal corporations would be swept away, but it was enough that they were constituted and renewed on a more modern and defensible basis – they were not expected to deliver much unless there were both a clear will locally and an explicit approval at Westminster from a cautious Parliament. Many in that Parliament, confident of Empire, would grudgingly accept local ambition and improvement – however, only so long as it involved no compulsion on other communities; no wider principle of universal standards; and provided that they could stand up and assure their constituents that they had voted against dangerous and detested centralisation, and had resisted creeping tyranny on behalf of the masses, whose freedom it was to live as they had always lived.

Once those in Parliament had accepted the *ends* of promoted local Bills, they had still to consider the *means*. On the floors of either House, there might be little focus on, or interest in, the drafting of particular provisions. In the Committee stages, however, wording would be carefully scrutinised – especially so if it gave the rights to take land, override private rights, or permit the levying of additional rates for any purpose. The material that enacted Bills contained in this respect – the basic apparatus of local legislation – has not been broadly studied before. Its content has much intrinsic interest, not least because of what it reveals about the approach to growing local powers and special interests at a time when the 'information state' – the whole machinery and scope of state government – was beginning to evolve so rapidly from limited beginnings into a major aspect of national life. The significance of the care given to matters of scope and drafting was acknowledged at the time: the Parliamentary agent Theodore Martin – a supporter of the system as it then was, who considered that 'The formal passage of these Bills through Committee does not impose any duty upon Members which they are not perfectly willing to discharge in the interests of their constituents' – opined in 1872 that

> The conformity of the framework of Bills with established principle and precedent is moreover secured by the careful supervision of the Chairman

of Committees in the House of Lords, by whom every Private Bill is narrowly scrutinised, and who not only strives to prevent the introduction of anything contrary to public interest or acknowledged principle, but to secure a uniformity and exactitude in the language of Private Bills which are often found wanting in Public Acts. How efficiently that work is done, with what regard to public objects, and with what vigilance for the protection of private rights, every practitioner in Parliament will rejoice to bear witness, though most of us have winced at times under the process of supervision.[112]

The ensuing chapters of this study follow on to consider in detail what the provisions were that the local Acts contained.

Notes

1 See Chapter 1.
2 *Hansard*, H.C. Deb. 3rd series, vol. 26, col. 155. At this time Sandon was M.P. for Liverpool, later succeeding as Earl of Harrowby.
3 *Hansard*, H.C. Deb. 3rd series, vol. 26, cols. 391–2. At this time Graham was a Cumberland M.P.
4 A *Return 'showing the several HIGHWAY DISTRICTS in each County in England constituted under the HIGHWAY ACTS 1862 and 1864 (25 & 26 Vict. c. 61 and 27 & 28 Vict. c.101), and the Names of the PARISHES comprised in each DISTRICT'* (Paper 143) was submitted by the Local Government Board (ordered to be printed 2 April 1873): *Parliamentary Papers* (1873) vol. LVIII p. 193. Throughout our period a wide variety of valuable Parliamentary returns is indexed, providing a wealth of detailed information not practically available from anywhere else.
5 The Public Libraries Act 1850 contained no powers to buy any books, and while the halfpenny rate product for maximum expenditure was raised to a penny in 1855, except where local Acts applied, it took until 1919 for this ceiling to be universally removed. See R.J.B. Morris, *Parliament and the Public Libraries* (1977), pp. 219, 228 and 291.
6 Angus Hawkins, *The Forgotten Prime Minister: The 14th Earl of Derby* (2008), vol. II, *Achievement, 1851–1869*, p. 24.
7 Pages 12–13. Somers Vine edited a number of annual yearbooks and statistical digests at this time: his book is a mine of information about all the various corporations that were or were not within the scope of the 1835 Act, and much else besides. See also note 60 to Chapter 2.
8 *Op. cit.*, p. 63.
9 H.C. Deb. 3rd series, 22 April 1858, vol. 149, col. 1555. See the Commons *Journal*, vol. 113 at pp. 129 and 130 for its introduction, and p. 131 for its withdrawal.
10 The Local Government Bill was introduced as Bill 59 on the same day, 23 April 1858, as his Public Health Act 1848 (Amendment) Bill was withdrawn: see also the Commons *Journal* at vol. 113, p. 131. Adderley had previously presented two Returns, one relating to the General Board of Health and the other to the Board of Health, recorded ibid. at p. 128; see *Parliamentary Papers*, 1857-8, vol. LII, pp. 517–18 and 519–20, Papers 222 and 223 respectively. The former lists, in section 5, three Public Health Bills, including that introduced in December 1857, prepared by the General Board, as well as others, including the Aldershot measure referred to in note 22 below.

132 *The wider context*

11 H.C. Deb. 3rd series, vol. CXLIX, col. 2095. Mr Bouverie, no doubt with an emphasis on *was*, percipiently 'remarked that there was a new principle involved in the Bill, as power was given to take lands without a previous application to Parliament': col. 2097. Sir Arthur Elton, M.P. for Bath, commented at col. 2096 that his constituency had waited 15 years for a Bill like this one.
12 This was Bill 166. It was passed as 20 & 21 Vict. c. 38. The *Justice of the Peace* journal reviewed the Act on 14 August 1858, vol. XXII, no. 33, pp. 510–11, opining

> let us hope that in the present instance we have more than a mere change of name, and that under the new regime sanitary reform will go hand in hand with practical science, instead of being subject as heretofore to the empirical vagaries of the school which was formerly dominant in Richmond-place.

The journal's articles were unsigned; this comment indicates the past struggles over whether, and how, sanitary reform should be carried forward.
13 Bill 124, introduced and ordered to be printed 15 July 1857. Leave to introduce this Bill had been given to Mr Cowper and Mr W. Monsell, M.P. for Limerick County, who was President of the General Board of Health from February to September 1857.
14 Bill 5, with 187 clauses, introduced and ordered to be printed 10 December 1857. Leave to introduce the Bill was given to Mr Cowper and Mr Massey. An article on the Bill in the *Justice of the Peace* for 2 January 1858, vol. XXII, no. 1, pp. 3–4 began 'Notwithstanding the discontent which has been occasionally manifested with regard to the working of the public health act, 1848, there can scarcely be a question that its operation has, on the whole, been fairly satisfactory'.
15 Clauses 25 and 23 respectively. Clauses in these Bills were numbered in Arabic in the 'Arrangement of Clauses' but set out in Roman numerals against the clauses themselves.
16 See the Commons *Journal* for 24 March 1858, vol. 113, col. 97. This was Bill 5.
17 See Mr Walpole's response to Mr Labouchere at H.C. Deb., vol. 151, cols. 606–07 (29 June 1858), and the Chancellor of the Exchequer's evasive reply to him two days later at vol. 151, cols. 756–57 (1 July). Mr Walpole's name is printed on the Bill as supporting Mr Adderley in bringing it in. As introduced, the original Bill 59 had 60 clauses; the clauses about adopting Local Board powers and their operation were soon augmented and other amendments made, so that as reprinted Bill 106 had 69 clauses, Bill 188 had 77 clauses, and the Act as passed had 82 sections.
18 Clause 67 of Bill 5, to be compared with section 29 of the 1858 Act, which received the royal assent on 2 August.
19 Clause 76 in Bill 5 (is the hand of Edwin Chadwick discernible here?), to be compared with section 32 of the 1858 Act.
20 Clauses 96 and 98–100 of Bill 5, to be compared with sections 50 and 51–53 of the 1858 Act.
21 Section 44 of the 1858 Act and clauses 93–95 of 1857's Bill 5 respectively.
22 20 & 21 Vict. c. 22 passed in 1857 had been an example of Parliament, in a public Act, creating a Local Board for Aldershot. The General Board of Health prepared the Bill: see the 1858 *Return* referred to in note 10 above. Another public Act, the Local Government Act (1858) Amendment Act 1864, 27 & 28 Vict. c. LXVIII (and referred to subsequently in the *Chronological Table and Index of the Statutes* as the Oxford Local Board Act), provided for early Local Board elections in Oxford.
23 See sections 12 and 15. In this respect it mirrored the 1857 Bills: see clauses 11 of Bill 5, which referred to adopting 'either wholly or partially'.
24 See H.C. Deb. 3rd series, vol. 149, col. 2015, in answer to a question from Mr (later Sir) Lawrence Palk (South Devon) about whether he intended to proceed with the Bill. There had, however, been some limited objections to the Bill expressed at the

The wider context   133

second reading by Mr Palk, Mr Cowper and Sir George Brooke-Pechell (M.P. for Brighton): vol. CLXIX, cols. 2095–97. It was passed as 21 & 22 Vict. c. 98. The *Justice of the Peace* for 30 October 1858, vol. XXII, no. 44, pp. 685–6, commented that the Act was 'no doubt, an improvement in many respects on the public health act ... But withal it is strange how many of the shortcomings of that act are noticeable in the new one.' The article is principally concerned, however, just with the powers to borrow on the credit of rating income; it comments of the General Board of Health that the journal 'cannot pretend to say whether they ever found themselves in any difficulty with reference to the construction of the borrowing powers conferred by the public health act. But if they did not, their minds must have been very differently constituted from those of the ordinary run of lawyers'.
25 See section 8.
26 As to Provisional Orders, see below in this chapter. There had been no equivalent of this provision in the 1857 Bills. In another commentary on its scope, the Local Government Act 1858 contained only 88 sections, as opposed to the 187 clauses in the 1857 Bill 5.
27 This had been introduced as Bill 88 on 17 May 1858 (Commons *Journal*, vol. 113, p. 180), and was passed as 21 & 22 Vict. c. 97.
28 This is reproduced in William Cunningham Glen, *The Law Relating to Public Health and Local Government in Relation to Sanitary and Other Matters etc.* (1858), pp. 409–13. The preceding pp. 405–8 usefully list 17 previous statutes confirming 126 Provisional Orders from 1849 onwards.
29 The significance of Acts such as these may be judged from the example of the Gasworks Clauses Consolidation Act 1847, 10 & 11 Vict. c. XV: '... the result was, that special gas Acts which in 1846 sometimes comprised over 200 clauses were, after the legislation of 1847, contained within forty'. Frederick Clifford, *A History of Private Bill Legislation* (1885), vol. I, p. 221. He also comments that 'Down to 1885, more than one thousand Gas Bills had passed the Legislature, and of these about sixty applied to the metropolis alone', *ibid.* A note adds that these included amending Acts.
30 10 & 11 Vict. c. XXXIV, section 136. Since the Act is too long and detailed to summarise here, the intention is to convey its broad scope, and to describe in outline the principles according to which it was enacted.
31 For example, section 160, allowing money to be borrowed for up to 30 years on the security of an adequate sewer rate that would not only 'defray the current Expences [sic] of maintaining the Sewers that shall have been purchased or made' but also pay off the debt and interest.
32 10 & 11 Vict. c. XIV.
33 10 & 11 Vict. c. XVII. Fire-plugs (see sections 38–41) were today's hydrants, from where water to fight fire could be drawn. The keys had to be kept where any public fire engine was kept, and in other conspicuous places.
34 Section 77(6).
35 Section 75.
36 The Local Government Act (1858) Amendment Act 1861, 24 & 25 Vict. c. 61, section 27.
37 Clifford, *op. cit.*, vol. I, Appendix A, p. 492. The Provisional Orders confirmation procedures covered other areas as well: see for instance 11 & 12 Vict. c. XXVII (inclosures), and 25 & 26 Vict. c. LVI (turnpikes). See generally on these Orders Clifford, *op. cit.*, (1887) vol. II, chapter XVIII, pp. 676–715. Vol. II was, with leave, dedicated to Queen Victoria in terms even more fulsome about private legislation than about Her Majesty's Golden Jubilee, referring to '*adding materially ... to the health, comfort and enjoyment of your Majesty's subjects in their ever-growing towns, and accomplishing these ends by measures of local self-government in harmony with the best English traditions*'. Clifford (1828–1904), a journalist and legal

writer, was also a barrister practising at the Parliamentary Bar. He later 'took silk', becoming a Q.C. in 1894.
38 34 & 35 Vict. c. 3. The Act did not enact a short title, but that volume of the statutes headed it as the Provisional Order Bills (Committees) Act.
39 38 & 39 Vict. c. 55. See sections 297–8.
40 Clifford, *op. cit.*, vol. II, chapter XVIII, pp. 676–715. He lists the 'sanitary and kindred subjects' on pp. 688–9 in 10 categories. Provisional Orders were used for a wide variety of other purposes besides those of local government and sanitary legislation (such as for example inclosures and the provision of school sites).
41 *Op. cit.*, p. 690. Clifford also comments on the differences between local Bills and Provisional Orders at pp. 710–11, but these are essentially issues about the nuances of differing departmental practice, and some perceptions –

> Indeed, it is commonly, though erroneously, supposed that a Provisional Order, once made, becomes 'a Government measure' ... Parliament has been careful to insert and retain, by way of safeguard and control, a special clause declaring that, when a confirming Bill is before Parliament, petitioners may appear and oppose it as though it were a private Bill.

42 (1850) 2 Mac. & G. 100; 42 E.R. 39.
43 *Op. cit.* at pp. 109 and 43 respectively.
44 *Op. cit.* at pp. 110 and 43 respectively.
45 *Op. cit.* at pp. 110 and 43 respectively.
46 (1848) 2 PH. 667; 41 E.R. 1101.
47 *Op. cit.* at pp. 670–1 and 1102 respectively.
48 (1850) 2 K. & J. 293; 69 E.R. 792.
49 *Op. cit.*, the headnote. An example of the Parliamentary viewpoint, although based on an allegation of sharp practice rather than breach of contract, is quoted in relation to the Bill that became the Somerset and Dorset Railway Leasing Act 1876, 39 & 40 Vict. c. cxv, the Committee Chairman saying 'If we are satisfied that the passing of the preamble of the Bill is a good thing for the public at large, we should not be deterred from doing so because one Company or the other had not acted quite fair and above Board'. See E.T. MacDermot, *History of the Great Western Railway* (1931, vol. II, pp. 99–100).
50 (1869) 5 Ch. App. 671. The report is also interesting for the aspersions cast by the Vice-Chancellor on Messrs. Baxter, Rose and Norton, 'solicitors of very extensive practice, very eminent, and whose character is very well known'. His first instance judgment is extensively set out in a long footnote, on which see pp. 675–6. See also on Baxter notes 3, 52, 70, 115 and 125 to Chapter 3. The involvement of solicitors etc. in railway Bills generally (with several references to Baxter) is the subject of R.W. Kostal's prize-winning *Law and English Railway Capitalism 1825–1875* (1994, corrected edition 1997). Kostal's conclusions are vigorously attacked by Sybil Jack and Adrian Jack in their article 'A reconsideration of nineteenth-century lawyers and railway capitalism and the use of legal cases' in the *Journal of Transport History* (2003), vol. 24, issue 1, pp. 59–85, suggesting *inter alia* that lawyers did not play the driving and self-interested roles in railway promotions that Kostal avers; that his finding that rating law bore deliberately and uniquely harshly on railway companies is based on failure to understand wider rating law provisions; and that he misunderstood the basis on which the courts decided many important cases. Nevertheless, the book is valuable in providing much unusual detail and portrayal of the context of much private Bill promotion in the middle years of the century.
51 At pp. 304 and 796 respectively.
52 At pp. 305 and 797 respectively. The 1839 case was *The Attorney-General v. The Manchester and Leeds Railway Company* (1 Railw. Cas. 436).

The wider context 135

53 Erskine May's *Treatise on The Law, Privileges, Proceedings and Usage of Parliament* (24th edn, 2011, p. 924). Earlier authorities were considered in *Bilston Corporation v. Wolverhampton Corporation* [1942] 2 All E.R. 447, a decision discussed both by Sir William Holdsworth (who had previously discussed the Victorian cases in 1938 in vol. XI of *A History of English Law*, pp. 359–62) at (1943) 59 *Law Quarterly Review* pp. 2–4 (untitled), and by Zelman Cowen at (1955) 71 *Law Quarterly Review* pp. 336–42 (titled 'The Injunction and the Parliamentary Process').
54 (1850) 2 Mac. & G. 225; 42 E.R. 87.
55 6 & 7 Will. 4, c. cxvi (96). The unreferenced section referred to was presumably section LXIV (64), although that alludes to 'this Act' rather than 'the Act'.
56 (1851) 13 Beav. 46; 51 E.R. 18.
57 *Attorney-General v. West Hartlepool Improvement Commissioners* (1870) L.R.10 Eq. 152. The commissioners did in fact get their Bill, which became the West Hartlepool Extension and Improvement Act 1870, 33 & 34 Vict. c. cxiii. Section 459, effectively reversing the court decision, provided that

> All costs charges and expenses preliminary to and of and incidental to the preparing applying for obtaining and passing of this Act shall be borne by the Commissioners and shall be paid by them out of the Improvement Fund or out of money borrowed under this Act.

58 *R. v. The Town Council of Dublin* [1863] *The Law Times*, vol. IX, p. 123 at p. 125. The Dublin Markets Bill was Bill 349 of the 1861 session. Its second reading, moved by the Duke of Leinster, was debated on 16 June 1862 at H.C. Deb., vol. CLXVII, cols. 630–31, and had aroused strong feelings with petitions against signed by 3,865 people, 1,514 of them Dublin market traders. It was not in the end enacted. Returns of Dublin Corporation's costs for 1849–64 on promoting and opposing private Bills were printed as *Parliamentary Papers* (1864, Paper 414, vol. L, p. 643–£31,962 7s. 10d.); for 1864–73 (1873, Paper 133, vol. LIII, p. 25–£18,099 19s. 2d., as corrected in the next return); and for 1873–78 (1878, Paper 132, vol. LXI, p. 365 against the name of Sir Arthur Guinness – £4,306 4s. 1d.). The Corporation spent £2,108 7s. opposing the 'Dublin Cattle Market Bill' as the 1864 return (which listed it against 1862) referred to it.
59 See note 57 in Chapter 3.
60 Clifford, *op. cit.*, vol. II, p. 690n., quotes the unusual case of the Westhoughton Local Board, whose Provisional Order was considered *ultra vires* by the Lords (because it would have conveyed compulsory purchase powers) though it had been approved by the Local Government Board. When a year later the Westhoughton Local Board Act 1878, 41 & 42 Vict. c. 62, was passed instead, duly conferring the required powers, 'It was necessary to provide in this Act for payment of the costs incurred by the Westhoughton Board in relation to the Provisional Order'. (This was in section 30.) The preamble to the Act set out the Lords' decision.
61 In *Rutherford v. Straker* in 1887, quoted in *Abergavenny Improvement Commissioners v. Straker* [1889] Ch. D. 83 at p. 85. In a wholly different context, section 28 of the 1854 Act was repealed by the Welsh Ministers in the Abergavenny Improvement Act 1854 (Repeal) Order 2012, S.I. No. 629 (W.87) – the last livestock market was finally held on the 1854 Act traditional site on Wednesday 11 December 2013.
62 [1869] *The Law Times*, vol. XX, p. 927 at p. 929. (Hannen J. read the judgment; the word 'nor' appears as 'not' in the report.)
63 [1865] *The Law Times*, vol. XIII, p. 180 at p. 183. (The word 'affect' appears as 'effect'.) Another report concerning the same parties follows at p. 185, holding that an offence under section 97 of the 1854 Act was 'not comprehended within the penalty clause, sect. 103'.
64 The Liverpool Library and Museum Act 1852, 15 & 16 Vict. c. iii, section 18.

136   *The wider context*

65 *R. v. The Justices of Liverpool* [1862] *The Law Times*, vol. VI, p. 241 at p. 242.
66 See note 93 in Chapter 3.
67 William Shakespeare Childe-Pemberton, *Life of Lord Norton 1814–1905* (1909), p. 166. Adderley accepted a peerage on the third offer in 1878. That he had invented the term 'local government' was repeated in the *Dictionary of National Biography*, seemingly based on his own claim.
68 *Punch* sketch, *The Last Man in the House*, 10 July 1858, p. 19.
69 H.C. Deb. 3rd series, vol. CXLIX, col. 2095 (3 May 1858; second reading).
70 Sidney Webb, *The London Programme* (1891), pp. v–vi.
71 *Op. cit.*, vol. I, pp. 255–6. In another comment of its time, he also stated at vol. I, p. 231 that 'Any serious rivalry between electricity and coal gas as a general means of lighting has yet to be established'. While it was correct that most transfers of undertakings were *to* municipalities, this was not universal: Dartford Local Board of Health was an example of an authority divesting itself of its water undertaking, in this case to the Kent Waterworks Company: Dartford Water Act 1868, 31 & 32 Vict. c. cxix. Paragraphs 1 and 8 of the agreement annexed to the Act as a schedule set out details of arrangements previously concluded about the Bill's promotion (Bill 121).
72 23 & 24 Vict. c. 16, sections 3 and 13. Where the Treasury authorised a sale of municipal land they were given the power to direct how the proceeds should be invested (section 4); the Act also gave cities and boroughs the power to buy land, if necessary on mortgage subject again, however, to Treasury permission (section 8). Section 15 of the Lands Clauses Consolidation Act 1845, 8 & 9 Vict. c. 18 had forbidden the sale of most lands by municipal corporations 'without the approbation of the Treasury'.
73 23 & 24 Vict. c. 106.
74 24 & 25 Vict. c. 61, section 1. Those making a requisition for the adoption process could be asked to provide a bond for the costs, 'with Two sufficient Sureties'.
75 Francis A.R. Bennion, *Statutory Interpretation: Codified with a Critical Commentary* (1984), section 181, p. 434.
76 23 & 24 Vict. c. 51. Accordingly a mass of fascinating detail is available about local expenditure – for instance, 135 improvement commissions (or equivalents) in England including Monmouthshire, and three in Wales, provided accounts abstracted in 1865 (*Parliamentary Papers*, vol. XLVI, p. 1 – Commons *Accounts and Papers* vol. 17 (of 29), Paper 447, pp. 331–7. We can see that Abergavenny then had secured debts of £18,505 12s. 7d., Birkenhead had an astonishing £325,254 14s. 5d., and Liverpool £194,544 11s. 8d., whereas Sheffield had none at all.
77 23 & 24 Vict. c. 30. Section 5 of this Act allowed any corporate body to vote at a meeting for levying a rate for improvement purposes 'by some Person to be deputed by them for that Purpose under their Corporate Seal'. A two-thirds majority was required for such rating. The maximum rate was sixpence in the pound: section VII.
78 24 & 25 Vict. c. 75.
79 26 & 27 Vict. c 17, sections 2–5. This Act was passed on 11 May 1863.
80 26 & 27 Vict. c. 70. The Act was passed *inter alia* to facilitate adoptions, receiving royal assent on 21 July 1863 only some ten weeks after the earlier Act, c. 17. Section 7(4) excluded the possibility of Local Government Act Amendment Act section 3 appeals against adoption resolutions for so long as c. 70 was in force, which for this purpose was until 1 July 1864. This provision was passed unamended, except that a reference to section 4 of the Amendment Act in the original public Bill 154 was altered at the Committee stage (Bill 192) to section 3. (Section 9 of this Act also enlarged the powers of section 4 of the Local Government Act Amendment Act 1863 for any place that could adopt the 1858 Act also to be able to abandon that

The wider context 137

adoption even where the population exceeded 3,000. This had not been included in the original Bill.)
81 32 & 33 Vict. c. 49.
82 32 & 33 Vict. c. 55.
83 34 & 35 Vict. c. 14. This Act amended the County Property Act 1858 (21 & 12 Vict. c. 92), also dealing with the vesting of property acquired before that principal Act had been passed.
84 34 & 35 Vict. c. 67.
85 (1870) L.R. 6 Q.B. 652 at pp. 658 and 659–60.
86 35 & 36 Vict. c. 91, section 4. (The Act itself did not include a short title, and is generally referred to just as the Borough Funds Act 1872 – as for instance when repealed by the Local Government Act 1933.) The polling requirement related to the constraint that 'no expense in promoting or opposing any Bill in Parliament' could be incurred without the consent of the district's owners and ratepayers, 'to be expressed by resolution in the Local Government Act (1858) for the adoption of that Act'. This was a reference to section XIII(4) of that Act. The Bill that led to the Sheffield case is Bill 98 of 1870. The narrative of events in Sheffield is fully set out in the *Report from the Select Committee on Municipal Corporations (Borough Funds) Bill*, ordered to be printed 1 May 1872 (H.C. Paper 177). The Corporation's costs, mostly unpaid at this time, were £4,113: see para. 76. The report lists the dozens who petitioned for and against the Bill, the latter almost entirely gas and waterworks companies.
87 35 & 36 Vict. c. 86.
88 Matlock Bath District had an unusual problem: its boundaries were undefined, though it was part of the larger Matlock parish. Having completed the initial 1858 Act procedures, the Secretary of State declined to continue, and the court – considering sections 14 and 16 – refused to compel him to do so, with the result that the District was unable to adopt: *Ex Parte the Matlock Bath District* [1862] *The Law Times*, vol. VI, p. 243. Section 16 of the Act had sought to provide for 'Adoption of the Act by Place not having a known or defined Boundary', but subsection (6) had stipulated that adoption could only be carried through once it was 'a place with a known and defined boundary'. Occasional problems of this kind persisted: the Kingsholm District Act 1871, a public Act 34 & 35 Vict. c. 54 concerning the Gloucestershire district of Kingsholm St. Catherine, had to be passed 'to settle a Boundary within which a vote may be taken for the adoption of the Local Government Act' – the problems there were recited in its preamble.
89 See notes 3–7 in Chapter 1, and the passages relating thereto.
90 *Edinburgh Review* (1855), vol. CI, no. 205, pp. 151–91. This is a perceptive and thoughtful article by Pulling, written from a more technically legal standpoint than that of Herbert Spencer published by the same journal in the previous year (see note 81 to Chapter 2), the tenor of which can be perceived from the beginning of its last paragraph on p. 191:

> If the preceding remarks are well founded, the system of Private Bill Legislation ought to be viewed by the public with jealousy and disfavour, and all attempts to extend its operation ought to be discouraged and repressed. Where it is introduced for local purposes, it is often a partial and imperfect attempt to remedy defects in the general law, which might be removed by a properly constructed public measure.

Referring earlier at p. 167 to the high costs of private Bills, and to the evidence of Robert Baxter to the 1847 Select Committee, Pulling drily observes that 'He gives us little information as to what proportion of these large sums gets into the pockets of the members of his own branch of the profession, but he does tell us a great

deal about the Bar'. (The *Review* did, however, publish a clarification in relation to Lord Redesdale in vol. CVI, no. 215 for July–October 1857 at p. 286.) On Baxter, see also the references in note 50 above. The *Edinburgh Review* article was also published in a longer form as a pamphlet in 1859: see note 16 to Chapter 3.
91 House of Commons *Journal*, 21 June 1859, p. 222. Those introducing the Bill were Mr Robert Aglionby Slaney, M.P. for Shrewsbury, and Mr William Francis Cowper (later Cowper-Temple and Lord Mount-Temple), M.P. for Hertford.
92 See note 77 above.
93 28 & 29 Vict. c. 75.
94 29 & 30 Vict. c. 90.
95 30 & 31 Vict. c. 113.
96 31 & 32 Vict. c. 115.
97 32 & 33 Vict. c 100.
98 31 & 32 Vict. c. 130.
99 33 & 34 Vict. c. 75. As a letter to *The Times* of 5 October 2012 noted, 'Contrary to popular belief the 1870 Education Act did not make elementary education compulsory or free', but its practical effect was to enable it to be brought within the opportunities of everyone. Section 17 provided for children's fees, though in some limited circumstances these could be remitted. This Act was soon amended, by 35 & 36 Vict. cc. 27 and 59, the latter of which related to elections of School Boards, and by 36 & 37 Vict. c. 86. Under 37 & 38 Vict. c. 39 (1874, without a formal short title), in a remarkable piece of seemingly contradictory drafting,

> for the purposes of the 'Elementary Education Act, 1870', the municipal borough of Wenlock shall not be deemed to be a borough, and the elections for school boards within the said borough shall take place and be conducted in the manner and under the regulations in such Act provided for a parish.

100 Occasionally an Act confirmed a single Order, but typically several were grouped together, and might achieve royal assent on the same day as another similar grouping. The largest group was that of 23 & 24 Vict. c. 44, which confirmed 15 Orders; 29 & 30 Vict. c. 24 confirmed 14. In the case of the Metropolitan Tramways Provisional Orders Suspension Act 1871, 34 & 35 Vict. c. 69, a public Act was passed to shorten the process still further so that eight tramways Orders could go through more quickly than would otherwise have been possible. (The promoters of Tramways (Metropolis) Bills were given leave accordingly to suspend further proceedings on their Bills, and to give notice if they would wish still to proceed in the next session: Commons *Journal*, 13 July 1871, vol. 126, p. 335.)
101 Morris, *op. cit.*, pp. 58–9 and 236. The 1871 Act was 34 & 35 Vict. c. 71.
102 *Journal*, vol. 125, p. 71. Mr Charles Buxton was Liberal M.P. for East Surrey, and Mr Thomas Hughes the Liberal M.P. for Frome. Buxton, however, died shortly afterwards on 10 August 1871. (A year earlier he had survived being shot at by a former employee: see H.C. Deb. 3rd series, vol. 200, cols. 2060–61.)
103 Queen Victoria's speech to Parliament on 21 August 1871 said of this measure 'The Local Government Board Act will, I trust, prepare the way for important sanitary and administrative improvements'. Commons *Journal*, p. 446; Lords *Journal*, p. 683.
104 The Local Government Board Act 1871 was 34 & 35 Vict. c. 70. The number of Local Boards reached its zenith in 1873 at 721; 419 had been created under the 1848 Act and the other 302 under the 1858 Act.
105 35 & 36 Vict. c. 79, section 3. The Rt. Hon. George Sclater-Booth, then M.P. for Hampshire North, who had been President of the Local Government Board from 1874 to 1880, reflected on *Local Government in Rural Districts* in an Address delivered on Friday 25 August 1882 to the 52nd Meeting of the British Association

for the Advancement of Science at Southampton; see *Transactions of Section F*, pp. 631–36.
106 Christine Bellamy, *Administering Central-Local Relations, 1871–1919: The Local Government Board in its Fiscal and Cultural Context* (1988), p. 33. Goschen transferred to the Admiralty from 24 March 1871.
107 38 & 39 Vict. c. 55.
108 Bellamy, *op. cit.*, p. 11.
109 Redlich and Hirst, *Local Government in England* (1903), vol. II, p. 300.
110 *Op. cit.*, vol. II, p. 227. There were innumerable instances of inconsistencies within adjoining areas, but perhaps the sheer volume and illogical diversity is best illustrated by Clifford's comment at p. 316 that 'Outside the City and Regent Street and Regent's Park, paving and cleansing were managed, in 1845, by no fewer than eighty-four separate bodies of commissioners, at whose instance at least 129 Acts of Parliament had been passed since 1829'.
111 *Op. cit.*, vol. II, p. 517.
112 Theodore Martin, *Notes on the Present System of Private Bill Legislation* (1872, J.B. Nichols and Sons, 25 Parliament Street, p. 9). Martin was head of Martin and Leslie, Parliamentary agents, and also author of *The Life of the Prince Consort*; he was later knighted.

5 The texts and technicalities of local legislation

There has been virtually no analysis nor study of the local legislation of the mid-Victorian years that attempts systematically to portray its content, in terms of both scope and drafting. Monographs dealing with one or more urban centres (usually in the north of England), or with specific industries like gas or water, do not convey impressions or conclusions that can safely be scaled up to generalise about local Acts overall. Nor do they, in narrating the events in a particular town in particular circumstances, necessarily present those events against the wider raft of practice and precedent of which competent Parliamentary agents of those days – and of course those who sat in Parliament itself – would, or should, have been aware. Promoting Bills in the face of local opposition was costly and uncertain enough; there was no point in complaining that clauses were struck out by a Select Committee if they were poorly drafted, or tried to secure novel provisions that clearly ran against the tenor of the times.[1]

This book seeks to provide that systematic portrayal of local legislation as a whole for the first time. Appendix 1 lists all the Bills that come within our definition, and makes clear those which received royal assent – 83 per cent, the great majority – and those that did not. This chapter and Chapter 6 divide considerations of the topics and texts of local legislation into two parts. First, this chapter provides insight into how those at Westminster regarded the Bills deposited with them from a technical viewpoint, and also provides – as an exemplar broadly typical of the years 1858–72 – more detailed consideration of the 14 local Acts passed in the session of 1863, which of course would tend to be seen by the Parliamentary authorities as a body of contemporary material rather than as a more or less random assembly of municipal promotions. Following that comes further analysis of the structure and 'apparatus' of the legislation; considering how the powers obtained were given; how what was permitted was to be paid for; and what constraints were imposed. Chapter 6 then considers the nature and scope of the powers themselves – the perceived local need for, or desirability of, which had provided the rationales for promotions in individual circumstances. Knowledge of the structure, scope and content of these local Acts is important, not only for the light it throws on the processes and content of what was after all a major (even if so far largely unremarked) aspect of Victorian constitutional activity, but also for the source material they provide for historians working on the health, industry, urbanisation and general context of local communities during a pivotal period of the nineteenth century.

The practice in drafting

Such is the mass and apparent diversity of local legislation that it may be thought to comprise a largely uncoordinated mass of provisions, possessing some themes and similarities but essentially the product of local demands and desires.[2] Systematic scrutiny, however, contradicts any such assumption; there are indeed some unusual or unique provisions, but as a whole the 278 local Acts on the statute book within our period 1858–72 (set out in Appendix 1, and analysed in this and the following chapter) reveal the consistency of approach that Lord Redesdale,[3] and others serving on and for the Select Committees, worked hard to achieve. Nevertheless, variations – sometimes small, but often significant and widely divergent in style and approach – commonly appear in the drafting of essentially familiar and repetitive sets of provisions, and while sometimes it is evident that this is to accommodate some particular individual circumstance, there is often no obvious reason. Different draftsmen, working for different Parliamentary agents, no doubt had their own styles; many different Select Committees deliberated on the Bills, and in most years the sheer bulk of material probably encouraged the Chairman of Committees and the House authorities concerned to focus mainly on those clauses or provisions that really mattered. Some flexibility and variation, in small and often incidental things, was not incompatible with broad conformity in the drafting of substantive proposals that had either intrinsic importance or were of potential significance for precedent.

Superficial comparison of the 1847 Clauses Consolidation Acts with subsequent 'special Acts' reveals apparently repetitive material about making works; taking lands; breaking open streets; laying and ownership of the necessary pipes; and so on. Careful analysis for the first time, however, reveals that while sometimes promoters found it helpful to have all the powers they needed consolidated in one place – found more commonly later in the period under review here, as earlier adoptions and enactments accumulated – in general the variations were sought to provide for gaps or shortcomings in existing legislation, or to complement existing provisions by supplemental powers required to make the Bill's objectives easier to achieve.

Whatever may be said about a broad consistency in relation to the Acts cannot necessarily be said of all the relevant Bills that were annually deposited in Parliament. Questioning his Counsel in a Select Committee hearing on *Parliamentary Agency* on 6 July 1876, Lord Redesdale asked Joseph Henry Warner whether he found 'a very great difference in the way in which Bills are prepared by different agents', receiving the reply 'Very great indeed'.[4] Warner added 'I have before me several examples of very badly drawn Bills'. In reference to two drafted in a rush to meet the session deadline, Lord Penrhyn asked 'Did they come before the Committee in that shape?' to be told 'No, they were much altered, in compliance with Lord Redesdale's directions ... a Bill once introduced in a bad shape can hardly be got into a satisfactory shape afterwards; it is a very difficult thing to manage'.[5] The Counsel to the Speaker, George Kettilby Rickards, similarly differentiated the good agents from the not so good based on his 25 years' experience: it was his 'duty to read and consider all the Bills that are deposited' and he confirmed that 'very frequently indeed' he had to have conferences with agents whose Bills appeared to him to require amendment.[6]

The practice in 1876 had evidently become much more exacting in the previous four decades: giving evidence to the Select Committee on Private Business on 15 July 1839, John Tyrrell, 'an eminent conveyancer' as the Report called him, whose letter to the Committee was printed as an Appendix, had been asked by Sir James Graham M.P. 'Does not each Private Bill, with all its clauses, undergo a certain scrutiny now in each House of Parliament?' He replied,

> Very little; every Private Bill, with reference to the clauses of which I have been speaking, so far as the public is concerned, undergoes no scrutiny except by Lord Shaftesbury, who is in the habit of saying, 'Take the usual clauses'.[7]

Tyrrell was then asked about the possibility of a defect being found in what were called 'the Standing Order Clauses' and what happened: 'does not the knowledge of such reach those interested in the preparation of the Standing Order clauses?' He responded

> sometimes, but they are not amended; and it is difficult to get any amendment of other usual clauses; Lord Shaftesbury does not like to admit amendments in a particular Bill: if counsel, in whom he had confidence, were to draw and send him new clauses to get rid of defects, without reference to any particular Bill, he would, I apprehend, consider them, and if they met with his approbation, would cause them to be adopted in future Bills; but then no one is interested in undertaking the labour of preparing such clauses.[8]

Accordingly, as we venture into more detailed consideration of what provisions were promoted in 1858 and beyond, and how those desired provisions were drafted, we must bear in mind that Bills as first deposited sometimes varied greatly from the versions of Bills that eventually received the royal assent. This was not only because Parliament declined to grant the powers sought, but often also because the Parliamentary authorities considered that their framing left much to be desired. Considerable resources and technical and procedural expertise had then to be expended if such Bills were to proceed.

Where the more experienced agents were concerned, this was far less of a problem.[9]

The notion that Bill Committees expended much energy in amending and correcting what came before them is not the only picture of their approach that recent commentators have given; writing in *The International Journal of Regional and Local Studies*, Garrard and Goldsmith assert that

> Over the decades [after 1835], municipal functions steadily expanded, partly via powers offloaded permissively or obligatorily by central government, more extensively for activist councils by local improvement Acts. But this latter route was hazardous, exposing municipalities to the fractious behaviour of parliamentary private bill committees, who could amend clauses, delete whole sections, or totally ravish what came before them. Sometimes this was due to aristocratic anti urban hauteur, more frequently due to committee susceptibility to pressure, particularly from local propertied groups.

There may well have been occasions when decisions were open to question, and the standards or ethics of the Parliamentary process fell short of those assumed in the various Select Committee reports on private Bill procedure; Garrard and Goldsmith, however, quote no example of any Bill or allegation where this capricious and jaundiced behaviour occurred,[10] and as a description of the overall local Bill process it seems at least unbalanced. A final verdict would require detailed examination – in practice more or less unachievable – of every local Bill deposited over many decades, comparisons of their texts with those of the subsequent Acts where the Bills were passed, and trawling for whatever local and other sources could be found to assess why it was that the particular changes or exclusions were made.

Private Acts are generally under-appreciated as a hugely rich source for local history. To leaf, for example, through the 745 Acts for 1865 (382) and 1866 (363) – following which an economic downturn much reduced the numbers[11] – is to be transported back to the frenetic climate of those years when literally hundreds of railway Bills were put forward, and the systematic characteristic they shared was not about a comprehensive and efficient national network (there was no such concept), but all about a race to invest and anticipate profits. The Caledonian Railway Company, for instance, promoted eight separate Bills in 1865 alone, and a ninth jointly with the Scottish Central Railway Company. In 1866 they promoted no fewer than ten Bills, plus a further joint one with the Scottish North Eastern Railway Company, though six of these ten were marked '*Not proceeded with*' in *Vacher's List of Private Bills*, and only three of their own plus the joint one later received royal assent. Some Acts illuminate well-remembered developments: Southport, for instance took powers to make new streets and widen existing ones in an Act[12] that received royal assent on 29 June 1865, but a few miles along the coast and a week later, on 5 July, Blackpool's Local Board of Health – reciting that 'the Population of the District and the Resort of Visitors to *Blackpool* have greatly increased, and the Streets of the Town are frequently inconveniently crowded' – obtained powers to construct what became the famous Blackpool Promenade.[13]

Companies named their initial directors in local Acts; commissioners were first appointed by Act of Parliament; and there were thousands of references to individual landowners – some august, but many certainly not so – whose lands were to be taken, or to be protected, or who were the 'owners or reputed owners' of properties subject to compulsory purchase. Schedules to the Westminster Improvement and Incumbered Estate Act 1865[14] set out 28 pages of these, and of occupiers too. Another especially noteworthy example comes from Scotland: the Aberdeenshire Roads Act 1865[15] contains only a modest two pages of preamble and an apparently unremarkable 91 sections. Section 7, however, runs for five pages, defining in detail the turnpike roads in the county. These five pages are then followed by 35 pages of schedules; they name hundreds of subscribers and the amounts of their subscriptions that are to be extinguished, their current valuations, the names of creditors, and so on. All this kind of information, moreover, will have been compiled with care – promoters had to prove compliance with standing orders, and had to survive scrutiny during the Parliamentary process, so that the reliability of whatever is recited or included is likely to be very high. This chapter now considers the regions from where promotions came, before giving detailed scrutiny to the provisions that were successfully obtained.

The sources of promotions

The origins of the 335 Bills from 1858–72, defined here as local in themselves, provide an interesting analysis of the scale and places of origin of local promotions. If an indicative line is drawn from the Mersey through and including Nottingham to the Wash, then 165, almost exactly half (49.25 per cent), of the Bills originated from authorities to the north. Rather more than another quarter were from Wales and the south (28.36 per cent), and the remainder from what we now call the Greater London area (22.39 per cent). Of the 335 Bills, 278 were enacted and 57 were not. Only 19, a third of these 57, came from the north – and of those, one (Tonge in 1861) was merged with Middleton and enacted anyway, and six more came from Sheffield in 1870 and 1872. Accordingly rather more than half of all the relevant local Acts of the period were promoted from the north of England.

Accepting London as a special case, this preponderance of northern over southern and Welsh promotions is more than a matter of which of the regions had the majority. The growth of industry and railways, and with it of both population and pollution, was particularly concentrated across south Lancashire and west and south Yorkshire, with their concentrations of coal mining, the cotton towns, and iron, steel, chemical and glass plants. Population density, together with growing economic strength and accompanying civic confidence, all combined to make living conditions for the new workforces unhealthy and intolerable. They also gave municipal leaders the business cases, and no doubt often also the religious or moral cases, to seek to do something about those conditions in a climate where Parliament had traditionally been disinclined to legislate across the country, but could be persuaded to allow local initiative. While intolerable conditions, as we have already seen,[16] were certainly not unique to industrialised areas, neither their sheer scale nor the rapidity of population growth had been experienced before.

Unsurprisingly Liverpool and Manchester, and the towns around them, feature repetitively in the lists of annual Bills set out in Appendix 1. The numbers are of course partly a function of what powers they had already obtained, but in the years 1858–72 Liverpool alone promoted 15 Bills, and Manchester 12, while Birmingham promoted only two. In addition, detailed comparisons of what was sought, and generally granted, in Parliament is instructive: the larger authorities tended to promote and run their own gas and water undertakings, for instance, whereas in most towns the companies established to run these utilities were private entities incorporated by Parliament at the behest of local businessmen. Northern industrial towns naturally sought powers that they felt particularly necessary for their areas: at a practical level, for instance, all five towns that between 1865 and 1869 prohibited the thatching of houses (Barrow-in-Furness, Farnworth, Oldham, St. Helens and Southport[17]) were the sorts of places where sparks and cinders from industrial premises were all too likely to be serious fire risks for the terraced houses built nearby, and even though all five employed different Parliamentary agents, it is easy to imagine that they copied such provisions from each other. Many larger conurbations were acquiring in the 1860s and 1870s the bases of municipal 'empires' that would grow and endure for at least the next hundred years, and whether their motivation was sheer necessity, or an admixture of 'civic boosterism',[18] they were prepared to spend the very considerable resources that were required to journey south to persuade small Select Committees that they were fit to be allowed to raise local taxes and spend public money on things that the general law did not permit.

The example of the 1863 local Acts

An overview of the session of 1863–26 & 27 Victoria in legislative terms – serves as an exemplar for the 15 years that are the subject of this study. In the middle of the period covered, 1863 was an average year for the promotion of private Bills generally: considering a single year allows analysis in terms of factors other than those purely relating to drafting or technical matters. Some 381 were deposited in that year (or session). It was also an average year for local Bills within our definition; there were 14 such (set out in Appendix 1), and all 14 were passed (though two were printed as public Acts). No such local Bills failed to receive royal assent. Of these 14, 6 came from the Midlands and north of England, 5 from the south, 2 from London and 1 from

Wales – proportions not dissimilar to those for the whole 1858–72 period set out on page 144 above. Together as passed, the 14 Acts comprised 604 sections (and a few schedules, sometimes separately numbered, and sometimes divided into parts). Their average of just over 43 sections per Act in this year was typical for local Bills generally, varying between 9 (Cambridge) and 114 (Rotherham and Kimberworth), though that of course is at best merely a broad indicator since sections were not of consistent length. No analysis of this kind of the local statute book has been published hitherto.

Four Acts (Rugby, Sowerby Bridge, Manchester, and Rotherham and Kimberworth) provided new or additional waterworks powers. They successively received royal assent over the course of two months, on 11 May, 8 June, 22 June and 13 July 1863 respectively. Manchester had already promoted a good deal of legislation, and as a community differed in nature from the other three. Rugby's Act, however, is typical. Essentially it gave (along with some incidental provisions) powers to the Local Board of Health to appoint a water committee; to break up streets under Local Board control without notice; to make new waterworks according to deposited plans; to lay pipes; to supply water; to supply domestic water at a fixed rate and non-domestic water by agreement; to prevent and penalise waste of water; to provide, read and remove water meters; to avoid liability if water pressure or supply were not consistent; and to borrow or re-borrow money on mortgage for the purposes of the Act. The others also needed very similar powers, depending to some degree on what they already possessed from earlier legislation. No reservoir was provided for at Rugby, but both Manchester and Rotherham and Kimberworth gave the justices strong powers to act promptly if it was reported to them that the reservoir was in a dangerous state; they could have it inspected, get work done and penalise the Local Board for failure to act.[19] Certain landowner rights, and local railway company land rights, were preserved, and it was provided that taking water on contract did not disqualify anyone under the Act who might otherwise be deemed to have a conflict of interest.

What is noticeable about all the foregoing provisions – except the specific identity of those whose interests were to be safeguarded – is that none of them was essentially *local* or unique to the community whose Local Board was promoting these additional powers. They could have been deemed incorporated, as the Waterworks Clauses Consolidation Act 1847 was deemed to be incorporated, by a single section in each Act. The degree of difference between the relevant sets of provisions that each promoter was granted was very small. In Rotherham and Kimberworth, they obtained an explicit power to pay for new works by means of levying 'The Improved Waterworks Rate' as it was called.[20] At Sowerby Bridge they were granted the power to supply water for washing the outside of houses.[21] Neither of these provisions appeared in the other Acts: they were partly a sign, no doubt, of the need to justify by explicit statutory detail, actions that would in later years be readily regarded as incidental to the principal powers of the Act in question. They were more powerfully indicative, however, of just how much statutory footage could have been saved by development of the Clauses Consolidation Acts of the mid-1840s,[22] and how, by leaving matters to local initiative, both government and Parliament ensured that the laborious and wasteful process of promoting, justifying and promulgating repetitive provisions, that public policy had already many times approved, would continue.

Some variations of the Clauses Consolidation Acts were minor in textual terms, but potentially significant for the promoters. Section XXVIII of the Waterworks Clauses Act 1847, for instance, gave powers for undertakers to break up streets, but section XXX required three clear days' prior notice. Section 11 of the Rugby Waterworks Act 1863, however, relieved the Local Board of the obligation to give that notice. Section XI of the 1847 Act set limits on lateral deviations from deposited works (ten yards in default of any other prescribed), whereas section 18 at Rugby and section 23 of the Rotherham and Kimberworth Local Board of Health Act 1863 (to quote two of very many examples) also provided for vertical deviation: 3 feet upwards and 5 feet downwards for reservoirs at Rugby and 5 feet otherwise, and 3 feet either way for reservoirs and 5 feet otherwise at Rotherham and Kimberworth. These apparently minor and inconsequential variations might be significant, according to local circumstances, in giving more scope to the promoters – or perhaps in providing more certainty to adjoining landowners whose objections had to be negotiated or removed for the powers to be granted at all. Again, section LXI of the 1847 Act provided a maximum £5 penalty for throwing rubbish into streams, reservoirs, aqueducts and waterworks used for supply; section 45 of the Sowerby Bridge Local Board Act 1863 provided quite similarly for the rivers Calder and Ryburn, but increased the penalty maximum to £20.

As stated above, while superficial comparison of the 1847 Clauses Consolidation Act with subsequent 'special Acts' does reveal apparently repetitive material, variations provided for gaps or shortcomings in existing legislation, or to make a Bill's objectives easier to achieve. The four Acts for Rugby, Sowerby Bridge, Manchester, and Rotherham and Kimberworth did nevertheless contain some provisions taking different approaches in what seem similar circumstances. Where compulsory purchase powers were granted, it was usual to specify the maximum period within which they might be exercised, and time limits too might be set for the completion of capital works. At Rugby, that time limit was 5 years,[23] the same as for compulsory purchase at Sowerby Bridge.[24] At Rotherham and Kimberworth, however, 10 years was allowed for the works, and 7 for compulsory purchase,[25] while Manchester had only 3 years to exercise their compulsory powers.[26] There were also some provisions where the variation was more apparent than real: section 7 of the Rugby Act, for instance, stated that 'This Act shall be executed by the Local Board with the Powers and Indemnities and according to the Provisions of the Public Health Acts' with the side-note reading 'Act to be executed by Local Board'. Section 7 of the Sowerby Bridge Act used exactly the same wording, but with quotation marks round 'The Public Health Acts', the side-note reading 'Act to be put in execution by Local Board'. This variation contained no subtlety of intent or meaning – it was simply a slightly different way of saying the same thing. So too was section 3 of the Rotherham and Kimberworth Act, which began 'Subject to the express provisions of this Act, this Act shall be executed by the Board, with the Powers and Indemnities and according to the Provisions of the Public Health Acts' and the side-note was shortened to just 'Act to be executed by Board'. This was possible because section 2 defined the term 'the Board' to mean the Local Board of Health, so that repetition of the word 'Local' was unnecessary. Nevertheless, it was still felt necessary to add the words 'as a Body Corporate' to section 10 when providing that all property and associated rights were to vest in the Board. The Act in fact contained no significant 'express provisions' to the contrary about carrying it into effect – this could only refer to the powers of justices about reservoir safety in sections 25–35.

The four Acts, the subject of the preceding paragraph, exemplified a typical set of communities at this period, seeking broadly similar powers for quite similar purposes. Not all Local Boards, indeed, were corporate bodies. Where they were created and elected from a district 'exclusively consisting of the whole or part of one corporate borough' by section XII of the Public Health Act 1848, and that council was accordingly able to 'exercise and execute the powers, authorities, and duties', corporate identity already existed, though the Board still required a distinct common seal. The Local Board of a non-corporate district had, however, to sue and be sued in the name of the clerk under section CXXXVIII; section XXXV laid down that they would still have a seal, but that validity also necessitated five Board member signatures. Local Act provisions about the capacity in which the responsible legal *persona* would carry the Act into effect were therefore not mere surplusage. The Northampton Waterworks Act 1861,[27] for instance, promoted by the Northampton Waterworks Company, defined 'the Town Council', 'the Town Commissioners', and 'the Local Board' as three separate entities, although the extent to which their membership was in practice distinct and unconnected was debatable. In another example from that year, the water supply contracts for Neath could be made between the company 'and the corporation acting by their council, and either as a municipal corporation, or as a local board for the district of Neath, or in both capacities'. Not only was this covering both possibilities, but 'the consent of two thirds of the members of the Council of the said Corporation' was also required.[28]

More pertinent, however, than small variations in drafting might be differences about how the costs were to be met of promoting the Bill that had now received royal assent (usually the subject of an Act's last section). As we have seen in Chapter 4,[29] the consequences could be severe of reaching the end of a promotion process without both the means to pay the costs incurred and the lawful authority to spend that money. The bodies obtaining Acts at Rugby, Sowerby Bridge and Rotherham and Kimberworth were all statutory

Local Boards of Health, but their authorisations to pay for their Bills were not expressed in the same terms. At Rugby (section 52),

> All the Costs, Charges, and Expenses of and preparatory and incident to the Surveys, Investigations, and Proceedings of the Local Board, with respect to obtaining Water, and the obtaining and passing of this Act, or otherwise in relation thereto, shall be paid by the Local Board out of any Monies which they have or may receive under the provisions of this Act or of the Public Health Acts.

At Sowerby Bridge (section 55),

> All the Costs, Charges, and expenses of and incident to the applying for and the obtaining and the passing of this Act, or otherwise in relation thereto, shall be paid by the Local Board out of any Monies they may have or receive under the Provisions of this Act, or of 'The Sowerby Bridge Gas Act, 1861', or of 'The Public Health Acts'.

Whereas at Rotherham and Kimberworth (section 114) it was simply provided that

> All the Costs, Charges, and Expenses attending or incident to the preparing, applying for, and passing of this Act shall be paid by the Board out of any Money now in their Hands, or to be received by them under this Act or any Act incorporated therewith.

Again, the last is the most concise form of words, but actually the sources for the lawful payment of promotions costs were to be the same in all three cases (Sowerby Bridge having also gas as well as water powers in their Act). Each local Act has accordingly to be examined to check whether differing forms of words actually stipulated different forms of financial provision; this would have been important to ensure not only that promotion costs were paid, but also that this was done from public funds in a lawful manner not open to challenge. Anyone who had objected to the Bill's promotion was likely to be vigilant in ensuring that the financial provisions it made were scrupulously respected.

All 14 local Acts of 1863 contained – as would be expected – a power to pay the expenses of the Act; in the Coventry Market House Act,[30] however, it was contained in section 12 (about the application of income from the Market House) rather than in a discrete section at the end. The Exeter Gaol Act[31] costs were first to be paid from the City Rate or City Fund, but to be repaid thereto out of the proceeds of sale of the City Gaol that it was the primary purpose of the Act to permit. St. John's College was to pay the whole promotion costs for what became the Cambridge Street Act.[32] These two latter cases involved peculiarly local circumstances, but the general principle is clearly that the costs of promotion were to be found from the benefits or rate income that would be derived from the exercise of the additional powers being sought. There was no general power or presumption that such costs could simply be taken from existing municipal funds or income sources. That principle is applicable to all the local Acts, not only of 1863 but of all the Parliamentary sessions within the scope of this work.

In addition to the four mainly water-related Acts, there were three more local Acts in 1863 that all conform to what we may expect of local legislation for that purpose at that time. The principal purpose of the Swansea Municipal Corporation Act,[33] to quote its long title, was 'to confer ... further Powers for the Improvement and Regulation of the Markets and Fairs in the said Borough'. Much of the Markets and Fairs Act 1847 was incorporated,[34] certain existing local legislation was replaced, and the new Act gave powers to appoint committees, erect a new cattle market and slaughterhouses, and to collect all the various tolls. In addition, there were four sections 52–55 regulating music and dancing premises, forbidding beer shops unless so licensed to have internal communications 'without passing into a public Thoroughfare', and penalising brothel keeping. A provision about the Corporation giving up the lease of the Garden and Postern of Swansea castle, one abolishing the Burrows and Greenhill fairs, and another about what were known as Town and Quay Dues were all special to Swansea,[35] but little else was so, apart from saving individual rights. The same was true of the Coventry Market House Act, already mentioned above. It gave power to erect a market house, with the associated provisions about acquiring the land; borrowing money on mortgage; forbidding anyone else to trade in the street except an auctioneer or public hawker; and of course to collect the tolls. Much of the legal mechanics of this were the same as at Swansea.

The third Act in this group was the Birkenhead Improvement Act of 88 sections.[36] Again it is a typical improvement Act of its time – powers to construct a Town Hall; to lay down street tramways and regulate minor highways matters about carriage crossings across footpaths, penalising driving across footways, and the like; new streets work; cleansing and public health powers about such things as privies in factories and keeping drains and cesspools properly, and for factories to consume their own smoke; and (in section 19) the power to appoint a Medical Officer of Health and pay 'such Salary as shall be approved of by One of Her Majesty's Principal Secretaries of State'. The power to make a higher night charge for the Woodside Ferry was genuinely local; so was a provision about Ferry Debt,[37] but for the rest there was nothing in the Act which – had you not known its title – would have identified it as being about Birkenhead and nowhere else.

Four of the remaining 5 of the 14 local Acts of 1863 seem genuinely local in the sense that their provisions were special to their locality and unlikely to be replicated elsewhere, at least contemporaneously. The Blackfriars Bridge Act[38] was made urgent by Bazalgette's plan for the Thames ('Whereas Blackfriars Bridge is in a dangerous State, and it is anticipated that the Safety thereof will be affected by the Embankment about to be constructed along the Northern Side of the River Thames...'). Exeter Gaol Act (the short title did not include 'The') was obtained to authorise the keeping of prisoners from the city gaol in the county gaol. The Southampton Harbour Act constituted the Southampton Harbour and Pier Board, and while some of its scope to do with tolls and tonnages was precedented elsewhere, there were also a number of special provisions about the Pier (such as not keeping any inn or hotel on it, or allowing any carriages drawn by steam along it).[39] The Cambridge Street Act made specific provisions about closing or widening existing passages and streets, and vesting certain resulting land in St. John's College for building. The other Act, the City of London Traffic Regulation Act 1863[40] was local, too, in the obvious sense of being peculiar to the City, even if the principle of regulating traffic could not be said to be unlikely to be replicated elsewhere.

We have seen in Chapter 4[41] that it was the attitude of central government that local communities and councils at this time should be required to decide and claim for themselves the powers and possibilities that they wanted in order to regulate and improve their areas. That may explain the need for their frequent approaches to Parliament; it scarcely justifies, however, the extent to which local authorities had to expend resources on provisions that were so often repetitive of what had gone before. The Clauses Consolidation Acts had been passed in the 1840s, and the advent of Provisional Orders did simplify to some extent the process of granting local provisions. Provisional Orders, though, were largely formulaic, both in their structure and content; that is, essentially they re-covered in another community or authority standard ground already covered elsewhere in other communities or authorities. If a Local Board or a corporation required a special provision, unique to them or unlikely to be repeated in similar terms elsewhere, that was unlikely to be secured without a local Act.

In 1863, the quantity of material in seven (the four for water-related powers plus those for Swansea, Coventry and Birkenhead) of the 14 local Acts that could be described as special or local in this way was remarkably small – just a few sections. All the rest of the 448 sections enacted in those seven statutes could be found in other similar local Acts dealing with powers about water supply, markets, improvements and cleansing powers, and so on. A large percentage of the clauses that the promoted Bills contained could have been applied or incorporated by a few words to that effect, drawing on already enacted general powers in standard form and so reducing the expense of promotion, the bulk of the statute book, and the growing diversity (in some cases as we have seen, superficial and pointless diversity) of the law from one place to another. There would still have been occasions where unique provisions were required, or some special local circumstance justified the differing of the law in Rugby from that in Sowerby Bridge; further Clauses Consolidation Acts, however, would have achieved for local Acts in the 1860s what those of the 1840s achieved for the railways, for gas and water companies, for markets and town improvements, and other cases. Of course, those 1840s Acts

152   *The texts and technicalities*

were not of universal application: they were applicable only where there was a 'special Act', which rendered them so. Nevertheless, there must be a sense of avoidable yet wasted resource about so much of the local statute book during this period we are studying, and this must be set beside what Joseph Warner stated to Lord Redesdale about the lack of conformity and care with which so many local Bills were apparently drafted.[42]

The local Acts of 1863 are typical of the sessions of this time, displaying variety of drafting, and sometimes also of substance, but set against an overall background of conformity with precedent and the expectations born of the recent experiences of Parliamentary agents. By 1870 there was more local legislation passed each year, and increasing instances of consolidating Acts, but the same general statement about their approach and content held good. The circumstances and examples described in this section provide a paradigm for the following analysis of the technical and constitutional content of local legislation – that is, the legislative *means* – to be followed in Chapter 6 by consideration of the scope of the substantive powers which promoters were seeking when they came to Westminster – their legislative *ends*. This is a critical distinction which categorises the thousands of provisions in the 278 local Acts passed between 1858 and 1872 studied in this work.

The legislative means: the structure and *vires* of Bills

A significant proportion of most Bills consisted of clauses which, while necessary to the overall technical acceptability and ultimate effectiveness of the measure, probably appeared to promoters to be incidental to their principal purposes in coming to Parliament at all. The Swansea Local Board of Health Act 1872,[43] for instance, is relatively succinct with just 24 sections and one schedule. It was obtained 'to provide for certain of [the Board's] existing debts by the issue of Annuities and Debenture Stock; and for other purposes'. Section 7 provided for that – and later on there were also unconnected powers in section 23 to buy up certain river water rights from the Duke of Beaufort. The other 22 sections provide supporting material in order to make the Act legally effective, to deal with past provisions and rights, and to ensure proper administration and record-keeping. Finally (section 24), the costs of obtaining the Act were to be paid for out of the Swansea Borough Fund. Those supporting provisions involve the Act's title, a statement that the Board might carry it into effect, how certain terms were defined or other statutory provisions incorporated, and so on. In other words, the *ends* of the resulting Act were expressed in just two sections, but the *means* of getting there required 22 other sections (and one schedule of two forms to be used). The proportions of ends and means sections were even more extreme than those of the Swansea Municipal Corporation Act 1863[33] referred to above, and illustrate the same point for the same locality even more starkly.

Local Acts almost invariably included sections at the outset that would follow the preamble, provide a short title and define terms, and – most importantly – give the promoting authority the power to carry the Act into effect: 'Act to be executed by Local Board' as the side-note to section 2 of the Swansea Local Board of Health Act 1872 puts it. Repetition of this power might not be necessary if the Act in question merely amended an earlier Act where it had already been provided, or fitted into it in some way, but otherwise it was necessary to state explicitly that Parliament was giving whichever local authority the power – and indeed the duty – to carry the Act's provisions into effect. The words used to effect this, while achieving the same outcome, are indicative of the typical local legislation characteristic of diversity of approach within conformity of purpose (well precedented principle, if you like), but even so display unexpectedly wide variety across different Acts.

Moreover, not all promoting authorities started from the same point in legal terms; some were long-established corporations, now deriving their constitutional legitimacy and much of the authorisation for their formal operations and transactions (apart from royal charters) from the Municipal Corporations Act of 1835 and its succeeding Acts. (Section XXV of the 1835 Act constituted the mayor, alderman and councillors of a borough as together constituting its council.) Others were Local Boards of Health, originally created under the Public Health Act 1848 and Local Government Act 1858, and with differing levels of already adopted powers under those enactments. Others were different kinds of bodies again – and indeed (as referred to above in discussing the local Acts of the 1863 session) neither all the continuing municipal corporations after 1858, nor all the Local Boards of Health, necessarily had come into being as corporate bodies. (See for instance the examples of the chartered borough Hedon[109] and the Wallasey Local Board below.[44]) Section XXIV of the Public Health Act 1848 constituted as Local Boards the mayor, aldermen and burgesses acting by the council in corporate boroughs; boards of improvement commissioners where they existed; and 'In other places, such number of elective members as may be determined by a resolution of the owners and ratepayers'.

The subject of 'interpretation of terms' – the definitions used in a Bill or Act – demonstrates how even outcomes intended to be exactly the same could vary in the way they were expressed, and that Parliament, which could have insisted on greater uniformity in drafting, accepted those variations. In 1860, for instance, all four Acts at Norwich, Swansea, Macclesfield and Wigan set out that, unless the contrary were provided, the terms used were to have the same meanings as in the public Acts that were incorporated with them.[45] All four, however, had different Parliamentary agents, and we can compare the results below –

NORWICH: Except as is by this Act expressly provided, the several Words and Expressions to which by the Acts wholly or partially incorporated with this Act Meanings are assigned have in this Act the same respective Meanings, unless there be in the Subject or Context something repugnant to or inconsistent with such Construction.

154   *The texts and technicalities*

SWANSEA: The several Words and Expressions to which by the Acts incorporated with this Act Meanings are assigned shall in this Act have the same respective Meanings, unless there be in the Subject or Context something repugnant to or inconsistent with such Construction.
MACCLESFIELD: The several Words and Expressions to which by the Acts incorporated with this Act Meanings are assigned have in this Act the same respective Meanings, unless there be in the Subject or Context something repugnant to or inconsistent with such Construction, or other Meanings be assigned to them by this Act.
WIGAN: The several Words and Expressions to which by any of the Acts incorporated herewith Meanings are assigned shall in this Act have the same respective Meanings, unless there be in the Subject or Context something repugnant to or inconsistent with such Construction.

The differences between these four sections were very small, carried no different nuances of meaning or intention, and yet allowed the four draftsmen and their promoters to express exactly what they wanted to say in their own way.

In some authorities, because of the way that Parliament had provided for Local Boards to be set up, the same membership constituted more than one legal entity, and consequently it was necessary for the local Act to contain two sections – one empowering the corporation to execute some of the provisions, and another empowering the Local Board of Health to execute others. That might be no mere technicality – it was likely that voters would have different numbers of votes to cast for these bodies, and certain that the different entities would have distinct legal powers to levy rates or borrow money, without which expenditure would be unlawful and void.

That unexpectedly wide variety referred to above can be illustrated by quoting another four examples. Section VI of the Lendal Bridge and York Improvement Act 1860[46] is succinct – 'The Corporation by the Council shall be and they are hereby empowered to carry this Act and the several Provisions thereof into execution'.

A very different approach was used in section 6 of the Oldham Borough Improvement Act 1865[47] –

This Act shall be carried into execution by the Corporation acting by the Council and according to the Municipal Corporation Acts and other Laws for the Time being affecting the Corporation, and with all the Authorities conferred by those Acts and Laws on the Corporation, and on the Council and Committees of the Council, and the Officers, Agents and Servants of the Corporation, with respect to Matters provided for or comprised in the Municipal Corporation Acts, and as nearly as may be in all respects as if the Powers, Duties and Property vested in, imposed on or enjoyed by the Corporation by or under this Act were vested in, imposed on, or enjoyed by them by or under the Municipal Corporation Acts.

The Leicester Improvement, Drainage, and Markets Act 1868[48] was one of the many that required two sections. Section 5 read –

> This Act so far as it is expressed to relate to the Powers of the Local Board shall (subject to the express provisions of this Act) be executed by the Corporation acting by the Council as the Local Board, with the Powers and Indemnities and according to the provisions of the Public Health Acts, which Acts shall in relation to the Corporation and the Purposes of this Act have effect as if the Purposes and Provisions of this Act were Purposes and Provisions of the Public Health Acts.

Section 6 then began 'This Act as far as it is expressed to relate to the powers of the Corporation shall be carried into execution ...' and (though drafted by different Parliamentary agents, so clearly working to precedent) continued in exactly the same elaborate terms as section 6 of the Oldham Act of the same session above, except that the 1868 version omitted the comma after the phrase '... Laws on the Corporation'. It was required in these empowering provisions not only that the local authority (and corporate body) concerned be specifically given the powers and duties enacted, but also that the Act should state *how* those powers and duties were to be executed, namely by the Council, or by the Council acting in a different legal capacity as the Local Board.

The shortest form, but still saying all that needed to be said in just 12 words, was that of section 4 of the Portsmouth Camber Quays Act 1868,[49] which simply stated that 'The Corporation acting by the Council shall carry this Act into effect'. A similarly direct provision (with a mix of capital and lower-case initial letters) was that of section 4 of the Salford Improvement Act 1870,[50] that 'The Corporation, by the council, are hereby empowered to carry this Act into execution'. Similar but slightly less succinct was section 6 of the Blackburn Improvement Act 1870[51] that 'The Corporation, by the council of the borough, shall be and they are hereby empowered to carry this Act into execution' – a slightly longer version of section 4 of the Park Lane Improvement Act 1869 whereby 'The Metropolitan Board of Works shall be and they are hereby empowered to carry this Act into execution'.[52] A different variant was used in section 4 of the Leeds Improvement Act 1869[53] that 'This Act shall be carried into execution by the corporation acting by the council of Leeds' – a plain English version that was not only shorn of legal verbiage but had also dropped all the capital letters hitherto traditionally printed for nouns. In section 4 of the Manchester Corporation Waterworks and Improvement Act 1869[54] the wording was 'The corporation, by the council, are hereby empowered to carry this Act and the several powers thereof into execution' – 'the several powers thereof' suggesting an abundance of caution that was neither necessary nor demonstrated in the succinct drafting of the section as a whole. Manchester used exactly the same wording in section 4 of the Manchester Improvement Act 1871,[55] and again in section 4 of the Manchester Corporation Waterworks and Improvement Act 1872,[56] except that the commas round the words 'by the council' had by then been dropped. Sherwood & Co. were the Parliamentary agents for both these Manchester Bills, but different agents had acted on all the others except for the interesting contrast that J. Dorington and Co. acted in the Bills cited here that contained both the longest form of this type of provision, at Oldham in 1865, and the shortest, at Portsmouth in 1868. Overall, however, a gradual – but not consistent – evolution towards more tightly drafted wording by the end of the 1860s is apparent, with the characteristics of statutes of earlier times – like a prolix style, and the use of Roman numerals and capital letters for nouns in the Germanic style – slowly becoming less the norm.

Is it significant, if all these varying forms were equally legally effective in bestowing on the Bills' promoters the powers they had sought and Parliament had granted, that they differed so much in style? At one level, apparently not – there seems to be no reported case where any authority was found to have not been given the capacity to use the powers that had supposedly been granted. It is, however, indicative of some of the realities of practical Bill promotion at this time. A much more likely ground for challenge, however, was provided for at Bolton; following a lengthy and now familiar section 133 establishing that the Act was to be executed by the Council, section 134 stated that –

> Every meeting of the council or of any committee of the council shall be presumed to have been duly convened and held, and all members of the council attending any such meeting shall be presumed to have been duly qualified.[57]

Had the Parliamentary authorities regarded it as important or essential that common, or at least basically consistent, wording was used for such technical provisions, they would surely have made that clear to promoting agents. Just as the Standing Orders were regularly reviewed and amended in the procedural context, so could drafting provisions have been. The principle of the various Common Clauses Acts of the 1840s[58] had, of course, already been well established, and could have been more widely extended. The evidence is, however – especially in years of very numerous promotions – that those in the Private Bill Office and sitting on the various Parliamentary Select Committees had more than enough work to do, and enough concerns about poorly drafted Bills generally, without worrying about style and variety in clauses that were in themselves both technically effective and unexceptionable in legal terms. We have seen at the outset of this chapter what in 1876 Lord Redesdale's Counsel thought of the quality of drafting in many of the Bills that he had to consider[59] – and in contrast we have also seen how relaxed Lord Shaftesbury was reported to have been about detailed drafting matters back in the 1830s.[7]

The prevalence of small drafting variations, however, did not go unnoticed outside Parliament. In 1871, a Memorandum was prepared at the Board of Trade, the Government Department responsible for provisional order applications for gas, water and tramways.[60] In October and November 1870, 52 applications – including those for Ireland and Scotland – had been received, of which 26 were for tramways, 12 for gas and 10 for water undertakings (with 3 not pursued). The Memorandum is of intrinsic interest in relation to these activities alone, but is noticed here primarily for the detailed scrutiny given to the differences between essentially similar applications. As the tendency to place more trust in municipal authorities grew as time went on, it observed that 'In comparing the Acts of last Session with the general Act of the preceding year, it will be found that the tendency is to give additional control to the local authorities'.[61] The 14 pages of the Memorandum provide a detailed critique of the relevant provisions, allowing – as in the following example – the unformed question 'why this disparity?' to come to the mind of the reader. Speaking of various Acts that transferred the ownership, for instance, of water companies, it states against the side-note 'Regulations' that –

> Eleven of these Acts confer powers more or less stringent upon the undertakers to make regulations for the prevention of waste and misuse of the water supplied by them, as a condition on which the supply is to be given. In some cases any difference as to whether the regulations are reasonable or have been complied with is to be decided by two justices, but in seven out of the eleven there appears to be no appeal from the decision of the undertakers.
>
> The Corporation of Burnley reserve to themselves the sole right of laying down all communication pipes at the expense of the consumer.[62]

By way of concluding summary, the Memorandum considered that –

> No material difference will be found in the principal provisions of the Acts and the Provisional Orders, and it is very desirable that such a general uniformity should, as far as possible, be maintained, in order that promoters may have no inducement to reject the mode of proceeding most suitable to the circumstances of each case, from any idea that better terms are to be obtained from one or the other.
>
> There will always be a large number of applications, *e.g.*, where compulsory powers are sought, or where there are strong competing interests, which must necessarily be proceeded with in the ordinary manner by Bill, but there appears to be no reason why Parliament, reserving to itself the hearing and adjudication of all important questions, and the final decision in all cases, should not require the promoters of schemes locally approved, and involving no serious principle, to adopt the means which have been provided for carrying out such proposals at a comparatively moderate cost, and thus lighten, to some extent, the heavy burden of private business which now falls on Parliamentary Committees.[63]

This latter paragraph has echoes of the arguments of long years before, about local inquiries, and whether it was acceptable in the interests of cost-saving for

158   *The texts and technicalities*

Parliament to concede the practical delegation of some of its present hearings.[64] To the extent that the former paragraph was a plea for precedent, conformity and consistency in drafting, it evidently did not find receptive ears. The variety and inconsistencies found in clauses and sections drafted to achieve identical or very similar purposes provides historians with evidence for the extent to which, while the process of authentication and enactment might be centralised and regulated through universally applicable Standing Orders, the process of generating and bringing it forward very definitely was not.

The legislative means: other powers and purposes

Bills contained many other powers of a structural or constitutional nature apart from the varied means of bestowing *vires* or validity described in the previous section above. Sometimes the borough was significantly extended, so bringing under their municipal direction areas previously outside the aegis of the promoters: this was the case at Middlesbrough in 1858[65] (where incidentally the centre line of a branch of the Stockton and Darlington Railway comprised part of the new boundary), and in consequence the Burial Board powers of the former Middlesbrough township were transferred and extended to the newly defined Local Board, which became the Burial Board for the township area.[66] At Halifax, as well as several sections elaborately defining the capacity and *vires* of the mayor, aldermen and burgesses, the 'fire engine establishment' (as the side-note called it) was transferred from them in their Local Board capacity to them in their Borough capacity.[67] At Wallasey in 1861, the Local Board required incorporation,[68] and at Farnworth the Local Board was created the Burial Board for the purposes of section 49 of the Local Government Act 1858,[69] while at Aberystwyth in 1872 the authority formally took the title 'The Aberystwyth Improvement Commissioners and Local Board'.[70] Darlington in 1861 took powers to purchase and abolish the office of Bailiff of the Borough.[71] Circumstances of a quite different character applied at Brecon in 1862, where – seemingly uniquely in our period – the Corporation was effectively bankrupt, and its market powers, undertaking and liabilities were taken over by the Brecon Markets Company.[72]

A number of Acts provided interesting insight into the negotiations and processes that preceded or accompanied the relevant Bill promotions – and were significant, as mentioned above, for the evidence they provided of the contrast between generally applicable Parliamentary Standing Orders governing the process of promotion and the wide diversity of local initiatives, politics and business deals that lay behind the appearance of any particular Bill in *Vacher*'s sessional lists. The Commons Select Committee considering the Sowerby Bridge Local Board of Health's Bill 268 in 1863 found its preamble not proved; the Board's area came within the scope of Halifax's water powers under an earlier Act, so that section 75 of the Public Health Act 1848 precluded the Committee's granting the proposed water powers that the Board was seeking. Nevertheless all was not lost: an agreement was reached between the Board and Halifax Corporation, and the amended Bill was passed.[73] At Cleckheaton in 1869 the Local Board petitioned against the Cleckheaton Gas Company's Bill 45, but it was subsequently agreed that the Local Board (subject to approval at a ratepayers' meeting) would buy the Company's undertaking, and the agreement was set out in the Cleckheaton Local Board Act 1870.[74] Such agreements did not always appear in Bills promoted by local authorities themselves: the schedule to the Mersey Docks (Liverpool River Approaches) Act 1871 comprised an agreement recording the terms on which Liverpool Corporation's earlier objections to proposals from the Mersey Docks and Harbour Board had been withdrawn.[75]

More unusual, considering the care that needed to be taken to pass Parliamentary Standing Orders and the critical scrutiny of both Select Committees and any objecting petitioners, were cases where statutory powers were prospectively granted to authorities that did not yet exist, or were granted subject to unfulfilled conditions. Perhaps the most extreme example of this was at Glossop, where no local authority existed at all, and yet powers were granted to the individuals who promoted the Glossop Water Bill 482 in 1865.[76] The Commissioners at Staines[77] obtained a provision that would confer the Act's market and town hall powers on the prospective Local Board if the Local Government Act 1858 were adopted for the current parish. For the avoidance of doubt, section XL of the London Railway Depôt and Storehouses Act 1862[78] provided that the Act would not be exempt from the contrary provisions of any other present or future Acts. On the other hand, assessment appeals to Quarter Sessions from Tranmere were to be final, with no certiorari to Westminster courts allowed.[79]

As well as the water powers referred to above, the Sowerby Bridge Local Board Act 1863 was notable for altering the qualifications for Board membership prescribed by the general law. Section XVI of the Public Health Act 1848 required residency in the relevant area or within seven miles, and also being possessed of real or personal property, or liable for rates, to the minimum levels prescribed by the relevant Order in Council or provisional order, not exceeding £1,000 or £30 respectively. For Sowerby Bridge those latter requirements[80] had been the standard £1,000 and £30 respectively; section 51 of their 1863 Act, however, fixed them instead at the lower levels of £500 or £15 rateable value. Generally, however, local Acts were careful to coordinate with, and not gainsay, the general law: it was usual for the provisions of the Municipal Corporations Act 1835, for instance, to be explicitly preserved and protected, as in section 366 of the Oldham Borough Improvement Act 1865,[81] stating that –

> Nothing in this Act shall take away or abridge any Right, Power, or Authority which the Corporation have or may enjoy under the Municipal Corporation Acts, or otherwise independently of this Act.

Middlesbrough, however, both appeared to respect, but in fact also amended, the 1835 Act in 1858 by obtaining a provision that where anything needing to

160 *The texts and technicalities*

be done under its terms would fall on a Sunday, the ensuing Monday should apply instead, and that also, in a somewhat extended provision –

> in every Case where, after any Meeting or Proceeding under any of the said Acts, Three clear Days Notice of any subsequent Meeting or Proceeding would be necessary, Two Days Notice thereof shall be sufficient in all Cases where less than Three Days intervene.[82]

Occasionally other authorities also sought to stipulate a minimum notice period for meetings. Just two clear days' notice sufficed for meetings of the Kings Lynn Paving Commissioners,[83] but for the Northampton Improvement Commissioners three clear days was stipulated.[84] Under section XXXIV of the Local Government Act 1858 it was for individual Local Boards to 'make byelaws with respect to the summoning, notice, place, management, and administration of ... meetings' and no minimum period of clear days' notice was prescribed.

Another important instance where authorities frequently sought to augment the general law concerned the appointment of committees. Section LXX of the Municipal Corporations Act 1835 had enabled 'the Council of any Borough' to appoint committees 'out of their own body', and gave wide powers to fix the purposes and size at discretion, 'Provided always', however, 'that the Acts of every such Committee shall be submitted to the Council for their approval'. Section XXXVI of the Local Government Act 1858 also provided for committees; that Act of course applied only to Local Boards of Health and not to municipal corporations or other local bodies, and there was similarly no power to delegate executive action; it was stipulated that 'the acts of every such committee shall be submitted to the said Local Board for their approval'. Accordingly in local Bills it was necessary not only to ensure that the appointment of committees would be inherently lawful if the Bill were not promoted by a Local Board – not an issue presumably if the 1835 Act powers applied – but also in some cases that they would have full authority to transact business validly in their own right – that is, with 'delegated' or 'plenary' powers as they are generally termed – so that their recommendations would not have to be referred to a full local authority meeting for confirmation and validity. In some local Acts Parliament provided not just the *power*, but rather the *duty*, to appoint a committee. The Halifax Park and Improvements Act 1858[85] required the Corporation annually to appoint a standing committee 'for the Management and Regulation of the Park'; even more specifically, the Corporation at Kings Lynn were obliged to appoint the Mayor and four other Council members as the Water Committee.[86] At Rugby, five also comprised the Water Committee (there was no mayor, this being a Local Board of Health), and the Local Board could in its discretion delegate the powers of the Act as thought fit.[87] A textbook example of a general provision not including delegated powers is provided by Swansea in 1863[88] –

> The Corporation may appoint out of their own Body from Time to Time such and so many Committees, consisting of such Number of Persons as they shall think fit, for all or any of the Purposes of this Act which in the Opinion of the Corporation would be better regulated and managed by means of such Committees, and may fix the Quorum of such Committees: Provided always, that the Acts of every such Committee shall be submitted to the Corporation for their Approval.

This drafting is almost identical to the earlier section VII of the Lendal Bridge and York Improvement Act 1859,[89] except that the latter refers to the Council and its discretion, rather than to the Corporation and its opinion, and the punctuation differs slightly. If, however, the desire to have provisions about committees is a common and increasingly prevalent theme in local legislation, yet again here – as in the case above of the drafting of the rights or standing to carry Acts into effect – the style in which that is done is very varied (and where there is a duty, as opposed to a power, to appoint committees it would be interesting to discover in each case what made the promoters write in or have to accept that compulsion, rather than merely enabling the option). A particularly prolix, though comprehensive, example is that of the Tynemouth Council in 1866[90] where there is both a power to appoint and a power to delegate, but with an important limitation relating to money –

> The Council may appoint out of their own body any Committee for the Execution of any of the Purposes of this Act, and may delegate to each Committee such of the Powers and Duties of the Corporation and Local Board respectively under this Act as the Council think fit (except the borrowing of Money) for the purpose of carrying into effect any specific Orders of the Council, and the Acts and Proceedings of every such Committee within the Limits of such Delegation shall be deemed the Acts and Proceedings of the Council, and the Quorum of each Committee shall be such as the Council direct; and the Council from Time to Time may make such Regulations as they think fit for the Guidance of any such Committee, and may remove any Members of any such Committee, and appoint in the Stead of them or any of them other Members of the Council.

Those opening words 'out of their own Body', included here and in the Swansea example above, were of course very significant: without an explicit statement to the contrary, committees could comprise only members of the appointing authority.[91] While some clauses were undoubtedly rather longwinded, promoters and their Parliamentary agents would not want to take any avoidable risk that their drafts might not prove fully effective, and would understandably feel that they might as well put in additional phrasing at the outset – after all, they were the ones promoting and paying the cost of the provisions they wanted, and we have seen that their experience of going before Select Committees was that the Committees did not usually systematically require precisely precedented wording where there was no technical need to do so.[92] When Ashton-under-Lyne and Stalybridge Corporations jointly promoted in 1864, careful provision was made both for each to appoint their own committees as well as for a joint committee, for which latter detailed regulation of proceedings was also provided.[93] Oldham in 1865[94] took a similar approach to that of Tynemouth above in the preceding year. Gateshead in 1867[95] obtained another lengthy committee clause, but were relatively economic in drafting overall because they incorporated provisions about both the Corporation and the Local Board into one section. Other local Acts continued to include committee powers closely similar, though not identical, to the approach passed in Tynemouth above: for instance, Congleton[96] in 1866, Barrow[97] in 1868, Leeds[98] in 1870, Huddersfield[99] in 1871, and Aberystwyth,[100] Birstal[101] and Rochdale[102] in 1872. None of these contained the exclusion of borrowing money that Tynemouth's Act had provided, but the Leeds, Aberystwyth and Birstal sections added that 'the attendance at and conduct of business at such committees shall be limited to the members of such committees and their officials' – something which presumably the others had neither experienced nor expected as a problem.

As well as committee appointments, provisions were necessary to bestow powers for certain kinds of individual appointments without which those acting would not have been able to establish unquestionably their powers to act. The Lord Mayor of York was given the power in 1859 to appoint temporary toll collectors;[103] while more significantly (and 17 years after Liverpool's pioneering provision[104]), Birkenhead was granted the power to appoint a medical officer of health.[105] The person appointed had to be a legally qualified medical practitioner, 'of Skill and Experience', but – revealing some unease perhaps on the part of Parliament as to how this power might be used – both the appointment and the salary had to be approved by 'One of Her Majesty's Principal Secretaries of State'. Just 4 years later Salford received the same power,[106] though the reference to skill and experience was modified to 'fit and proper person' and the need for Secretary of State approvals had gone. Stockton also was granted the power in 1869,[107] in a more succinct form suggesting that the lack of trust implied when Birkenhead had applied for powers was no longer such an issue –

> The Corporation may from time to time, if they shall think fit, appoint a fit and proper person, being a registered medical practitioner, to be and be called the officer of health, who shall be removable by the Corporation, and the Corporation may pay to him out of the general district rates to be levied under this Act such remuneration by way of annual salary or otherwise as the Corporation may by order in writing determine and appoint.

Salford extended the ambit of their appointment in 1870,[108] so that –

> The officer of health for the time being appointed by the Corporation under the provisions of the Act of 1867 shall have and may exercise all

such powers as are by any public and general Act, or by any local and personal Act, in force within the borough vested in the inspector of nuisances.

Another kind of confirming appointment was required at Hedon in 1860,[109] where the Town Clerk was appointed by statute as the returning officer for the first elections of the councillors, aldermen and mayor when the former borough was reconstituted; under section XXXII of the Municipal Corporations Act 1835 – which was concerned with existing boroughs and in itself created no new ones – elections in boroughs were held before the mayor and assessors. Liverpool provided in 1864 that notices could be signed not just by the Town Clerk personally but also by 'any Deputy appointed by him'.[110] This was the sort of sensible provision that might have been expected to be universal, but at Norwich in 1867 it was simply enacted that any document requiring authentication could be signed by the Clerk to the Local Board or the Town Clerk according to the legal entity on whose behalf it was being done, and there was no provision for anyone else.[111] The term 'proper officer' to denote the official specifically appointed by an authority to carry out a particular task – much used in modern local government legislation – has a long history, and is for example used in the Barrow-in-Furness Corporation Act 1868 in the context of recording the quashing of a conviction.[112]

The whole structure and style of local legislation tended to be better internally organised and constructed by the late 1860s than a decade earlier. An occasional mistake might slip through (as for instance the wrong section number references corrected by section 20 of the Manchester Corporation Waterworks Act 1865),[113] but there were more instances of helpful drafting that better placed a new Act against its legislative background. The 12-section Metropolitan Subways Act 1868[114] had a schedule listing seven related Acts. Another Act in the same context, the Thames Embankment (North and South) Act 1868,[115] clarified which borrowing powers would be applicable should a current Bill in Parliament be passed, cancelling one set, while another did the opposite, providing for the extension of other borrowing powers should yet another Bill then going through Parliament in that session be passed.[116]

Later legislative trends

Not only the drafting, but also the presentation of Acts had largely changed by 1870. Roman numerals for sections had already been replaced a decade earlier,[117] but capital letters were no longer used for all nouns, and that – together with the more direct and relatively 'plain English' style – had moved the image of the private statute book away from the almost eighteenth-century atmosphere of enactments prior to the start of our period in 1858. These characteristics, while superficial in one sense, are also significant in providing evidence of a slowly modernising trend – the gradual replacement of antiquated styles with more accessible ones at this time that was part of the gradual growth of business or bureaucratic practice in the emerging information state, and which started to place more emphasis on efficacy and convenience than on outmoded forms redolent of a passing age.

Other growing trends were for authorities with more extensive or well-ordered local legislation (and, presumably, a more go-ahead outlook on the part of the town clerk or someone else of influence) either to replace the relevant public general law entirely with their own local code of provisions, or to consolidate the accumulated results of past promotions into a single convenient Act. Section 4 of Oldham's 1865 Act referred to above was an example of the former, declaring that –

> the said Local Act[118] shall be repealed, and the Parts of the Public Health Act 1848, and the Local Government Act 1858, and the Local Government Act (1858) Amendment Act 1861, adopted and applied to the Borough as aforesaid, shall cease to apply to the Borough.

The preamble had declared that there were now in force locally 'a Variety of Provisions affecting the Improvement and Government of the Borough comprised in different Acts not harmonizing in their language, and frequently conflicting in their effect'.[119] Section 6 of the 1869 Stockton-on-Tees Act above provided another example, that –

> the Public Health Act 1848, the Local Government Act 1858, the Local Government Act, 1858, Amendment Act 1861 and the Local Government Act Amendment Act 1863 shall cease to apply to the borough.

The year before, Barrow-in-Furness had simply recited in the preamble[120] that the Corporation was 'desirous and it is expedient that all the Provisions relative to the Supply of Gas and Water, and to the Improvement and Government of the Borough, should be comprised in One Act of Parliament'. St. Helens in 1869[121] expressed the same intention, but – as we have so often seen with provisions like this – in quite different wording –

> to avoid the inconvenience and difficulty arising from various enactments relating to the same purposes being in force within the borough at the same time, it is expedient to reduce into one Act the provisions relating to the local government and improvement of the borough.

The preamble for the Wolverhampton Improvement Act 1869,[122] which received royal assent just a fortnight after that for St. Helens, again expressed the same sentiments; it also went further, however, in seeking not only to remove overlapping public general provisions, but also to extend the operation of the relevant consolidated local ones, so that yet again we see Parliament accepting situations that were similar in principle, and endorsing the kinds of provisions being promoted to deal with or change them, but allowing that to be effected in different ways, using differing drafting approaches and with minor – but to the promoters by no means necessarily insignificant – variations of legislative outcome. We also see Parliament accepting not only the repeal and replacement of individual general provisions for specific local reasons, but much more surprisingly endorsing the wholesale replacement of public general codes that Parliament had relatively recently enacted, and which the municipal authorities concerned had therefore also quite recently adopted.

While not consolidating or re-enacting as such, Liverpool – long a particularly active promoter – set out in the preamble to the Liverpool Improvement and Waterworks Act 1871[123] a set of 17 local Acts going back to 1842 that not only provided a useful compendium of references but also made it easier to amend them in a manageable and accessible way. Other places, however, did promote fully consolidating Bills. Early to do this was Salford in 1862, with 'An Act for consolidating and amending the Acts relating to the Corporation of Salford; for extending their Powers; and for other Purposes'.[124] It ran to 442 sections and 12 schedules (A.) to (L.) inclusive. A few years later – by then with more legislation, both general and local, steadily accumulating – consolidating Bills became more frequent. West Hartlepool's 1870 Act[125] ran to 459 sections and nine schedules, for instance; Huddersfield's in 1871[126] to 429 sections and four schedules; Burnley's in 1871[127] to an enormous 537 sections and five schedules; and Rochdale's in 1872[128] to a more modest 264 sections but no fewer than 11 schedules. Wolverhampton's Act[129] referred to above was unusual in terms of geography: otherwise northern towns promoted all of these immediate examples. This was another indication, no doubt, of both the volume of previous promotions there, and also of the degree of energy for legislative initiative in places that had previously needed and secured local Acts; that had probably found the slow pace of general municipal law reform inadequate for their challenges; and that were prepared to plan and to pay to do something about it.

Conclusion

Whatever the aim and intent of a private Bill, it had to be paid for, and – as we have seen in Chapter 3 – the costs involved would almost certainly be substantial. Promoters, private or public, had to take the risk that if their Bill was not passed with an adequate source of funding to pay for it, they would have to meet those costs themselves or, in the case of a local authority, the expenditure would be unlawful. Almost invariably, therefore, the Acts with which we are concerned in this study included a section (generally at or very close to the end) stipulating how the costs of obtaining the Act were to be met. Once again, however, that common principle was met by a variety of different kinds of provision, illustrated by the following four examples. In some cases the necessary money would be raised from the newly permitted activities (perhaps making lawful payment in the interim a moot point), but in others, funds already to hand could be spent.

In most case the costs were treated as revenue expenditure out of income, generally to be found out of a rate the levying of which the Act authorised, or maybe out of the proceeds of a trading undertaking such as water or gas. Bradford's 1866 Act[130] is typical, although the expenses were to be borne not out of a special rate levy but out of the already authorised general rate –

> All the Costs, Charges and Expenses of and incident to the preparing, applying for, obtaining, and passing of this Act shall be borne by the Corporation, and paid by them out of the General District Rate, as if the same were Expenses of carrying into effect with respect to the Borough 'The Public Health Act 1848', and 'The Local Government Act 1858'.

In the same session, however, Liverpool[121] were also allowed to pay their costs out of capital monies –

> All Costs, Charges, and Expenses of and attending to obtaining and Passing of this Act or incidental thereto shall be paid by the Corporation out of any Capital Monies that may be in their Hands, or that they may hereafter receive on the Water Account.

Yet again in 1866 Aberavon[131] were accorded a mixed permission for the promotion of the Bill and the purchase of the gasworks that its passing enabled; the costs were to be met 'out of any Monies which they have received or may receive under this Act or the Public Health Acts'. Diversity of a different kind occurred at Wolverhampton in 1869,[132] where it was stipulated that all the relevant costs 'shall be paid by [the Corporation] out of the borough fund and improvement fund in equal shares'. The cost of the Lincoln City Commons Act 1870[133] was to come out of the proceeds of selling Holmes Common, the authorisation of which was one of the objectives of the Corporation's Bill 226, while the costs of passing the Buckinghamshire County Rate Act 1860 were to be 'borne and paid by the Justices out of the County Stock of the County of Buckingham'.[134] At Brecon, where the Council had run out of money, the costs of the necessary Act were to be borne initially by the Markets Company, but as soon as the Council received an anticipated £200 for their Gaol Field, £150 of that was to be paid to the Company towards the Bill promotion costs.[135]

***

Throughout this chapter the point has been made that local Acts were at the same time both formulaic, mindful of precedent, and repetitive (all characteristics to be expected from their technical legal nature, and from the constitutional climate of the times), but also within that framework surprisingly varied and individual (particularly in the narratives of their preambles and the ancillary contextual background that is often apparent from promoters' agreements annexed as schedules). If the powers principally sought and the drafting styles that were adopted differed almost imperceptibly from one session to the next, the cumulative change is much more obvious between 1858 and 1872, and seems to accelerate from the mid-1860s onwards. Analysis of this kind has never been published before.

The world of private legislation was, as we have seen, a significant 'industry' at Westminster, yet it was but a minor aspect of the outputs and interests of a Parliament at the zenith of the Empire, fully seised of foreign affairs but still to be persuaded of the necessity of looking after the governing of local affairs in the home country. Nevertheless, it is always as well in considering private legislation, as earlier chapters have sought to do, to bear in mind what was happening in the wider world outside the Select Committees, with their doctrine of *locus standi* and their worries about what municipal authorities of one kind or another should be allowed to do in the name of social progress.

The number of private Bill promotions reached its peak in 1866.[136] It was never sustainable at that zenith anyway, but economic downturn had an immediate impact (apart from the fact that the country was running out of space to plan yet more railways). The more obvious changes in the annual *Vacher* lists were fewer numbers of private Bills in total but a growing number of local ones as we define them here; more accessible drafting; and more places consolidating and modifying the still halting attempts of the state to provide any kind of minimal standards in the social basics of food, shelter and public health. While considering factors such as the changing economy and the realities at this point of constrained or declining railway and other business promotions, historians must also reflect on the contrast that *municipal* promotions of Bills were continuing and even growing. The local appetites for reform, improvement and civic advancement were undiminished as municipalities all over the country continued to invest in their own development and progress in a climate where central government was still not wholeheartedly engaged in doing – or, just as likely, controlling – it for them. More subtle, yet more significant for the longer term, was the nature of the change in the constitution itself that Walter Bagehot observed in 1872. 'The change since 1865' he wrote, 'is a change not in one point, but in a thousand points; it is a change not of particular details but of pervading spirit'.[137] We may concur all the more readily today, having the benefit of long hindsight, with what Bagehot perceived at the time. The same might be said of the municipal mood – and hence of the mood of municipal legislation – of those years.

After considering here the statutory *means* – the technical apparatus necessary to achieve a workable enactment on which its promoters could rely – the next chapter considers the legislative *ends* – the sorts of provisions the demands for which brought promoters to Westminster in the first place.

Notes

1 See note 10 below in relation to John Garrard's examples.

168   *The texts and technicalities*

2 See, for example, Oliver MacDonagh, *Early Victorian Government 1830–1870* (1977), p. 155: 'The hotch-potch at the centre was more than matched on the periphery. First came the local health authorities ... Moreover many places chose to work under their own local acts and these statutes often created further and still more exotic administrative bodies.'
3 Lord Redesdale (1805–1886) served as Chairman of Committees in the House of Lords from 1851 until 1886. He was created Earl of Redesdale in 1877.
4 *Minutes of Evidence* taken before the Select Committee on *Parliamentary Agency*, q. 276 (ordered to be printed 17 July 1876, Paper 360; see *Parliamentary Papers*, vol. XII, p. 539).
5 *Op. cit.*, qq. 280–2. Warner agreed with Mr Raikes M.P. at q. 299 that 'the present system is only workable in consequence of the careful supervision and the great authority exercised by Lord Redesdale'. He gave an extreme example of incompetent drafting at qq. 316–17:

> I have a Bill here in which there were four paragraphs of the preamble which required alteration, and an addition was also required to be made to the preamble. Thirty clauses required alteration out of 55, and probably still more consequentially ... A considerable number of Bills every Session require nearly as much alteration as that. Common form Bills, ordinary Railway Bills, and so on, ought to be almost without a mistake.

In every case where individual Bills are referred to in evidence, they are not identified in the transcript, though presumably the principal parties involved in the taking and giving of evidence generally knew well enough which they were.

6 *Op. cit.*, qq. 335–6. A 'filled-up Bill', that is, a complete text, had to be submitted before 23 December under Commons Standing Order 38 (1866 edn). Back in 1824 it had been recommended that 'a filled up Bill, signed by the Agent for the Bill, as proposed to be submitted to the Committee, be deposited in the Private Bill Office ...' *Report From Committee of the Whole House on the Private Business of the House*, Paper 453, 22 June 1824, p. 2 (*Parliamentary Papers*, vol. VI, p. 507).
7 *Second Report from Select Committee on Private Business*, ordered to be printed 25 February 1839, q. 51. This Lord Shaftesbury (Chairman of Committees) was the sixth Earl, father of the famous social reformer. Sir James Graham, a former Whig M.P. now a Tory, was M.P. for Pembroke in 1839. In 1841 he became Peel's Home Secretary. The *Second Report* is at *Parliamentary Papers*, vol. XIII, p. 105 (Paper 520), the *First Report* being at vol. XIII, p. 101 (Paper 51).
8 *Op. cit.*, q. 53.
9 *Minutes of Evidence* taken before the 1876 Select Committee on *Parliamentary Agency*, *op. cit.*, qq. 283, 286 and 318.
10 John Garrard and Michael Goldsmith, *Municipal Progress and Decline in Britain Since 1835*, *op. cit.*, 2nd series, vol. 7, nos. 1 & 2, 2011–12, pp. 38–64 at p. 41. As a whole, however, the article convincingly narrates a surely incontrovertible truth about local government generally, and the passage about Bill committees is somewhat redeemed by the further passage *ibid.* at p. 51 that

> Parliament and/or government, at various nineteenth century points, diluted national legislation empowering municipalities, rendering their clauses weaker, more permissive, or altogether inoperative. Meanwhile parliamentary private Bill committees expunged clauses or whole sections from local improvement Bills, believing them improper uses of government, or impelled by local private interests so to think. In reality, matters are more complex.

Again no evidence or example is cited. Garrard had, however, included some examples in his book *Leadership and Power in Victorian Industrial Towns 1830–80*

The texts and technicalities 169

(1983), pp. 101–3, in a passage beginning 'The expense might have been more bearable if the process had not been so fraught with risk' and quoting the editor of the *Rochdale Standard* in 1854. His examples mostly lie outside our period here (Rochdale 1853 and 1872, Bolton 1854 and 1877). The comment on p. 102 that 'Sometimes such horrendous things were done because a given Bill was ill designed or conflicted with national legislation' does somewhat undermine the strength of the argument: seen from Parliament's point of view, and the experience of the House authorities in receiving poorly drafted Bills, it would be hardly surprising if Select Committees were impatient at their shortcomings, and wont to reject clauses that they considered unsatisfactory for technical, if not for intrinsic, reasons.

11 See the annual table in Chapter 1.
12 28 & 29 Vict. c. cxcv, section 70.
13 28 & 29 Vict. c. ccxiv, section 12.
14 28 & 29 Vict. c. clxxxvii. It had been Bill 484.
15 28 & 29 Vict. c. ccxl. It had been Bill 371.
16 See note 23 in Chapter 2.
17 See note 56 in Chapter 6.
18 See note 13 in Chapter 1.
19 These provisions might have been stronger had the mechanism for intervention been more effective, but that they were prudent in principle was demonstrated by what happened the following year in 1864, when 'On the 11th of March the Dale Dyke reservoir gave way ... causing fearful loss of life and property'. This is recounted by Ralph Blakelock Smith, the Secretary of the Sheffield Water Company (whose reservoir it was), to the Select Committee on the *Municipal Corporations (Borough Funds) Bill*, 22 April 1872, at qq. 533ff. esp. qq. 547–8. The witness was questioned about Sheffield Corporation's 'threatened opposition' (q. 541) to the Company's Bill. The Bill, whose preamble recites what had happened, became the Sheffield Waterworks Act 1864, 27 & 28 Vict. c. cccxxiv, part of the scope of which was to settle the 7,000 claims arising from the disaster. (More than 200 died; the reservoir was re-built in 1875.) The 1864 Act made provision for what could be termed a 'class action' by creating (section 6) the Sheffield Inundation Commissioners, and under section 40 barring any claims not made under the Act. The Select Committee's report is at *Parliamentary Papers*, vol. XI, p. 627 (Paper 177). See also G.M. Binnie, *Early Victorian Water Engineers* (1981), pp. 263–77, and Samuel Harrison, *A Complete History of the Great Flood at Sheffield on March 11 and 12, 1864* (1864).
20 26 & 27 Vict. c. cxvii, s. 59.
21 26 & 27 Vict. c. lii, s. 22.
22 See Chapter 1.
23 26 & 27 Vict. c. xxxiii, s. 21.
24 26 & 27 Vict. c. lii, s. 15.
25 26 & 27 Vict. c. cxvii, ss. 24 and 8. The compulsory purchase limit was only 3 years for the lands of Sir George Reresby Sitwell.
26 26 & 27 Vict. c. lxviii, s. 19.
27 24 & 25 Vict. c. xlvii.
28 24 & 25 Vict. c. xlv, section XLIII.
29 See notes 57–60 to Chapter 4.
30 26 & 27 Vict. c. xcii. The preamble refers to the Corporation, in their capacity as the Local Board of Health, being unable to afford to execute a provisional order confirmed by the Local Government Supplemental Act 1860 (23 & 24 Vict. c. 44); it was replaced by this Act, section 7 of which made the previous order effectively inoperative.
31 26 & 27 Vict. c. lxxiii. In a remarkable local Act provision, s. 20 empowered the city sheriff to execute prisoners in the county gaol.

170 *The texts and technicalities*

32 26 & 27 Vict. c. i.
33 26 & 27 Vict. c. xiii.
34 Section 14.
35 Sections 48–50.
36 26 & 27 Vict. c. cvi.
37 Sections 72 and 75 respectively.
38 26 & 27 Vict. c. lxii, preamble.
39 26 & 27 Vict. c. cxix, ss. 30 and 46 respectively.
40 26 & 27 Vict. c. ccvi.
41 See note 69 in Chapter 4.
42 See note 4 above.
43 35 & 36 Vict. c. xv.
44 See note 68 below.
45 All were 23 & 24 Vict. – Norwich Corporation Markets Act 1860, c. xxxiv, section VII; Swansea Local Board of Health Waterworks Act 1860, c. cxlviii, section X; Macclesfield District Gas Act 1860, c. clxxxi, section V; and Wigan Waterworks Act 1860, c. clxxxvi, section V. Their dates of royal assent were respectively 15 May, 23 July, 6 August and again 6 August, 1860.
46 23 & 24 Vict. c. xix.
47 28 & 29 Vict. c. cccxi.
48 31 & 32 Vict. c. xxiv.
49 31 & 32 Vict. c. cxxviii.
50 33 & 34 Vict. c. cxxix.
51 33 & 34 Vict. c. clx.
52 32 & 33 Vict. c. cxxxiv. This wording for the Metropolitan Board of Works was not unique: see for instance section 4 of the Kensington Improvement Act 1866, 29 & 30 Vict. c. cl.
53 32 & 33 Vict. c. xi.
54 32 & 33 Vict. c. cxvii.
55 34 & 35 Vict. c. lxv.
56 35 & 36 Vict. c. xxxi.
57 Bolton Corporation Act 1872, 35 & 36 Vict. c. lxxviii.
58 See Chapter 1.
59 See notes 3–5 above.
60 *Return to an Order of the Honourable the House of Commons dated 8 February 1872; for COPY 'of a MEMORANDUM prepared at the BOARD OF TRADE concerning LEGISLATION in 1871 on the subject of GAS, WATER, and TRAMWAYS'. Parliamentary Papers*, 1872, vol. LIV, pp. 301–314 (Paper 8).
61 *Op. cit.*, p. 7.
62 *Op. cit.*, p. 12. Footnotes in the original cite the Acts referred to.
63 *Op. cit.*, pp. 13–14.
64 See, for example, note 25 in Chapter 3.
65 21 & 22 Vict. c. cxl, section III, which took two and half pages to define the new boundaries.
66 *Op. cit.*, section LXXIV.
67 21 & 22 Vict. c. xci, sections VI–XI and LXVIII.
68 24 & 25 Vict. c. iv, sections VIII and IX. Local Boards of Health were not automatically corporate; the Wallasey Improvement Act 1858, 21 & 22 Vict. c. lxxiii, had been passed only 3 years earlier, and had even been granted compulsory purchase powers. Section IX of the 1861 Act confirmed that everything previously done by the Local Board was as valid as if that Act had already been passed.
69 30 & 31 Vict. c. lxxiii, section 51.
70 35 & 36 Vict. c. xxx, section 8.

71 Darlington Local Board of Health Act 1861, 24 & 25 Vict. c. lxxvii, section LXIII. (On the vellum copy in the Parliamentary Archives, on which the royal assent 'La Reyne le veult' is inscribed on the first page, the number of this section is printed as 63. Practice did vary at this period between prints of Bills and Acts.)
72 25 & 26 Vict. c. clxxxvi. The six pages of preamble recite much of the financial difficulties that beset the Corporation.
73 26 & 27 Vict. c. lii, Part II of the Schedule. See the Commons *Journal* for 27 March 1863, vol. 118, p. 144 referring to the deletion of the waterworks part of the preamble and consequential amendments. The Bill was further amended in the House on 20 April (vol. 113, p. 169), and yet another verbal amendment was made on 24 April (vol. 118, p. 180) when a new title was provided. The experience of this Bill, when occasion demanded, counters the notion that the Parliamentary process was wholly unforgiving over procedural or indeed more substantial difficulties.
74 33 & 34 Vict. c. lxix, Schedule (B.). At Dartford an agreement provided for the undertaking to be sold, not acquired, by the Local Board: see note 71 to Chapter 4.
75 34 & 35 Vict. c. cxcvii.
76 See note 6 to Appendix 1. Because it was promoted in this way, however, this Bill is strictly not within our 'local Bill' definition here.
77 35 & 36 Vict. c. xxii, section 4.
78 23 & 24 Vict. c. cxcvii.
79 25 & 26 Vict. c. xxvi, section 17.
80 The Provisional Order was annexed to and confirmed by the public general Act 19 & 20 Vict. c. XXVI.
81 28 & 29 Vict. c. cccxi.
82 Middlesbrough Improvement Act 1858, 21 & 22 Vict. c. cxl, section VIII. The draftsman omitted the apostrophes that might have been expected after 'Days' in each case, and might also have said 'fewer than' rather than 'less than'!
83 Kings Lynn Waterworks and Borough Improvement Act 1859, 22 & 23 Vict. c. xxxii, section CII.
84 Northampton Improvement Act 1871, 34 & 35 Vict. c. cxxxix, section 7 (varying the seven days required by section XXXI of the Northampton Improvement Act 1843, 6 & 7 Vict. c. lxxviii).
85 *Op. cit.*, section XV.
86 *Op. cit.*, section XXVII. Section XXVIII gave delegated powers, though these were revocable by the Corporation.
87 Rugby Waterworks Act 1863, 26 & 27 Vict. c. xxxiii, section 8.
88 Swansea Municipal Corporation Act 1863, 26 & 27 Vict. c. xiii, section 17.
89 23 & 24 Vict. c. xix.
90 Tynemouth Improvement Act 1866, 29 & 309 Vict. c. li, section 7. Section 8 made further provisions about committee quorums and meetings, etc.
91 There seems to be no case during the period under review of individual or general co-option to committees being allowed, though it might occur that individuals would be given rights of membership or participation in parent bodies for reasons such as donation for public benefit of land previously owned. See for instance section XVI of the Halifax Park and Improvements Act 1858, referred to in note 67 above, appointing the benefactor Francis Crossley (and any successor 'Protector of the Park') as an *ex officio* member of the standing committee without his being a member of the Council.
92 This was hardly surprising when one considers how many Select Committees were sitting at the same time, particularly when the number of Bills promoted in one session numbered several hundred.
93 Ashton-under-Lyne and Stalybridge (Corporations) Waterworks Act 1864, 27 & 28 Vict. c. xlvii, sections 5, 6 and 72.

172   *The texts and technicalities*

94   Oldham Borough Improvement Act 1865, 28 & 29 Vict. c. cccxi, section 7.
95   Gateshead Improvement Act 1867, 30 & 31 Vict. c. lxxxiii, section 9.
96   Congleton Gas and Improvement Act 1866, 29 & 30 Vict. c. lii, section 9.
97   Barrow-in-Furness Corporation Act 1868, 31 & 32 Vict. c. civ, section 9.
98   Leeds Corporation Gas 1870, 33 & 34 Vict. c. lvi, section 4.
99   Huddersfield Improvement Act 1871, 34 & 35 Vict. c. cli, section 12.
100 Aberystwyth Improvement and Water Act 1872, 35 & 36 Vict. c. xxx, section 7.
101 Birstal Local Board Act 1872, 35 & 36 Vict. c. lxxiii, section 5.
102 Rochdale Improvement Act 1872, 35 & 36 Vict. c. cxlix, section 7.
103 The Lendal Bridge and York Improvement Act 1860, 23 & 24 Vict. c. xix, section XLII.
104 9 & 10 Vict. c. cxxvii, section CXXII. The city's first appointee, Dr William Henry Duncan, took up his appointment in 1847, his appointment and salary being confirmed by the Secretary of State (as the Act, which had no short title, required) on 1 January that year. See W.M. Frazer, *Duncan of Liverpool: Being an Account of the Work of Dr. W.H. Duncan, Medical Officer of Health of Liverpool 1847–63* (1947), p. 43. The 1846 Act also required that a civil engineer be appointed as a 'Surveyor of the Drainage and Other Works': section XXII. In the Liverpool Improvement and Waterworks Act of 1871 (34 & 35 Vict. c. clxxxiv) it was termed 'the Sanitary Act 1846'.
105 Birkenhead Improvement Commissioners Act 1863, 26 & 27 Vict. c. cvi, section 19.
106 Salford Improvement Act 1867, 30 & 31 Vict. c. lvii, section 40. The appointee was to be called simply 'the Officer of Health' without the addition 'Medical', though still required to be a legally qualified medical practitioner.
107 Stockton-on-Tees Extension and Improvement Act 1869, 32 & 33 Vict. c. lxxiv, section 316.
108 Salford Improvement Act 1870, 33 & 34 Vict. c. cxxix, section 78.
109 Hedon Corporation and Borough Improvement Act 1860, 23 & 24 Vict. c. xxxi, section XVIII. Hedon was an interesting place; its preamble recited that 'Hedon is a Corporate Borough by Charter, and certain of the inhabitants of the existing Borough are a Body Politic and Corporate' whose Mayor and Bailiffs exercised jurisdiction as magistrates, and where only the freemen were burgesses. Hedon was one of five boroughs that by 1879 had been placed under the Municipal Corporations Act 1835 since its passing, the others being Aberavon, Conway, Hartlepool and Yeovil: J.R. Somers Vine, *English Municipal Institutions; Their Growth and Development From 1835 to 1879, Statistically Illustrated* (1879), p. 11.
110 Liverpool Sanitary Amendment Act 1864, 27 & 28 Vict. c. lxxiii, section 16.
111 City of Norwich Act 1867, 30 & 31 Vict. c. cii., section 95.
112 31 & 32 Vict. c. civ, section 232(8).
113 28 & 29 Vict. c. cxlv. This had probably occurred when the clause numbering had altered following amendment.
114 31 & 32 Vict. c. lxxx.
115 31 & 32 Vict. c. cxi, section 22.
116 Hornsey Local Board Act 1871, 34 & 35 Vict. c. cxxix, section 33.
117 The last session when Roman numerals were used to number private Act sections in the Queen's Printer's copies was 1861.
118 A reference to 7 Geo. 4, c. cxvii (1827).
119 For an example from elsewhere, see note 61 to Chapter 4, referring to a case involving the Abergavenny Improvement Act 1854.
120 Barrow-in-Furness Corporation Act 1868, 31 & 32 Vict. c. civ.
121 St. Helens Improvement Act 1869, 32 & 33 Vict. c. cxx, preamble. (A hundred years later the present writer, employed at St. Helens C.B.C. from 1967 to 1972,

would occasionally rely on the provisions of this Act rather than the more constrained public general legislation by then applicable!)
122 32 & 33 Vict. c. cxxxi. Strictly speaking this was not a consolidation Act as such, but it provided widely for the extended Rochdale Borough, which absorbed the Local Board of Buersil.
123 34 & 35 Vict. c. clxxxiv.
124 Salford Improvement Act 1862, 25 & 26 Vict. c. ccv. (There was no schedule (J.).) Even earlier, though outside our immediate scope here, was the Mersey Docks and Harbour (Consolidation of Acts) Act 1858, 21 & 22 Vict. c. xcii, with 368 sections and 11 schedules.
125 West Hartlepool Extension and Improvement Act 1870, 33 & 34 Vict. c. cxiii.
126 Huddersfield Improvement Act 1871, 34 & 35 Vict. c. cli.
127 Burnley Borough Improvement Act 1871, 34 & 35 Vict. c. cliv.
128 Rochdale Improvement Act 1872, 35 & 36 Vict. c. cxlix.
129 Bradford Corporation Act 1866, 29 & 30 Vict. c. ccxxii, section 87.
130 Liverpool Corporation Waterworks Act 1866, 29 & 30 Vict. c. cxxvi, section 43.
131 Aberavon Local Board Act 1866, 29 & 30 Vict. c. ccxl, section 51.
132 Wolverhampton Improvement Act 1869, 32 & 33 Vict. c. cxxxi, section 416.
133 33 & 34 Vict. c. lxxxvii, sections 43 and 86.
134 23 & 24 Vict. c. lxxxvi, section V.
135 *Op. cit.*, section 92. See note 72 above.
136 See the table in Chapter 1.
137 Angus Hawkins, *The Forgotten Prime Minister: The 14th Earl of Derby* (2008), vol. II, *Achievement, 1851–1869*, p. 423, quoting *Introduction to the Second Edition, 1872* from Walter Bagehot, *The English Constitution*, pp. 194–5 (2001, edited by P. Smith).

6 The powers and purposes of local legislation

The previous chapter distinguished the statutory *means* – the technical apparatus of an enactment – from the legislative *ends* – the sorts of required provisions that promoters were really seeking. Obtaining what statute then called a 'special Act'[1] can be compared to the procurement by an authority of an expensive and sophisticated piece of equipment: an elaborate, time-taking and detailed procedure would be involved, with a detailed specification. Its successful acquisition might well be a source of considerable pride; essentially, however, the equipment would not have been bought for its own sake, but rather for what it could do. In this chapter we consider the powers and purposes that authorities were primarily seeking when they promoted local Bills.

While the thousands of relevant provisions from the years 1858–72 are of course very diverse, they can be categorised into broad groups – there are far fewer unique, unusual or 'maverick' provisions (at least in the resulting enactments, as opposed to the deposited Bills) than sometimes supposed.[2] The pages that follow concentrate on provisions that are particularly interesting in their style, content, scope or drafting approach, and for the picture they help collectively to build of the whole *corpus* of 'special Act' local powers at this period. They are selected to illustrate both the subject matter and the approaches involved, and also the places (very often in the north of England) that were promoting the local legislation from which the various sections are drawn. There are of course, as Chapter 5 has shown, very numerous other provisions dealing with matters that were minor, incidental or simply generally repetitive across the local legislation of these years as a whole. The broad groupings below relate first to what we may term constitutional matters and the general exercise of powers. Those then following concern rating, financial and charging powers; building, safety or public health standards of various kinds; highways and streets; and finally a spectrum of diverse other local and exceptional provisions. These latter are often unique (to the years 1858–72 at least), but even when precedented elsewhere they provide insights into the sorts of local problems and concerns – real or potential – for which authorities were willing to bear the expense and trouble of coming to Parliament. This is important in understanding the relationship between the central Government at this time and the many local authorities and communities that had the initiative and the resources to procure solutions, and obtain authorisation for developments, that would otherwise not have been possible.

Constitutional matters and the general exercise of powers

At a time when the public legislation framework for local government was far less comprehensive and prescriptive than it later became, authorities often found that they had little option but to seek additional legislation to fill gaps, or to make alternative provisions to what was otherwise available to them. Obvious problems arose, for example, when there was a need – or desire – to extend the boundaries, or to remedy some defect or problem with the legal status, of an authority.

Under section 30 of the Halifax Extension and Improvement Act 1865,[3] 'The Borough as extended by this Act is by this Act made to all Intents and Purposes the District of the Local Board of Health...' and a suite of provisions divided the extended Borough into ten wards (section 14); extended the Municipal Corporations Act 1835 across the whole area (section 17); and made ancillary and consequential provisions. At Stourbridge[4] any of the constituent townships might vote to adopt the Improvement Act, in which case 'the Limits of this Act shall be extended so as to comprise the respective Township'. The preamble to the Bath Act 1870[5] referred to Bath as both a city and a borough – the former term more about civic status, and the latter about municipal definition. Unusually, at Rochdale in 1872[6] 'So much of the royal charter as is inconsistent with or contrary to the provisions of the Act shall be repealed, but in all other respects the said charter is hereby confirmed'. Not only is any provision of this kind unusual in itself (apart from its rarity, charters are usually regarded as separate or parallel sources of law alongside statutes), but also of course it is the Sovereign, and not Parliament, who grants charter powers from the royal prerogative, putting it outside the usual powers or role of Parliament to confirm a charter.[7] The Rochdale Act also provided for the Borough name, and that the Corporation should 'have perpetual succession, and use a common seal' – provisions that might be thought unnecessary in a local Act, except that the preamble recited the unextended Borough, chartered on 9 September 1856, as styled 'the mayor, aldermen and burgesses of the town and borough of Rochdale' and section 16 styled the 'one body politic and corporate', instead as 'The Mayor, Aldermen, and Burgesses of the Borough of Rochdale'.[8] Letters patent establishing the Borough of St. Helens in 1868 were similarly confirmed by local Act in the following year.[9] Communities wanted no doubts to exist about such matters, and for the basics of civic existence to be clearly included when they sought their own wide-ranging enabling statutes.

In some cases authorities used local Acts *inter alia* to alter or stipulate the numbers and distribution of council membership. The 1865 Halifax Act referred to above[10] provided for a mayor, ten aldermen and 30 councillors,

176 *The powers and purposes*

with ten three-councillor wards, and sections 22–29 provided in some detail for the transitional arrangements as the former council was replaced by the new membership. At Salford less detailed transitional arrangements were required, as the Council was to continue to consist of a mayor, 16 aldermen and 48 councillors – again in three-member wards with an alderman also for each.[11] At Burnley,[12] however, the council of 32– 8 aldermen and 24 councillors – *included* the mayor, who was not additional as in the other places not far away. Differences like these showed that the formalities of local government structures were not yet fixed, and that Parliament would allow variations that, perhaps, they felt were of little significance beyond the boundaries of the authority concerned. Two sections of the Newcastle-upon-Tyne Improvement Act 1865[13] provided both for byelaws made under now repealed local Acts there to remain in force, unless and until repealed, and for the council itself to be able to make and revoke byelaws under the Act at a quarterly meeting.

Powers over land have also always been very important for local authorities – and particularly the principle of being able to justify compulsory acquisition of land necessary for the achievement of public purposes. The requirements of the Lands Clauses Consolidation Act 1845 and the amending Act of 1860[14] would be incorporated with any local Act authorising lands to be acquired, whether by agreement or compulsorily. Bradford[15] were authorised to take possession of certain lands, at least on a temporary basis, without paying for them; the powers were limited, could not include ornamental or garden areas, and there was no immunity to liability for nuisance if they were adversely exercised. The enactment of clauses like these, however, showed that Parliament recognised that it was not always possible to conclude all the consequential formalities before programmes of publicly authorised works could proceed. The Bath Act 1870[16] provided a different example of flexibility: section 24 helpfully provided that

> The Corporation may at any time or times purchase by agreement for the purposes of this Act, in addition to any lands authorised to be taken by any other Act or by any other provision of this Act, any quantity of land not exceeding in the whole ten acres.

A very useful and innovative provision was obtained by Newcastle-upon-Tyne in their 1865 Act.[17] If land originally acquired for the purposes of the Act under section 116 were transferred to a third party so that the original 'privity of contract' (but not necessarily 'privity of estate') were lost, restrictive covenants could be enforced at common law, but not positive covenants. While section 125 did not cure that problem, it did strengthen the Corporation's capacity to enforce stipulations for adjoining owners' benefit, and the ease of doing so:

> Any Stipulations or Provisions contained in any such Conveyance [...] may at all Times be enforced in a Court of Equity by the Corporation

for the Benefit of the Parties entitled to the other Property adjoining to that comprised in such Conveyance or held under the same Title, in such Manner in all respects as the Corporation think fit.

The 'labouring classes' might find that compulsory powers meant that they would be evicted from their houses. There was no obligation to re-house, or to pay tenants any compensation, but Kensington's Act of 1866 was typical of this sort of provision in requiring notice to be given:[18]

> The Board shall, not less than Eight Weeks before they take in any Parish Fifteen Houses or more occupied wholly or partially by Persons belonging to the Labouring Classes as Tenants or Lodgers, make known their intention to take the same by Placards, Handbills or other general Notice placed in public View upon or within a reasonable distance from such Houses, and the Board shall not take any such Houses until they have obtained the Certificate of a Justice that it has been proved to his Satisfaction that the Board have made known their Intention to take the same in manner hereinbefore required.

At Norwich, Inclosure Commissioners were empowered under the local Act of 1867[19] to certify Schemes for 'the draining levelling lighting watching and improving by the Corporation of a common' (section 103), but they required confirmation by Act of Parliament to become effective. It was provided that

> If in the Progress through Parliament of a Bill confirming any Scheme certified under this Act by the Commissioners a Petition is presented to either House of Parliament against the Scheme, the Bill, as far as it relates to the Scheme petitioned against, may be referred to a Select Committee, and the Petitioner shall be allowed to appear and oppose as in case of a Private Bill.

Other limitations were enacted for less elaborate needs. Frequently powers – especially compulsory purchase powers – were given with a variety of time limits within which they could be exercised; examples included Tynemouth street improvements (3 years);[20] Victoria Park Approach (5 years);[21] Halifax Park (8 years for the waterworks, 3 years for the cemetery and 5 years for the gas works);[22] and Leeds (5 years for land purchases).[23]

The longer that potential compulsory purchase powers affected an area, of course, the longer the lands or properties affected were blighted. Even within a given category, however, not all places were authorised to the same extent. For Manchester's waterworks,[24] 3 years were allowed for such powers to be used, but for Aberdare's waterworks[25] it was 5 years, with 7 allowed to complete the authorised works. The completion period, however, was only 5 years at Bradford[26] ('except Works for the Distribution of Water'). For land disposal duties, much longer periods were sometimes stipulated: any surplus land not required after the completion of the street for which the

178   *The powers and purposes*

Newcastle-upon-Tyne Improvement Act 1865 provided had to be disposed of within 20 years,[27] while the similar provision relating to the relevant park or street at Burnley was a remarkable 50 years.[28]

In contrast to these limits, at Malvern[29] markets powers were instead given on the basis that they *could not* be utilised for 5 years, and then only after a confirming vote at a meeting of those ratepayers having votes for the elections of Improvement Commissioners. A range of detailed markets provisions was also enacted against the day when the Malvern Commissioners' powers became effective.

It should not be overlooked that private Acts not promoted by a given local authority could sometimes provide for significant powers or duties there. The Birmingham Waterworks Act 1870, for instance, conferred powers on Birmingham Corporation in relating to testing water, and using it for Corporation purposes.[30] The Memorandum of Agreement of 18 July 1871 annexed as a schedule to the Mersey Docks (Liverpool River Approaches) Act 1871 revealed the parties' agreement that had resulted in Corporation opposition to the relevant Bill being withdrawn.[31] Provisions and scheduled agreements like these, which would have been the subject of negotiations either before the deposit of the Bill or in order to forestall hostile petitioning, show the growing importance of the local authorities involved. Recognition of their roles, and acknowledgement of their developing regulatory powers in particular, was vital for private companies who were also coming to Parliament to acquire powers without which they could neither fulfil their business objectives nor, no doubt, raise the capital that they needed.

Rating, financial and charging powers

Rating powers were of course critical for all authorities: such powers were generally founded on specific municipal purposes rather than generically based, and as their product was then hypothecated to their authorised purposes they were closely scrutinised for lawfulness. The limits on the leviable rates were increased at Bingley[32] (four shillings – 20p – in the pound without the ratepayers' consent, and five shillings – 25p – with consent). The different purposes and contexts for rating powers meant that there could be no direct comparison of poundage limits alone: that for improvement purposes, for example, was capped at two shillings in the pound for the Reading Local Board.[33] Any unusual business practice in levying and collecting rates would certainly require explicit statutory authorisation; accordingly Blackburn obtained powers 'if they think fit' to allow up to a 10 per cent discount for payment within a prescribed time limit,[34] while Oldham[35] was granted powers to lessen the rate burden:

> If at any Time the Rate for the Relief of the Poor is in the Judgment of the Corporation an unfair Criterion by which any Rates under this Act

should be made, they may cause a Valuation to be made of all or any Part of the rateable property within the Borough by some competent Person, and any Rate under this Act shall, as to the Property comprised in such Valuation, be made upon such Valuation.

An innovative provision was granted to Burnley[36] in 1871 to levy an annual lamp rate not exceeding sixpence (2½p) in the pound

> on the occupiers of lands and property within the borough, situate or within a distance (in a direct line) of two hundred yards from any public lamp for the time being lighted by the Corporation under the authority of this Act.

Living near a lamp in Burnley was presumably a mixed blessing! Ratepayers did sometimes possess more control over local taxation levels than simply the power of the next elections: at Chiswick,[37] for instance, levying an improvement rate of more than 2s. 6d. (12½p) in the pound necessitated approval by at least three-fifths of those ratepayers present 'in Person or by Proxy' at a public meeting.

It was no doubt practical experience that led authorities sometimes to seek variations (rather than more fundamental changes of principle) to the generally applicable rating law. These would typically be additional provisions included in a more wide-ranging Bill, or one promoted primarily for some other specific purpose. The Liverpool Improvement Act 1858[38] granted powers both to levy rates prospectively 'to raise Money to pay Charges and Expenses to be incurred thereafter' and retrospectively for those already incurred. Oldham obtained similar powers in 1865, but with the condition that retrospective rates had to be made within six months of the relevant expenditure being incurred.[39] Liverpool also provided that, were anyone about to quit, they were liable to pay rates immediately on demand.[40] Across the Mersey at Tranmere, the Local Board was empowered to make a rate for a period more or less than a year, so long as the period neither exceeded 18 months nor made the total payable in any one year more than it otherwise would have been.[41] At Sowerby Bridge, any rate made could include not only the expenditure it was being made to cover, but also 'what is in their Judgment a due Proportion of the Expenses incurred and to be incurred in and about making and recovering the Rate'.[42] As part of a suite of rating provisions in their 1865 Act, Oldham provided for rates to be amended (that is, in terms of who was liable to pay, rather than the rate-fixing resolution itself), and for anyone aggrieved that the 'Inequality, Unfairness or Incorrectness' in their rateable value to have a right of appeal.[43] Once 'the Objects and Purposes of this Act shall have been effected' as one of Liverpool's two 1864 Acts expressed it, with the expenses, loans and interest paid, then the power to levy an improvement rate was to cease.[44] Halifax achieved a notable outcome in securing exemption of their

Park 'from all Municipal, Parochial and other local Rates, Impositions and Assessments whatsoever'.[45]

A number of Acts contained ancillary financial powers of various kinds. The City of London was empowered to borrow money at a lower rate of interest, if that were possible, in order to pay off an existing loan at a higher rate of interest.[46] Oldham replaced the Borough Fund provisions of the Municipal Corporation Acts with their own.[47] Liverpool provided for annual accounts made up to the end of August to be open to inspection by no later than the end of the following May.[48]

Payments for gas and water that later would be called rates or charges were often termed 'rents' at this time. Reflecting the differing terminology then in use, the Merthyr Tydfil Act 1858 used both terms, referring to 'Rates for Water supplied or Water Rents'.[49] Manchester referred to 'Water Rents or Sums of Money' for supply,[50] while Loughborough's interpretation section set out that 'The term "Water Rent" or "Water Rate" shall be taken to include every Sum of Money paid to the Local Board for a Supply of Water.'[51]

Burnley, however, were content simply to refer to 'water rent' in 1871,[52] and Macclesfield similarly used the term 'gas rents',[53] while Bradford referred to both 'gas rates or rents'.[54] Aberdare defined what 'domestic water' meant – nothing ornamental, industrial, or for animals, and for no more than one water-closet and one bath, so long as the bath 'shall not be constructed so as to contain when filled for use more than fifty gallons of water'![55]

Different approaches like these show authorities using their own experience and judgment – and no doubt, if any were available, the experiences of others with similar or related local Acts already in force – to provide practical solutions for administrative, management and regulatory problems where little or nothing was available by way of national legislation, advice or guidance. Nevertheless, whatever was promoted would have to fit, in the most general terms, with the structure and assumptions of the general law; as we have seen, Parliament would permit variations, but was not going to pass clauses that were outside the recognised parameters of the jurisprudence of the day.

Building, safety and public health provisions

To the extent that the growth of modern local government was founded on the recognition (locally to begin with, if not always nationally) that industrialisation, population growth and tolerable living conditions required powers and resources that custom, common law or contract could never deliver, it is unsurprising that local Acts contained wide-ranging provisions about matters of public health and safety – 'sanitary matters', as people would no doubt have termed them in the mid-Victorian period. Whereas, however, we have noted that more than half of the local Acts of the years 1858–72 came from the northern half of England, the innovative provisions about these 'sanitary matters' overwhelmingly did so. Unsurprisingly, it was the towns and cities with the industrial raw materials, factories, pollution, overcrowding, and with evident physical and health problems, that led in trying to legislate their way to better living standards.

The prohibition of thatch provides an excellent example of this. What in some parts of the country was a traditional and effective roofing material was an immediate danger in places where sparks, smoke pollution and caustic or corrosive fallout were a constant risk. Within a four-year period, five northern towns banned the use of thatch for roofing: Oldham, Southport, Farnworth, Barrow and St. Helens.[56] The textual similarity of their provisions, and the quick succession in which the bans appeared on the statute book, make it probable that provisions like this were copied from one place to another when wide-ranging Bills were being considered and prepared for promotion. Other places, like West Bromwich, were also taking powers to improve fire safety and means of escape – in this case by incorporating and extending sections 110–12 of the Towns Improvement Act 1847.[57] West Bromwich, in fact, secured powers to make a range of safety byelaws about a variety of matters including regulating the height of industrial chimneys, preventing chimneys generally from catching fire, and cleansing footpaths and pavements adjoining properties,[58] and was not unique in doing so.

At a time of rapidly expanding urban populations, and growing appreciation of how disease spread, provisions about house construction were sought as the concept of building regulation developed. Manchester Corporation was empowered in 1858 to regulate the front elevations of new houses, at least on land they owned or controlled, by the approval of plans.[59] By 1872 more comprehensive codes of building regulations were obtaining Parliamentary sanction, like those at Birstal, Haworth and Keighley.[60] More specific or single-purpose provisions, however, were also promoted by authorities with more limited objectives. The size of underground rooms was a concern: letting or allowing occupation of an underground room below the acceptable minimum size (400 cubic feet of space for every individual sleeping there) was made an offence in Barrow in 1868.[61] No living or sleeping room was to be let if over a cesspool (Southport 1865; St. Helens 1869[62]), and at Farnworth the same requirement was more expansively drafted to refer to any 'Privy, Cesspool, Middin or Ashpit'.[63] Lodgers required at least 300 cubic feet each in any sleeping room in Wolverhampton, though at Cardiff the minimum requirement for each sleeper was 500 cubic feet,[64] while at Stockton it was an offence to let any kitchen, scullery or room of which more than a third was below the immediate ground level.[65] Southport went further in 1871, normally forbidding dwellings to be subdivided unless the resulting units each had a front and back entrance and some open yard space; moreover 'There shall not be more than one storey in any part of the roof of any house hereafter built or rebuilt, except with the consent of the Corporation'.[66]

The heights of rooms, and the necessity of providing windows (especially in the years following the repeal in 1851 of the long-standing window tax), were addressed by provisions that shared principles and intent, and sometimes shared the same Parliamentary sessions, but – if anyone expected precedent to be closely followed in matters such as this – often varied to a surprising degree in detail. At Newcastle-upon-Tyne, every habitable room in new houses had to be at least 9 feet high, or 8 feet if in the roof, with one room at least on each floor having 'an area of one hundred and eight superficial feet of floor'. Each habitable room had also to have a window, with detailed rules prescribed about their sizes, heights, and ability to be opened.[67] At Salford, the equivalent height limits (though expressed slightly differently) were 8 and 7 feet respectively, and there was no prescribed minimum room floor space. Furthermore, at Newcastle the clear glass in windows in habitable rooms had to amount to at least one-tenth of the floor space, while at Salford at least one window of 9 square feet of clear glass per habitable room sufficed, though in both cases the prescribed height requirements above the floor were similar.[68] Blackburn opted for the same minimum room heights as Newcastle, but – in a longer section combining several detailed size requirements – persuaded Parliament to approve a glazing minimum of one-twelfth rather than one-tenth of the relevant floor space.[69] Sunderland, 3 years before Newcastle in 1867, had adopted the 9 and 8 feet high minima as well, but in addition required 10 feet on the ground floor and at least 4 feet of perpendicular wall in the attics, where the floor below that part of the horizontal ceiling that was at least 8 feet high had also to comprise at least a quarter of the floor area of that room. In addition no dwelling house was to be built 'immediately adjoining any Back Street without the special Permission in Writing of the Corporation'.[70] The penalties for breach varied considerably: at Salford they were £5 and 40 shillings daily, but at Sunderland as much as £20, though only 20 shillings daily.[71] These Acts also variously contained other related provisions about ancillary matters like connecting to or building over sewers; providing ventilation; and protecting the small yard or open space that newly constructed housing had to have. They also illustrate again the recurrent theme of so much local legislation – that of general and broadly systematic principles varied by differing, and sometimes seemingly quixotic, detail.

Buildings might not only be inherently unhealthy to live in; they might also be structurally dangerous. The preamble to the Liverpool Sanitary Amendment Act 1864[72] repeated a recital from their 1842 Act[73] that

> it had happened and might happen that some of the Buildings and Walls in several parts of the Borough were sometimes in so ruinous a Condition that Passengers passing by or Persons dwelling near the same were in danger of their Lives or some bodily Harm arising from the falling thereof, or of Bricks, Stone, Timber, or other Materials therefrom.

The Corporation took powers to reduce the risks (and also to deal with houses deemed unfit for human habitation) by serving notices on owners, requiring works to be done, and enabling the purchase of any premises where the owner, refusing to do necessary works, required the Corporation to buy the property instead. (The same lengthy preamble referred to 'the great benefit of the inhabitants of the Borough' from the appointment of a medical officer of health and his exercise of his powers.) Leeds Corporation shortly afterwards in 1866 obtained a provision[74] to prohibit the construction of any cellars or passages under streets unless permission were first obtained. In a different subterranean context, a 'Coffin containing a Corpse' (as the section carefully expressed it) was not to be buried in Hove without at least 4 feet of soil on top.[75] The same Act made disturbing one grave by a person having, as it was put, 'the preparation' of any other grave an offence (maximum penalty £5);[76] if authorised disturbance for some reason were necessary in the implementation of Newcastle's 1865 Act,[77] the graves or vaults involved were to be affected as little as possible. Concerns like these reflected Victorian attitudes and anxieties generally about burials, the overcrowding or worse of some urban cemeteries in particular, and a society where child mortality rates and low life expectancy for many were in stark contrast to the burgeoning population growth overall.[78]

Authorities also began to seek powers to regulate, license or penalise a variety of activities, risks or problems for which they found the general law inadequate. Some enactments were concerned with what must always have seemed relatively trivial annoyances when considered against the general state of public health and well-being at the time, but are indicative of a different attitude to good public order and, perhaps, to enforceability: in 1870 West Hartlepool secured a law[79] that

> Any householder personally or by his servant, or by any constable, may require any street musician or singer to depart from the neighbourhood of the house of such householder, and every person who sounds or plays upon any musical instrument or sings in any street near or within hearing of such house after being so required to depart shall be liable to a penalty not exceeding forty shillings.

Rochdale included the same provision in their Act of 1872.[80] Examples of rather more significance for long-term public well-being were sections 95 and 96 of Newcastle's 1865 Act,[81] making it an offence either to sell butter short-weight or to refuse to have it weighed.

One method was to include a section that directly covered a wide range of minor matters or public nuisances, making them offences, or which would enable byelaws to be made about a wide range of relatively lesser matters, as for example of the kinds that came to be known as building regulations or 'good rule and government'.[82] Another was simply to ask Parliament for powers over specific issues: Hove, for instance, wanted to control dangerous dogs, to inspect hackney carriages, and also to license (via the Police Commissioners) sailing and rowing boats and 'Hand Chairs'.[83] Such activities were not always wholly at the instigation of the authority alone: in Leeds[84]

> If and whenever any four or more householders living in or near to any court or alley, by writing under their hands, represent to the officer of health that disease exists in any premises in or near to the court or alley, he shall forthwith inspect the premises and report thereon, but the absence of any such representation shall not excuse him from inspecting any premises and reporting thereon.

The officer of health had to pass the report to the town clerk, who in turn had to lay the report before the council, and give the owner of the premises three clear days' notice when 'at such meeting the owner shall be entitled to attend and be heard for his interest'.[85] Similar provisions had been enacted a few years earlier at Liverpool under their 1864 Act; the procedure was very similar (except that there the official title was *medical* officer of health), but, in place of the right to be heard at a council meeting before any decision was taken, the owner had 14 days to object to any plan of the Borough Engineer for remedial works, with an appeal to Quarter Sessions.[86] Disease might well be furthered by the lack of adequate clean water; at Liverpool the owner of any house of less than £13 annual rateable value without a proper supply could be compelled to obtain and pay for it, with the Corporation empowered to do the necessary works in default.[87] Clean water could not be supplied to large populations without reservoirs and extensive infrastructure: Barnsley was just one of a number of places[88] where 'in order to provide against Accidents to Life or Property by the Bursting of any Reservoir authorised to be made or maintained under the provisions of this Act' those powers included provisions to allow two justices to compel the Local Board to do repair works – and in cases of urgent danger to lower the water level.

The initiatives set out in this section reveal some of the responses to that recognition in many places, referred to at its outset, that without self-help the intolerable living conditions of pollution and disease – and indeed the inter-relation of those two – were not going to be improved in the foreseeable future. They also underline the predominant position of northern towns and cities in this respect; not surprisingly, the greatest problems drove the greatest urgency to do something about them – but it is important, too, not to overlook the many places where lesser problems existed, or where the political and public will, or the money and general capacity, to tackle local conditions was lacking, so that another decade or more would pass before broadening national public health powers became available without going to Westminster to deposit a local Bill.

Anyone left in any doubt about the prevalent risks of disease, even in places that might be thought healthier to live, had only to consider two consecutive recitals of the preamble to the Rhyl Improvement Act 1872:[89]

> And whereas the sewage of the town is discharged on to the foreshore at a point above low-water mark:
> And whereas the said town has for many years been and still is a place of great resort during the summer season as a bathing and watering place ...

Highways and streets provisions

Perhaps because the law of highways was relatively well developed, local authorities tended to seek fewer local provisions of their own – though the need to augment their powers over streets (particularly in the context of undertaking works) was rather greater. Many local Acts, including for instance those where a local authority's area was being extended, incorporated a range of provisions about private streets, other streets and highways.[90] Common law primarily governed the 'dedication or creation of highways, the right to use them, the liability to repair them, and the mode of enforcing that liability, and of otherwise maintaining a free passage over highways for the use of the public'. Statute law on the other hand, in particular at this time the Highway Acts 1862 and 1864,[91] was described as 'modifying and amplifying it to some extent'.[92] Nevertheless Oldham found it necessary to have their Act of 1865 declare that the Corporation were exclusively the 'Surveyors of Highways' for their area,[93] and Leicester required the power to cover over any water that formed part of any highway.[94] The proprietors of a street, not being already a highway, were given the right in Rhyl in 1872[95] to object to its being declared a highway, with section 54 of the Towns Improvement Clauses Act 1847 accordingly being disapplied.

If authorities could be granted the power to close a street (or to break open its surface) without notice, that would of course prove very useful to them – since it would simplify procedures, remove the possibility of troublesome objections, and generally lessen the need to plan ahead – notwithstanding any inconvenience for those affected. York Corporation were successful in obtaining this in the Lendal Bridge and York Improvement Act 1860,[96] the section succinctly providing that

> It shall be lawful for the Corporation to alter, divert, stop up or inclose the whole or any Part of any Street which the Corporation shall at any Time and from Time to Time deem necessary to be altered, diverted, stopped up, or inclosed for the Purposes of this Act.

Sunderland was granted effectively the same power in 1867,[97] but in a section drafted in a different style:

> The Corporation may stop up and discontinue as Thoroughfares, and appropriate for the Purposes of this Act, the Sites of so much of the Streets, Roads, Quays, Thoroughfares, Courts, Alleys, and Passages and Places widened, altered, improved, or interfered with by the Works, and all such other Courts, Passages and Approaches as it may be necessary to stop up in order to the Construction and Execution of the Works.

Halifax, however, in a section drafted differently again (though more similar to that in York than in Sunderland) was granted the closure powers only with the inclusion of the condition 'but with the Consent of the Owners of the Houses or other Property immediately adjoining'.[98] At Barrow, while consent as such was not required for stopping-up, the Corporation had to agree 'such Terms as to the Vesting of the Soil and other Matters'.[99] Birstal could, in the event of emergency, break open any street under the Board's own control (with equivalent powers for any bridge, sewer, drain or tunnel) without notice.[100] Farnworth, however, obtained a concise power in 1867[101] that

> It shall not be necessary for the Board before they proceed to open or break up any Street, Sewer, Drain or Tunnel, being under their own Control, to give any Notice of their Intention to do so.

Cleckheaton was similarly authorised in 1870[102] (though the section did have a qualification about exceptional provisions elsewhere in the same Act), as was Lymm in 1872,[103] so long as the London and North Western Railway Company were not involved. Similar powers over footways and footpaths, public or private, were granted to Bradford in 1858; no prior notice or consent was needed, but disturbance had to be kept to a minimum, alternative footways provided and compensation paid 'to all Parties interested'.[104] At Chiswick in the same year the responsibility for taking (and paying for) all necessary precautions in the carrying out of road works was explicitly laid on the Improvement Commissioners, and 'the Roads Commissioners [were] hereby discharged from all Liability by reason of any Accidents or Damage which may happen or ensue by reason or in consequence of any of the Works of the Commissioners'.[105] It would usually be appropriate for new streets to become highways, and to vest accordingly in the local authority, as for example at Norwich.[106]

While the relatively mature law of highways, therefore, occasioned less local initiative, it was still found wanting where regulatory powers were needed, and accordingly where highways and streets were to be stopped up, diverted, or simply temporarily opened up for works like laying sewers and drains, or pipes for new supplies of water and gas, special powers still had to be obtained.

The diversity of other provisions

The variety and diversity of provisions in local legislation – particularly of those provisions that are unique or nearly so – are a source of much interest. They seem to epitomise the 'local' element, and it is sometimes assumed that the vast recesses of the private statute book harbour many improbable Parliamentary approvals that promoters have 'bought' in contexts of questionable public interest. This work, however, has shown that so far as local authority legislation is concerned any such reputation would be ill-founded. Taken as a whole, the 278 local Acts from 1858–72, as noted both in this chapter above and the preceding one, do reveal differing, and sometimes seemingly quixotic, detail – but they also show to a considerable degree that Parliament granted this legislation along general and broadly systematic principles. There is no evidence of significant abuse either of the right to petition Parliament, or of Parliament's own constitutional authority in granting to a locality special powers not ordinarily available to the contemporary organs of local government across the land. That is not to say that deals were never done (some are manifest in the texts of Acts themselves) – nor that no untenable provisions lie within the clauses of Bills as deposited, only to have been rejected by the Select Committee – but the rules on Bill promotion, on the right or 'standing' to petition and so on, were elaborate, well administered, and of necessity respected in their observance by the parties who came to Westminster.

There are, nonetheless, some very interesting and innovative provisions to be found, and they are significant because they often reveal local authorities going beyond immediate public health or regulatory demands. The need to relieve distress provides two particularly compelling examples of a kind of local government initiative perhaps more associated with the later twentieth century than with the nineteenth. The preamble to Oldham's comprehensive Act of 1865[107] recites that on 28 August 1863 the Corporation 'with a view to alleviate the Distress existing among the Factory Operatives' took adoption steps to enable a loan application to be made under the newly passed Public Works (Manufacturing Districts) Act 1863.[108] Even more explicit is part of the preamble to Blackburn's 1870 Act:[109]

> And whereas for better enabling the Corporation to give employment, by the execution of works of public utility and sanitary improvement, to the labouring and manufacturing classes within the said borough thrown out of employment by reason of the closing of mills and factories.

To this end the Corporation had borrowed two loans under the 1863 Act totalling £144,125. These recitals, with the statutory powers sought – and granted – provide unusually graphic examples of local authorities taking direct action to try to assist their local populations (even though, presumably, at this date not many of the 'labouring and manufacturing classes' would have been voters).

Few provisions are more directly expressed than this for the object of directly benefiting local residents. Often the benefit would be longer term, incidental or unquantifiable – as where the power to regulate, for example, removed a source of danger or nuisance but it would later take the measurement of a negative to demonstrate the outcome that the promoters wanted. Practical arrangements about elections were unlikely to enthuse the public, but provided an obvious context in which the public interest, in a more philosophic sense, was served by improving the machinery of local democracy.[110] West Bromwich[111] provided for the returning officer at elections to be able to appoint a deputy. This certainly happened elsewhere, but if that were merely a prudent precaution, the problems of plural voting were more immediate –

188 *The powers and purposes*

> Whereas, when a Person is entitled to vote, not only as an Owner but also as an Occupier of Property, a Doubt has arisen as to the Number of Votes to which he may be entitled: For Remedy thereof be it enacted, That such Person shall be entitled to the Number of Votes to which he may be entitled as Owner, in addition to the Number of Votes to which he may be entitled as an Occupier, and the Votes to which he may be entitled in each Capacity shall be so stated in the Voting Paper signed by him.[112]

The number of votes depended on the value of the property on which entitlement to vote was based – anything from one to six at West Hartlepool, for instance, the fourth schedule to whose 1870 Act[113] set out the scale for commissioner elections. At Northampton[114] it was enacted that a poll need not be taken if the number of those standing for election were not greater than the number of vacancies to be filled.

Several authorities sought to amplify their powers to control matters relating to their employed officers. West Bromwich also included in their 1865 Act[115] a requirement that

> One of the Auditors of the Accounts of the Commissioners appointed by the Ratepayers shall be a person following the Profession or Business of a Public Accountant, and he need not be qualified to be a Commissioner.

A provision of this kind is evidence of the growing expectation of professional standards and integrity in the conduct of local affairs. A more unusual provision was obtained by Hove in 1858,[116] that

> The attendance of the Clerk at the Offices of the Improvement Commissioners under Section Fifty-three of 'The Commissioners Clauses Act 1847' need not be oftener than One Day in each Week, unless the Improvement Commissioners so direct.

This does not suggest an excess of duties to be performed, but may simply have been a means of encouraging suitable local appointees wary of the implications for their other business activities. In any case the Commissioners also excluded the duty in that 1847 Act for them to hold monthly meetings 'except when the Amount of Business to be transacted by them shall in their Judgment render it desirable to do so'.[117] At West Hartlepool,[118] if any Commissioner or someone on their behalf believed that an officer were about to abscond, there was a process for bringing them before two justices. Not all provisions about employees were about discipline and control, however – pension arrangements (commonly termed superannuation) had begun to appear in legislation some years earlier, and a number of places obtained powers to allow the payment of benefits in some instances. These, though, were not pensions based necessarily on contributions, discrete funding and employee rights – they were sometimes merely discretionary benefits, as at West Ham, where there was no employee contribution rate but the Local Board could pay 'retiring Pensions or Allowances of such Amounts and upon such Terms as they may deem just, not exceeding in any Case Two Thirds of their average annual Salary during the last 5 Years of their Service'.[119] Manchester already had superannuation provisions: they extended these to 'the fire police and members of the fire brigade' in 1872, but set the contribution rate at 3 per cent per annum.[120] In the same year Bolton also obtained powers to compensate firemen, or their widows and any children, 'by way of annuity or otherwise' where injury or death had occurred.[121] In a more everyday context, Liverpool provided that they had powers to appoint officers for the purposes of their 1867 Act.[122] They might have been confident of such powers for other purposes, but if there were any doubt that the new legislation was included within their scope it was easier to include a safety section than be sorry – so the drafting here included employing existing officers for the purposes of the new Act as well as for their previous duties. Authorities were well aware that powers to levy rates for any purpose at all would be vigorously tested if there were any possibility that they were not valid, and the prerogative remedies – in this case usually certiorari – were available to challenge that validity in court.

Public order was always, and would remain, a concern for the authorities at both national and local level – though the approach that could, or would, be adopted naturally varied according to the mood of the times and the perceived risks. In a number of places – Newcastle-upon-Tyne, Gateshead, St. Helens and West Hartlepool – powers were obtained in the years after the mid-1860s over street processions. The mayor at Newcastle could make regulations about the routes to be taken for public festivities, if there were any apprehension of danger from overcrowding, or potential obstruction near the Town Hall.[123] Two years later in 1867, Gateshead just across the Tyne was granted very similar provisions.[124] At St. Helens in 1869 the powers were again very similar, except that the regulations were to be made by the Council,[125] not by the mayor, and the penalty for breach had risen to £5 although the alternative of a prison sentence was not repeated. West Hartlepool in 1870 followed that same approach, with the same £5 penalty,[126] although it was for the chairman of the Improvement Commissioners to make the regulations.

Exceptional local provisions

No review of local legislation can overlook the unique, unusual and sometimes rather esoteric provisions that survived from deposited Bills into subsequent local Acts. Such provisions neither define the importance of the statutes that contain them nor exemplify the kinds of clauses that, year after year, Parliamentary agents deposited at Westminster on behalf of their principals. Nonetheless, they provide a degree of contrast and colour to the supposedly grander and more worthy legislative purposes on achieving which so much local public money was spent.

Some of that colour relates simply to language used then that is no longer used now – terms like 'fire police',[127] 'fire plugs',[128] 'basket men',[129] 'hand chairs',[130] 'hoards',[131] 'voices',[132] and 'strangers'.[133] There is also an obvious difference of type between a provision that occurs only once because it is special to a local circumstance – such as for instance about the payment of the income of the Buerdsell's, Broster's and Cuthbertson's Charities in Salford[134] – and another that occurs either once only (or very seldom) not because it would be incapable of application elsewhere, but because nobody (or hardly anybody) else sought, or was successful in seeking, an enactment to that effect. One section that appears to meet both descriptions was the duty in Exeter to carry out an execution.[135] Powers of capital punishment would, of course, not normally have been the subject of local legislation, but this exceptional declaration arose from the interrelation of the high sheriff of the city and the Devon county justices and gaol. Provisions of the second type, however, are not as numerous as might be supposed – at least not during the 1858–72 period.

Liverpool in 1859 obtained powers to make byelaws that, for 7 years to come, would exempt already constructed wagons, carts and the like from the effect of section XXVIII of their 1854 Act, which had regulated the maximum permissible width (or 'breadth' as the section had termed it).[136] That might arguably be regarded as 'special to a local circumstance', but a provision that certainly was not, and which anticipated widespread future practice, was section 91 of the Bolton Corporation Act 1872[137] whereby the Corporation could charge for police service 'on any special duty for the benefit of any individual, or of any body other than the Corporation'. At all events that seemed much more significant in its innovation than the preceding section,[138] whereby Bolton Corporation might accept statues and other monuments, and keep them in good repair without, apparently, also being given the explicit power to commission and erect their own. The Local Board at Farnworth was granted powers to establish and manage public libraries in 1867;[139] the Board, having a population exceeding 5,000, could have adopted the Public Libraries Act 1855[140] with a two-thirds majority in favour at a public meeting, but this provision removed that necessity (and also would have removed the penny rate limitation of section 15 of the 1855 Act). The Board seems not to have used this power, however, since the adoption of library powers there is not recorded until 1908, with the service itself starting in 1911.[141]

Not all authorities, even those in relatively close proximity, were necessarily moving in step with each other. Burnley persuaded Parliament in 1871[142] that

> Whenever any baths or wash-houses or bathing places established by the Corporation, having been carried on for one year or upwards, are determined by the council to be unnecessary or too expensive to be kept up, the Corporation may discontinue the same, or any part thereof, and sell or dispose of the same or any part thereof.

Meanwhile, it was enacted at Birstal[143] that

> The number of baths for the use of the working classes in any building provided by the Local Board shall not be less than twice the number of the other baths of any higher class.

Language used then that is no longer used now was not confined to simple terms!

Other kinds of powers about facilities were granted: for Leamington there was permission to let the Pump Rooms and associated pleasure grounds,[144] while Bradford were enabled to close 'any park or place of public resort or recreation under their control' to admit private groups, whether or not for payment.[145] The West Ham Local Board, in providing suitable Board offices, was given an obligation to provide 'in such Building proper and suitable Offices for the Use and Occupation of the Churchwardens and Overseers of the Poor'.[146] Bearing in mind also the extent of technical and scientific innovation at this time, in the case of Southport[147] it was enacted that

> The Corporation may take and hold any license or authority under any letters patent to use any invention relative to the manufacture or distribution of gas, or the utilisation of the residual products arising in the manufacture of gas, but they shall not acquire by any such license or authority any right or privilege in any respect of an exclusive character.

A few years earlier Tynemouth[148] had successfully promoted that

> The Corporation from Time to Time may establish, provide, maintain, and regulate, or may contribute towards the Establishment and Maintenance of all such Electrical Time Guns, Barometers, Electric or Barometric Signals, and other like Apparatus as they think fit for public Information and Use, and may pay the Expenses of keeping the same in operation out of the Borough Fund and Borough Rates of the Borough.

If at one extreme were the provisions of Oldham and Blackburn[149] about the relief of distress in the local population, at the other extreme was making offences of playing at pitch and toss, flying a kite, or making or using a slide on ice or snow (and dozens of other misdemeanours) at Stockton-on-Tees,[150] or of throwing or leaving any 'orange-peel or other refuse of fruit' on any footway in Bolton.[151]

Overview

The enactments described in this chapter, not noticed before in local government or legal literature, and taken from the many thousands of sections in the local Acts of the 15 years 1858–72, together say several things about the nature and context of local legislation at this period. While the scope and effectiveness of public local government legislation was slow to develop, local authorities – particularly in the northern half of England – were prepared to take the initiative, and to pay what it cost, to obtain the powers they felt they needed to possess in order to improve the quality of life and the wellbeing of their areas. These areas were predominantly urban; not only were the necessary units of local government still largely lacking in the rural shires, but factors equivalent to the pollution and overcrowding that prompted so much urban local self-help were less apparent (and so probably less compelling and urgent) in places where the old agricultural economy still masked the different kinds of deprivation and danger that were often prevalent there.

Those who promoted Bills did not do so lightly – the procedures were too cumbersome and too costly for that. Local Bills were but a small part of the private Bill 'industry' that had grown up from the 1840s onwards at Westminster. Given an intention to promote a Bill for some significant purpose, however, ancillary objectives would often be added on. As the 1860s passed, some authorities – in this case almost exclusively northern – began to deposit Bills that not only consolidated past provisions but in some cases sought entirely to replace the code of public local government legislation with their own 'to avoid the Inconveniences arising from several Acts of Parliament, relating to the same Purposes being in force at the same time' as the preamble to Salford's Act of 1862 put it.[152] The precise drafting of individual Bills, and hence Acts, did vary, but often in ways that were matters of style rather than having any differing legal significance. The *corpus* of local legislation as a whole, however, exhibits a high degree of conformity in terms both of the technical approach to the construction of enactments and of the principles underlying the powers and provisions that Parliament granted.

While the range and diversity of enacted local provisions, as we have seen above in this chapter, varied greatly, it must also be remembered that so did the willingness and energy of communities to seek these powers. There were many places where no local Bills at all were promoted – still less enacted – to supplement or supplant national public legislation, and many again where the additional powers obtained were minimal. When the Prime Minister the Earl of Derby declined in 1852 to pursue statutory state solutions,[153] and in 1858 the responsible Minister Charles Adderley spoke of allowing 'all those towns which desired to possess the power of self-administration to constitute local boards',[154] this patchwork outcome was what they considered appropriate. Local government has ever since equivocated between the merits of local determination and the necessity for consistent national standards.

Notes

1 See section 2 of the Towns Improvement Clauses Act 1847, 10 & 11 Vict. c. 34, and Chapter 2 *passim*.
2 The suggestion that one local Act contained a final provision to the effect 'that the Town Clerk be divorced' is thought to be apocryphal! The sorts of issues and concerns remarked here were, however, not by any means confined to the mid-Victorian

period, but seem endemic in the concept of private legislation. Speaking on 26 November 2013 of the London Local Authorities and Transport for London (No. 2) Bill, which had taken 6 years from its promotion to reach its Commons third reading, Christopher Chope, M.P. for Christchurch, remarked that

> The whole process of private legislation should perhaps be revisited by the Procedure Committee, because this Bill shows that too often Bills are brought to this House and presented without being sufficiently thought through in advance. Great chunks of the Bill have been removed as a result of the scrutiny that this House has given to it ... a Bill that originally had 39 clauses now has only 20, so it is much tighter ... I have noticed a distinct drying up of the number of private Bills being brought before the House. I hope that the thorough scrutiny to which they have been subject has become part of a deterrent process whereby people realise that one cannot just dream up some idea, put it in the form of legislation, present it, and hope that it will go through the House without anybody taking too much notice of it. H.C. Deb. 6th series, vol. 571, cols. 210–211.

If there were no precedent for a provision, that would be evident to the Lord Chairman of Committees from the Precedent Bill (on which see the reference from page 84 of Maurice F. Bond's *Guide to the Records of Parliament* (1971) set out at the beginning of the Bibliography).

3 28 & 29 Vict. c. cxl.
4 Stourbridge Improvement Act 1866, 29 & 30 Vict. c. clxix, sections 5 and 6.
5 33 & 34 Vict. c. liii.
6 Rochdale Improvement Act 1872, 35 & 36 Vict. c. cxlix, section 5.
7 Since the Sovereign in Parliament can in principle do anything, and that is the constitutional power from which statutes are derived, this confirmation was not in any real sense unlawful or invalid.
8 *Op. cit.*, sections 16 and 17.
9 St. Helens Improvement Act 1869, 32 & 33 Vict. c. cxx, section 7.
10 *Op. cit.*, section 18. Three-member wards were the norm under the general law.
11 Salford Improvement Act 1870, 33 & 34 Vict. c. cxxix, section 110.
12 Burnley Borough Improvement Act 1871, 34 & 35 Vict. c. cliv, section 24.
13 28 & 29 Vict. c. ccl, sections 155 and 156.
14 8 & 9 Vict. c. 18 and 23 & 24 Vict. c. 106 respectively.
15 Bradford Corporation Waterworks Act 1858, 21 & 22 Vict. c. lxxvi, section XI.
16 *Op. cit.*; see note 5 above.
17 Newcastle-upon-Tyne Improvement Act 1865, 28 & 29 Vict. c. ccl, section 125. The power to enforce positive covenants appeared in local legislation from time to time for well over a century afterwards; see for instance section 45 of the Grimsby Corporation Act 1962, 10 & 11 Eliz. 2, c. xxvi.
18 Kensington Improvement Act 1866, 29 & 30 Vict. c. cl, section 42. 'The Board' was the Metropolitan Board of Works, defined in section 3, whose Act this was.
19 City of Norwich Act 1867, 30 & 31 Vict. c. cii, sections 119–120. Commissioners were defined in section 102(e).
20 Tynemouth Improvement Act 1866, 29 & 30 Vict. c. li, section 12.
21 Victoria Park Approach Act 1858, 21 & 22 Vict. c. xxxviii, section XXIX.
22 *Op. cit.*, section XXIX.
23 Leeds Improvement Act 1866, 29 & 30 Vict. c. clvii, section 11.
24 *Op. cit.*, section 19.
25 Aberdare Local Board Waterworks Act 1870, 33 & 34 Vict. c. xliii, sections 15 and 16.
26 *Op. cit.*, section XXVI.
27 28 & 29 Vict. c. ccl, section 126.

194 *The powers and purposes*

28 *Op. cit.*, section 427.
29 Malvern Improvement Amendment Act 1858, 21 & 22 Vict. c. xxxi, sections XVII and XVIII–XXVI.
30 33 & 34 Vict. c. cxxviii, sections 35 and 36.
31 34 & 35 Vict. c. cxcvii. See paras. 10, 11 and 13 – and paras. 1 and 14 also, about the parties having agreed to allow the Bill to proceed, subject to various works being done and the striking out of a clause that had already been passed by the Commons.
32 Bingley Extension and Improvement Act 1867, 30 & 31 Vict. c. lxxxviii, section 40.
33 Reading Local Board Waterworks, Sewerage, Drainage and Improvement Act 1870, 33 & 34 Vict. c. cxxxiii, section 57.
34 Blackburn Improvement Act 1870, 33 & 34 Vict. c. clx, section 88.
35 Oldham Borough Improvement Act 1865, 28 & 29 Vict. c. cccxi, section 300.
36 *Op. cit.*, section 439.
37 Chiswick Improvement Act 1858, 21 & 22 Vict. c. lxix, section XLVII.
38 Liverpool Improvement Act 1858, 21 & 22 Vict. c. lxxx, section XX.
39 *Op. cit.*, section 295.
40 *Op. cit.*, section XXX.
41 Tranmere Improvement Act 1862, 25 & 26 Vict. c. xxvi, section 76.
42 Sowerby Bridge Local Board Act 1863, 26 & 27 Vict. c. lii, section 39.
43 *Op. cit.*, sections 306 and 307.
44 Liverpool Improvement Act 1864, 27 & 28 Vict. c. lxxii, section 20.
45 Halifax Park and Improvement Act 1858, 21 & 22 Vict. c. xci, section XXVI.
46 Metropolitan Meat and Poultry Market Act 1860, 23 & 24 Vict. c. cxciii, section XXIV. An account of their toll rates and receipts had to be laid annually before Parliament: section XLI.
47 *Op. cit.*, section 294.
48 *Op. cit.*, section 22. Under section XCIII of the Municipal Corporations Act 1835 accounts were to be submitted and audited twice a year, in March and September. The municipal financial year was not finally standardised as ending in all cases on 31 March until the passing of the Local Government Act 1933, 23 & 24 Geo. 5, c. 51.
49 Merthyr Tydfil Act 1858, 21 & 22 Vict. xii, section XXXIII.
50 Manchester Corporation Waterworks Act 1863, 26 & 27 Vict. c. lxviii, section 22.
51 Loughborough Local Board Act 1868, 31 & 32 Vict. c. xvi, section 3.
52 *Op. cit.*, section 193.
53 Macclesfield District Gas Act 1860, 23 & 24 Vict. c. clxxxi, section 6.
54 Bradford Corporation Gas and Improvement Act 1871, 34 & 35 Vict. c. xciv, section 38.
55 *Op. cit.*, section 18. Whether this meant filled to the brim or to the point where you could still get in without overtopping is a moot point!
56 Oldham *op. cit.*, section 53; Southport Improvement Act 1865, 28 & 29 Vict. c. cxcv, section 110; Farnworth Park and Improvement Act 1867, 30 & 31 Vict. c. lxxiii, section 44; Barrow-in-Furness Corporation Act 1868, 31 & 32 Vict. c. civ, section 91; and St. Helens *op. cit.*, section 136. All provided a penalty of £10, with power for the authority to remove the offending material in default.
57 West Bromwich Improvement Amendment Act 1865, 28 & 29 Vict. c. clx, section 25. The 1847 public Act was 10 & 11 Vict. c. 34.
58 *Op. cit.*, section 29.
59 Manchester Improvement Act 1858, 21 & 22 Vict. c. xxv, sections XVIII–XIX.
60 Birstal Local Board Act 1872, 35 & 36 Vict. c. lxxvii, fourth schedule; Haworth Local Board of Health Act 1872, 35 & 36 Vict. c. cvii, fifth schedule; and the

The powers and purposes 195

schedule to the Keighley Waterworks and Improvement Act 1872, 35 & 36 Vict. c. cviii. (Curiously, the Haworth schedule was numbered in Roman numerals, whereas that for Keighley in the next numbered private Act was numbered in Arabic.)
61 *Op. cit.*, sections 121(4) and 122.
62 Southport *op. cit.*, section 106; St. Helens *op. cit.*, section 157.
63 *Op. cit.*, section 50.
64 Wolverhampton Improvement Act 1869, 32 & 33 Vict. c. cxxxi, section 127; Cardiff Improvement Act 1871, 34 & 35 Vict. c. clxi, section 17. Section 18 and the third schedule at Cardiff also regulated the minimum sizes and occupation of lodging houses that did not come under the Common Lodging Houses Act 1851, 14 & 15 Vict. c. 28.
65 Stockton-on-Tees Extension and Improvement Act 1869, 32 & 33 Vict. c. lxxiv, section 111.
66 Southport Improvement Act 1871, 34 & 35 Vict. c. cxl, sections 71 and 73. For discussion of Henry Roberts' work on model houses after 1849, see James Stevens Curl, *The Life and Work of Henry Roberts (1803–1876), Architect* (1983), esp. chapter four, pp. 87–110.
67 The Newcastle-upon-Tyne Improvement Act 1870, 33 & 34 Vict. c. cxx, sections 74 and 75.
68 *Op. cit.*, sections 58 and 59. So while an individual window at Salford might be larger than at Newcastle, the latter required rather more glazing overall.
69 *Op. cit.*, section 29. Two of these latter three Bills, Newcastle-upon-Tyne and Salford, were allocated to the same Group F for consideration by the Commons Committee of Selection, while Blackburn was placed in Group E: 1870 *Parliamentary Papers*, vol. VI, pp. 157 and 159 (Papers 81 and 81-I).
70 Sunderland Extension and Improvement Act 1867, 30 & 31 Vict. c. cxvii, sections 71 and 72.
71 Salford *op. cit.*, section 77; Sunderland *op. cit.*, section 72.
72 27 & 28 Vict. c. lxxiii.
73 5 & 6 Vict. c. xliv.
74 *Op. cit.*, c. clvii, section 56.
75 Hove Improvement Act 1858, 21 & 22 Vict. c. cxx, section XXXV.
76 *Op. cit.*, section XXXVI.
77 *Op. cit.*, section 46.
78 See for instance Sylvia M. Barnard, *To Prove I'm not Forgot: Living and Dying in a Victorian City* (1990). The city studied here was Leeds.
79 West Hartlepool Extension and Improvement Act 1870, 33 & 34 Vict. c. cxiii, section 264.
80 *Op. cit.*, section 203.
81 *Op. cit.*
82 See for instance section 189 of the Stockton-on-Tees Extension and Improvement Act 1869, *op. cit.*, for an example of the former, and section 28 of the Rhyl Improvement Act 1872, 35 & 36 Vict. c. civ, for an example of the latter.
83 *Op. cit.*, sections LXXVIII, LXXIX and LXXX. Section LXXIX actually covered 'Hackney Carriages, Boats and Hand Chairs' and was about inspecting them, whereas section LXXX was about controlling the numbers permitted.
84 Leeds Corporation Gas and Improvements, &c. Act 1870, 33 & 34 Vict. c. xciii, section 12.
85 *Op. cit.*, sections 13 and 14.
86 *Op. cit.*, sections 4–12.
87 Liverpool Corporation Waterworks Act 1866, 29 & 30 Vict. c. cxxvi, section 36. Presumably it was not thought necessary to coerce the owners of larger houses!

196 *The powers and purposes*

88 Barnsley Local Board Act 1862, 25 & 26 Vict. c. xxxii, sections 43–53. See also note 134 to Chapter 3, and note 19 to Chapter 5 about the Dale Dyke Reservoir burst that occurred not long afterwards in 1864.
89 *Op. cit.* These recitals were in marked contrast to the idyllic scene painted in David Cox's picture *Rhyl Sands* circa 1854 (Manchester Art Gallery)!
90 See for example the Darlington Extension and Improvement Act 1872, 35 & 36 Vict. c. cxii, sections 38 and 39 (private streets) and 40–51 (streets and highways).
91 25 & 26 Vict. c. 61 and 27 & 28 Vict. c. 101.
92 William Cunningham Glen, *The Law Relating to Highways, Highway Authorities, Bridges, Railways Crossing Highways, Locomotives on Highways, and Tramways* (second edn by Alexander Glen, 1897), p. vi.
93 *Op. cit.*, section 9.
94 Leicester Cattle Market, Town Hall, and Improvement Act 1866, 29 & 30 Vict. c. xxvi, section 41.
95 *Op. cit.*, section 32.
96 Lendal Bridge and York Improvement Act 1860, 23 & 24 Vict. c. xix, section LXXXIX.
97 *Op. cit.*, section 42.
98 Halifax Extension and Improvement Act 1865, 28 & 29 Vict. c. cxl, section 98.
99 *Op. cit.*, section 71.
100 *Op. cit.*, section 99. The sidenote reads 'Streets under Control of Local Board' though this phrase does not occur in the section itself.
101 *Op. cit.*, section 37.
102 Cleckheaton Local Board Act 1870, 33 & 34 Vict. c. lxix, section 7.
103 Lymm Local Board (Gas) Act 1872, 35 & 36 Vict. c. lxxv, section 7.
104 Bradford Corporation Waterworks Act 1858, 21 & 22 Vict. c. lxxvi, section XXV.
105 *Op. cit.*, section LXVII. 'The Roads Commissioners' were 'the Commissioners of the Metropolis Turnpike Roads North of the Thames', defined in section LXIII.
106 Norwich Corporation Markets Act 1860, 23 & 24 Vict. c. xxxiv, section XVIII.
107 *Op. cit.*
108 26 & 27 Vict. c. 70.
109 *Op. cit.*
110 A summary of what the authors call 'this system of disorganisation' is contained in note 2 on pp. 194–5 of vol. I of Redlich and Hirst's *Local Government in England* (two vols., 1903). It refers to 1885, but the situation a few years earlier was no different.
111 West Bromwich Improvement Amendment Act 1865, 28 & 29 Vict. c. clx, section 6.
112 *Op. cit.*, section 8. This section captures much about the Victorian voting system at the time, before the advent of the secret ballot in 1872.
113 *Op. cit.*
114 Northampton Improvement Act 1871, 34 & 35 Vict. c. cxxxix, section 6.
115 *Op. cit.*, section 28.
116 *Op. cit.*, section XXII.
117 *Op. cit.*, section XXI.
118 *Op. cit.*, section 438.
119 Local Board of Health for West Ham, in Essex, Extension of Powers Act 1867, 30 & 31 Vict. c. lvi, section 34.
120 Manchester Corporation Waterworks and Improvement Act 1872, 35 & 36 Vict. c. xxxi, section 33. The contribution rate for police pensions under the Manchester General Improvement Act 1851, 7 & 8 Vict. c. xl, section CXCVI, had been a maximum of only 1.25 per cent.
121 Bolton Corporation Act 1872, 35 & 36 Vict. c. lxxviii, section 92.

122 Liverpool Improvement Act 1867, 30 & 31 Vict. c. clxviii, section 56.
123 *Op. cit.*, section 92.
124 Gateshead Improvement Act 1867, 30 & 31 Vict. c. lxxxiii, section 18. The drafting of the penalties (a 40-shilling fine or a maximum one month's imprisonment) was slightly different at Gateshead to clarify the justices' discretion.
125 *Op. cit.*, section 263. The Act used both the terms 'Corporation' and 'Council' in its drafting; the 'Corporation' was defined as 'the mayor, aldermen, and burgesses of the borough of St. Helens', acting by 'the Council' of the Borough, whose charter of incorporation was dated 5 March 1868.
126 *Op. cit.*, section 265.
127 For example at Halifax, 21 & 22 Vict. c. xci (1858, section LXX), and at Manchester – see note 120 above.
128 For example Salford Improvement Act 1862, 25 & 26 Vict. c. ccv, section 50.
129 See Brecon, *op. cit.*, section 73. The term occurs in the side note rather than the section itself, referring to people offering goods for open sale in public, similarly to pedlars.
130 For example in section LXXIX of the 1858 Act at Hove – see note 75 above.
131 For example at West Hartlepool – *op. cit.*, section 104. This was the Victorian usage for 'hoardings'.
132 'Voices' was the term used for members of the public coming to be heard at Parliamentary Committees – see Chapter 3.
133 'Strangers' were people from outside the Borough – see the sidenote to section LXXIV of the Halifax Park and Improvement Act 1858, *op. cit.*
134 *Op. cit.*, section 113.
135 Exeter Gaol Act 1863, 26 & 27 Vict. c. lxxiii, section 20. It will be noticed that it provided duties, rather than merely powers.
136 Liverpool Sanitary Amendment Act 1859, 22 & 23 vict. c. cxxxii, section I. The similarly titled 1854 Act was 17 & 18 Vict. c. xv. The maximum allowed at the 'widest part' was 7ft. 6ins.
137 35 & 36 Vict. c. lxxviii.
138 *Op. cit.*, section 90.
139 *Op. cit.*, sections 42 and 43.
140 18 & 19 Vict. c. 70. See also R.J.B. Morris, *Parliament and the Public Libraries* (1977), pp. 227–30.
141 Thomas Kelly, *A History of Public Libraries in Great Britain 1845–1975* (2nd edn, 1977), p. 473.
142 *Op. cit.*, section 300.
143 *Op. cit.*, section 63.
144 Leamington Priors Local Board (Extension of Powers) Act 1868, 31 & 32 Vict. c. xxvii, section 13.
145 Bradford Corporation Gas and Improvement Act 1871, 34 & 35 Vict. c. xciv, section 55.
146 *Op. cit.*, section 6.
147 *Op. cit.*, section 37.
148 *Op. cit.*, section 44.
149 See the text referred to in notes 107 and 109 above.
150 *Op. cit.*, section 189.
151 *Op. cit.*, section 103.
152 *Op. cit.*
153 See note 6 to Chapter 4.
154 See note 9 to Chapter 4.

7 Conclusion

Close scrutiny of 'local legislation' – as defined in this work – reveals for the first time a great deal of interest and significance for mid-Victorian studies of Parliament, government at both national and local levels, and indeed the overall state of England and Wales at this period. By way of summary, this short concluding chapter offers first some general observations about the sources; then considers those areas of particular interest and significance in turn; and finally suggests where further local legislation research may be profitably directed.

The scope, extent and approach of local legislation

The scope, extent and approach of local legislation have hitherto been more or less unknown in its impact as a discrete body of statutory material. There have of course been the thousands of private Acts themselves, with the Law Commission's *Chronological Table*, and the Indexes published over the years by both HMSO (or its predecessors) and more recently Ms. Rosemary Devine.[1] There have also been individual studies or monographs about particular places and their local politics, but other references to local legislation as a whole are usually generalised, and largely lack specific citation of individual enactments. No doubt this is mainly the product of the sheer bulk of the private statute book: 3,448 private Acts in the years 1858–72. It is now clear from the distillation here that just 8 per cent of them, 278, were local government-related.

Nevertheless, those 278 in themselves comprise thousands of sections and schedules, and while indexes sometimes make it possible to find particular subject-matter (such as water, public health, markets powers and the like), there has been no way of readily identifying and then surveying the coverage and impact of the 278 Acts as a whole.[2] They are all listed and referenced in Appendix 1 here. The commentary in other chapters portrays the evolution in legislative style after 1858 – when Acts as texts had changed relatively little since the late eighteenth century – towards 1872 and beyond, when Roman numerals, and capital letters for every noun, had disappeared and the drafting appears much more 'modern', not just by comparison with today but also with the contemporary style of most formal documentation of that era.

Despite the passing of some reforming public Acts beginning in the 1840s – such as the Towns Improvement Act 1847,[3] and the various Clauses Acts[4] – the powers available to local or municipal authorities were limited and patchy. They depended on the existence of municipal corporations, improvement commissions or adopted Local Boards of Health, and so predominated anyway in urban rather than rural areas. Ability to use the 1840s reforms in the 25 years following the late 1840s often depended on already possessing a 'special Act' – an individual local Act for that authority. Acquiring local facilities, particularly those needing significant capital investment or borrowing, required further dedicated local legislation – and obtaining that was likely to be expensive, often contentious locally, and procedurally complex. Most gas, water and market undertakings at this time, for instance, were private companies that had obtained their own private Acts of incorporation, so that local authorities, with little tradition of publicly funded service provision, had further to justify to populace and Parliament alike why private enterprise was not a satisfactory way to meet the identified need in their areas.

Where powers were granted by Parliament, their principles and structuring largely complied with precedent, and conformed to the systematic approach of other Bills that had been enacted. As the 1860s passed, a few of the authorities that had promoted Bills before began to consolidate their local legislation, and even to replace the national law with their own codes. Most, in fact virtually all, of those authorities were from the northern half of England. There was often a surprising degree of minor, and usually legally insignificant, variation in the drafting of individual sections across all local Acts, but any idea that they comprised a vast mass of inconsistent and self-serving provisions that contradicted the general law of the land is simply wrong.

An additional point, not apparent without a survey of the scope and extent of local legislation, is that it has also to be considered how relatively few authorities had the benefit of any local Acts at all. The 1871 Census listed 938 places that were 'municipal boroughs, places under Improvement Acts for sanitary purposes, and places of 2,000 or more inhabitants'[5] – well over three times the number of local Acts passed in the 15 years from 1858 to 1872, and four times or so when you take into account those 57 authorities or places, some 17 per cent of the total, which obtained local Acts more than once. Even where a local Act contained provisions that were well precedented, and in no way novel in legislative terms, it must be remembered that they were also in no way typical of the statutory setting under which most people in the country lived.

The attitude of Parliament

It is difficult to attribute a specific policy or approach to Parliament's attitude to local legislation. On the one hand, the majority of local Bills promoted by local authorities – 278 out of 335, or some 83 per cent – were passed, even if amendments were made, and a rigorous and frequently reviewed Standing Orders procedure ensured that Bills were considered in a systematic way, and with safeguards for the interests of those involved. On the other hand, Parliament for many years seemed unwilling to go beyond the Clauses Acts of the 1840s, and to recognise or act on the fact that relatively straightforward reforms in, or additions to, public legislation could have swept away much of the need for local expense and initiative. This reluctance was voiced more in the Commons than the Lords; imposing general duties, or acknowledging the desirability of any sort of national control or national standards, was anathema to some – and those who thought differently had still in the 1850s and early 1860s very little precedent to support their arguments. A community could in effect *buy* the powers it wanted, at a price, but the notion died hard that any hint of social or municipal compulsion would be interfering with the Englishman's inalienable right to live as he had always lived. William Lubenow's 1971 study of early Victorian attitudes to state intervention[6] aptly quotes Walter Bagehot, who 'caught this spirit' when he observed:

> our freedom is the result of centuries of resistance, more or less legal, or more or less illegal, more or less audacious, or more or less timid, to the executive Government. We have, accordingly, inherited the traditions of conflict, and preserve them in the fullness of victory. We look on State action, not as our own action, but as alien action; as an imposed tyranny from without, not as the consummated result of our own organized wishes.

Moreover, the circumstances of local legislation were largely submerged, particularly up to the economic downturn of 1866, by the flood tide of other private legislation, most of it railway-related. Where local Bills were counted in single figures, railway Bills were counted in dozens. Taking them through Parliament had become a lucrative industry for all concerned, including Parliament itself; it stood to earn huge fees from the leviathan that the private legislation industry, with all its vested interests, had become. The 504 Bills of 1864 for instance, had they all passed the Commons, would have yielded £115,035 in House fees alone.[7] Throughout the period under review, direct references to local legislation in the Select Committee examinations of private Bill procedure[8] were scant; those inquiries were prompted by an oft-repeated view that change was needed because Parliament was struggling with the huge mass of private business coming before it. Time and again, however, references to railway Bills dominated the evidence given; both Houses were jealous of their rights to consider all Bills; and any changes of practice or procedure made were trifling.

The attitude of government, national and local

The initial attitude of national Government is summed up in the two quotations that close Chapter 6. The Prime Minister Lord Derby in 1852 was not going to pursue statutory state solutions, while in 1858 the responsible Minister Charles Adderley played down the significance of his Local Government Bill (while claiming credit for inventing the term itself), referring to 'all those towns which desired to possess the power of self-administration' with the apparent assumption that many did not.[9] By the early 1870s, neither attitude could have been expressed in the same way, or at least in the same context, and Government had begun to legislate to a different agenda (as, for example, with the case of compulsory education). From 1868, Provisional Orders had made some access to local legislation easier, and the advent of the Local Government Board after 1871 was imminent. Before then, however, local authorities that had ambitions had been obliged to use the only route open to them to enable that power of self-administration – the route of coming to Westminster to petition for, and in effect buy, the powers that Government and Parliament might concede that they individually needed or could justify, but which would not otherwise be voluntarily conceded either to them or to everyone in like circumstances across the country.

The attitude of local government authorities themselves, and the communities behind them, also varied greatly. When one considers the appalling filth, overcrowding, disease and death rates of some; the civic pride and ambition of others; and the initiative and capability of yet more – with the fact that some authorities possessed most or even all of the foregoing – it is also important to consider, as already noted above, that the majority of places, whatever else they may have done, promoted no Bills and obtained no local Acts. Yet in the face of indifference from the centre, those places listed alphabetically in Appendix 3 did have the will, the determination and the resources to promote self-help, and to do for themselves what central Government would not do for them. As E.P. Hennock put it,

> before the introduction of massive Treasury grants the precarious financial basis of English local government meant that in the growing towns successful administration required among other things a marked flair for business, and ... it was essential in order to achieve anything to be able to think *adventurously* about finance.[10]

The quality of initiative and determination so often depended primarily on one or two forceful people, frequently business leaders, who could see what needed to be done locally, or what might be made of their town, and could – in the phrase – think 'adventurously' about how to achieve it. No doubt there were some who achieved more modest objectives using the powers and the possibilities that they already had without going to Westminster for more. (It is surprising, for instance, that during these 15 years there were only 2 Bills about Birmingham, though 8 each about Bradford and Leeds, 13 about Manchester, and a remarkable 15 about Liverpool.) There seems little doubt, however, that most of the drive for municipal improvement in this period came from local sources, and a very large part of that from northern England.[11]

The overall state of England and Wales

A few lines cannot portray fully the overall state of England and Wales at this time, considered particularly here in Chapters 1 and 2 in this book. Nevertheless, some circumstances seem obvious, and much can be told from the contrasts to be discerned. A country at the apogee of its international influence and wealth, whose Governments were extremely active in seeking to shape and influence international events to national advantage, found those same Governments still, in the 1860s, disinclined to effect the internal shape of their own nation to the significant degree that would come to be normal a couple of generations later. The result was private legislation about nationally unplanned and uncoordinated infrastructure, mainly railways, which distorted capital markets and certainly distorted the work of Parliament in trying to cope with its formal requirements.

Local communities had to use that same system of authentication that railway companies and others were using, to secure improvement powers for themselves that they could not otherwise obtain. The huge growth in population, and everything that came with that, meant that the old ways of living could no longer cope with the new realities. The 'information state' began only slowly to evolve,[12] but medical and public health understanding of the causes of so much mortality and disease evolved rather more rapidly. It was not surprising that those communities who felt their needs to be most urgent could not wait for a change in national mood on procuring social and physical improvements. This study has shown which places promoted local Bills, and how often, and in what parts of the country they were; what kind of provisions the authorities concerned included in those Bills; how often they promoted, and at what cost; and what was the context and climate of private local government legislation in the period of change between the late 1850s and the early 1870s. It enables historians of law, local government and social development to derive specific conclusions from the identified and enumerated Acts that were passed, and to focus on specific provisions much more readily. It also provides more evidence in the continuing debate about the emergence of the 'information state' and the relative roles (or reluctances) of Government, Parliament and the mood of public opinion, as the country – and the local authorities of the day – began to grapple with the aftermath of the embrace of technology and the industrial revolution two or three generations earlier. By taking the legislative initiatives that many of those authorities did, they themselves helped to bring about a fundamental change in that mood – and neither the local statute book, nor indeed local government itself, would ever be the same again.

Further research

Any perception that examining the scope, extent and approach of local legislation simply involves its scrutiny through a metaphorical magnifying lens is mistaken. Indeed, the opposite is true. Far from narrowing, the visible parameters hugely expand. Beyond the 335 local Bills and resulting 278 Acts lies an immense field of further inquiry and research, capable not only of illuminating the places involved but also casting much further light on the much-studied world of mid-Victorian Britain. The lens shows not merely a narrow focus of inconsequential local detail, but a wide angle of potential inquiry for which an immense trove of archival material lies largely untapped. Each Bill carries its own narrative of how it came to be proposed, drafted, deposited, opposed or supported, and (so far as it progressed) carried through Parliament. Outside the monograph studies – predominantly based on the larger northern towns and cities[13] – there are dozens of places, many promoting Bills only once or very seldom, where the story is as yet untold.

In addition to those histories, other themes abound in the hinterland of local legislation. Who were the driving forces behind local promotions? To what extent did places collaborate with each other, or actively share and benefit from their legislative experiences? How did the numerous Parliamentary agents obtain their clients, and how much did those clients spend on their services? How did they compile their legal advice, and how did those Bills that were deposited come to be framed in the way that they were? How frequently did would-be promoters never even make it to Westminster, because they could not achieve the required local support? How were communities faring that never had any 'special Acts', and had to rely on what was possible under public legislation for whatever municipal steps they wanted to take? What information may emerge from the broadening digitisation, for instance, of local newspapers, and from contemporary journals, the range of which has hitherto made extensive research almost impracticable? And finally, how does the local legislation or charters evolution of the period 1858–72 fit into its setting – that of the generation or so before 1858 since the dawn of the railway age, and the generation or so after 1872 to the end of the nineteenth century?

Questions like these deserve far more research and inquiry than they have had so far. Local legislation may have seemed forbidding to many because of its bulk, and because it was perhaps thought – by the very fact of being only *local* – to be unlikely to yield results and insights of wider consequence. Possessed now of a map of these 15 years at least, so many more places to travel become clear.

Notes

1 See Chapter 1 and the Bibliography.
2 Class V in the *Index to the Local and Personal Acts 1801–1947* (and *Supplementary Index 1948–1966*) (HMSO 1949 and 1967) is headed *Local Government (Including Judicial Matters, and Public Health)*, and while the topic information is provided, the nature of specific provisions about each topic is very limited.
3 10 & 11 Vict. c. 34.
4 See Chapter 1.

5 J.R. Somers Vine, *English Municipal Institutions; Their Growth and Development From 1835 to 1879, Statistically Illustrated* (1879), p. 254.
6 William C. Lubenow, *The Politics of Government Growth: Early Victorian Attitudes Toward State Intervention 1833–1848* (1971), p. 184, quoting Walter Bagehot, *The English Constitution* in a 1966 Ithaca New York edition at p. 262. (See also World's Classics edn, 1928, p. 254). *The English Constitution* first appeared in 1867, with a 2nd edition and additional chapter in 1872.
7 *Private Bills (Petitions, &c., 1864)*: Commons Return dated 9 February 1864 in *Parliamentary Papers*, vol. XLVIII, p. 85 (Paper 167).
8 See Chapter 3.
9 See notes 153 and 154 to Chapter 6, citing notes 6 and 9 respectively to Chapter 4.
10 E.P. Hennock, 'The Social Composition of Borough Councils in Two Large Cities, 1835–1914': essay in H.J. Dyos (ed.), *The Study of Urban History* (1968), pp. 315–36 at p. 319, quoting his own article 'Finance and politics in urban local government in England, 1835–1900' in the *Historical Journal* vi, No. 2 (1963), pp. 212–25.
11 This is apparent from the list of places promoting in Appendix 3. It is not always so explicit in general commentaries: for example, Oliver MacDonagh (speaking primarily of the 1840s) refers to 'a handful of the largest northern cities, including Manchester, Liverpool, Leeds and Newcastle. These were the cities with the best record for civic enlightenment.' He also refers to the 'development and hardening of the opposition to sanitary reform, particularly in London' in the period 1842–47. This falls short of the endorsement, particularly *after* the public health reforms of the Acts of 1848 and 1858, which many northern towns, as well as these, deserve. See *Early Victorian Government 1830–1870* (1977, p. 143).
12 See for instance notes 4 and 5 to Chapter 1.
13 See for example those cited in note 30 to Chapter 2.

Appendix 1
Local Bills promoted 1858–1872

It may appear that the study of individual pieces of local legislation involves narrow focus on extreme detail. In one sense it does; however, like examining drops of pond water through a microscope, it opens up new and very broadranging fields. Every Bill was the product of local initiative; the culmination of much work; and often the subject of vigorous local support or opposition. Behind every Act lay its history also in Parliament, in particular in a Select Committee, so that extensive study of local legislation leads to almost limitless consideration of history, development and municipal context in hundreds of localities across England.

This Appendix lists the 335 local Bills promoted (or the subject of notice to be promoted) in the 15-year period from 1858 to 1872 inclusive that have been identified as coming within the definition set out in Chapter 2 – that is Bills

> that were promoted by existing municipal corporations, or by parishes, or by equivalent bodies in London; by improvement commissioners and other entities already possessing separate legal identity and status; and by individuals who if successful would bring about a new corporate body for municipal objects.

These 335 represent a relatively small proportion of all the local and private Bill activity (as defined in Parliamentary Standing Orders terms) in these years. Most of these Bills – 278 of them – were duly enacted; the relevant statutory citation is added in the lists below.[1] The individual Bill numbers – and titles, not by any means always identical to the short titles given to the subsequent Act – are taken from *Vacher*'s annual *Lists of Private Bills*. Any Bills that at the outset (as noted in *Vacher*) did not pass Standing Orders; or the preamble for which was not proved; or were not proceeded with; or were withdrawn or postponed; are omitted below.[2] The Bills mostly originated in the Commons and have numbering accordingly, but *Vacher* marks some as 'H.L.' From 1870, *Vacher* also included a classification of the Bills and a numerical list of them, in addition to the alphabetical one taken from the Examiners' list. A note opposite the alphabetical list indicates that 'A New edition is published at Easter, showing the proceedings of Parliament on Private Bills to that time'. (The numerical list Bill titles are often not identical: for example, the 1870 Bill 3 shown alphabetically as 'Bath Corporation (Waterworks Increase and

Extension)' is simply 'Bath Corporation' in the numerical list. The *Vacher* titles, however, are often longer, and sometimes more descriptive of a Bill's scope, than the subsequent formal titles.) In 1871 and 1872 *Vacher* provided also more detailed lists of Provisional Orders applied for, under headings for tramways, rivers and harbours, and gas and water.

The *Journals* recorded petitions and subsequent stages for private Bills in a common form. For instance, the Commons *Journal* for Bill 195, the 1860 Macclesfield Gas Bill, sets out the initial formal stage on 3 February at vol. 115, p. 40 as follows:

> A Petition of the Mayor, Aldermen and Burgesses of the Borough of *Macclesfield*, for leave to bring in a Bill to confer upon the Local Board of Health for Macclesfield further Powers with reference to the Supply of Gas, and for other purposes, was presented, and read; and referred to the Select Committee on Standing Orders.[3]

Provisional orders, confirmed by Acts which from 1868 were placed in the private Acts statute book rather than listed with the public general Acts, are not included below. It would, however, somewhat distort the impression given by the lists of individual Bills for those later years were no reference at all to be made to them: accordingly Appendix 2 sets out the places for which from 1868 Provisional Orders were confirmed by Acts indexed in the local statute book. A glance at the sessional lists is enough to see, however, that outside London the majority of local legislation was promoted in the northern half of England.

Copies of Bills in the Parliamentary Archives were annotated in manuscript, and the wordings of amendments passed were interleaved into Bill copies under the vellum covers. Norman French was used in the 1860s – as apparently it still is – to record that a Bill had been passed to the Lords (*Soit brillé aux Seigneurs*), or that the Lords or Commons had concurred in amendments (*A certe bille avesque des amendemens les Seigneurs sont apertus* and *A ces amendemens les Commons sont apertus*).

In Victorian times, and indeed up to and including 1962, it was the custom to insert a comma between the words of an Act's short title and its date. (This applied to both public and private Acts.) Throughout this work those commas are for consistency omitted; thus for example 'Thames Embankment Act 1864' referred to below was actually enacted as 'Thames Embankment Act, 1864'. Clauses or section numbers in local Bills or Acts respectively (since the convention is to refer to them differently) were printed in Roman numerals up to and including 1861, when regular Arabic numerals were substituted. All nouns in the texts of Queen's Printer's copies of Acts were similarly printed with capital letters in the old style up to and including 1868, when that practice also ceased – though by then Bills and the blue-paper copies of Acts as passed that promoters printed had dropped capital letters, except where common usage demands them still today. In themselves these printing modifications mattered little, but they are indicative of the changing and modernising mood and practice that occurred during the years we are studying.

The definition of Bills

No definition, as Chapter 2 makes clear in its section *Defining 'Local' Private Bills*, is without its qualifications or exceptions. There are instances of joint or cooperative approaches, such as between the City of London and the Metropolitan Railway Company in 1860 in 23 & 24 Vict. c. cxcvii; in 27 & 28 Vict. c. xlvii, the Ashton-under-Lyne and Stalybridge (Corporations) Waterworks Act 1864; or in 28 & 29 Vict. c. ccxxviii, the Liverpool Gunpowder Regulation &c. Act 1865, for which latter the promotion costs were to be equally divided between Liverpool Corporation and the Mersey Docks and Harbour Board. Another apparent joint promotion, but without cost sharing, is the Bill that became the Cambridge Street Act 1863, 26 & 27 Vict. c. i. The *London Gazette* notice published on 25 November 1862, pp. 5754–55, gives both the Town Clerk of Cambridge C.H. Cooper and Messrs. Francis, Webster, and Riches of Cambridge as solicitors for the Bill, which provided for the closure of two lanes or passages, vesting the land in St. John's College, and for widening 'St. John's-street and Bridge-street'. Both St. John's College and the Borough (as it then was) benefited, but the Act provided for the College alone to pay for the promotion. Other joint promotion examples from the City of London and from Oxford are marked in the lists below in 1868, and involved Dukinfield and Denton Local Boards (though not passed) in 1869. A joint promotion led to the creation of a Sewerage Board by the Nottingham and Leen District Sewerage Act 1872, 35 & 36 Vict. c. cv.

There were also arrangements of necessity, such as 25 & 26 Vict. c. clxxxvi, where Brecon Corporation in 1862 had to dispose of much of its assets because it was effectively insolvent and deeply in debt. Both are included here. Bills are listed under the year in which they appear in *Vacher*. Other variations occur; in 1861, for instance, *Vacher* listed two relevant deposited plans 'in respect of which Bills have not been deposited' – Barnsley Local Board of Health and Birkenhead Improvement Commissioners. Barnsley, however, was promoted as Bill 222 in 1862 and Birkenhead as Bill 207 in 1863, both being passed.

Local authorities of course not infrequently appeared in legislation that they had not promoted. They might be given protective or similarly incidental provisions. Sometimes the degree of involvement went further: for instance, the cost of promoting what became the Leicester Waterworks Act 1866[4] was to be paid by the Leicester Waterworks Company, but it gave the Local Board of Health for the Borough of Leicester a contingent right to accept half of the profits, and to take up certain shares and borrow on mortgage if necessary (they already held £17,000 worth of shares under the Company's Act of 1851).[5] At Glossop a Bill was even promoted and passed in 1865 for the benefit of a local authority that did not yet exist.[6]

In a few cases below, the relevant Bill (or supposed Bill) is noted as not recorded in either of the House *Journals* or in *Vacher*. Sometimes Bills might be prepared and advertised but never promoted as such. There might be formal objections from the Examiners on Standing Orders, or want of funds, or a change of intent locally, or evidence that the promotion was bound to fail and so a waste of resources to continue. Whatever the reasons, it seemed worthwhile to record the limited traces left in the record by such measures, and count them in the totals below; they occasionally re-appear in a later session, and something can perhaps be deduced from the original negative outcome. Detailed local research, for instance, would probably reveal why the Parliamentary Archives contain a deposited plan for sewage irrigation works for Kingston-upon-Thames Corporation in 1872, and a manuscript copy of the notice of intended promotion that was published in the *London Gazette*, but no actual Bill.

London

London always amounts to a special case in legislative terms. Then, as now, legislation about London became part of both the public and private statute books (sometimes for purely incidental reasons – see note 18 below to the Bill that became the Metropolitan Meat and Poultry Act 1860 – this is annotated extensively to illustrate by way of exemplar just how detailed the narrative of some Bills can become, with their associated records and implications). The Bills listed below were primarily promoted by the Corporation of the City of London (chartered since early medieval times), or by the Metropolitan Board of Works, created by the public Metropolis Management Act 1855.[7] They included Bills for construction of major public works – in 1867, for instance, the creation of the Embankment and for Blackfriars and Southwark Bridges, as well as in 1869 Finsbury Park, Great Tower Hill and Holborn Valley Improvement. The lists show how many more London schemes of one sort or another were being brought forward in the later years considered below. The various Thames Embankment Bills, for instance (see notes 31, 32 and 36 below), which appear below in nearly every session from 1862 to 1872 inclusive, were mostly (but not all) private Bills – though the Thames Embankment Acts passed in 1862 and 1863 were classed as public Acts. So, too, had been the Metropolis Improvement Act 1863 (26 & 27 Vict. c. 45, introduced as Bill 23, the Thames Embankment (North) Bill), although it might from its title be expected to have been a private measure. This may apparently blur the supposedly clear distinction between public and private Bills, but it must be remembered that for most purposes the provisions that matter in practice are those that are passed into law, and that all Bills that are passed and ultimately receive royal assent become part of the overall statute book.

Corporation Bills had their own petition process, recorded in a set form in the Commons *Journal*. For example, the petition for the Epping Forest Bill is recorded there on 8 February 1872[8] as follows:

> The House being informed, That the Sheriffs of the City of *London* were at the door, they were called in; and at the Bar presented, – A Petition

of the Lord Mayor, Aldermen, and Commons of the City of *London*, in Common Council assembled: – And then they withdrew.

And the said petition, praying for leave to bring in a Bill for enabling the Mayor and Commonalty and Citizens of the City of *London* etc.

Petitions for the Corporation's Holborn Valley and Metage on Grain Bills follow on in the same form.

A helpful additional source for London is *London Statutes. A Collection of Public Acts Relating Specially to the Administrative County of London and of Local and personal Acts Affecting the Powers and Duties of the London County Council from 1750 to 1907* (vol. I, 1907). This was prepared by G.L. Gomme and Seager Berry, Clerk and Solicitor respectively to the L.C.C.

Other difficulties of definition

The Tyne Improvement Acts exemplify another kind of difficulty in tightly defining 'local Acts'. The Corporation of Newcastle-upon-Tyne had been recited in the Tyne Improvement Act in 1850[9] as being the conservators of the port, in receipt of 'Town and Quay Dues', which were thereby transferred to a Tyne Improvement Fund, with Tyne Improvement Commissioners established. Several further Acts followed, in 1859, 1861, 1865, 1866, 1867 and 1870, all promoted by the Commissioners. The last of these was 'An Act to authorise the Tyne Improvement Commissioners to collect certain coal and other dues now collected by the [Corporation], and to apply the whole thereof to the Tyne Improvement Fund'. These were accordingly *port*, rather than *town*, improvement commissioners, and accordingly – as other harbour Acts and commissioners have also been excluded – they are not included here.

On the other hand, sewerage commissioners are included: where a Bill was promoted to establish a new body of commissioners, or existing commissioners promoted a further Bill, they were similar to improvement commissioners in comprising a body set up to carry out what was a municipal function as commonly understood at that time. Drainage commissioners, however, were concerned with rather different issues, so that Bill 246 of 1861, which was passed as the Baggymoor Drainage Act that year and appointed a number of named individuals (24 & 25 Vict. c. xlviii), is not included. The six-page preamble to the Newcastle-under-Lyme Burgesses' Lands Act 1859 set out the arrangements and reasons for the creation of new trustees to hold and manage the burgesses' lands, approved at a public meeting; the trustees did not comprise a local authority in our usual sense here, but they were established for public benefit in apparent close conjunction with the Borough, and it seems appropriate to include the Act accordingly.

It must be acknowledged that these are narrow distinctions, and could be debated. There was then no equivalent of the modern section 270(1) of the Local Government Act 1972 defining what is meant by 'local authorities' – though even this has been variously amended in scope too, since it was originally enacted.

Bill promoters

It is usually obvious from the title who has promoted a given Bill; if not there, or implied by the preamble, then there will almost always be a clause at the end stipulating how the Bill costs are to be met, and the principle is of course that the promoter pays. A response to the author from the Parliamentary Archives dated 15 February 2013 notes that

> there would not appear to be a straightforward way of confirming who promoted a Local and Private Bill. ... Private Bills are started by a petition to the House by the promoters, these petitions as per most petitions don't seem to have been kept and as per all petitions the only real record is found in the *Journal*. But as you would have no doubt found the record of the petition varies from giving the name of the railway company to record of 'A Petition of Suitors for a Bill'.

This can make it difficult to be certain of promoters in cases where the Bill was not enacted and, in default of an available text, reliance has to be placed on the possibly ambiguous Bill title given in the House *Journals*, or listed in *Vacher*. Where a copy of the original printer's text of the Bill as now enacted is available (often printed on pale blue paper – some sets of Private Acts of that time are made up from them) it will have the solicitor's and/or Parliamentary agent's name on it, and from the former – the name of a Town Clerk, for instance, if it was a municipal promotion – the promoter is usually (but by no means always) clear.

Fortunately, there is a further resource that usually solves the problem of identifying who was promoting. A notice of intention had to be published in the *London Gazette* by the due date stipulated in the Houses' Standing Orders. Such notices had to set out in some detail the objectives of the proposed Bill, and would be undersigned by the party or parties publishing them.[10] Those notices are still available for consultation; most would be published on or shortly before the last day permitted under the Standing Orders. (Under Commons Standing Order 18 in the 1866 edition (Paper 480), for instance, publication was required in either October or November immediately preceding the application for a Bill.) A few Bills appear in the *London Gazette* but not in *Vacher*, and again some cannot be found in the Commons or Lords *Journals*. This is probably because an intended Bill has for some reason not been promoted when expected, or that for some other reason it has been rejected by the Examiners under Standing Orders, and so has not reached the stage of formal Commons or Lords consideration. One hundred and fifty years later, all this makes a complete record (and absolute numerical accuracy) virtually unachievable – but it does illustrate, however, something of the scale and uncertainty of the private Bill promotion process at this time. There could be many reasons, other than purely technical ones, why an intended or published Bill did not in the event proceed.

Totals of Bills promoted

In total during the years 1858–72, 3,448 of the 5,458 deposited private Bills listed in the official Parliamentary returns – that is 63.17 per cent – eventually received the Royal Assent and thereby became Acts. (The 5,458 fall just 20 short of averaging one for every day during those 15 years.) The individual annual totals are tabulated in Chapter 1; the reason that the Bill totals given there are derived from the official returns rather than *Vacher* concerns the numbers of intended Bills which for one reason or another were withdrawn, held over, or failed to pass preliminary procedural stages etc. The bulk of the private statute book is huge; in 1858, for instance, the 150 Acts passed comprise some 2,434 pages. Bill promotions rose to their peak in the mid-1860s: in 1865, the 382 private Acts set out in the *Chronological Table* occupied 6,358 pages, and in 1866, when there were 363 such private Acts, they occupied 5,739 pages. The general subject matter of a Bill is evident from its title. In order to establish precisely which Bills or Acts come within the definition used here, the relevant texts have wherever possible been examined.

The Bills set out below are listed alphabetically by place in Appendix 3.

***

Sessional lists of local Bills promoted by defined local authorities, etc.

Each Bill number given below is described in *Vacher* (to quote the 1858 rubric) as 'that on the Petition List, and indicates the order in which the respective bills as will be taken up by the Examiners'. As noted above, the titles are similarly those given in *Vacher*, and often differ from short titles provided in subsequent Acts. A few Bill numbers have not been able to be traced.

Bill		Statute Cap.
1858	**21 & 22 Vict.**	**16 Bills; 16 Acts**
208	Birkenhead Improvement Commissioners (Bondholders' Arrangements)	lxxxv
143	Birkenhead Improvement Commissioners (Gas and Water)	cxxi
52	Bradford Corporation Waterworks	lxxvi
139	Chiswick Improvement	lxix
153	Halifax Park and Improvements	xci
175	Hove Improvement	cxx
101	Liverpool Improvement	lxxx
93	Malvern Improvement	xxxi
105	Manchester Assize Court House	xxiv
131	Manchester Corporation Water	lxxxvii
132	Manchester Improvement	xxv
47	Merthyr Tydfil Water	xii
87	Metropolitan Board of Works (Victoria Park Approach)	xxxviii
107	Middlesbrough Improvement	cxl
11	Vauxhall Bridge Road	xxxii
205	Wallasey Improvement	lxiii

(continued)

212 *Appendix 1*

1859[11]	22 Vict.	2 Bills; 2 Acts
82	York Improvement[12]	xix
122	King's Lynn Borough and Port and Harbour Improvement	xxxii

1859	22 & 23 Vict.	6 Bills; 6 Acts (1 Private and Personal)
54	Ipswich (Borough) Fishery	lxxii
180	Liverpool Sanitary Amendment	cxxxii
145	Newcastle-under-Lyme Burgesses' Lands[13]	ciii
70	Portsmouth New Docks and Railway	lx
79	Salford Borough (No. 2)[14]	xix
258	Westminster Improvements	*3*[15]

1860	23 & 24 Vict.	17 Bills; 15 Acts (1 Public)
232	Abergavenny Improvement	cxxxvii
63	Bucks County Rate[16]	lxxxvi
78	Gas (Metropolis)[17]	125
101	Hedon Corporation and Borough Improvement	xxxi
213	Leicester Cemetery	xxii
8	Liverpool Corporation Water	xii
70	Llandaff and Canton District Markets	
279	London Railway Depôt and Storehouses[18]	cxcvii
195	Macclesfield Gas[19]	clxxxi
155	Manchester Corporation Water	xciii
156	Manchester Improvement	xlviii
158	Smithfield Markets, Streets, and Improvements[20]	cxciii
249	Norwich Corporation, Markets, &c.	xxxiv
210	Swansea Local Board of Health	cxlviii
302	Westminster Improvements	
104	Wigan Water	clxxxvi
31	York Improvement, &c.	xix

1861	24 & 25 Vict.	17 Bills; 14 Acts
51	Bolton Corporation	clxxiii
161	Birmingham Improvement	ccvi
287	Clifton and Durdham Downs (Bristol)	xiv
277	Darlington Local Board of Health	lxviii
94	Dewsbury, Batley and Heckmondwike Water	xxxiii
202	Liverpool Cemetery	civ
154	Liverpool Improvement	xlii
307	Middleton and Tonge Improvement[21]	c
170	Newgate and Metropolitan Meat and Poultry Markets	lii
171	Preston Markets	vii
386	Richmond Improvement[22]	
25	Ryde Water	lviii

Appendix 1   213

210	South Shields Improvements and Quay	xxiii
	Sutton Coldfield Corporation Estate (H.L.)[23]	
308	Tonge Improvement[24] *(Consolidated with Middleton Improvement)*	
152	Wallasey Improvement	iv
380	Westminster Improvements	cxxvi

1862   **25 & 26 Vict.**   **19 Bills; 17 Acts (1 Private and Personal; 1 Public)**

Acts up to and including liv were styled 25 Vict. only as printed (a general practice in the early part of a regnal year). From this session onwards, the section numbers in Acts, hitherto in Roman numerals, were printed in Arabic numerals.

27	Barnsley Local Board of Health	xxxii
156	Bollington (Prestbury) Improvement and Lighting	xxxvii
117	Bradford Corporation Water	xviii
310	Brecon Markets and Fairs	clxxxvi
39	Cardiff Borough and Llandaff and Canton Markets	cxxiii
299	Crystal Palace District Improvement	
142	Halifax Corporation	xli
200	Kent County Gaol and Lunatic Asylum (Water Supply)	xxv
189	Leeds Water	lii
107	Liverpool Corporation Water	cvii
212	London Railway Depôt and Storehouses	lvii
154	Metropolitan Meat and Poultry Market (Western Approach)[25]	clxxiv
169	Norwich Corporation	iii
	Saint Thomas's Hospital	4[26]
254	Salford Improvement	ccv
63	South Molton Corporation	xxvii
199	Thames Embankment	93[27]
318	Thames Embankment (South Side)	
243	Tranmere Local Board	xxvi

1863   **26 & 27 Vict.**   **14 Bills; 14 Acts (2 Public)**

207	Birkenhead Improvement	cvi
161	Blackfriars Bridge	lxii
189	Cambridge Saint John's Lane Stoppage, &c.[28]	i
324	Coventry Market House	xcii
304	Exeter Gaol[29]	lxxiii
162	London (City) Traffic Regulation	ccvi
68	Manchester Corporation Water	lxviii
254	Rotherham and Kimberworth Local Board of Health[30]	cxvii

(continued)

214 *Appendix 1*

104	Rugby Water	xxxiii
202	Southampton Port, Harbour and Pier	cxix
268	Sowerby Bridge Local Board	lii
133	Swansea Municipal Corporation	xiii
23	Thames Embankment (North Side)	45[31]
65	Thames Embankment (South Side)	75[32]

1864	**27 & 28 Vict.**	**11 Bills; 10 Acts**
156	Ashton-under-Lyne and Stalybridge (Corporations) Water[33]	xlvii
260	Bolton Improvement	cci
64	Holborn Valley Improvement[34]	lxi
345	Lancaster Local Board of Health	cviii
166	Liverpool Improvement	lxxii
165	Liverpool Sanitary	lxxiii
42	Metropolitan Subways[35]	
160	Metropolitan Meat and Poultry Market	xv
159	Southwark Park	iv
158	Thames Embankment (South Side)[36]	cxxxv
298	Wallasey Improvement	cxvii

1865	**28 & 29 Vict.**	**24 Bills; 24 Acts**
536	Blackpool and Layton-with-Warbrick Improvement	ccxiv
161	Bolton Improvement	xii
400	Carnarvon New Water	xcix
376	Halifax Extension and Improvement	cxl
163	Leicester Lunatic Asylum and Improvement	vii
578	Liverpool Gunpowder Regulation, &c.	cclxxviii
141	Liverpool Improvement	xx
404	Llanelly Local Board of Health	lxv
143	Manchester Corporation Waterworks	cxlv
142	Manchester Improvement	xc
403	Merthyr Tydfil Local Board of Health	cxxxviii
	Metropolitan Market[37]	ccviii
355	Newcastle-upon-Tyne Improvement	ccl
390	Oldham Borough Improvement	cccxi
251	Oswestry Local Board	ix
285	Ripon Local Board	cxxvi
407	Ross Improvement	cviii
307	Southampton Corporation	clxii
531	Southport Improvement	cxcv
263	Sunderland Corporation	lxx
510	Tunbridge Wells Water	cciv
466	West Bromwich Improvement	clx
484	Westminster Improvements	clxxxvii
208	West Worthing Improvement	xxvii

Reference must also be made to Bill 482, Glossop Water, passed as the Glossop Waterworks Act 1865, c. cxv. See also note 6.

Appendix 1   215

1866	29 & 30 Vict.	24 Bills; 17 Acts (1 Private and Personal)
503	Aberavon Local Board Banbury Extension[38]	ccxl
499	Barnsley Local Board of Health	xcviii
387	Bath Corporation	
388	Bradford Corporation	ccxxii
	Rawson's Estate	5[39]
466	Bury Gas	xlii
337	Congleton Gas and Improvement	lii
375	Kensington Improvement	cl
324	Leeds Borough[40]	cli
325	Leeds Improvement Acts Amendment	clvii
222	Leicester Cattle Market, Town Hall, and Improvement	xxvi
326	Liverpool Corporation Waterworks	cxxvi
491	London (City) Corporation Gas	
492	London (City) Traffic Regulation	
216	Manchester Improvement	xxix
579	Middlesbrough Extension and Improvement	cxliii
395	Nelson Local Board	lxxvi
374	Park Lane Improvement	
265	Stockton Gas	cvi
592	Stourbridge Improvement	clxix
373	Thames Embankment (Chelsea)	
372	Thames Embankment (North) Approaches	
497	Tynemouth Improvement	li

See also note 41 on the total cost of the four Metropolitan improvements promoted in Bills 372, 373, 374, and 375 above.

1867	30 & 31 Vict.	31 Bills; 27 Acts
232	Bingley Extension and Improvement	lxxxviii
248	Birkenhead Improvement Commissioners	xcii
152	Blackfriars and Southwark Bridges	iii
229	Brighton Improvement	xxii
247	Dewsbury, Batley, and Heckmondwike Water	lxii
270	Farnworth Park and Improvement	lxxiii
182	Gateshead Improvement	lxxxiii
91	Heywood Improvement	lxiv
155	Holborn Valley Improvement	lv
6	Ipswich Fishery	xlvi
233	Keighley Water, &c.	liv
205	Leeds Corporation Water	cxli
206	Liverpool Improvement	clxviii
154	London City Municipal Elections[42]	i
116	Manchester Corporation Water	xxxvi

(*continued*)

216   *Appendix 1*

249	Metropolis Subways[43]	
191	Norwich Local Board of Health	cii
35	Nottingham Improvement	x
38	Park Lane Improvement	
57	Plymouth Corporation Water, &c.	cxxviii
104	Salford Borough	lviii
273	Stockport Corporation Water	xcix
193	Sunderland Extension and Improvement	cxvii
194	Sunderland Ferry	lxxix
37	Thames Embankment (Chelsea)	
36	Thames Embankment (North) Approaches	
115	Wallasey Improvement	cxxxii
172	West Ham Local Board of Health	lvi
272	Widnes Gas, Water, and Improvement	cxxvi
103	Wolverhampton New Water	cxxxiii
39	Worcester County and City Gaols	xxiii
1868	**31 & 32 Vict.**	**25 Bills; 23 Acts**
78	Barrow-in-Furness Corporation	civ
5	Bradford Waterworks and Improvement	cxl
28	Caversham Bridge	lx
150	Chichester Cattle Market	lxvii
121	Dartford Water	cxix
190	Halifax Corporation Waterworks and Improvement	cxxvii
1	Haverfordwest Borough	xxxiv
131	Leamington Priors Local Board of Health	xxvii
64	Leicester Improvement, Drainage, and Markets	xxiv
202	Lincoln Corporation (Canwick and Monks Leys Commons)	xxii
66	London (Corporation) Gas[44]	cxxv
151	Loughborough Local Board	xvi
115	Marylebone (Stingo Lane) Improvement	vii
41	Metropolis Subways[45]	lxxx
219	Oxford Police[46]	lix
37	Park Lane Improvement	
59	Portsmouth (Borough) Water	xxix
60	Portsmouth Camber Quays	cxxviii
29	Reading Local Board of Health	lxxxi
104	Saint Mary Church Local Board	cxxix
148	Salford Hundred and Manchester (City) Courts of Record	cxxx
36	Thames Embankment (Chelsea)	cxxxv
35	Thames Embankment (North and South)	cxi
24	Tynemouth (Borough) Quays and Improvement	
41	Wolborough Local Board	lxxv[47]
1869	**32 & 33 Vict.**	**21 Bills; 18 Acts**
3	Bradford Water	cxxxv

Appendix 1 217

76	Dukinfield and Denton Local Boards of Health	
192	Finsbury Park Act, 1857, Amendment[48]	
141	Great Tower Hill[49]	xii
75	Grimsby Corporation	x
95	Holborn Valley Improvement	xx
92	Huddersfield Water	cx
173	Keighley Water	cxxix
31	Leeds Improvement	xi
96	London (City) Subways[50]	xxx
198	Manchester Corporation Waterworks, and Improvement	cxvii
172	Melton Mowbray Cattle Market, &c.	xxvii
211	Milford Improvement	xcvii
68	Oldham Corporation Water, &c.	
130	Oswaldtwistle Local Board	lxvi
93	Park Lane Improvement	cxxxiv
34	Preston Corporation	lxxxvii
193	Ross Improvement Act, 1865, Amendment	lxxix
183	Saint Helens Borough Improvement	cxx
97	Stockton-on-Tees Extension and Improvement	lxxiv
187	Wolverhampton Borough Improvement	cxxxi
1870	**33 & 34 Vict.**	**28 Bills; 22 Acts**
217	Aberdare Local Board Water	xliii
51	Ashton-under-Lyne, Stalybridge and Dukinfield (District) Waterworks	cxxxi
3	Bath Corporation (Waterworks Increase and Extension)	liii
225	Blackburn Corporation Improvement	clx
159	Brighton Intercepting and Outfall Sewers	c
138	Cleckheaton Local Board	lxix
114	Fosdyke Bridge	xxxiv
151	Halifax Water and Gas Extension	xcv
83	Hyde Local Board	xvii
61	Leeds Corporation Gas and Improvements, &c.	xciii
62	Leeds Corporation Gas (Purchase of Existing Gasworks, &c.)	lvi
82	Leicester Lunatic Asylum	iv
226	Lincoln City Commons	lxxxvii
29	Liverpool Improvement and Waterworks	
95	Newcastle-upon-Tyne Improvement	cxx
32	Northampton Markets and Fairs	xlv
31	Oldham Corporation Waterworks, &c.	cxliv
66	Reading Local Board of Health	cxxxiii
157	Rotherham and Kimberworth Local Board of Health	cxxxiv
116	Saint Alban's Borough Extension and Improvement	
64	Salford Borough Improvement	cxxix
158	Sheffield Corporation Gas (New Works)	

(*continued*)

218   *Appendix 1*

213	Sheffield Corporation Gas (Purchase)	
25	Sheffield Corporation Water	
60	Thames Embankment (North)	xcii
41	West Hartlepool Extension and Improvement[51]	cxiii
152	Yeovil Improvement	lxxxviii
195	York Markets and Fairs and Improvement	
1871	**34 & 35 Vict.**	**37 Bills; 24 Acts**
155	Abergavenny Improvement	xcii
192	Batley Corporation Water	xl
112	Beckenham Sewage[52]	
106	Billingsgate Market	lv
154	Bradford Corporation Gas	
128	Bradford Corporation Gas and Improvement	xciv
256	Burnley Borough Improvement	cliv
	Cambridge Improvement[53]	
67	Cardiff Improvement	clxi
235	Chorley Improvement	lxvi
108	City of London Court	iii
215	County of Northampton (Vesting of Land, &c.)	
109	Court of Hustings (London) Abolition	
21	Hornsey Local Board	cxxix
91	Huddersfield Improvement	cli
92	Huddersfield Water	xxiii
231	Ilkley Local Board	xlv
120	Ince Water	c
107	Leadenhall Market	liv
143	Lincoln Water[54]	cxlix
147	Liverpool Improvement and Water	clxxxiv
104	Manchester Improvement	
46	Metropolitan Board of Works (Leicester Square Improvement)	
47	Metropolitan Board of Works (Metropolis Sewage and Essex Reclamation)	
45	Metropolitan Board of Works (Purchase of Hampstead Heath)	lxxvii
44	Metropolitan Board of Works (Shoreditch Improvement)[55]	
37	Newcastle-upon-Tyne Improvement	cxxxv
36	Northallerton Borough Gas	
240	Northampton Improvement	cxxxix
242	Poplar and Greenwich Ferry Roads	
252	Richmond Sewage	cxxiv
144	Salford Borough Drainage and Improvement	cx
239	Sheffield Improvement	lxxix
226	Southport Improvement	cxl
118	Surrey County Offices[56]	clix
66	Todmorden Local Board	
55	Walsall Improvement and Markets	

Appendix 1   219

1872	35 & 36 Vict.	43 Bills; 29 Acts
280	Aberystwyth Improvement, Water, &c.	xxx
21	Barrow in Furness Corporation	cxiii
241	Birmingham Sewerage	
279	Birstal Local Board	lxxiii
93	Bolton Corporation	lxxviii
230	Brighton Corporation Water	lxxxvi
146	Bury Improvement and Waterworks	cxlvi
221	Darlington Borough Sewage Irrigation	xxxiv
186	Darlington Improvement	cxii
222	Elland Board of Health (Gas Transfer)	
86	Epping Forest[57]	
20	Haworth Local Board of Health	cvii
276	Hereford Improvement	cxix
256	Hindley Local Board (No. 1)	
50	Hindley Local Board (No. 2)	lxxx
85	Holborn Valley and Farringdon Market Improvement	lxxxi
214	Keighley Water	cviii
220	Kingston-upon-Hull Water and Court of Record	cc
	Kingston-upon-Thames Corporation[58]	
126	Leeds Improvement	xcvii
35	Liverpool Tramways	cxxii
224	Lymm Local Board Gas	lxxv
143	Manchester Corporation Water and Improvement	xxxi
87	Metage on Grain (Port of London)	c
57	Metropolitan Street Improvements	clxiii
18	Nottingham and Leen District Sewerage[59]	cv
303	Pontypridd District Stipendiary Magistrate[60]	xiv
228	Rhyl Improvement	civ
99	Rochdale Borough Extension and Improvement	cxlix
290	Sheffield Corporation (Payment of Costs)	
269	Sheffield Corporation Tramways[61]	
	Sheffield Corporation Water[62]	
277	Staines Town Hall and Market	xxii
148	Stanford (Hove) Estate Improvement[63]	
88	Sun Street (City of London) Maintenance[64]	
158	Swansea Local Board of Health	xv
82	Thames Embankment (Land)	
72	Thames Embankment, North[65]	lxvi
281	Thames Sewerage Commission[66]	
102	Tormoham Local Board of Health	
302	Wallasey Improvement	cxxv
125	Warwick Local Board Water	ci
197	West Worthing Improvement	

220 *Appendix 1*

Notes

1. The total of Bills passed included three cases (all noted against their passing) where the resulting Acts were printed as personal and private Acts, and another four cases where what were promoted as private Bills were printed as public Acts. All seven had occurred by 1866.
2. For example, the Bath Corporation Bill, nod. 387, of 1866 did not pass the Standing Orders. It was referred to the Select Committee on Standing Orders, which could authorise that the Bill should continue to be considered notwithstanding its failure to pass. It was decided in this case, however, that the Standing Orders 'ought not to be dispensed with' – see House of Commons *Journal*, 8 March 1866, vol. 121, pp. 441–2 and 16 March, p. 168 respectively. Sometimes it might be some time before a Bill was rejected on Standing Orders grounds following formal Select Committee consideration of whether in the face of some technical challenge or defect it should be allowed to proceed, and such cases are included here, as the Bills have been the subject of evidence and debate – as for instance in the case of Bill 44 in 1871, the Metropolitan Board of Works (Shoreditch Improvement) Bill.
3. The Bill proceeded, however, only after a dispensation – see note 19 below.
4. 29 & 30 Vict. c. xxvii. See the preamble and sections 35–47 and 56. The Act was passed as just 29 Vict. c. xxvii.
5. The 1851 Act was 14 Vict. c. xxxiii.
6. This Bill was promoted by individuals when, to quote the preamble, 'there is not as yet any Local Authority constituted for the said Town or Township of Glossop or any Part thereof'. Section 32 and those following proceeded to provide for the sale to any local authority for the district, and to give that local authority powers accordingly. It was exceedingly unusual for this to occur in this fashion, so that – while not technically a local Bill as defined here – it nevertheless gave what amounted to royal assent to local Act powers. Glossop achieved borough status in 1866.
7. 18 & 19 Vict. c. 120. For a list of the Acts then affecting the Metropolitan Board of Works see Appendix 7 to the *Third Report* of the 1867 Select Committee referred to in note 42 below. Appendix 13 set out the local Acts of the metropolis itself.
8. Vol. 127, p. 13.
9. 13 & 14 Vict. c. lxiii.
10. The notice for the Banbury Extension Bill intended for 1866, published in the *London Gazette* on 28 November 1865, pp. 6019–20 was – very unusually – not undersigned, and gave no indication of who were the promoters. (Though it is presumed to have had a municipal origin, it is possible that the Bill was the result of independent local initiative.)
11. Parliament was prorogued on 19 April 1859 ahead of the general election. On 11 April, in anticipation, the Commons made a Standing Order that

    the promoters of every Private Bill which has been introduced into this House, or brought from the House of Lords in the present Session of Parliament, shall have leave to suspend any further proceedings thereupon, in order to proceed with the same Bill in the next Session of Parliament.

    Where this happened, fees paid and petitions submitted were also to be carried forward. The Order was printed that day as Paper 206, *Parliamentary Papers* (session 1), vol. XXIII, p. 3.
12. The York Improvement Bill was enacted as the York Improvement (Foss Abandonment) Act 1859.
13. It is not apparent from the *London Gazette* notice dated 9 November 1858 who was actually promoting, as opposed to who was acting for them (19 November 1858, p. 4938).

Appendix 1 221

14 An earlier Bill the same title and apparently the same number was withdrawn, this Bill being passed as the Salford Gasworks Act.
15 Included in the separate italic numbering of Private and Personal Acts.
16 This Bill is listed in *Vacher* (which, like the Bill itself and the eventual Act, prints the name as just 'Bucks') but with no number. It appears in the Commons *Journal* for 10 February 1860 (vol. 115, p. 62) where leave was given to deposit a petition for a Bill, since 'the Standing Orders ought to be dispensed with'. The number 63 is printed on the deposited Bill in the Parliamentary Archives.
17 *Vacher* also lists the Gas (Metropolis) Bill, notice for which had been given under the title 'London Metropolitan Gas Regulation' in the *London Gazette* on 18 November 1859 at pp. 4144–6. Unnumbered in *Vacher*, it is identified as Bill 78 in the Commons *Journal*, and is recorded there through all its stages as a private Bill, presumably because it referred specifically to a number of gas companies in the metropolitan area, though under section LVI its costs of promotion were to be paid by the Metropolitan Board of Works from levies on the respective Vestries and Local Boards proportionate to their annual rateable value – the 'enormous sum of money ... expended in contesting the Bill' was the subject of comment by Lord Stanley of Alderley in the Lords on 14 August 1860 (three days before he joined the Cabinet as Postmaster-General) at *Hansard* vol. CLX, col. 1247. It received royal assent, however, as a public Act – the Metropolitan Gas Act 1860, 23 & 24 Vict. c. 125 (and is also listed in Part II of the *Classified Index to the Journals of the House of Lords: From 1833 to 1863, both inclusive* at p. 218 as public). It is included here as it was regarded as a hybrid Bill – a term applied to it in the Commons by Lord Robert Cecil on 10 July 1860 at *Hansard*, 3rd series, vol. CLIX, col. 1687. The Bill, renumbered 276, was the subject of a special report recorded in the Commons *Journal* on 18 July at vol. 115, p. 397. (Meanwhile a notice had been published in the *London Gazette* on 29 November 1859 at p. 4500 that the United Gas Consumers' Company (Limited) proposed also to bring in a Bill for the 1860 session. This Bill, however, did not appear in *Vacher* and was not passed.) In 1866, *Vacher* also records Bill 601, the Metropolis Gas Act Amendment Bill, but it is noted as 'not proceeded with'.
18 This Act was linked to the Smithfield Markets, Streets, and Improvements Act (Bill 158), c. cxcvii giving powers to both the Corporation of the City of London and the Metropolitan Railway Company, following on from the authorisation of the new Market House by c. cxciii, passed as the Metropolitan Meat and Poultry Market Act 1860. (Lord Berners had brought a petition about the metropolitan markets to the Lords on 17 May 1858: *Hansard*, 3rd series, vol. 150, cols. 761–63.) The Bill for this latter 1860 Act does not appear in *Vacher*: it was introduced as a public Bill nod. 158 (later Bill 212), entitled Smithfield Markets, Streets and Improvement Bill. The reason was explained at second reading by Mr Edward Pleydell-Bouverie, M.P. for Kilmarnock Burghs,

> that this Bill, which was essentially a private Bill, had been introduced as a public one by a Motion in the house. Such a course was permitted only when a measure of this sort was brought forward by a Member of the Government, because the Crown could not appear as petitioner for a private Bill before the House.
> (*Hansard*, 3rd series, vol. 159, col. 21, 7 June 1860)

The Crown had land ownership rights affected; clause X of Bill 158 made the market site part of the City of London, but this was amended, and clause XI of Bill 212 placed the market site more specifically within the City of London's Ward of Farringdon Without, and added that it was to continue to be rated by the existing responsible Parish of Saint Sepulchre, Middlesex. Following amendment it became Bill 212; see the Commons *Journal*, vol. 115 variously on 24 March (p. 269); 15 June, when the several previous Select Committees on this subject and site were set out and referred to the current Committee on the Bill (p. 305); 27 June (p. 337); and 10 July (p. 370). Questions and concern in the Commons about the site and its future continued: see *Hansard* for 2 April (vol. 157, cols. 1715–17); 20 April (vol. 157, col. 2050); and 30 April (vol. 158, cols. 305–311). A statement about the site addressed to the Secretary of State by the Governor of St. Bartholomew's Hospital had earlier been printed in *Parliamentary Papers* for 1857–8 at vol. XLVIII, p. 417 (Paper 224). See also the representations about the 'dead meat market' by St. Sepulchre's Wardens at *Parliamentary Papers* (1866) vol. LIX, p. 183 (Paper 103). The Act included a provision (clause XIX in Bill 212, the drafting of which the Commons had slightly amended) to lay a wood pavement in Duke Street to protect the Hospital.

The preamble to the Metropolitan Railway Act 1860, 23 & 24 Vict. c. lviii, also refers to the then current Bill promotion by the Corporation. (The London Railway Depot and Storehouses Act 1860 was repealed by the similarly named Act of 1862–25 & 26 Vict. c. lvii – and the powers to undertake the 1860 Act works thereby abandoned, but the 1862 Bill appears to have been promoted by the Company alone.)

19 This is an interesting example of the working of the Standing Orders procedures. One of the Examiners of Petitions reported on non-compliance with the Standing Orders, and the Bill was referred by the Commons to that Select Committee (*Journal*, vol. 115, p. 39, 3 February). On 10 February, the House accepted a recommendation from the Select Committee that the Standing orders ought to be dispensed with provided that provisions be inserted into the Bill that no works be erected – without their consent – within 300 yards of various cottages and houses occupied or owned by certain named individuals. Leave to bring in the Bill was later given accordingly (vol. 115, pp. 62, 63). The required protective provisions were duly enacted in section XVI of the Macclesfield District Gas Act 1860.

20 See footnote 18.

21 Marked (*Consolidated Bill*) in *Vacher*. Accordingly the Tonge Bill is not counted again in the list above.

22 This Bill comes after the withdrawn Bill 245 of 1859, Richmond Improvement, for which Muggeridge & Co. had also been the agents.

23 No Bill number; marked *Petition in Lords, Feb. 12* in *Vacher*. Accordingly this Bill does not appear in the Commons *Journal*.

24 See footnote 21.

25 The scope of compulsory purchase powers under this Act and the Holborn Valley Improvement Act 1864, deemed wider in principle for a public than a private body, was the subject of *Galloway v. Mayor and Commonalty of London* (1866) L.R. 1 H.L. 34.

26 This was listed with the private and personal (as opposed to the local and personal, declared public) Acts, but is included here as it empowered the Corporation of London to convey away the St. Thomas's Hospital site, and to acquire a new one. It was brought from the Lords to the Commons (*Journal*, 27 June 1862, vol. 117, p. 295), but the number was not recorded and *Vacher* does not list it. At its third Commons reading on 29 July 1862, Standing Orders 174 and 214 were suspended: *Journal*, vol. 117, p. 377. These concerned the timing of, and notice for, third readings of an opposed Bill, and are printed in 1861 *Parliamentary Papers*, vol. XVI, p. 133 (Paper 373). (Coincidentally 29 July 1862 was the date on which the next revised Standing Orders were ordered to be printed: 1862 *Parliamentary Papers*, vol. XLIV, p. 223 (Paper 462)).

27 Passed as a public Act. Its lengthy preamble includes reference to Her Majesty's Commission 'to examine into Plans for embanking the River Thames within the Metropolis', and the previous legislation passed concerning the land and riverbed ownership involved. This Act gave rise to *Duke of Buccleuch and Queensberry*

Appendix 1 223

v. *Metropolitan Board of Works* (1871–72) L.R. 5 H.L. 418, in relation to the loss of value that the works occasioned in the Duke's riparian mansion's garden frontage.

28 See the reference to this joint Bill under *The Definition of Bills* above.
29 The short title (section 1) was 'Exeter Gaol Act 1863' with no 'The'.
30 The minutes of Committee evidence on this Bill were ordered to be referred to the Committee on the Doncaster Water Bill 1872 (though that, no. 187, was not a local Bill as defined in this schedule): see the Commons *Journal* for 9 April 1872, vol. 127, p. 129.
31 Passed as a public Act, the Metropolis Improvement Act 1863.
32 Passed as a public Act, the Thames Embankment Act 1863.
33 A joint promotion of the two Corporations.
34 William Haywood, Engineer and Surveyor to the Commissioners of Sewers of the City of London, designed this scheme; he also gave evidence on 27 May 1864 to the Select Committee considering the Metropolitan Subways Bill: *Minutes of Evidence* (*Parliamentary Papers*, vol. XI, pp. 37 and 645; Paper 378 and 378-I), q. 4495. In the preceding 7 years, gas and water companies had opened metropolitan streets 10,377 times, and there had been many thousands more applications: see qq. 1–46.
35 See footnote 34.
36 This Act is unusual in that it was to be construed as one with 26 & 27 Vict. c. 75, which was a public, not local, Act. The short title given by section 1 was 'Thames Embankment Act 1864' with no 'The' – unlike the public Act entitled 'The Thames Embankment Act 1863'. See also note 25 above to the Metropolitan Meat and Poultry Market (Western Approach) Act 1862.
37 This Bill has no number in the Commons *Journal*, and does not appear in *Vacher*.
38 This Bill, to extend the municipal borough boundary and for other associated and improvement purposes, is not listed in *Vacher* (nor in the Commons *Journal*) but notice was given in the *London Gazette* on 28 November 1865, pp. 6019–20. Unusually, the notice was not undersigned by any solicitor or Parliamentary agent.
39 This personal Act is included as it empowered the grant of a lease to Bradford Corporation of part of the settled estate devised by (i.e. left in his will by) Benjamin Rawson, Esq.
40 This Bill was passed as the Leeds Improvement of Becks Act 1866, and is not to be confused with Bill 325, passed as the Leeds Improvement Act 1866.
41 See para. 33, p. xli, of Appendix 2 to the second report referred to in note 42 below. Each of the four schemes was costed, the total being £669,000.
42 A London City Improvement Rates Bill (nod. 153) had also been deposited, but is not included in those listed for 1867 as the preamble was found not to have been proved. Three *Reports From the Select Committee on Metropolitan Local Government &c. (London City Improvement Rates Bill)* were published (*Parliamentary Papers* nos. 135, 268 and 301 + 301–I, ordered to be printed on 15 March, 6 and 20 May respectively 1867; vol. XII, pp. 431, 435, 443 and 661). The minutes of evidence provide a fascinating insight into attitudes to London, the City and its local government system at that time. The fourteen appendices set out a wealth of detail about such matters as traffic in the City, and barriers to its free movement; health statistics; all those (including the City Corporation) who had petitioned against the Metropolitan Improvement Rate Bill (appendix 5 at p. 164 of Paper 301); the powers and duties of the City's Commissioners of Sewers; and a list of the local Acts of the metropolis.
43 This Bill was promoted again the following year in identical terms. It is not in *Vacher*, which does not list the deposit of any plan without a Bill either.
44 Promotion costs were to be shared equally with the companies concerned.

224 *Appendix 1*

45 The Commons and Lords *Journals* both refer to this as 'Metropolis' not 'Metropolitan'. The latter was the term prescribed for the Act's short title. The text of the Bill (which was not listed with the private Bills in *Vacher*) was identical to that of the Metropolis Subways Bill of 1867.
46 Promotion costs were to be shared equally with the University.
47 The short title of this Act was the Newton Market Act 1868.
48 This Bill was the subject of a demand for the production of papers in connection with a pending legal action, *Wing v. Metropolitan Board of Works*: see House of Commons *Journal*, 9 February 1870, vol. 125, p. 17. There had been a private Finsbury Estate Bill in 1866 (Bill 97, not listed in *Vacher* but recorded as introduced in the Commons *Journal* on 10 April 1866 at vol. 121, p. 208) that had not passed.
49 Notice was given in the *London Gazette* on 24 November 1871 at p. 5025 of a Great Tower Hill Ratepayer's Relief Bill. This appears to be the intended promotion not of a municipal authority but of disgruntled interests. It does not appear in the Commons *Journal*.
50 The Commons *Journal* for 14 April 1869, vol. 124, p. 133, records that the 'Minutes of the Evidence taken before the Select Committee on the Metropolis Subways Bill, in Session 1867, be referred to the Committee on the London (City) Subways Bill'.
51 This very large Bill (the Act had 459 sections and nine schedules) was originally allocated for consideration by the Commons Committee of Selection to Group E, but then withdrawn from E on 1 March and added instead on 5 April to K: 1870 *Parliamentary Papers*, vol. VI, pp. 157, 159 and 163 (Papers 81, 81-I and 81-II).
52 This Bill is not in the Commons *Journal*. See the *London Gazette* for 29 November 1870, pp. 5559–60 and the Beckenham Vestry notice following. The Beckenham Sewerage Act was, however, passed in 1873 as 36 & 37 Vict. c. ccxviii.
53 This Bill is not in *Vacher* or the Commons *Journal*. See the London Gazette for 29 November 1870, pp. 5554–6. A Cambridge Improvement Bill was promoted in 1874 (Bill 43), but withdrawn.
54 This was an unusual example of a Bill not promoted, and indeed originally opposed, by the Lincoln Corporation, which however later took over its promotion; see section 83.
55 After long consideration, on 27 March 1871 the Commons Select Committee by five votes to two found the preamble to this Bill not proved (1871 *Parliamentary Papers*, vol. XI, p. 281, Paper 142).
56 This Bill was promoted by the County Justices of the Peace.
57 The public Epping Forest Act 1871, 34 & 35 Vict. c. 92 had appointed commissioners. For the 1872 session they gave notice of a Bill to extend their powers (not in *Vacher*, but published in the *London Gazette* on 24 November 1871 at pp. 4923–4. This Bill 86, however, was promoted by the Corporation of London in turn to extend their powers, the requisite *London Gazette* notice being published on the same day at pp. 5115–16.
58 This Bill, to take certain lands for sewage irrigation purposes, is not listed in *Vacher*. See the *London Gazette* for 28 November 1871, pp. 5396–8. The Parliamentary Archives contain a deposited plan (for which the reference is HL/PO/PB13/plan1872/K3), but no actual Bill.
59 This was a joint local authority promotion for the creation of a Sewerage Board. The *London Gazette* notice (17 November 1871, pp. 4761–3) was over the name of '*Sam. Geo. Johnson*, Town Clerk, Nottingham' as well as the Parliamentary agents J. Dorington and Co.
60 The *London Gazette* notice for this Bill (14 November 1871, pp. 4683–4) refers *inter alia* in paragraph 7 to conferring exemptions from the payment of poor rates or

other local rates, but there is no wording to this effect in the relevant sections 19–22 of the Act.
61 The Select Committee merged this Bill with the Sheffield Tramways Bill, passed as 35 & 36 Vict. c. cxliii, the whole costs of obtaining which were to be paid by the company: s. 78. The second schedule comprises the agreement for lease dated 8 May 1872 between the Corporation, the Bill promoters and the Tramways Company. See also the Commons *Journal* for 4 June 1872, vol. 127, pp. 230–1.
62 This Bill is not in *Vacher*. See the *London Gazette* for 28 November 1871, pp. 5187–8. The Parliamentary Archives contain neither a plan nor a Bill. A Sheffield Water Bill (nod. 11) appeared in the following session in 1873, but was promoted by the company whose undertaking would, had the prospective Bill of 1872 become law, have been vested in the Corporation. The Corporation gave notice of a similar Bill in the following session (*London Gazette*, 26 November 1872, pp. 5711–12).
63 It is recorded in the Commons *Journal* on 8 February 1872 at vol. 127, p. 14 that this Bill should originate in the House of Lords, but it is not in the Lords *Journal*. See also the *London Gazette* for 21 November 1871, pp. 4868–9.
64 It is recorded in the Commons *Journal* on 8 February 1872 at vol. 127, p. 14 that this Bill should originate in the House of Lords. The Bill as such is not in the Lords *Journal*, but a petition against the closing of Sun Street is minuted there on 15 June 1872 at vol. 104, p. 562. See also the *London Gazette* for 21 November 1871, p. 4875.
65 There had been a public Thames Embankment Act 1862 (25 & 26. Vict. c. 93), and a public Thames Embankment (Land) Bill nod. 82 was also introduced in 1872. For background to this Bill and the (Land) Bill, see David Owen, *The Government of Victorian London 1855–1889: The Metropolitan Board of Works, the Vestries, and the City Corporation* (1982), pp. 98–9; this work also refers to other Metropolitan Board measures.
66 This Bill is not in the Commons *Journal*.

Appendix 2
Provisional Orders 1868–1872

Part one of this second Appendix lists the 15 confirming Local Government Acts which from 1868 were defined as local Acts, together with the 139 places or local authorities in 1868–72 inclusive (many occurring more than once) whose Provisional Orders (see pp.116–18 above) were confirmed, and so given the force of law without the need for individual private Bill promotion. Other Provisional Orders had, prior to 1868, been confirmed by public general Acts.[1] It should be noted that these 15 are the *local government* Provisional Orders, for which the procedures were authorised by section LXXV of the Local Government Act 1858; there were other separate provisional Act confirmation procedures, for example, for piers and harbours under the General Pier and Harbour Act 1861, 24 & 25 Vict. c. 45 (as amended by 25 & 26 Vict. c. 19), for which deposits were also recorded in *Vacher*'s annual *Lists of Private Bills*.

Vacher additionally set out from 1871 Provisional Order applications under the Gas and Water Works Facilities Act 1870–33 & 34 Vict. c. 70 – and the Tramways Act 1870–33 & 34 Vict. c. 78; as with piers and harbours, however, these by no means all concerned local governments: in fact almost all such confirmed orders gave powers to companies, commissioners and 'undertakers' rather than corporations and local boards.[2] (As to metropolitan tramway promotions, see note 100 to Chapter 4.) Part two below lists five cases of other Provisional Orders confirmed for bodies that came within the local authority definition that we are using in this study.

Local government confirming Acts, with the addition of a serial number in the short title where there was more than one in a Parliamentary session, would be styled – as in the first set out below, 31 & 32 Vict. c. x – 'The Local Government Supplemental Act 1868'. Often they contained ancillary matters described in the long titles as 'for other purposes'.

Section LXXV of the Local Government Act 1858 enabled Local Boards to obtain land acquisition powers according to the petition and inquiry procedure laid down; orders had no validity unless confirmed by Act of Parliament, and all costs incurred by the Secretary of State had to be met by the district concerned: section LXXV(6) and (7). (Orders in confirming Acts were not necessarily printed in alphabetical order.) Provisional Orders, although more limited in scope, were likely both to cost less and to be less vulnerable to procedural hazards on the way to royal assent, and sometimes authorities might seek both at more or less the same time. The circumstances might, on the other hand, be very different. The Local Board of Health, for instance, obtained the Keighley Waterworks and Improvement Act 1867 (30 & 31 Vict. c. liv), but the Keighley Provisional Order of the following year arose not from the Board as such but from a petition 'signed by owners and ratepayers in the hamlet of Stanbury', who had successfully sought to have their area added to that of the Keighley Local Board (so necessitating the complementary Oxenhope and Stanbury Provisional Order confirmed by the same Act). Keighley were back again at Westminster in 1869, obtaining 32 & 33 Vict. c. cxxix.

Part I – Local government provisional orders

1868	31 & 32 Vict.	38
c. x	Workington, Walton-on-the-Hill, West Derby, Eton, Llanelly, Oxenhope and Stanbury, Keighley	
c. lxxxiv	Southampton, Bradford (twice), Whitchurch and Doddington, Royton, Kendal, Sunderland	
c. lxxxv	Tormoham	
c. lxxxvi	Malvern, Cowpen, Bristol, Sheffield, Margate, Bognor, Otley	
c. clii	Tunbridge Wells	
c. cliii	Harrogate, Layton-with-Warbrick, Bury, Lower Brixham, Hexham, Tipton, Gainsborough, Worthing, Aberystwith, Cockermouth, Burnham, Wednesbury, Burton-upon-Trent, Hornsey, Keswick	
1869	**32 & 33 Vict.**	**25**
c.cxxiv	* Bideford, Bournemouth, Bowness, Bristol, Croydon (twice), Fleetwood, Harrogate, Hanley, Litchurch, Litherland, Portsmouth, Rochdale, Ryde, Worthing	
c. cl	Aberystwith, Ashton-under-Lyne, Bath, Cleckheaton, Crompton, Newport (Monmouthshire), Reading, Southport, Stalybridge, Weston-super-Mare	

* This Act also corrected a mistake affecting Burton-on-Trent's Provisional Order of the previous year (putting back in the word 'not', which had wrongly been taken out the first time). Its sections 3 and 4 also confirmed uncertainty that had arisen in relation to the status of the council at Huddersfield as being the validly constituted Local Board of Health for all the districts then comprising that council's area.

1870	**33 & 34 Vict.**	**13**
c. cxiv[3]	Blackpool, Bristol, Eton (twice), Heckmondwike, Kidderminster, Lincoln, Nottingham, Plymouth, South Molton, Wallasey, Ware	
c. clxv	Merthyr Tydfil	

(continued)

228   *Appendix 2*

1871	34 & 35 Vict.	54
c. i	Barton, Eccles, Winton, Monton, Bognor, Bolton (twice), Burton-on-Trent, Chippenham, Chiswick, Derby, Harrogate (three times), Kidderminster (twice), Merthyr Tydfil, Northam, Ryde, Stroud, Trowbridge, Worthing	
c. lix	Dawlish, Kingston-upon-Hull, Morley, Nelson, Sheerness, Skipton, Todmorden, West Derby, Willenhall, York	
c. clxxxvii	Acton, Altrincham, Bognor, Bolton, Harrogate (twice), Henley-on-Thames, Kingston-upon-Hull, Litchurch, Malvern, Nelson, Over Darwen, Pensarn, Prescot, Ramsgate, Redcar, St. Leonards, Stamford, Tottenham, Ware, Widnes, Wimbledon	

1872	35 & 36 Vict.	9
c. xlv	Kingston-upon-Hull	
c. xcii	East Barnet, Banbury, Glastonbury, Knaresborough and Tentergate, Nottingham, Shipley, Soothill Upper, Swadlincote	

Part II – Other provisional orders

1. The Gillingham Pier Order 1869 – confirmed by 32 & 33 Vict. c. lxxi.
2. The Penrhyn Harbour Order 1870 – confirmed by 33 & 34 Vict. c. lxxxii.
3. In 1872 there was a Provisional Order (not given a formal title) for the School Board for London (which had been recently constituted under section 37 of the Elementary Education Act 1870 (33 & 34 Vict. c. 75)) – the Education Department Provisional Order Confirmation Act 1872, 35 & 36 Vict. c. lxv.
4. The Birmingham (Corporation) Tramways Order 1872 – confirmed by 35 & 36 Vict. c. clvii.
5. The Bristol Corporation Tramways Order 1872 – confirmed by 35 & 36 Vict. c. clviii.

Notes

1 See notes 37–41 and 100 to Chapter 4.
2 For many years the Commons received separate returns of gas undertakings for both local authorities and private companies, providing great detail by county and by authority or company of the private Acts involved, their share capital, loan commitments etc. as applicable, and in the case of each company the maximum price of gas authorised. See for example those ordered to be printed on 19 August 1881, Paper 315 (local authorities) and 19 June 1882, Paper 239 (private companies): *Parliamentary Papers* (1881) vol. LXXIII, p. 179 and (1882) vol. LXIV, p. 287 respectively.
3 This Act also contained four additional provisions not contained within Provisional Orders. Section 2 gave the Bangor Local Board the powers of a Board for the purposes of the Public Libraries Act 1855, so that a gift of a museum and library from a local benefactor could be accepted. Section 3 transferred part of a local turnpike in Chatham to that Local Board. Section 4 gave the Kidderminster Local Board power to protect the River Stour from fouling and inappropriate building. Section 5 confirmed and validated the change of name of the Monks Coppenhall Local Board to Crewe, by which it was 'usually and commonly known'.

Appendix 3
Alphabetical list of places promoting local Bills 1858–1872

This Appendix lists alphabetically those places or authorities promoting local Bills (or in respect of which they were promoted) in the years 1858–72 set out in Appendix 1. Promotions by the City of London and by the Metropolitan Board of Works are usually listed against the names of the relevant locations or subjects. Not all of these Bills were of course enacted, though 278 out of 335 were passed – 83 per cent. Fifty-seven places promoted more than once – some 17 per cent of all those promoting.

Aberdare	1870
Aberavon	1866
Abergavenny	1860, 1871
Aberystwyth	1872
Ashton-under-Lyne and Stalybridge	1864, 1870
Banbury	1866
Barnsley	1862, 1866
Barrow-in-Furness	1868, 1872
Bath	1866, 1870
Batley	1871
Beckenham	1871
Billingsgate	1871
Bingley	1867
Birkenhead	1858 (twice), 1863, 1867
Birmingham	1861, 1872
Birstal	1872
Blackburn	1870
Blackfriars	1863, 1867
Blackpool and Layton-with-Warbrick	1865
Bollington (Prestbury)	1862
Bolton	1861, 1864, 1865, 1872
Bradford	1858, 1862, 1866 (twice), 1868, 1869, 1871 (twice)
Brecon	1862
Brighton	1867, 1870, 1872
Bucks County	1860
Burnley	1871
Bury	1866, 1872
Cambridge	1871

(continued)

230   *Appendix 3*

Cardiff	1862, 1871
Carnarvon	1865
Caversham	1868
Chichester	1868
Chiswick	1858
Chorley	1871
Cleckheaton	1870
Clifton and Durdham Downs	1861
Congleton	1866
Coventry	1863
Crystal Palace	1862
Darlington	1861, 1872 (twice)
Dartford	1868
Dewsbury, Batley and Heckmondwike	1861, 1867
Dukinfield and Denton	1869
Elland	1872
Epping Forest	1872
Exeter	1863
Farnworth	1867
Finsbury Park	1869
Fosdyke	1870
Gas (Metropolis)	1860
Gateshead	1867
Great Tower Hill	1869
Grimsby	1869
Halifax	1858, 1862, 1865, 1868, 1870
Hampstead Heath	1871
Haverfordwest	1868
Haworth	1872
Hedon	1860
Hereford	1872
Heywood	1867
Hindley	1872 (twice)
Holborn Valley	1864, 1867, 1869, 1872
Hornsey	1871
Hove	1858
Huddersfield	1869, 1871 (twice)
Hyde	1870
Ilkley	1871
Ince	1871
Ipswich	1859, 1867
Keighley	1867, 1869, 1872
Kensington	1866
King's Lynn	1859
Kingston-upon-Hull	1872 (twice)
Lancaster	1864
Leadenhall Market	1871
Leamington Priors	1868
Leeds	1862, 1866 (twice), 1867, 1869, 1870 (twice), 1872
Leicester	1860, 1865, 1866, 1868, 1870
Leicester Square	1871
Lincoln	1868, 1870, 1871

Liverpool	1858, 1859, 1860, 1861(twice), 1862, 1864 (twice), 1865 (twice), 1866, 1867, 1870, 1871, 1872
Llandaff	1860
Llanelly	1865
London (City of)	1866 (twice), 1867, 1868, 1869, 1871 (twice), 1872
London (Port of)	1872
London Railway Depot	1860
Loughborough	1868
Lymm	1872
Macclesfield	1860
Malvern	1858
Manchester	1858 (three times), 1860 (twice), 1863, 1865, 1867 (twice), 1866, 1869, 1871, 1872
Marylebone (Stingo Lane)	1868
Melton Mowbray	1869
Merthyr Tydfil	1858, 1865
Metropolis Sewage and Essex Reclamation	1871
Metropolitan Market	1865
Metropolitan Meat and Poultry	1860, 1862, 1864
Metropolitan Streets	1872
Metropolitan Subways	1864, 1868
Middlesbrough	1858, 1866
Middleton and Tonge	1861
Milford	1869
Nelson	1866
Newcastle-under-Lyme	1859
Newcastle-upon-Tyne	1865, 1870, 1871
Northallerton	1871
Northampton	1870, 1871
Northamptonshire	1871
Norwich	1860, 1862, 1867
Nottingham	1867, 1872
Oldham	1865, 1869, 1870
Oswaldtwistle	1869
Oswestry	1865
Oxford	1868
Park Lane	1866, 1867, 1868, 1869
Plymouth	1867
Pontypridd	1872
Poplar and Greenwich	1871
Portsmouth	1859, 1868 (twice)
Preston	1861, 1869
Reading	1868, 1870
Rhyl	1872
Richmond	1861, 1871
Ripon	1865
Rochdale	1872
Ross	1865, 1869
Rotherham and Kimberworth	1863, 1870

(*continued*)

Appendix 3

Rugby	1863
Ryde	1861
Saint Alban's	1870
Saint Helens	1869
Saint Mary Church	1868
Saint Thomas's Hospital	1862
Salford	1859, 1862, 1867, 1868, 1870, 1871
Sheffield	1870 (three times), 1871, 1872 (twice)
Shoreditch	1871
Southampton	1863, 1865
South Molton	1862
Southport	1865, 1871
South Shields	1861
Southwark Park	1864
Sowerby Bridge	1863
Staines	1872
Stanford	1872
Stockton-on-Tees	1866, 1867, 1869
Stourbridge	1866
Sunderland	1865, 1867 (twice)
Sutton Coldfield	1861
Surrey	1871
Swansea	1860, 1863, 1872
Thames Embankment	1862 (twice), 1863 (twice), 1864, 1866 (twice), 1867 (twice), 1868 (twice), 1870, 1872 (twice)
Thames Sewerage	1872
Todmorden	1871
Tormoham	1872
Tranmere	1862
Tunbridge Wells	1865
Tynemouth	1866
Vauxhall Bridge Road	1858
Victoria Park Approach	1858
Wallasey	1858, 1861, 1864, 1867, 1872
Walsall	1871
Warwick	1872
West Bromwich	1865
West Ham	1867
West Hartlepool	1870
Westminster	1859, 1860, 1861, 1865
West Worthing	1865, 1872
Widnes	1867
Wigan	1860
Wolborough	1868
Wolverhampton	1867, 1869
Worcester	1867
Yeovil	1870
York	1859, 1860, 1870

Bibliography

Primary sources

Statutes are published in sessional, usually annual, volumes, which are officially published. Since 1797 they have been divided between either the public general or the local and private statute books. Each year a small number of personal statutes has usually also been passed, listed with the latter private Acts but – especially in early years – not always printed. For the HMSO *Chronological Table* and *Indexes*, see the Annex to Chapter 1 on *The Sources for and Existing Discussion of Local Legislation*. Local Acts from 1797, though not all private and personal Acts, are now available online at www.justis.com on a subscription basis. *Private Bills* are annually deposited with the Private Bill Office according to the Parliamentary Standing Orders being printed or reprinted on behalf of the promoters. The materials held in the Parliamentary Archives and Libraries are listed in Maurice F. Bond's *Guide to the Records of Parliament* (1971) – for the Lords at pp. 82–92 and for the Commons at pp. 5 and 228–31. Page 84 notes that

> Since 1849 ... two official series of printed Private Bills have been preserved: *Table Bills* and *House Bills* ... Occasionally after 1849, and continuously from 1936, the following three additional classes of prints have been preserved, either with the Main Papers or as separate classes: *Precedent Bills* in which the precedents for each clause are noted in the margin for the use of the Lord Chairman; *Proof Bills* produced before the L. Chairman containing consents and proofs that the preamble has been approved; and *Filled Bills* in which the Parliamentary Agent has entered amendments made during the passage of the Bill. ... A collection of printed Private Bills and Private Acts has been formed by the H.L. Library of 200 vols., 1713–1867, which is fairly complete from about 1760 (the 18th c. vols. Principally contain Bills, the 19th c., Acts). ... A bound set of Private Bills, 1860-date [in the Commons Library] includes prints of various stages.

The *Journals* of the House of Commons and House of Lords are published by the authority of each House. The Parliamentary Archives contain a Classified Index to the Journals of the House of Lords: from 1833 to 1863, both inclusive, the first part dating from 1865. Part V dealing with Local and Personal and Private Bills was printed in 1869, and the Archives have other Journal Indexes etc. and source materials, relating to both Houses. E.R. Poyser wrote House of Lords Record Office Memorandum No. 16 on *The Private Bill Records of the House of Lords* (1957). It contains, however, only a list reference to local Bills in the sense that with which we are concerned here, and gives no commentary on them.

Parliamentary Papers are ordered by either House of Parliament to be printed, and are cited according to their session, title and given number. Apart from individual papers, lists and returns are particularly valuable in revealing material either unsuspected or difficult to find: for instance, Commons paper 483 ordered to be printed on 27 July 1858 is a *List of the Bills, Reports, Estimates, and Accounts and Papers* from the 1857–58 session, with a general alphabetical index. It runs to 102pp. and is at vol. LXII, p. 1. A similar *List* was compiled each year. The detail provided by the various returns etc. scheduled in these *Lists* is normally unobtainable elsewhere, and – like the preambles to private Bills, which had to be proved to Examiners, often in the face of opposition – they have a high degree of accuracy and reliability. For example, the *Papers* for 1864 include returns of the fees paid for the stages of private Bills (vol. XLVIII, p. 39, Paper 184), and of the share capital and loan amounts proposed to be raised under private Bills for that year for which petitions had been lodged (vol. XLVIII, p. 85, Paper 167).

Hansard's Parliamentary Debates were technically a private publication until 1909. There was not even a reporter regularly in the Commons gallery till 1878: the history and status of these reports is summarised in G. Kitson Clark, *The Critical Historian* (1967) at pp. 77–78. Those published during the years 1858–72 were part of the Third Series. Also useful in this context is *Who's Who of British Members of Parliament*, vol. I, 1832–85 (1976), compiled by Michael Stenton.

Thomas Vacher commercially published an *Alphabetical List of Private Bills, Deposited in the House of Commons* for each sessional year of Parliament. In 1868 and 1869 he altered the title to *Alphabetical List of Petitions for Private Bills, Deposited for 1868 [1869]*, and then from 1870 he published *The Private Bills in the Session [1870], Arranged in Two Lists: Alphabetically, and in Numerical Order; From the Examiners' List. And Orders Relating to Private Bills.*

A useful source for the metropolitan area is *London Statutes. A Collection of Public Acts Relating Specially to the Administrative County of London and of Local and Personal Acts Affecting the Powers and Duties of the London County Council from 1750 to 1907* (vol. I, 1907). This was prepared by G.L. Gomme and Seager Berry, Clerk and Solicitor respectively to the L.C.C.

The *London Gazette* printed the statutory notices required before Bills were deposited. Notices are generally fully descriptive of the clauses intended to be promoted, and most appeared in late November shortly before the deadline imposed by Parliamentary Standing Orders. They can be found online.

Law Reports are cited in the footnotes according to their series.

Secondary sources

Books (place of publication is usually London unless otherwise stated)

Albert, William, *The Turnpike Road System in England, 1663–1840* (1972)
Allen, Carleton Kemp, *Law and Orders: An Inquiry Into the Nature and Scope of Delegated Legislation and Executive Powers in England* (1945)
Arnold, Thomas James and Johnson, Samuel George, *A Treatise on the Law Relating to Municipal Corporations in England and Wales* (1883)
Ashton, Rosemary, *142 Strand: A Radical Address in Victorian London* (2006)

Bagehot, Walter, *The English Constitution* (1867, 1872; World's Classics edition 1928)
Barker, Theo C. and Harris, J.R., *A Merseyside Town in the Industrial Revolution: St Helens 1750–1900* (1959)
Barnard, Sylvia M., *To Prove I'm Not Forgot: Living and Dying in a Victorian City* (1990)
Bellamy, Christine, *Administering Central-Local Relations, 1871–1919: The Local Government Board in its Fiscal and Cultural Context* (1988)
Bennion, Francis A.R., *Statutory Interpretation: Codified with a Critical Commentary* (1984)
Binnie, G.M., *Early Victorian Water Engineers* (1981)
Blake Odgers, William and Naldrett, Edward James, *Local Government*; one of the Macmillan series *The English Citizen: His Rights and Responsibilities*, 2nd edn, 1913
Boas, Frederick S., 'Historians in the Sixties: A New Era': essay at pp. 175–200 in *The Eighteen-Sixties* (Royal Society of Literature, 1932)
Bond, Maurice Francis, *Guide to the Records of Parliament* (HMSO, 1971)
Bramwell, George, *An Analytical Table of the Private Statutes Passed Between 1727 and 1812* (1813)
Bready, J. and Wesley, J. *Lord Shaftesbury and Social-Industrial Progress* (1926)
Briggs, Asa, *Victorian Cities* (1963, 1968)
Bristowe, Samuel Boteler, *Private Bill Legislation, Comprising the Steps Required to Be Taken by Promoters or Opponents of a Private Bill Before & After Its Presentation to Parliament: & the Standing Rules of Both Houses* (1859)
Brockington, C. Fraser, *Public Health in the Nineteenth Century* (1965)
Brundage, Anthony, *England's 'Prussian Minister': Edwin Chadwick and the Politics of Government Growth, 1832–1854* (1988)
Cannadine, David (ed.), *Patricians, Politics and Power in Nineteenth Century Towns* (1982)
Carr, E.H., *What is History?* (1961)
Carter, *An Historical Geography of the Railways of the British Isles* (1959)
Chester, Sir Norman (D.N.), *The English Administrative System 1780–1870* (1981)
Childe-Pemberton, William Shakespear, *Life of Lord Norton 1814–1905* (1909)
Clark, G. Kitson *The Critical Historian* (1967)
Clarke, John J., *A History of Local Government of the United Kingdom* (1955)
Clifford, Frederick, *A History of Private Bill Legislation* (2 vols., 1885 and 1887)
Clifton, Gloria C., *Professionalism, Patronage and Public Service in Victorian London: The Staff of the Metropolitan Board of Works 1856–1889* (1992)
Coleman, Terry, *The Railway Navvies* (1965)
Collinge, J.M., *Office-Holders in Modern Britain* in J.M. Collinge (ed.), *Officials of Royal Commissions of Inquiry 1815–1870* (vol. IX, 1984)
Collini, S., *Liberalism and Sociology: L.T. Hobhouse and Political Argument in England, c. 1880–1914* (Cambridge, 1979)
Cooke Taylor, W., *The Natural History of Society* (two vols., 1840)
Crook, Tom and O'Hara, Glen (eds.), *Statistics and the Public Sphere: Numbers and the People in Modern Britain, c. 1800–2000* (2011)
Curl, James Stevens, *The Life and Work of Henry Roberts (1803–1876), Architect* (1983)
Davis, Richard W., *Political Change and Continuity 1760–1885: A Buckinghamshire Study* (1972)
Disraeli, Benjamin, *Sybil or the Two Nations* (1845)
Dyos, H.J. (ed.), *The Study of Urban History* (1968)

Finer, S.E., *The Life and Times of Sir Edwin Chadwick* (1952)
Forsyth, R.A., 'Nature and the Victorian City: The Ambivalent Attitude of Robert Buchanan', essay 6 in *The Lost Pattern: Essays on the Emergent City Sensibility in Victorian England* (Nedlands, W.A., 1976)
Fraser, Derek (ed.) *Municipal Reform and the Industrial City* (1982)
Fraser, Derek, *Power and Authority in the Victorian City* (1983)
Frazer, W.M., *Duncan of Liverpool: Being an Account of the Work of Dr. W.H. Duncan, Medical Officer of Health of Liverpool 1847–63* (1947)
Gardiner, Patrick, *The Nature of Historical Explanation* (1952)
Garrard, John, *Leadership and Power in Victorian Industrial Towns 1830–80* (1983)
Gaskell, S. Martin, *Building Control: National Legislation and the Introduction of Local Bye-laws in Victorian England* (1983)
Glen, William Cunningham, *The Law Relating to Public Health and Local Government in Relation to Sanitary and Other Matters etc.* (1858)
Glen, William Cunningham, *The Law Relating to Highways, Highway Authorities, Bridges, Railways Crossing Highways, Locomotives on Highways, and Tramways* (2nd edn by Alexander Glen, 1897)
Greaves, John Neville, *Sir Edward Watkin, 1819–1901: The Last of the Railway Kings* (2005)
Green, David R., *Pauper Capital: London and the Poor Law, 1790–1870* (2010)
Hadfield, Charles, *British Canals: An Illustrated History* (1950, 3rd edn, 1966)
Hadfield, Charles, *The Canal Age* (1968)
Halcomb, John, *A Practical Treatise on Passing Private Bills Through Both Houses of Parliament* (London, 1836)
Halliday, Stephen, *The Great Stink of London: Sir Joseph Bazalgette and the Cleansing of the Victorian Metropolis* (1999)
Hamlin, Christopher, *Public Health and Social Justice in the Age of Chadwick: Britain, 1800–1854* (1998)
Hanham, H.J., *The Nineteenth Century Constitution 1815–1914: Documents and Commentary* (1969)
Harper, Roger H., *Victorian Building Regulations: Summary Tables of the Principal English Building Acts and Model By-laws 1840–1914* (1988)
Harris, Bernard, *The Origins of the British Welfare State: Society, State and Social Welfare in England and Wales, 1800–1945* (2004)
Harris, Jose, *Private Lives, Public Spirit: Britain 1870–1914* (1993)
Harrison, Samuel, *A Complete History of the Great Flood at Sheffield on March 11 and 12, 1864* (1864).
Hawkins, Angus, *The Forgotten Prime Minister: The 14th Earl of Derby* (vol. II, Achievement, 1851–1869, 2008)
Henthorn, Frank (ed.), *Letters and Papers Concerning the Establishment of the Trent, Ancholme and Grimsby Railway, 1860–1862* (1975)
Higgs, Edward, *The Information State in England* (2004)
Holdsworth, Sir William, *A History of English Law* (vol. XI, 1938)
Hole, James, *An Essay on Literary, Scientific and Mechanics' Institutions* (1853)
Hoppen, K. Theodore, *The Mid-Victorian Generation: England 1846–1886* (1998)
Hoppit, Julian (ed.), *Failed Legislation 1660–1800: Extracted From the Commons and Lords Journals* with an Introduction by Julian Hoppit and Joanna Innes (1997)
Hurren, Elizabeth T., *Protesting About Pauperism: Poverty, Politics and Poor Relief in Late-Victorian England, 1870–1900* (2007)

Innes Joanna, *Inferior Politics: Social Problems and Social Politics in Eighteenth-Century Britain* (2009)
Jackman, W.T., *The Development of Transportation in Modern England* (1916; 3rd edn by W.H. Chaloner, 1966)
Jenkins, T.A., *The Parliamentary Diaries of Sir John Trelawny, 1858–1865* (Royal Historical Society, Camden Fourth Series, vol. 40, 1990)
Jennings, W.I., *The Law Relating to Local Authorities* (1934)
Joby, R.S., *The Railway Builders: Lives and Works of the Victorian Railway Contractors* (1983)
Keith-Lucas, Brian, *The Unreformed Local Government System* (1980)
Kellett, John R., *The Impact of Railways on Victorian Cities* (1969)
Kelly, Thomas, *A History of Public Libraries in Great Britain 1845–1975* (2nd edn, 1977)
Kostal, R.W., *Law and English Railway Capitalism 1825–1875* (1994)
Lambert, Sheila, *Bills and Acts: Legislative Procedure in Eighteenth Century England* (1971)
Lawrence, Jon, *Speaking for the People: Party, Language and Popular Politics in England, 1867–1914* (1998)
Lewis, R.A., *Edwin Chadwick and the Public Health Movement, 1832–54* (1952)
Lipman, V.D., *Local Government Areas 1834–1945* (1949)
Lubenow, William C., *The Politics of Government Growth: Early Victorian Attitudes Toward State Intervention 1833–1848* (1971)
McCalmont's *Parliamentary Poll Book: British Election Results 1832–1918* (1879; 8th revised edn, 1971) edited by J. Vincent and M. Stenton
MacDermot, E.T., *History of the Great Western Railway* (vol. I, 1833–1863, 1927; vol. II, 1863–1921, 1931)
MacLeod, Roy (ed.), *Government and Expertise: Specialists, Administrators and Professionals, 1860–1919* (1988, paperback edn 2003)
Maltbie, M.R., *English Local Government of Today: A Study of the Relations of Central and Local Government* (1897)
Martin, E.W., *The Book of the Country Town* (1962)
Martin, Theodore, *Notes on the Present System of Private Bill Legislation* (J.B. Nichols and Sons, 25 Parliament Street, 1872)
Maximo, Carleton Olegario (ed.), *Local and Personal Acts of Parliament in the United Kingdom* (2012)
May, Erskine, *The Law, Privileges, Proceedings and Usage of Parliament* (20th edn, 1983)
Middlemas, Robert Keith, *The Master Builders* (1963)
Morris, R.J.B., *Parliament and the Public Libraries* (1977)
Neeson, Jeanette, M., *Commoners, Common Right, Enclosure and Social Change, 1700–1820* (1993)
Ottley, George, *Bibliography of British Railway History* (2nd edn, 1983)
Overton, Mark, *Agricultural Revolution in England: The Transformation of the Agrarian Economy* (1996)
Owen, David, *The Government of Victorian London 1855–1889: The Metropolitan Board of Works, the Vestries, and the City Corporation* (1982)
Page, Sir Harry, *Local Authority Borrowing: Past, Present and Future* (1985)
Pawson, Eric, *Transport and Economy: The Turnpike Roads of Eighteenth Century Britain* (1977)

Phipps, J.S., *Leicester in Parliament: A Record of the Use of Private Bill Legislation to Benefit and Improve the City* (1988)
Pratt, Edwin A., *A History of Inland Transport and Communication in England* (1912)
Priest, John, *Liberty and Locality: Parliament, Permissive Legislation, and Ratepayers' Democracies in the Mid-Nineteenth Century* (1990)
Priestley, J.B., *Victoria's Heyday* (1972)
Pulling, Alexander, *Private Bill Legislation: Can Anything Be Now Done to Improve It?* (16pp. pamphlet, 1859)
Pulling, Alexander, *Proposal for Amendment of the Procedure in Private Bill Legislation: In a Letter Addressed to Colonel Wilson Patten M.P.* (pamphlet, 1862)
Redlich, Josef and Hirst, Francis W., *Local Government in England* (two vols., 1903)
Reed, M.C., *Investment in Railways in Britain 1820–1844: A Study in the Development of the Capital Market* (1975)
Roebuck, Janet, *Urban Development in 19th Century London: Lambeth, Battersea and Wandsworth 1838–1888* (1979)
Rydz, D.L., *Parliamentary Agents – A History* (1979)
Scott, James John, *Railway Practice in Parliament: The Law and Practice of Railway and Other Private Bills* (1846)
Shenton, Caroline, *The Day Parliament Burned* (2012)
Smellie, K.B., *A History of Local Government* (4th edn, 1968)
Smethurst, James Mellor, *A Treatise on the Locus Standi of Petitioners Against Private Bills in Parliament* (1866, 1867)
Somers Vine, J.R., *English Municipal Institutions: Their Growth and Development From 1835 to 1879, Statistically Illustrated* (1879)
Spencer, F.H., *Municipal Origins: An Account of English Private Bill Legislation Relating to Local Government, 1740–1835; with a Chapter on Private Bill Procedure* (1911)
Spencer, Herbert, *Essays: Scientific, Political, and Speculative* (1854)
Spencer, Herbert, *An Autobiography* (two vols., 1904)
Stebbings, Chantal, *Legal Foundations of Tribunals in Nineteenth Century England* (2006)
Stebbings, Chantal, *The Victorian Taxpayer and the Law: A Study in Constitutional Conflict* (2009)
Szreter, Simon, *Fertility, Class and Gender in Britain, 1860–1940* (1996)
Thompson, James, *British Political Culture and the Idea of 'Public Opinion', 1867–1914* (2013)
Thornhill, W., *The Growth and Reform of English Local Government* (1971)
Vacher, Thomas, *List of Private Bills* (annual)
Vardon, Thomas, *Index to the Local and Personal and Private Acts 1798–1839* (1840)
Vaughan, Adrian, *Railwaymen, Politics and Money: The Great Age of Railways in Britain* (1997)
Warburg, Jeremy, *The Industrial Muse in English Poetry* (1958)
Ward, Benjamin, *The Health of Nations: A Review of the Works of Edwin Chadwick* (vol. I, 2008)
Ward, J.R., *The Finance of Canal Building in Eighteenth-Century England* (1974)
Ware, Michael E., *Britain's Lost Waterways, Inland Navigations* (vol. I, 1979)
Watson, Roger, *Edwin Chadwick, Poor Law and Public Health (Then & Now)* (1969)
Webb, Sidney, *The London Programme* (1891)
Webb, Sidney and Beatrice Potter, *Statutory Authorities for Special Purposes* (1922)

Webster, Edward, *Parliamentary Costs: Private Bills, Election Petitions, Appeals, House of Lords* (3rd edn, 1867)

Wheeler, Gerald John, *The Practice of Private Bills: With the Standing Orders of the House of Lords and House of Commons, and Rules as to Provisional Orders* (1900)

Williams, O.C., *The Historical Development of Private Bill Procedure and Standing Orders in the House of Commons* (HMSO, two vols., 1948 and 1949)

Willis, John, 'Parliament and the Local Authorities', essay in *A Century of Municipal Progress* (NALGO, 1935) pp. 400–416

Wohl, Anthony S., *Endangered Lives: Public Health in Victorian Britain* (1983) p. 170

Articles

Albert, William, 'Popular Opposition to Turnpike Trusts and its Significance', *Journal of Transport History* (1984) 3rd series, vol. 5, no. 2, pp. 66–8

Cowen, Zelman, 'The Injunction and the Parliamentary Process', *Law Quarterly Review* (1955) 71, p. 336

Denault, Leigh and Jennifer Landis, 'Motion and Means: Mapping Opposition to Railways in Victorian Britain', https://www.mtholyoke.edu/courses/rschwart/ind_rev/rs/denault.htm (December 1999)

Dodson, John G., 'The Private Business of Parliament', *Edinburgh Review* (1867) vol. CXXV, no. CCLV, January, pp. 85–107

Garrard, John and Goldsmith, Michael, 'Municipal Progress and Decline in Britain Since 1835', *The International Journal of Regional and Local Studies* (2011–12) series 2, vol. 7 nos. 1 & 2, pp. 38–64

Hennock, E.P., 'Urban Sanitary Reform a Generation Before Chadwick', *Economic History Review* (1957), vol. 10, pp. 113–20

Holdsworth, Sir William, Untitled Comment on Injunctions and the Parliamentary Process, *Law Quarterly Review* (1943) 59, p. 2

Jack, Sybil and Adrian, 'A Reconsideration of Nineteenth Century Lawyers and Railway Capitalism and the Use of Legal Cases', *Journal of Transport History* (2003) vol. 24, issue 1, pp. 59–85

Leys, Colin, 'Petitioning in the Nineteenth and Twentieth Centuries', *Political Studies* (1955) vol. III, pp. 45–64

Morris, R.J.B., 'Finding and Using Local Statutory Instruments', *Statute Law Review* (1990) vol. 11, no. 1, summer, pp. 28–47

Murphy, John Joseph, 'The Private and Local Business of Parliament', *Journal of the Dublin Statistical Society* (1856) vol. 1, part VI, pp. 311–21

Pawson, Eric, 'Debates in Transport History: Popular Opposition to Turnpike Trusts?', *Journal of Transport History* (1984) 3rd series, vol. 5, no. 2, pp. 57–65

Pulling, Alexander, 'Private Bill Legislation', *Edinburgh Review* (1855) vol. CI, no. CCV, January, pp. 151–91

Pulling, Alexander, 'The Failure and Fate of the Statute Law Commission', *Law Magazine and Law Review, or Quarterly Journal of Jurisprudence* (1859) 3rd series, vol. VII, May to August, pp. 122–45

Sclater-Booth, Rt. Hon. George, 'On Local Government in Rural Districts', *Report of the British Association for the Advancement of Science*, 52nd Meeting, Southampton, Transactions of Section F, pp. 631–6, Address delivered Friday, 25 August 1882

Sheail, John, 'Local Legislation: Its Scope and Content', *Archives* (2005) vol. XXX, no. 113, October, pp. 36–50

Spencer, Herbert, (untitled), *The Westminster and Foreign Quarterly Review*. July 1853, vol. LX (no. CXVII), New Series vol. IV, no. 1, pp. 51–84

Spencer, Herbert, 'Railway Morals and Railway Policy', *Edinburgh Review* (1854) vol. C, no. CCIV, October, pp. 420–61

Stobart, Jon, 'Identity, Competition and Place Promotion in the Five Towns', *Urban History* (2003) vol. 30

Stobart, Jon, 'Building an Urban Identity: Cultural Space and Civic Boosterism in a "New" Industrial Town: Burslem, 1761–1911', *Social History* (2004), vol. 29, no. 4, pp. 485–98

Szreter, Simon, 'A Central Role for Local Government? The Example of Late Victorian Britain', www.historyandpolicy.org (May 2002)

M. Whittaker, 'The Bury Improvement Commissioners', *Transactions of the Lancashire and Cheshire Antiquarian Society* (1935), vol. XLIX for 1933, pp. 113–49.

Table of Cases

Ashbury Railway Carriage and Iron Co. v. Riche [1875] LR 7HL 53 23
Attorney General v. Andrews [1850] 2 Mac. & G 225; 42 ER 87 120
Attorney General v. West Hartlepool Improvement Commissioners [1870]
    LR 10 EQ 152 . . . . 135n57
Duke of Buccleuch and Queensberry v. Metropolitan Board of Works 222n27
Galloway v. Mayor and Commonality of London [1866] LR 1HL 34 . . . . 222n25
Heathcote v. The North Staffordshire Railway [1850] 2 Mac. & G 100;
    42 ER 39 118
In re London, Chatham and Dover Railway Arrangement Act, Ex parte
    Hartridge and Allender [1850] 2 K & J 293; 69 ER 792 119
London County Council v. Attorney-General [1902] AC 165 23
Pearson v. the Local Board of Health of Kingston-Upon-Hull 121
R. v. The Town Council of Dublin [1863] 135n58
Rutherford v. Straker [1887] 135n61
Stevens v. The South Devon Railway Company [1856] 13 Beav. 46; 51 ERT 18 120
The Earl of Derby v. The Bury Improvement Commissioners 121
The Lancaster and Carlisle Railway Company v. The North-Western
    Company [1848] 2PH 670-1; 41 ER 1102 119
The Queen v. The Mayor and Town Council of Sheffield [1870] LR 6 QB 652 125
The Stockton and Hartlepool Railway Company v. The Leeds and Thirsk
    and the Clarence Railway Companies [1850] 2 Mac. & G 110; 42 ER 43 119
Wing v. Metropolitan Board of Works 223n48

Table of Statutes and Bills

Below, the reader will find a list of all the Acts and Bills significantly discussed in the main text. Readers may also consult the Annex at the end of Chapter 2 for a list (derived from *Vacher*) of private Bills originating in the House of Commons in 1858 (pp. 52–57); Appendix 1 (pp. 211–219) for local Bills promoted 1858–1872; and Appendix 3 (pp. 229–232) for places promoting local Bills in that period.

Aberdeenshire Roads Act 1865 143
Abergavenny Improvement Act 1854. . . . . 121, 135n61
Alkali Act 1863. . . . . 63n72
An Act for making preliminary Inquiries in certain Cases of Application
   for Local Acts 1846. . . . . 15, 20
Artizans and Labourers Dwellings Act 1868. 127–128
Ashton-under-Lyne and Stalybridge (Corporations) Waterworks Act 1864 207
Baggymoor Drainage Act 1861 209
Ballot Act 1872. vii
Banbury Extension Bill 1866 . . . . 220n10
Barrow-in-Furness Corporation Act 1868. 163–164
Bath Act 1870. 175–6
Bath City Prison Act 1871 . . . . 99n40
Bath Corporation Bill 1866 . . . . 220n2
Belfast Award Act 1864 . . . . 101n86
Belfast Town Improvement Bill 101n86
Birkenhead Commissioners Gas and Water Act 1858. 49
Birkenhead Improvement (General Mortgages) Act 1858 . . . . 49, 75, 150
Birmingham Gas Act 1855. . . . . 104n103
Birmingham Gas Bill 104n103
Birmingham Waterworks Act 1870 178
Blackburn Improvement Act 1870. . . . . 155, 187
Blackfriars Bridge Act 1867. 208
Blackpool Improvement Act 1865 143–4
Board of Health Act 1848 112
Bolton Bill. 22
Bolton Corporation Act 1872 190
Borough and Local Courts of Record Act 1872 125
Borough Funds Act 1872. . . . . 137n86
Bradford Corporation Waterworks Act 1858 . . . . 49, 65n101
British Plate Glass Company Act 1862 . . . . 99n51
Buckinghamshire County Rate 1860 166
Burial Act 1852. . . . . 48, 65n98

Table of Statutes and Bills 243

Bury Improvement Act 1846 ....22–3, 85, 105n111, 121
Cambridge Street Act 1863 ....146, 149–151, 207
Cemeteries Clauses Act 1847 .... 65n98
Chester Courts Act 1867 .... 99n40
Chiswick Improvement Act 1858 49
City of London Traffic Regulation Act 1863............................ 151
Clauses Consolidation Act 1847 147
Cleckheaton Local Board Act 1870.................................... 159
Colchester Improvement and Navigation Bill 23
Costs Taxation Act 1847 68
Costs Taxation Act 1849 68
County of Sussex Act 1865 .... 99n40
County Property Act 1850.. 137n83
County Property Act 1871... 125
Coventry Market House Act 1863 149–50
Darlington Extension and Improvement Act 1872 .... 196n90
Darlington Local Board of Health Act 1861........................... 171n71
Dorking Water Bill.. 84
Dublin Markets Bill 120
Education Act 1870 .... 26n4, 48, 138n99
Elementary Education Act 1870 127
Exeter Gaol Act 1863... 149–51
Falmouth Borough Act 1865 .... 99n40
Gas and Water Works Facilities Act 1870 226
Gasworks Clauses Consolidation Act 1847............................ 133n29
General Board of Health Continuance Bill............................. 114
General Pier and Harbour Act 1861 226
Glossop Water Bill 1865... 159
Halifax Extension and Improvement Act 1865 175–6
Halifax Park and Improvements Act 1858..................... 49, 160, 171n91
Health of Towns Improvement Act.................................... 88
Highway Act 1835 .... 32, 36, 48, 65n100
Highway Act 1862 .... 26, 48, 65n100, 185
Highway Act 1864 .... 36, 185
Hove Improvement Act 1858 49
House of Lords Costs Taxation Act 1848 .... 96n12
Huddersfield Water Bill 1866.. 100n58
Hull Improvement Act 1848... 121–2
Interpretation Act 1850 12
Keighley Waterworks and Improvement Act 1867 227
Kensington Improvement Act 1866................................... 177
Kent Waterworks Company: Dartford Water Act 1868 .... 136n71
Kingsholm District Act 1871.. 137n88
Lands Clauses Consolidation Act 1845............... 104n98, 123–4, 136n72, 176
Lands Clauses Consolidation Act 1845 (Amendment 1860)............. 123, 176
Leeds Improvement Act 1869.. 155
Leicester Improvement Drainage and Markets Act 1868 155
Leicester Waterworks Act 1866 207
Lendal Bridge and York Improvement Act 1859......................... 161
Lendal Bridge and York Improvement Act 1860...................... 154, 185
Lincoln City Commons Act 1870...................................... 166
Liverpool and Manchester Railway Bill................................. 77
Liverpool Gunpowder Regulation &c. Act 1865....................... 207

244 *Table of Statutes and Bills*

Liverpool Improvement Act 1858 .... 49, 179
Liverpool Improvement and Waterworks Act 1871....................... 165
Liverpool Library and Museum Act 1852........................... 135n64
Liverpool Licensing Bill 1865..................................... 99n40
Liverpool Sanitary Amendment Act 1864......................... 179, 182
Local Government Act 1858 .... 40–1, 60n53, 61n57, 61n6089, 92, 104n98,
　　　　　　　　　　　　　　　　　　109–26, 137n86, 153, 159–60, 164–6, 201, 226
Local Government Act 1858 (Amendment 1861)............... 122–3, 132n36, 164
Local Government Act 1858 (Amendment 1863)............... 125, 136n80, 164
Local Government Act 1858 (Amendment 1864)..................... 132n22
Local Government Act 1888 .... 27n13, 65n96
Local Government Act 1894 .... 27n13, 65n96
Local Government Act 1933 .... 194n48
Local Government Act 1972 .... 25, 209
Local Government Board Act 1871.................................... 128
Local Government Supplemental Act 1860........................... 169n30
Local Government Supplemental Act 1861........................... 104n98
Local Government Supplemental Act 1868............................... 226
Local Legislation Bill 1873... 92
Local Legislation (Ireland) Bill 1873................................... 92
Local Stamp Act 1869 125
Local Taxation Returns Act 1860 .... 124, 128
London Local Authorities and Transport for London Bill................ 193n2
London Railway Depot and Storehouses Act 1862................. 159, 222n18
Macclesfield District Gas Act 1860 153–4
Malvern Improvement Amendment Act 1858............................. 49
Manchester Assize Courts Act 1858 49
Manchester Corporation Waterworks Act 1858 49
Manchester Corporation Waterworks Act 1865 163
Manchester Corporation Waterworks and Improvement Act 1869 155–6
Manchester Corporation Waterworks and Improvement Act 1872 155–6
Manchester Corporation Waterworks Bill............................... 77
Manchester Improvement Act 1858..................................... 49
Manchester Improvement Act 1871.................................... 155
Manchester Overseers Act 1858.................................... 65n99
Markets and Fairs Clauses Act 1847 .... 116, 121, 150
Mersey Docks (Liverpool River Approaches) Act 1871 .... 159, 178
Mersey, Weaver, Irwell &c. Protection Bill........................ 106n120
Merthyr Tydfil Act 1858... 180
Merthyr Tydfil Water Act 1858 49
Metropolis Improvement Act 1863 208
Metropolis Local Management Act 1858 .... 61n58
Metropolis Management Act 1855.............................. 96n17, 208
Metropolitan and County Borough Police Act 1829..................... 26n4
Metropolitan and County Borough Police Act 1856..................... 26n4
Metropolitan Meat and Poultry Act 1860 .... 109, 208, 221n18
Metropolitan Subways Act 1868 163
Metropolitan Tramways Provisional Orders Suspension Act 1871......... 138n100
Middlesbrough Improvement Act 1858.................................. 49
Morayshire Railway Bill.. 78
Municipal Corporations Act 1835.............. 5–6, 9–10, 32, 36, 57n6, 112, 153,
　　　　　　　　　　　　　　　　　　　　　　　159–60, 163, 175, 194n48
Municipal Corporations Act (Amendment 1861)........................ 125

Table of Statutes and Bills 245

Municipal Corporations Act 1859 (Amendment 1871)..................... 125
Municipal Corporations Act 1883... 25
Municipal Corporations (Borough Funds) Act 1872...................... 125
Municipal Corporations (Bridges) Act 1850............................. 112
Municipal Corporations Elections Act 1869............................. 125
Municipal Corporations Mortgages Etc. Act 1860........................ 123
Nene Valley Act 1862.. 106n119
Newcastle Coal Turn Act 1845...................................... 107n103
Newcastle-under-Lyme Burgesses' Lands Act 1859........................ 209
Newcastle-upon-Tyne Improvement Act 1865..................... 176–8, 183
Northampton Improvement Bill 81
Northampton Waterworks Act 1861....................................... 148
Nottingham and Leen District Sewerage Act 1872........................ 207
Nottingham Inclosure Act 1845.. 46
Norwich Corporation Markets Act 1860................................. 153–4
Nuisances Removal Act 1855.. 121–3
Oldham Borough Improvement Act 1865................... 154–6, 159, 164, 187
Park Lane Improvement Act 1869.. 155
Parliamentary Costs Act 1865............................. 21, 30n53, 71
Parliamentary Costs Act 2006....................................... 30n53
Poor Law Amendment Act 1834.. 26n4
Portsmouth Camber Quays Act 1868 155
Preliminary Inquiries Act 1846 .... 23, 97n21
Preliminary Inquiries Act 1851 15
Private Bill Costs Act.. 98n31
Provisional Order Bills (Committees) Act 1871....................... 134n38
Public Health Act 1848.............. 9, 26n4, 38–41, 60n41, 60n42, 60n44, 60n53,
                                    60n54, 61n60, 65n96, 88, 92, 112–17,
                                    121, 148, 153, 158–60, 164–6, 204n11
Public Health Act 1848 (Amendment Bill) 114
Public Health Act 1872.. 128
Public Health Act 1875....................... 33, 57n10, 65n100, 117–18, 127
Public Health Bill 1847.. 35
Public Improvements Act 1860 125
Public Libraries Act 1850.................................... 59n32, 111
Public Libraries Act 1855................................... 190, 228n3
Public Libraries Act 1855 (Amendment 1871)........................... 111
Public Works (Manufacturing Districts) Act 1863 .... 125, 187
Railways Clauses Consolidation Act 1845........................... 14, 68
Reform Act 1832... 9
Rhyl Improvement Act 1872 184–5
Roads Act 1765... 63n77
Rotherham and Kimberworth Local Board of Health Act 1863 147–9
Rugby Waterworks Act 1863 147–9
St. Helens Canal and Railway Bill 65n108
St Helens Improvement Act 1869....... 145, 164, 172n121, 175, 181, 193n9, 194n56
Salford Improvement Act 1870 .... 155, 197n128
Sanitary Act 1868... 126
Sanitary Loans Act 1869 126
Sewage Utilization Act 1865... 126
Sewage Utilization Act 1867... 126
Sheffield Water Company Bill 125
Sheffield Waterworks Act 1864...................................... 169n19

Table of Statutes and Bills

Sirhowy Railway Bill 1868 13
Somerset Central Railway (Narrow Gauge) Act 1859.................. 107n133
Somerset and Dorset Railway Leasing Act 1876...................... 134n49
Southampton Harbour Act 151
Southport Improvement Act 1865 181
Sowerby Bridge Gas Act 1861 148
Sowerby Bridge Local Board Act 1863 ....147–9, 158–9
Stokes Bay Railway and Pier Bill................................... 65n108
Swansea Local Board of Health and Waterworks Act 1860.............. 153–4
Swansea Local Board of Health Act 1872............................. 152–3
Swansea Municipal Corporation Act 1863 150–2
Thames Embankment Act 1862... 225n65
Thames Embankment Act 1864... 206
Thames Embankment (North and South) Act 1868....................... 163
Torbay and Dartmouth Shipping Dues Act 1870 .... 106n121
Town Police Clauses Act 1847 115
Towns Improvement Act 1847................... 33, 40, 115, 181, 185, 182n1, 199
Tramways Act 1870 226
Tyne Improvement Act 1850 209
Vale of Crickhowell Railway (Eastern Extension) Bill 1865............ 77, 101n61
Vale of Llangollen Railway Bill.................................... 95n1
Vauxhall Bridge Road Act 1858....................................... 49
Victoria Park Approach Act 1858 49
Wallasey Improvement Act 1858 49
Waterworks Clauses Consolidation Act 1847 .... 116, 146
Westhoughton Local Board Act 1878 .... 135n60
Westminster Improvement and Incumbered Estate Act 1865.............. 143
Westminster Life Insurance Society (Dissolution) Act 1861........... 99n51
Wigan Waterworks Act 1860 153–4
Wolverhampton Improvement Act 1869 164
York Improvement (Foss Abandonment) Act 1859....................... 220n12

Index

Bold headings indicate those principal entries that have sub-entries.

Aberavon 166
Aberdare 177
Aberdeenshire 143
Abergavenny 121, 135n61
Aberystwyth 158, 162
Acts: categories of 12; definition of 226; Provisional Orders 116–18, 124–7, 151, 157, 201, 206, 226–8, 134n38; *see also* Bills; Table of Statutes and Bills
art galleries 5, 22
Ashton-under-Lyne 162, 207

'baby-farming' 26n3
Bagehot, Walter 167, 200
Baggymoor 209
Banbury 220n10
Barnsley 184, 207
Barrow 162, 181
Bath 175–6, 99n40, 220n2
Bidder, George Parker 87–8, 106n121
Bills: Breviates of 15–16, 21; Court of Referees 70–2, 78; definition of 49–52, 205–9; drafting of 141–4, 169n10; fees derived from considering *see* financial matters; French, Norman 206; hybrid 73, 99n39, 221n17; Private Bill Committees *see* Select Committees; Private Bill Office viii, 19, 48; Private Bill procedures 67–78; structure of 152–8; style of 163–5; *Vacher's List of Private Bills see* Vacher; *see also* Acts; Table of Statutes and Bills
Bingley 178
Birkenhead 150–1, 162; legislation relating to 49, 75, 150
Birmingham 63n77, 104n103, 178, 201
Birstal 162, 181, 186, 191
Blackburn 155, 178, 182, 187, 191
Blackpool 143–4

Board of Admiralty 15, 20
Board of Health *see* public health
Board of Trade 14–16, 28n32, 70–1, 82, 86, 91, 94, 97n22, 101n67, 106n125, 156
Bolton 156, 189–191; *Bolton Chronicle* 22, 30n57; legislation relating to 22, 190
Booth, James 16–17, 29n32, 86–8, 107n134; *see also* Speaker of the House, Counsel to
Bradford 176–7, 180, 186, 191, 201; legislation relating to 49, 65n101
Brecon 158, 166, 207
bridges 32, 36, 50, 67–9, 73; legislation relating to 112, 208; *see also* rivers
British Empire 1, 9, 112, 127, 130, 167
Buckinghamshire 59n30, 166
building 30n58, 60n45, 180–4; roofing materials 145, 181; windows 181–2; *see also* towns, improvement of
burial: Burial Boards 48, 65n98; cemeteries 14, 32, 73, 85, 112, 115, 177; certification of death 26n3, 105n111; coffins 183; legislation relating to 48, 65n98
Burnley 165, 176–180
Bury 22–3, 85, 105n111, 121

Cambridge 146, 149–51, 207
canals 2, 6, 42, 50; legislation relating to 51, 65n108, 67, 96n17, 97n28
capital punishment 169n31, 190
Cardiff 181
cases *see* Table of Cases
Chadwick, Edwin 38, 41, 58n27, 59n37, 60n51, 81, 102–3n82, 112, 132n19
Chester 99n40
child labour 24, 38

Chiswick 49, 179, 186
Cleckheaton 159, 186
Clifford, Frederick 6–7, 21–2, 28n29, 63n79, 75–76, 96n17, 117–19, 123, 129, 133n37
coal 2, 35, 107n103, 144 *see also* pollution
Cockburn, C.J. 125
Colchester, legislation relating to 23
commissioners 14, 32–3, 115, 120, 124, 178, 188–9
committees: Clerk of Commons 7; Private Bill *see* Bills; Railways *see* railways; Select *see* Select Committees; Ways and Means 1, 17, 66, 72, 75, 90–1, 97n28
Congleton 162
constitutional matters 175–8
Coventry 149–51
Crimean War 46
Crook, Tom 43

Darlington 158, 171n71
docks and harbours 7, 14, 35, 44–5, 115, 159; legislation relating to 65n108, 151, 155, 226
drainage *see* sewerage, sanitation and drains

education 33, 38; legislation relating to 26n4, 48, 127
electricity 2, 191; electric telegraph 73
Erskine May, T. 29n35, 88, 97n21, 101n65-6, 106n127, 135n53
Exeter 149–51

factories 2, 35, 42
Farnworth 158, 181, 186, 190
financial matters 21–3, 43, 46, 50, 92–3, 152–4, 165–6, 174; attitudes to 201; charging powers 178–80; cost of building a railway 67, 72–3; fees derived from considering private Bills 21, 75, 82–5, 97n28, 98n31, 200; Ferry Debt 150; financial legislation 21, 68, 71, 123–8, 166; loans 126, 186; parliamentary expenses 40, 68; rent 39; parliamentary returns 21–2, 41; rates 116, 125, 146, 154, 159, 178–80, 189–91, 227; 'water rent' 180; window tax 181–2
First World War vii, 2

gas: companies 2; gasworks 6, 14, 45, 49, 85, 111, 115, 123, 206; legislation relating to 32–3, 49–51, 73, 83, 104n103, 133n29, 148, 151, 156–7, 177, 226, 228n2; payment for 180
Gateshead 162, 189
Glossop 159, 207
gunpowder 207

Halifax 158–60, 177–9, 185; legislation relating to 49, 160, 171n91, 175–6
Hamlin, Christopher 40–1, 58n27, 60n40
Hansard viii, 52, 58n24, 73, 113, 234
Harris, Bernard 41
Haworth 181
Hedon 162
Hennock, E.P. 45, 201
highways 36, 50, 129, 150, 174, 185–6; Highway Boards 48; legislation relating to 26, 32, 36, 48, 59n29, 63n77, 65n100, 143, 151, 185; *see also* bridges; turnpikes
Higgs, Edward 3–4, 37
Hirst, Francs W. 38, 128
His/Her Majesty's Stationery Office (HMSO) 7, 13, 25–6, 198, 233
Hole, James 37–9
Hove 49, 183–4, 188
Huddersfield 100n58, 162, 165
Hull 121–2

inclosure 2, 6, 42–6, 67, 177; legislation relating to 15, 46
Innes, Joanna 7–8
Ireland 157; famine 1; legislation relating to 92, 120
Ironbridge 42

Jennings, W.I. (later Sir Ivor) 8–9

Keighley 181, 227
Keith-Lucas, Brian 6–7
Kent 136n71
King's Printer 12, 110; *see also* Queen's Printer
King William IV 129
King's Lynn 160

land, compulsory purchase of 176–8
Law Commission, The 2–3, 198
Leamington 191
Leeds 155, 162, 177, 183–4, 201
Lefevre, Sir John George Shaw 85, 105n112
Leicester 8, 35, 58n10, 185; legislation relating to 155, 207

Lewis, R.A. 39–40
Lincoln 166; *Lincoln, Rutland and Stamford Mercury* 28n22
Liverpool 81, 107n130, 145, 163–6, 184, 190, 201; legislating relating to 49, 77, 99n40, 135n64, 165, 179, 182, 207; *see also* rivers, Mersey
local legislation: context of vi–viii, 8–11, 109–39; definition of vii; drafting of 141–4, 167; financing of 66–108, 208–10; joint promotion of 207; Local Government Acts *see* Table of Statutes and Bills; passing of 66–108; powers of 174–97; promotion of 18–23, 31–56, 67–71, 83, 90, 95, 109–10, 118–22, 143–5, 210–19; purposes of 23–4, 174–97; sources of 1–26; structures of 1–26; scope of 11–18, 198–9; style of 167, 185–6; technicalities of 140–73
locus standi 19–20, 70, 75–9, 87, 92–3, 119–20, 167
London 26, 48, 60n56, 61n58, 180, 208–9; legislation relating to 49, 61n58, 96n17, 109, 143, 151, 155, 159, 163, 177, 189–91, 208; *London Gazette* viii, 41, 61n59, 80, 207–10; Metropolitan police 26n4; *Westminster Review* 46; *see also* rivers, Thames
Loughborough 180
Lymm 186

Macclesfield 153–4, 180, 206
MacDonagh, Oliver 31
Maltbie, M.R. 10–11
Malvern 49, 178
Manchester: 81, 145–6, 177, 180–1, 189, 201; legislation relating to 49, 54, 63n77, 65n99, 77, 155–6, 163
markets and fairs 14, 32, 49–50, 111, 114–16, 149–150, 178; legislation relating to 54–5, 116, 120–1, 150, 153–5
Mathew, Mr. Justice 121
Members of Parliament: Adair, Hugh Edward 87; Adderley, Sir Charles 9, 112–15, 122–3, 128, 192, 201; Cecil, Lord Robert 70–1, 98n29, 221n17; Clarke K.C., Sir Edward 5, 34–6; Cowper, William F. 113, 123, 132n13-14, 138n91; Dodson, John George 1, 26n1, 47, 72, 77, 90; Ewart, William 9, 24; Fortescue, Chichester 91; Gibson, Milner 71, 98n29, 106n127; Graham, Sir James 111, 142; Granby, Marquess of 38; Griffith, Christopher Darby 71, 97n27; Hodgson, Richard 71, 97n26; Hume, Joseph 22, 68, 97n21; Leeman, George 90–1; Massey, William N. 17, 71, 77, 103n90, 114; Morpeth, Lord 36; Newdegate, Charles Newdigate 36; Patten, Colonel John Wilson 69, 75, 86–8, 96n17, 100n55, 107n133, 108n153; Pim, Jonathan 90; Sandon, Viscount 110–11; Sibthorp, Colonel 9; Trelawney, Sir John 78, 95n1; Walpole, S.H. 40, 132n17; Whalley, G.F. 86–9, 95n1, 107n136
Members of the House of Lords: Beaufort, Duke of 152; Cottenham, Lord 118–20; Redesdale, Lord 17, 89, 94, 100n55, 101n59, 105n118, 106n125, 138n90, 141–2, 152, 156; Shaftesbury, seventh Earl of 24, 38, 59n37, 60n51, 112, 142, 156; Stanley of Alderley, Lord 70, 74, 88, 94, 107n137
Merthyr Tydfil 49, 54, 180
Middlesbrough 49, 158–9
Morayshire 78
museums 5, 22, 135n64

Napoleon 4; Napoleonic War vii
Neath 148
Nene Valley 106n119
Newcastle-under-Lyme 209
Newcastle-upon-Tyne *see also* rivers, Tyne 182–3, 189; legislation relating to 107n103, 176–8, 183
newspapers and journals 43; *Bolton Chronicle* 22, 30n57; Commons and Lords *Journals* viii, 50, 64n92, 98n30, 102n79, 127, 206–10; *Edinburgh Review* 45, 63n71, 71, 96n17, 126; *International Journal of Regional and Local Studies* 143; *Law Magazine and Law Review or Quarterly Journal of Jurisprudence* 96n16, 97n18; *Lincoln, Rutland and Stamford Mercury* 28n22; *London Gazette* viii, 41, 61n59, 80, 207–10; *Northampton Herald* 79–80, 102n72, 102n75-8; *Punch* 61n58, 122–3; *Rochdale Standard* 169n10; *Scotsman, The* 78; *Solicitors' Journal and Reporter* 71, 78, 97n26-7, 98n29-32, 100n53; *Surrey Advertiser, The* 84; *Times, The* 37; *Westminster Review* 46, 64n86

250 *Index*

Northampton 79–81, 160, 188; legislation relating to 81, 148; *Northampton Herald* 79–80, 102n72, 102n75–8
Norwich 163, 177, 186; legislation relating to 153–154
Nottingham 46, 64n88, 207

Oldham 162, 178–81, 185, 191; legislation relating to 154–6, 159, 164, 187
Oxford 207

Parliamentary agents 5, 20–3, 74–7, 97–8n28, 100n59, 103n93, 141–5, 153–6; Coates, Thomas 83–4, 89, 103n92, 106n119, 106n127; Gregory, G.B. 22; Martin, Theodore 74–5, 130; Pritt, George 77, 86, 101n65; Thomas, Charles Evan 23, 100n59, 104n103
Pawson, Eric 18, 61n66
Peterborough 81
police *see* London, Metropolitan police; towns, police in
pollution vi, 3, 10, 35, 42, 90, 144, 150, 180–1, 184, 192; 'Great Stink' 61n58, 93, 100n52; Smoke Acts 90
population growth 183, 202
Portsmouth 155–6
poor law 5, 11, 32–33, 36, 59n37, 60n56, 129; boards 127; legislation relating to 26n4; overseers 48, 191; unions 4
prostitution 32, 150
Prime Ministers: Derby, Earl of ixn1, 111–14, 192, 200–1; Disraeli, Benjamin 35, 61n58; Gladstone, W.E. 9, 28n32, 63n70, 93; Grey, Earl 87–90, 106n127, 111; Palmerston, Viscount 29n47, 60n51; Peel, Sir Robert 28n32, 168n7
public baths 116, 191
public clocks 116
public health 2, 9, 17, 33–5, 59n37, 109–18, 129, 148–66, 174, 180–4; Board of Health, abolition of 40, 61n58, 89, 113–15; disease 41, 184, 201–2; legislation relating to *see* Table of Statutes and Bills; Local Boards of Health 38–41, 124; medical statistics 26n3
public libraries: 5, 9, 22–4, 122; legislation relating to 111, 135n64, 190, 228n3
public nuisance 183; legislation relating to 121–3

public opinion 1, 36–41, 64n80, 72
public parks 22, 177–80; legislation relating to 49, 160, 171n91
Pulling, Alexander 68, 126, 137n90

Queen's Printers vii, 13, 110, 206 *see also* His Majesty's Printer
Queen Victoria: accession of 3, 8; death of 3; reign of vii, 1–3, 6–8, 36, 68;

railways vii–viii, 2, 6, 35, 99n37, 144; Committee 68, 93; companies 76, 68, 75, 80, 87, 98n32, 143, 158–9, 186; legislation relating to 13–17, 28n32, 41–8, 51, 65n108, 66–78, 81–89, 92–5, 95n1, 98n28, 101n61, 107n134, 115, 126, 134n49, 143, 151, 159 'mania' 15–18, 28n32, 42–4, 73, 82; narrow gauge 107n133
Rea, John 78, 101n68
Reading 178
Redlich, Josef 38, 127
Returns *see* financial matters
revolution of 1848 4, 9, 38
Rhyl 184–5
Rivers: improvement of 7; Mersey 106n120, 159, 178; penalties for throwing rubbish into 147; Ribble 28n29; Thames 100n52, 122, 150–1, 163, 206, 225n65; Tyne 209; *see also* bridges
roads *see* highways
Rochdale 162, 165, 173n122, 175, 183; *Rochdale Standard* 169n10
Rotherham and Kimberworth 146–9
Royal Commission 32
Rugby 146–51, 160

St. Helens 43, 61n65, 164, 175, 181, 189; legislation relating to 65n108
Salford 162, 165, 176, 182, 190–2; legislation relating to 63n77, 55, 197n128
Scott, James John 81, 102n80
Select Committees viii, 4, 17, 23, 67–78, 82–9, 93–5, 115, 141–7, 161–2, 205–6; on Private Bills 1, 15–17, 21, 68–70, 74, 82, 87, 93, 126, 156; on Private Business 14, 67, 142
sewerage, sanitation and drains 73, 112–16, 126, 180–6, 207–10; legislation relating to 126, 155, 179, 182, 207–9
Sheffield, legislation relating to 125, 169n19

Sirhowy 13
Smethurst, James Mellor 19, 76, 121
Speaker of the House 21, 66, 73, 78, 83; Counsel to 16, 69, 83, 88, 141–142, 156
Spencer, F.H. 5–8
Spencer, Herbert 45–7, 63n71, 96n17, 100n52, 137n90
Somerset, legislation relating to 107n133, 134n49
Somers Vine, J.R. 112
Southampton 120, 151
Southport 181
Sowerby Bridge 146–51, 179; legislation relating to 147–9, 158–9
Stalybridge 162
stamps 125
Standing Orders vii–viii, 13, 18–21, 66–70, 73–7, 86, 95, 126, 142, 156–9, 205–10; Examiners of 68–74
Stockton 162–4, 181, 191
Stourbridge 175
Sunderland 182, 185–6
Sussex 99n40
Swansea 150–4, 160–1
Swift, John 94–5
Szreter, Simon 27n13, 41, 61n63

Taylor, Tom 61n58, 122
theatres 22
Thomson, James 35
Torbay 106n121
towns: civic pride 5, 22–24, 31, 81, 109, 201; cleansing of 33, 36, 112–16, 139n110, 150; drains of 33, 36 *see also* water; fire services in 132n33, 158, 189–90; halls of 5, 22, 150, 189; Health of Towns Association 35; improvement of 14, 32–4, 151–67, 182n1; lighting of 2, 33–4, 68, 115, 179; markets in *see* markets and fairs; paving of 2, 33–4, 139n110, 160; police of 14, 26n4, 32–3, 85, 115, 189

tramways 2, 7, 50, 138n100, 150, 156–7, 226
Tranmere 159, 179
turnpikes 50, 77 *see also* highways; legislation relating to 48, 65n100, 85–6, 143; movement 18; trusts 42, 61n66
Tynemouth *see also* rivers, Tyne 161–2, 177, 191
Tyrell, John 142

ultra vires 24, 34

Vacher's List of Private Bills viii, 13–14, 50–7, 64n92, 81, 122, 143, 205–19, 226–8, 234
Vale of Crickhowell 77, 101n61
Vale of Llangollen 95n1
voting vii, 187–8; legislation relating to 125; rights 3, 112

Wallasey 49, 158
Warner, Joseph Henry 141, 152
water: cleanliness of 112, 184; companies 2, 6, 14, 35, 151; costs of obtaining 149–52; supply of 38, 49, 77, 84–5, 111–16, 123, 151–60, 164; legislation relating to 49–51, 73, 77, 83–4, 100n58, 125, 136n71, 146, 153–6, 159, 163–5, 169n19, 177–8, 207, 226–7; 'water rent' 180; waterworks 65n101, 107n134, 146–7
Webb, Beatrice and Sidney 45, 57n7, 123
Webster, Edward 20–1, 83
West Bromwich 181, 186
West Hartlepool 165, 183, 188–9
Wigan 153–4
Willes, J. 121
Williams, O. Cyprian 7
Wolverhampton 59n30, 164–6, 181
Wordsworth, William 35

York 154, 161–2, 185, 220n12

Taylor & Francis eBooks

Helping you to choose the right eBooks for your Library

Add Routledge titles to your library's digital collection today. Taylor and Francis ebooks contains over 50,000 titles in the Humanities, Social Sciences, Behavioural Sciences, Built Environment and Law.

Choose from a range of subject packages or create your own!

Benefits for you
- Free MARC records
- COUNTER-compliant usage statistics
- Flexible purchase and pricing options
- All titles DRM-free.

REQUEST YOUR FREE INSTITUTIONAL TRIAL TODAY

Free Trials Available
We offer free trials to qualifying academic, corporate and government customers.

Benefits for your user
- Off-site, anytime access via Athens or referring URL
- Print or copy pages or chapters
- Full content search
- Bookmark, highlight and annotate text
- Access to thousands of pages of quality research at the click of a button.

eCollections – Choose from over 30 subject eCollections, including:

Archaeology	Language Learning
Architecture	Law
Asian Studies	Literature
Business & Management	Media & Communication
Classical Studies	Middle East Studies
Construction	Music
Creative & Media Arts	Philosophy
Criminology & Criminal Justice	Planning
Economics	Politics
Education	Psychology & Mental Health
Energy	Religion
Engineering	Security
English Language & Linguistics	Social Work
Environment & Sustainability	Sociology
Geography	Sport
Health Studies	Theatre & Performance
History	Tourism, Hospitality & Events

For more information, pricing enquiries or to order a free trial, please contact your local sales team:
www.tandfebooks.com/page/sales

Routledge
Taylor & Francis Group

The home of Routledge books

www.tandfebooks.com